Books abound on church planting. Few go
This is not a book written by an ivory towe
Whether you are a church planter or not you are a member of a planted church. This book sheds great light on what a church ought to be and how it can reach out in church planting. Get it and read it!

RALPH D. WINTER
Founder, U. S. Center for World Mission

Students of church planting and church planting practitioners often ask me what one book I would recommend for this growing discipline. To this point, I have pointed them to multiple resources since no one book covered the breadth of church planting. Now that book exists, and it is a masterpiece. J. D. Payne has written the single comprehensive guide to church planting that covers biblical foundations, missiological principles, historical paradigms, and contemporary issues. I am immensely proud of Dr. Payne, my former student. He has quickly risen to become one of the world's leading voices in church planting. I see *Discovering Church Planting* as becoming the textbook for the discipline for years to come.

THOM S. RAINER
President and CEO, LifeWay Christian Resources

J. D. Payne has here gifted the church with a missiologically sound, theologically literate, and practically thorough guidebook on the vital task of multiplication church planting. Of the plethora of books on the subject, this is a standout work.

ALAN HIRSCH
Author, *The Forgotten Ways* and *reJesus*
Founder, Forge Missional Training Network.

This is quite simply an excellent, excellent book. In *Discovering Church Planting*, J.D. Payne has woven together biblical exegesis, missiology, church history, and practical insights from across the spectrum of church planting literature and experience into a seamless tapestry of church planting wisdom that is sure to be a classic in the field. I believe Payne's work will richly reward students, pastors and church planters for generations to come. *Discovering Church Planting* is a must read for anyone who wants to grasp the scope, meaning and state of church planting in our world today.

DAVID GARRISON, PHD
Missionary and author, *Church Planting Movements*
Researcher, International Mission Board, SBC

J. D. Payne knows church planting from personal experience, research, and training of those called to this task in North America and around the world. He reflects strong convictions that church planting is the heart of our mission to reach a lost world. It is only as our evangelistic witness results in local, indigenous, healthy, biblical congregations that become a growing, reproducing network of churches that witness can be extended to all people in every location and community. Much has been written on practical church planting methods, but Dr. Payne combines in this volume a comprehensive presentation of not only those practical strategies, but a biblical and historical overview applied to the contemporary challenges of this vital aspect of our mission task.

JERRY RANKIN
President, International Mission Board, SBC

My only criticism of Paynes' *Discovering Church Planting* is that it should have been published 50 years ago—I'd have avoided years of floundering in needless complexities! A friendly writing style makes it a joy to discover valuable facets of church planting, including some that have been overlooked in other analyses. Penetrating questions challenge one to think through crucial issues. Rarely does a scientific approach to mission work also show such a passionate devotion to Christ, the Holy Spirit, and Scripture. I'd have my students read this!

DR. GEORGE PATTERSON
Co-author, *Church Multiplication Guide*

*Discovering Church Planting* is a book that delivers what it promises. I am convinced it will become a standard in its field. In what can only be described as a truly comprehensive treatment, J.D. Payne analyzes church planting biblically, theologically, missiologically, historically, and practically. Important contemporary issues also receive attention, issues that are crucial to successful church plants that reflect the New Testament pattern. The book is well written and the research is superb. I am delighted to commend its widest possible use both for the academician as well as the on-the-field practitioner. All will profit from its reading.

DANIEL AKIN
President, Southeastern Baptist Theological Seminary

*Discovering Church Planting* by Dr. J.D. Payne gives us a very broad overview of church planting. Dr. Payne's research is phenomenal and sound. He touches almost any question one would have about church planting. There is a great section on the historical background of mission evolvement through the decades. I especially like his treatment of the team approach to church planting. For anyone who wants a good read—this is a clinic in church planting. Dr. Payne not only writes well, but he has been a practitioner in church planting. That gives great credibility to his writing. I highly recommend this book.

CHARLES BROCK
President, Church Growth International

*Discovering Church Planting* hits the triple crown of church planting books, theologically centered, historically refreshing, and missiologically driven. J.D. offers a stellar work in the field of church planting that is a must read for all serious students of church multiplication.

GARY P. ROHRMAYER
National Director, ConvergeUSA, www.convergeusa.org
President, Your Journey Resources, www.yourjourney.org

Church Planting is the most effective method of reaching people who need to hear the good news of the new life available through a personal relationship with Jesus Christ. This is a must read for anyone pastoring or thinking about planting a church. I am impressed with the biblical approach that challenges some of today's thinking. The beginning of any new church plant needs to be the winning the lost. Every church planter needs to be a missionary.

DR. GERRY KRAFT
Outreach Canada

J.D. Payne's treatise on church planting focuses on the theological, historical, and missiological underpinnings of how the church grows and spreads. If you want a comprehensive case for church planting today—one that will challenge your ecclesiology—this is a must-read. As Payne writes: "Church planters must be both outstanding theologians and missionaries. To be one without the other is a liability to the Kingdom."

DR. BOB LOGAN
CoachNet International Ministries

This book by J.D. Payne, which brings together the essential considerations for effective church planting, also has the added benefit of dealing with relevant and current issues that make it an invaluable resource for church planters today. The beginning chapters alone, where Payne masterfully weaves together biblical foundations and principles of church planting that are typically missing in most church planting books, makes this book a must read. With that foundation in place, the rest of this professionally written yet readable book unfolds the practical steps of church planting. This fresh contribution to the church planting endeavor will become a standard resource that will benefit many.

MARVIN J. NEWELL
Executive Director, CrossGlobal Link

I know of nothing that has so impacted the people in our church as much as church planting. Nothing so multiplies the Church and inspires the people than to see their own work replicated in this nation and around the world. Dr. Payne has done us the Church a great service in giving us truth that will chart the course in Christ-honoring church planting.

JOHNNY HUNT
Pastor, First Baptist Church, Woodstock, Georgia

My sense is that far too many Next Generation pastors and church planters are slipping away from the importance of Scripture to their ministry. No one could say this about J.D. Payne's *Discovering Church Planting*. I appreciate so much his love for and exposition of the Scriptures in the context of planting missional churches.

AUBREY MALPHURS
President of the Malphurs Group
Senior Professor, Pastoral Ministries, Dallas Seminary

J.D. Payne has done a masterful job of unpacking the core elements of church planting. In a day of instant programs, quick fixes and chic planting methodology, J.D. challenges us to understand planting from a much more solid and deeper level. He takes us beyond simply planting a church to planting the right kind of church. He takes us beyond simply growing a church to multiplying churches. He combines the streams of theology, biblical integrity, well thought out philosophy and strong leadership to provide a mighty river that we can ride to effective church planting. The questions at the end of each chapter provide a platform for thoughtful conversation to be used by planters, planting teams, and parent church leaders. This is a must resource for any interested in starting strong, effective, and multiplying congregations.

PHIL T. STEVENSON
Director, Evangelism & Church Growth, The Wesleyan Church

I have written many blurbs and a few forewords on some good church planting books. But, only one made it into my required reading list when I teach church planting—*Discovering Church Planting*. J.D. Payne brings a theologian's mind, a missiologist's passion, and a church planter's heart. If you are thinking about church planting, you should be reading this book.

ED STETZER
Author, *Planting Missional Churches,* www.edstetzer.com

Finally . . . a comprehensive introduction to church planting that applies to both North America and international fields. The bonus is that it reads well and connects with our next generation of church planters. It's the best new text on church planting I've seen. *Discovering Church Planting* will serve us well in formal classrooms as well as field training venues. Thank you J.D.!

MIKE BARNETT, PHD
Missions strategy coach, Professor of Missionary Church Planting,
Columbia International University (CIU)

J.D. Payne who himself has been a church planter, a passionate advocator for church planting, and currently a seminary professor of missions has written an excellent introductory volume on church planting. The author, in 25 chapters and 400+ pages, comprehensively covers multiple dimensions of church planting, e.g.

historical, biblical, practical, etc., including an eleven-page bibliography of the most current publications on the subject.

ENOCH WAN
President, Evangelical Missiological Society
Research Professor, Intercultural Studies, Western Seminary

J.D. Payne's *Discovering Church Planting* is thorough without being wordy, scholarly without being burdensome, challenging without being overwhelming, and practical without ignoring the work of the Spirit. I highly recommend it!

DR. TOM NEBEL
Director of Multiplication, Converge Worldwide
Author, *Empowering Leaders Through Coaching, Big Dreams in Small Places,* and *Church Planting Landmines*

Payne's writing makes a considerable contribution for those in the school of church planting. As a church planter, this book will resonate with other church planters. Payne has grasped the key issues we face when planting churches and he gives practical steps and solutions for working through many of these issues. His understanding of the roles of the apostolic missionary and the pastoral missionary in planting churches is crucial for new pioneer workers to grasp and apply. This is a must read for all church planters.

PATRICK LAI
Author, *Tentmaking: Business as Missions*

J.D. Payne provides a fine introductory text on church planting by investigating the past and present, identifying universal principles, and providing a firm scriptural foundation for evangelism that results in new churches.

TOM STEFFEN
Biola University

I wish I had read this book twenty years ago. It will put any church planter light-years ahead when it comes to planting a healthy biblical church. In *Discovering Church Planting* J.D. moves us far beyond the gadgets and widgets that now flood the church planting market and focuses on the issues that every church planter should consider prior to planting.

DAVID PUTMAN
Pastor, Mountain Lake Church in the Atlanta area, co-founder of www.churchplanters.com, co-author, *Breaking the Missional Code*, and author, *Breaking the Discipleship Code*

J.D. Payne covers the entire range of church planting practices from A to Z. More a workbook than an ivory tower text, Payne's experience and down-home approach are refreshing as well as challenging. The practitioner who wants a helpful book that is solidly grounded will find just that in *Discovering Church Planting*.

A. SCOTT MOREAU
Professor, Intercultural Studies, Wheaton College
Editor, *Evangelical Missions Quarterly*

*Discovering Church Planting* is a collection of solid, thought-provoking insights into church planting, but without the quick-fix answers of too many church-planting manuals. Even after putting the book down, many of Payne's quandaries still challenge me: After more than three decades of cross-cultural church planting, how much more extra-biblical fluff do I still carry around in my own Westernized church-thinking and practice? And how can our church planting teams coach tribal churches into the razor-sharp simplicity of New Testament living that can quickly be reproduced in their own church planting efforts? *Discovering Church Planting* will be a valuable training tool for both rookie and veteran church planters.

DAVID SITTON
President, To Every Tribe Ministries

This is a very comprehensive and thorough book on church planting. It spans all different types of churches one might plant from small house churches to large churches. The book is definitely for practitioners who are interested in being challenged by a number of different approaches to the complex task of church planting. J.D. uses wonderful case stories to illustrate his points. He also quotes many masters of the art of church planting over the last hundred years. He draws on books, but also articles and unpublished works of practitioners. J.D. opens the door to understanding the apostolic nature of church planting. It will be interesting to see where this develops in his future books!

DICK SCOGGINS
Head of Leadership Development, Frontiers
Author, *Building Effective Church Planting Teams* and co-author of *Church Multiplication Guide*

Few people I know have the passion for church planting that J.D. Payne has. His commitment to planting healthy local congregations echoes throughout this work, and you will not read this work without catching some of this enthusiasm. I am particularly challenged by the chapters on spiritual warfare in church planting and church planting in an urban context—*must* topics for the 21st century church. Read this book, be challenged by it (even when you may disagree), and then find your role in starting a new congregation.

CHUCK LAWLESS
Dean, Billy Graham School of Missions, Evangelism, and Church Growth, Southern Baptist Theological Seminary

This volume is broad in scope, but detailed in its approach—a rare set of attributes in a text book. In addition to many facts about church planting in North America and worldwide, Dr. Payne offers his own insights from years of experience. His well-defended suggestion that North American churches adopt a missional and discipleship approach to church planting, rather than a plant-and-pastor model makes this volume not just applicable to new church planters, but seasoned ministers as well. Payne's frankness and honesty about the need for a biblical vision and prayer in church planting is sobering. But the greatest strength of the volume is when Payne tells us why church planting is *not* the goal, and why making disciples of Christ is. Payne's unprecedented and well researched book is a must-have for the novice, scholar, the well-seasoned pastor, and almost every serious Christian. Read this book front to back. It is convincing and convicting.

JOHN D. BARRY
Editor in Chief, *Bible Study Magazine* and Minister

J.D. Payne

# DISCOVERING CHURCH PLANTING

## AN INTRODUCTION TO THE WHATS, WHYS, AND HOWS OF GLOBAL CHURCH PLANTING

Foreword by David Hesselgrave

# DISCOVERING CHURCH PLANTING

## AN INTRODUCTION TO THE WHATS, WHYS, AND HOWS OF GLOBAL CHURCH PLANTING

J.D. Payne

Paternoster:
thinking faith

COLORADO SPRINGS • MILTON KEYNES • HYDERABAD

Authentic Publishing
We welcome your questions and comments.

| | |
|---|---|
| USA | 1820 Jet Stream Drive, Colorado Springs, CO 80921 www.authenticbooks.com |
| UK | 9 Holdom Avenue, Bletchley, Milton Keynes, Bucks, MK1 1QR www.authenticmedia.co.uk |
| India | Logos Bhavan, Medchal Road, Jeedimetla Village, Secunderabad 500 055, A.P. |

Discovering Church Planting
ISBN-13: 978-1-60657-029-6



11 10 / 6 5 4 3 2

Published in 2009 by Paternoster


Cover design: Sarah Hulsey
Interior design: projectluz.com
Editorial team: Bette Smyth, Daniel Johnson, John Barry

Printed in the United States of America

To my heavenly Father and to Sarah, my earthly partner
whom he allowed me to discover years ago

# CONTENTS

# ACKNOWLEDGMENTS

I must begin by acknowledging the great blessing it has been to be able to write this book about discovering church planting. I greatly thank the Lord for the opportunity and the ability to work on this project to its completion. It is my prayer that if you do not know him, you will come to discover this great God personally through Christ, who is the way, the truth, and the life (John 14:6).

Over the years it has been a tremendous privilege to serve with the North American Mission Board and the Southern Baptist Theological Seminary. I have colleagues with both of these agencies who are outstanding saints. Our interactions across the years influenced this book. Thank you very much for your commitment to the Lord and for your friendship.

I must say thank you to two particular colleagues at Southern, Gregg Allison and Tom Nettles. Gregg provided me with some helpful feedback on the ecclesiology chapters and Tom did likewise with the three history chapters. Thank you, brothers, for your assistance and for having offices near mine so I did not have to walk too far to con you in to reading my writing.

I have to say thank you to my numerous students from the past seven years at the seminary. Our interactions helped shape the contents of this book as well. Also, the students who were required to read an early rough draft of this book deserve recognition. They survived . . . I think. I am thankful for them; they provided some good insights regarding this book in the early days.

Kari Plevan, my secretary in the Church Planting Center, deserves a word of thanks as well. She assisted me in compiling the bibliographic material and biblical index for this book. Thank you, Kari, for putting up with me over the past few years.

I appreciated David Schattschneider's feedback on my history chapter regarding the Moravian Church. David's knowledge and experience with the Moravian Church were of great assistance.

A word of thanks goes to all of the brothers who wrote endorsements for this book. You all were very gracious and kind. Many of you freely offered specific feedback that assisted me in honing certain chapters. Also, thank you, David Hesselgrave, for contributing the foreword to this book.

This work is my second book with Authentic/Paternoster. And once again, I must say I have enjoyed working with the folks of this company. Keep up the great work, guys! Bette Smyth and her proofing skills took my rough, sandpaper-esque writing style that would appall even the most backwoods of all English speakers and made it as smooth as porcelain. Thanks, Bette, for your outstanding work. (Your work ain't bad. You did real good. Makin' me sound nice and all.) I started this project with Dana Carrington and later transitioned to working with John Dunham, the editorial manager with Authentic/Paternoster. Thank you, Dana and John, for your contributions and endeavors on this project. Of course, I could not forget to say thank you to Volney James, the publisher of Authentic/Paternoster. From the very beginning, he has been a great encourager and supporter of this work and a delight to work with.

Last, but not least, I must say thank you to Sarah, Hannah, Rachel, and Joel. These loved ones make up the Payne household and have encouraged and supported me over the course of the research and writing of this book. This book would not be the same without their love and prayers. I love you guys.

Though many folks in some way have contributed to this work, at the end of the day, I take full responsibility for any shortcoming contained in the final product.

—J. D. Payne
*February 2009*

# FOREWORD

How does one best characterize and commend *Discovering Church Planting: The Whats, Whys, and Hows of Global Church Planting*—one of the finest books on church planting to appear in recent years? The breadth of treatment it embraces is made clear by simply perusing the table of contents. The depth of research it displays is made apparent by examining the bibliography. The extensive experience it reflects is made evident by reading the author's preface. What, then, remains other than wholeheartedly to commend Professor Payne's book to the reading and study of every serious teacher, student, and practitioner of church planting—indeed, to the reading of every lover of the Christian Church and every supporter of Christian mission?

That is what I propose to do here. In doing so I will take a clue from the likes of Henry Venn and Rufus Anderson, who propounded the "Three Selfs" of the indigenous church, and also from John Nevius, who advanced nine principles of what we now know as the "Nevius Method" of church planting. Though more could be said in commending *Discovering Church Planting*, I will point to five sound and solid reasons for concluding that this book should be one of the very first books of recent vintage that missionaries, church planters, and all mission-minded Christians should access immediately and study carefully.

First, from the first word of the first chapter ("understanding") to some of the last words of the text ("lizard churches"), this book has to do with what the Great Commission is actually all about—the proclamation of the gospel and the planting of "responsible churches" (Peter Beyerhaus's phrase). Looking at the title, such a statement may seem to be redundant and completely unnecessary. But even if the former proposition be true, the latter does not necessarily follow. By sometimes curious alchemies, Christian mission has often become "any *good* thing Christians ought to do" (Donald McGavran's complaint) or just "*every* thing" Christians may decide to do. That's too bad because it flies in the face of the gospel mandate. More than that, "when mission becomes *everything*, mission becomes *nothing*" (Stephen Neill's assertion).

Second, from start to finish, this book is anchored in the authority and veracity of sacred Scripture. Obviously, I do not mean to say that every proposition emanates from the Bible or that this book contains "only truth, all the truth, and nothing but the truth." Of course not. *Discovering Church Planting* is replete with the ideas of literally scores of very human scholars and practitioners, to say nothing of the fact that their ideas are filtered through Payne's personal, mental exertions and field involvements. Dr. Payne offers much more than the results of human cogitation, however. He reminds his readers that the Bible is the divine *magnum opus* on church planting as well as on all matters of faith and conduct. He examines church-planting proposals in the light of Scripture and urges his readers to do the same. And he explores the rudiments of biblical theology in order to bring theological principles and implications to bear on the church-planting task. In this book church planting is informed by ecclesiology—by a study of the nature and functions of the church as revealed in the Word of God. Here kingdom theology and ethics find their rightful place in Great Commission mission without preempting the priority of evangelism and world evangelization. That is indeed commendable.

Third, *Discovering Church Planting* is both comprehensive and contemporary—amazingly so! Professor Payne is extremely well informed. His bibliography is extensive and impressive, but it is more than that. It is a *working* bibliography. His text exudes familiarity with a whole range of relevant literature. It reaches into the past in order to bring to light the best thinking of faithful missiological forebears who labored hard and long to extend the geographical and intellectual frontiers of church growth. At the same time, Payne is by no means captive to the past. He ranges over the whole gamut of relevant current literature. In fact, and in a profound sense, his thinking is more up-to-date than a good deal of current literature because he does not get hung up on this or that new model or novel strategy purported to be *the* key to church planting and growth. He is more concerned with timeless principles than with either the traditional or the trendy. This is important because, if it is possible to be mired in the past, it is also possible to follow new rabbit trails or wind up in side eddies. Payne is familiar with most digressions of this kind but is diverted by none of them.

Fourth is the matter of student and classroom friendliness. This book is not a difficult read, but neither is it an easy read. It does not purport to be. After all, it grows out of a deep concern for the future of church and mission. For that reason it deals with abiding questions having to do with the biblical text and its interpretation and contextualization; with the histories of Moravian, Methodist, and Baptist evangelism and church development and their implications; with proposals of past and present missiologists and their relevance. In the process it also deals with concepts and terms that, while familiar to some, will not be familiar to all—*pneumatology*, *paternalism*, *pragmatism*, *spiritual warfare*, *oikos*, and, yes, *lizard churches*, to name just a few. It is one thing to *read* a book like this. It is something else to *understand* it, *learn* from it, and *practice* it. Professor Payne is a classroom lecturer and teacher. He knows all of this. Accordingly, at the close of each chapter he provides a summary of the content, questions for group discussion, and a list of terms for personal review. Teachers and students will appreciate this greatly.

Finally, at the risk of being misunderstood, I want to suggest that this book is made more commendable by the fact that it grows out of a Southern Baptist ethos. All will be aware that the Southern Baptist denomination is the largest Protestant denomination in the United States. Many will know that its overseas mission is one of the largest of our Protestant missions. Both of these facts are noteworthy, but I have something else in mind here. Down through the years Southern Baptist churches, theological institutions, missions, and organizations have gone through significant struggles of various kinds. Nevertheless, overall, no other single denomination or organization that approaches their size can match Southern Baptists when it comes to a combination of ecclesiastical leadership, theological education, evangelical advocacy, literature production, and evangelistic involvement. Speaking very personally, I believe that before they finish a reading of *Discovering Church Planting*, the majority of readers will come to appreciate the richness that accrues to the fact that its author has been informed by his roles as student, pastor, church planter, and elder in various Southern Baptist contexts in the United States and Canada and, most recently, as professor in one of its finest seminaries.

With that I rest my case in the assurance that all who become acquainted with this book will greatly profit from it; with a prayer that the Lord of the Church will use it to the glory of his name and the extension of his kingdom; and with an expression of thanks to the author and all who aided him for the writing and publication of one of the foremost works on church planting available today.

—David J. Hesselgrave, Ph.D.
*Professor Emeritus of Mission*
*Trinity Evangelical Divinity School*
*Deerfield, Illinois*

# PREFACE

Discovering new things can be fun. This past summer I had the joy of watching my children make a discovery. It happened at a birthday party that my mother gave for one of my daughters. Of course, we had the standard cake, ice cream, and presents. But Mom did something unique this year—she organized a treasure hunt around her yard.

Both of my daughters, Hannah and Rachel, are just now starting to learn the value of money. They love getting and counting their coins. If they happen to find a penny or nickel in a parking lot, a great celebration takes place as they rejoice over their new discovery.

When my mom heard of their new interest in coins, she decided to surprise them with something special. She took two empty coffee cans, filled them almost full with loose change, and buried them in her yard. Next, she created and hid a series of clues around her yard, leading Hannah and Rachel on a quest to discover the treasure.

After several minutes of traveling from clue to clue (not to mention the great assistance provided by their father), my daughters finally found the *X*'s that marked the spots where they had to dig for their treasures.

You can imagine the excitement on their faces when they opened the cans to discover something they had never had before—a can full of coins.

## What You Will Discover in This Book

It is my hope that this book will provide you with the opportunity to make some discoveries of your own. For some readers this may be your first introduction to church planting. You may have heard about this aspect of the Great Commission but have very little understanding of it. If such is the case, I pray that this book will supply you with a biblical foundation in this subject. For others, church planting has been part of your life for a long time, and I pray that this book will assist you in becoming even more effective at making disciples of all nations.

However, regardless of your knowledge of church planting, this work was written as an introduction to the *whats*, *whys* and *hows* of global church planting. I hope that at times you will want to pursue some of the material covered in this book in greater depth. You will find additional resources in the bibliography. At the time of this writing, this is one of the most extensive church-planting bibliographies. Some of the books and articles were published just weeks before the completion of this writing. Also, you may want to consult my website at www.northamericanmissions.org, where I regularly post articles, book reviews, podcasts, and links related to church planting.

The weight of this work is on providing you with the biblical and missiological principles of church planting while assisting you and your church-planting team in thinking through how to apply those principles to your context. Each chapter includes many questions to assist you in this process. Because this book focuses on church-planting principles—and not on methods or models—I have written this text to be used in both the North American context and non-North American context. Though the methods for church planting are numerous and relative to their contexts, principles are universal and not limited to location or people.

The first section of this book deals with the biblical and theological foundations for church planting. The second section addresses some of the more important missiological principles that church planters need to apply to their ministries. The third section will take you on a brief historical journey, looking at the missionary approaches of the eighteenth-century Moravians in Europe and the Methodists and Baptists on the early North American frontier. The final section focuses on some of the most pressing contemporary issues related to church planting today.

## My Journey of Discovering Church Planting

But before we begin our journey together, I would like you to know a little about me and my unexpected introduction to church planting.

Shortly after coming to know and follow Jesus when I was a teenager, the Lord guided me in the undesired direction of serving his Church as a pastor. Though I initially resisted his leading in this direction, the journey became very sweet as I stopped rebelling and followed obediently. As I simply began seeking first his kingdom and his righteousness (Matthew 6:33), I came to know him better. For the next few years I preached in as many locations as I possibly could, and shortly after college I was called to pastor a church in central Kentucky. Church planting was nowhere on my radar screen.

While I was serving in the new pastorate, the Lord allowed me to gain additional knowledge and training through seminary education. Though I had no plans of changing directions in my ministerial journey, the Lord was about to take me down a different path of discovery.

After completing approximately half of a master of divinity degree, I realized I needed a three-hour evangelism course, and I needed to complete this course during that one particular summer. My only option was a course entitled Introduction to Church Planting taught by Dr. Charles Brock, a former missionary to the Philippines. The Lord used that class to change the direction of my life and ministry. Over the next several years, I would have the opportunity to serve alongside church planters on several church-planting teams as well as pastor churches in Indiana and Kentucky while pursuing my Ph.D.

So, in one sense, the unexpected journey of writing this book can be traced back to Dr. Brock's class several years ago. In another sense, this work has come about through both my research as a missiologist and my missionary labors.

Several years ago I noticed that many church planters in the United States and Canada were attempting to impose many of their cultural preferences regarding the local church onto the people they were trying to reach, while I noticed many church planters serving outside of North America were intentionally working to contextualize as much as possible. On this continent I saw church planters enter into an area and have a vision of planting one church that would, it was hoped, plant another church three years later, or, at best, one church per year. Whereas, in the Majority World, I observed many church planters developing strategies to multiply churches throughout a population segment, city, or people group, while serving on a team to plant several churches simultaneously.

Although some of the differences observed on the field were related to radically different contexts, most of the differences were theological issues related to ecclesiology. How the church planters answered the question, What is the local church? affected everything they did in their contexts. It affected the way they approached the people, served them, preached the gospel to them, baptized them, gathered them together as local churches, taught them obedience to the commands of Christ, and raised up leaders among them.

In North America I observed and experienced a failure to recognize the apostolic (or missionary) nature of church planters. This was no surprise, for the majority of the church-planting books and conferences geared toward a U.S. or Canadian audience expect that the person who plants a church will also pastor that church. Rather than beginning with the expectation that all church planters are missionaries, such resources are generally designed for the church planter to begin as a missionary, but then, as quickly as possible, change to become the pastor over the newly planted church.

Such matters greatly concerned me. First, I had a very difficult time finding biblical support for a plant-and-pastor model for kingdom expansion. Of course, I am not opposed to such a model and even encourage that paradigm in certain contexts. However, the weight of the Scriptures is on the church planter functioning in an apostolic role while raising up pastors/elders from out of the harvest.

Second, I was troubled because no matter how contemporary, progressive, postmodern, avant-garde, edgy, or creative the church-planting strategies were, the majority of the churches planted in the United States and Canada in the last thirty years were the same as the conventional (or traditional) churches that existed here before these new congregations.

Even though new worship services had been conducted in darkened rooms with candles and sermons had been as relevant as the latest felt need and PowerPoint presentations had been as prevalent as funnel cakes at the state fair, little had changed theologically and missiologically. Great praise music, excellent family programs, and even solid biblical preaching (and I'm a very strong advocate for each of these), in many cases, did not result in new healthy churches taking the gospel to the highways and hedges of society. Even many of the newly planted, conservative, evangelical churches were still market driven; the faith once for all delivered to the saints was still a private, individual matter separated from the local community of the saints; and the missional aspects of the church were still primarily understood in terms of bringing in as many people as possible to the worship gathering so they could hear the gospel in a foreign environment.

Third, I realized that by continuing to follow the dominant U.S. and Canadian paradigm for church planting, we will not experience a significant advancement of the kingdom among the approximately

200,000,000 nonkingdom citizens living in North America and most definitely not among the *four billion* others across the globe.

So, my unexpected journey in discovering church planting caused me to return to the Scriptures and begin asking questions such as: What is the local church? What is necessary for a church to exist among any people, at any time, in any location across the globe? What is a church planter? and What are the functions of church planters? As I read the Scriptures for answers, searched Church history, reflected on my own ministry, and consulted with other kingdom citizens, I came to realize that, for the most part, the people asking these same questions were laboring in fields in the Majority World.

What I discovered was *not* that church planters serving outside of the United States and Canada have all the answers to the problems facing the Church on this continent, but rather they were attempting to be guided in their missionary labors by biblical and missiological principles for kingdom expansion and not by their cultural preferences.

What they had learned was learned the hard way over the nineteenth and part of the twentieth centuries. The Church and many missionaries from the United States and the United Kingdom had embraced colonialism as a part of the advancement of the kingdom of God. To make a long story short, the church planters brought the gospel to the peoples of Asia and Africa, but it was so entwined with the Christian subcultures of the missionaries that many nationals equated Jesus and the newly planted churches with products of the West. Such religion was a white man's religion, and following Jesus was equated with loss of ethnicity and becoming a westerner. Missiologists such as Henry Venn, Rufus Anderson, J. Wascom Pickett, Roland Allen, and Donald McGavran, among others, called for a return to the Scriptures for belief and practice, as well as dissolving whatever would smack of colonialism.

Knowledge of such historical problems in the growth of the Church has caused many contemporary church planters serving the Majority

World to be cautious in their missionary practices. Unfortunately, those of us serving in the Western world, for the most part, continue to perpetuate a variation of the problems that our brothers and sisters encountered in the nineteenth and twentieth centuries outside North America.

Global church planting, regardless of the geographical location, must be guided by the biblical and missiological principles leading to making disciples of all nations. *Church planters must be both outstanding theologians and outstanding missionaries.* To be one without the other is a liability to the kingdom. Paul contended for the faith (2 Timothy 4:7), proclaimed the whole counsel of God (Acts 20:27), and appropriately contextualized his work (1 Corinthians 9:19–23) for the multiplication of disciples, leaders, and churches.

So, it was in the matrix of all of these influences over the past several years that I have taken this unexpected journey in church planting, resulting in the writing of this book.

## Discovering the Nomenclature Used

You need to be aware of some of the terms that I frequently use throughout the text. First, I use the word *Church* with an uppercase *C* to refer to the Church universal or to a denomination (e.g., the Anglican Church) or to the Church in a region or on a continent (e.g., the North American Church). I use the word *church* with a lowercase *c* in reference to the local expression of the body of Christ (i.e., the local church). In some contexts I will refer to the universal *and* local expressions of the body of Christ, and at these times, I will use the term *C/church.*

Second, though not all missionaries are church planters, I believe that all church planters are missionaries. Therefore, unless the context reveals otherwise, I will use the terms *missionary* and *church planter* interchangeably, even within the same paragraph.

Third, at times I will use the phrases *church planting* and *church multiplication* interchangeably as well. Again, unless the context notes otherwise, I am thinking of the same concept: the multiplication of churches across a population segment, community, or people group.

Fourth, though more will be stated later, throughout this book I often refer to *kingdom citizens* and the *kingdom ethic*. Such terms refer to followers of Jesus who by God's grace live according to the ethic set forth in his Word that guides their relationships with God, other kingdom citizens, and with nonkingdom citizens.

## Discovering Your Author

I would like you to know a little more about me before you begin reading this book. As a follower of Jesus, I love and believe in his Church. My family and I have spent the last several years laboring to build up local churches and see churches planted across the globe. While I have a global vision, the Lord has allowed the majority of my pastoral and church-planting experience to be in the North American context.

I love church planters regardless of where they are serving across the globe. These men and women are daily in the trenches of frontline spiritual warfare and need our support and encouragement. I am thankful to be a fourth-generation Southern Baptist. Though I work with Great Commission Christians of many denominational or nondenominational affiliations to see the kingdom advance, the Lord has led me to spend the majority of my time with Southern Baptists. I presently have the honor and privilege of serving as a national missionary with the North American Mission Board—the largest Protestant missions agency in the United States—and as an associate professor of church planting and evangelism at the Southern Baptist Theological Seminary in Louisville, Kentucky.

I have always attempted to wed the biblical and the practical aspects of missions. As a professor who teaches such courses, I have always striven to walk with one foot in the classroom, training missionaries and pastors, while walking with the other foot in the field of practical ministry through the local church. Presently, I am serving with the elders of my church in Louisville as we work to send out missionary teams across our city, our nation, and our world.

Though *Discovering Church Planting* was written as an introduction to the ministry of church planting, it was also designed as a refresher for those of you who have served in such a capacity for many years. Whether you are preparing for the field or needing a different perspective on church planting, this work was written for you. It is my hope and prayer that the Lord of the harvest will greatly bless you from what you read here. It is also my hope and prayer that these thoughts will not remain locked within in your head, but rather that you will apply what you learn and be involved in the multiplication of disciples, leaders, and churches across the globe. As we follow Jesus, he promises to never leave us or forsake us (Hebrews 13:5). As we follow the sovereign Lord in discovering church planting, he will always take us on an unexpected journey for our good and his glory.

Section I

# DISCOVERING BIBLICAL AND THEOLOGICAL FOUNDATIONS

While discovering church planting, it is vitally important that we begin with the biblical and theological foundations for such missionary activity. In chapter one, you will be exposed to the biblical basis for church planting. Chapters two and three examine the importance of ecclesiology, or the doctrine of the C/church. We must understand what the C/church is in order to be involved in properly planting it among the peoples of this world. Chapter four addresses the importance of the role of the Holy Spirit in church planting. Chapter five combines the topics of prayer and spiritual warfare, noting that church planting is frontline spiritual warfare. Chapters six, seven, and eight examine the importance of evangelism, discipleship, and leadership development in church planting.

Chapter 1

# UNDERSTANDING BIBLICAL CHURCH PLANTING

It is not about planting churches. These may be unusual words to begin a book on the topic of church planting; however, it is necessary that this point is made from the beginning. There is no command in the Bible to go into all the world and plant churches. The Church is never told to plant churches until the end of the age or search out all people groups and plant churches among them.

It seems everywhere we turn today both churches and mission agencies in North America and outside this continent are training and sending missionaries to plant multiplying churches across the globe. Over the past twenty years in North America and Europe, numerous books and articles have been published addressing this topic. Conferences and practical resources are being provided every year to potential church planters. As a professor of church planting at the Southern Baptist Theological Seminary, I represent a small minority of theologians who have recently emerged in the academy. More and more seminaries are offering courses and emphases in church planting. As a national missionary with the North American Mission Board of the Southern Baptist Convention, in conjunction with my teaching responsibilities, I am also responsible for recruiting and equipping church planters through our school's Church Planting Center.

So, why is there so much talk about church planting if there is no scriptural mandate?

Though there is no direct command to plant churches, our Lord was very clear about the Great Commission to make disciples of all nations (literally, "peoples," not nation-states). The best way to fulfill this mandate of evangelizing, baptizing, and teaching obedience is through the planting of contextualized churches among the various people groups and population segments of the world. For it is in the process of evangelizing, baptizing, and teaching that local churches are planted. Though our Lord gave the Great Commission before his ascension, it was the apostolic Church that later followed in obedience, setting the example of church planting for all believers to emulate.

> **"We'd be wrong to send out planters with organizational, strategic, and marketing tools but not the fundamental truths of God's Word and the principles of Scripture from which to work."**
>
> —Ed Stetzer, *Planting Missional Churches* (Nashville, TN: Broadman and Holman Publishers, 2006), 37.

**Biblical church planting** is evangelism that results in new churches. There are many ways to plant churches; however, the model in the Scriptures is one that begins with evangelism and ends with those new churches following the Lord in obedience.

A few years ago I wrote a chapter in the book *The Challenge of the Great Commission* by Thom S. Rainer and Chuck Lawless. In that work I set forth the following detailed description of biblical church planting.

> Biblical church planting follows the way modeled by Jesus and imitated by the Apostolic Church for global disciple making. It

is a methodology and strategy for bringing in the harvest, raising up leaders from the harvest, and sending leaders to work in the harvest fields. It is evangelism resulting in congregationalizing. Under the leadership and work of the Holy Spirit, biblical church planting seeks to translate the gospel and the irreducible ecclesiological minimum into any given social context, with the expectation that new communities of believers in turn will continue the process in their contexts and throughout the world.[1]

## Biblical Basis

The first obvious and most significant component of this definition is that biblical church planting has a *biblical* foundation. The Scriptures are our source of guidance for doctrine and practice. Church planters who fail to base their theological framework on the Bible tread on the shifting sands of contemporary fads, trends, and whims.

Before the birth of the Jerusalem Church, the essence of the Church existed in the community of believers who followed Jesus before the ascension. Many church planters are quick to turn to the pages of Acts for understanding church planting and missionary practice; however, much of what is revealed in Acts was established by Jesus in the Gospels.

An examination of the life and manner of Jesus demonstrates that his missionary activity was relational, simple, and highly reproducible—all necessary characteristics for the simple, uneducated Galileans to continue after the ascension. Yet, before his return to the Father, Jesus modeled a lifestyle that he expected the Twelve to imitate. For example, a comparison of Jesus sending the Twelve and the Seventy-two demonstrates considerable similarities with what Jesus had been doing before their commissioning (Matthew 10; 28; Luke 9; 10), particularly, a lifestyle of preaching, healing, and casting out demons.

Paul told the newly planted churches that they should imitate him as he imitated Christ (1 Corinthians 4:16; 11:1; Ephesians 5:1; Philippians 3:17; 1 Thessalonians 1:6; 2 Thessalonians 3:9). Peter wrote that his readers should follow the example of Jesus (1 Peter 2:21). Just as Jesus departed from areas when the people resisted him (Mark 5), he admonished the Twelve and the Seventy-two to do likewise. Paul continued this practice of concentrating on receptive peoples (Acts 13:49–51; 18:6).

> **"Church planting is not an end in itself, but one aspect of the mission of God in which churches are privileged to participate."**
>
> —Stuart Murray, *Church Planting: Laying Foundations* (London: Paternoster Press, 1998), 30.

## Missiological Basis

**Missiology** is the science and art of missions. Though there is much more to missiology than church planting, church planting is missions in action. Biblical church planting derives principles primarily from the Scriptures, although other areas of God's truth located in fields such as sociology, anthropology, communications, linguistics, economics, and philosophy can be extremely advantageous in assisting missions activities.

Church planting is both a method and a strategy of fulfilling the Great Commission. As a method, church planting tells us how to make disciples. C. Peter Wagner wrote that "the single most effective evangelistic methodology under heaven is planting new churches."[2] Though Wagner definitely stated a missiological truth, not all church planting methods are the same; and all church planting cannot be labeled "the single most effective evangelistic methodology." For there are many churches being planted with little or no evangelism taking place. Yet, despite this limitation, church planting is a biblical, effective, and efficient method of carrying out the Great Commission.

As a strategy, church planting offers a paradigm for reaching villages, tribes, urban enclaves, and entire cities with the gospel. It provides the Church with a great potential of multiplying disciples, leaders, and other churches.

As stated above, biblical church planting focuses on bringing in the harvest, raising up leaders from the harvest, and sending leaders to work in the harvest fields. Believers are not commanded to go into all the world and plant churches, but rather *make disciples*. It is in the process of making disciples (evangelization) that new churches (congregationalization) result. Biblical church planting is about using contextualized methods in a strategic manner to reach unbelievers, equip them as church leaders, and send them as evangelists and church planters throughout the world.

## Theological Framework

In his work *Church Planting: Laying Foundations,* Stuart Murray wrote of the need to develop a theological framework for church planting. He argued for the need to establish the biblical parameters for this aspect of the Great Commission, rather than attempting to locate proof texts for such a practice. His words are helpful to all church planters, reminding us of the need for a healthy theological framework for this missionary practice. He noted, "An inadequate theological basis will not necessarily hinder short-term growth, or result in widespread heresy among newly planted churches. But it will limit the long-term impact of church planting, and may result in dangerous distortions of the way in which the mission of the church is understood."[3] Murray encouraged us to keep in mind that church planting is located at the intersection of **ecclesiology** (doctrine of the Church) and missiology (science and art of missions). (See figure 1.1.) Murray also explained that church planting stands in relationship to the theological concepts of *missio dei,* incarnation, and the kingdom of God.[4]

Figure 1.1 **Church Planting: A Theological Framework**

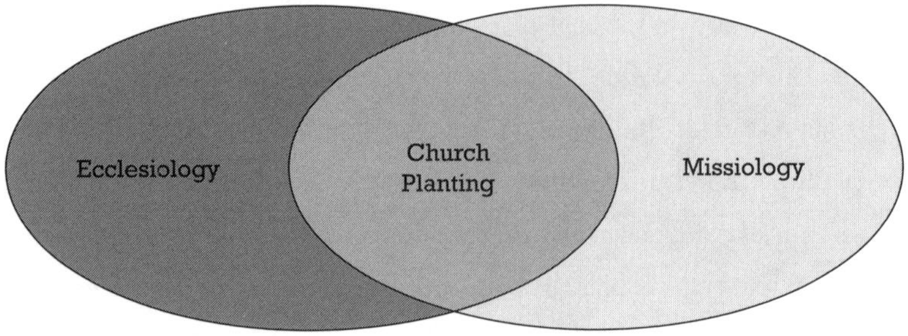


## Missio Dei

*Missio dei* is a Latin phrase that means the "mission of God." God is a missionary God. He takes the initiative to engage his creation with his plan of salvation for his glory. Part of this work involves the birth, maturation, and multiplication of the local expression of his Church. Just as he sent the Son and the Spirit into the world, his Church is also sent into the world to be a part of the outworking of salvation history. As church planters carry the gospel into the kingdom of darkness and people become citizens of the kingdom of light, local churches are birthed and continue the mission of God.

## Incarnation

In the fullness of time God sent his Son into the world (Galatians 4:4) to fulfill the promise of crushing the Serpent's head (Genesis 3:15).

The incarnation of the Son of God was part of the Father's plan to redeem people. Church planters have much to learn about their missionary work from this doctrine. Since the missionary God made his dwelling among us (John 1:14) to both build his Church (Matthew 16:18) and show kingdom citizens how to live according to the kingdom ethic (John 10:10), we must view church planting in the light of an incarnational approach to missions—that is, an approach to missions that involves living among the people and serving them. The early church used this contextualized paradigm for its missionary activity. The apostle Paul wrote of this when he reminded the recently planted church at Thessalonica that it was a blessing for the church-planting team to be able to share with them the gospel *as well as their very lives* (1 Thessalonians 2:8).

## Kingdom of God

The Church is a part of the kingdom of God. The planting of local expressions of the body of Christ—local churches—however, is no guarantee that the kingdom has expanded. Our focus should not be on planting churches or birthing church-planting movements, but rather disciple-making movements. For it is out of a disciple-making movement that church-planting movements occur.

I am amazed at the number of church planters who are content with having a large number of churches planted, even if there has been no regenerative work of the Holy Spirit in the lives of the people. Particularly in the West, the Church is number hungry. We want to equate the advancement of the gospel and the expansion of the kingdom with the number of new churches started. Church planters must make certain that they have a clear understanding of the kingdom of God and are working toward its advancement, rather than attempting to start a new church with people who are already kingdom citizens.

Figure 1.2 **Great Commission Passages**

| Text | Passage | Contents |
|---|---|---|
| Matthew 28:18-20 | "And Jesus came and said to them, 'All authority in heaven and on earth has been given to me. Go therefore and make disciples of all nations, baptizing them in the name of the Father and of the Son and of the Holy Spirit, teaching them to observe all that I have commanded you. And behold, I am with you always, to the end of the age.'" | Evangelism<br>Baptizing<br>Teaching of Obedience<br>Global Witness |
| Luke 24:45-47 | "Then he opened their minds to understand the Scriptures, and said to them, 'Thus it is written, that the Christ should suffer and on the third day rise from the dead, and that repentance and forgiveness of sins should be proclaimed in his name to all nations, beginning from Jerusalem.'" | Evangelism<br>Global Witness |
| John 20:21-23 | "Jesus said to them again, 'Peace be with you. As the Father has sent me, even so I am sending you.' And when he had said this, he breathed on them and said to them, 'Receive the Holy Spirit. If you forgive the sins of any, they are forgiven them; if you withhold forgiveness from any, it is withheld.'" | Forgiveness of Sins |
| Acts 1:8 | "But you will receive power when the Holy Spirit has come upon you, and you will be my witnesses in Jerusalem and in all Judea and Samaria, and to the end of the earth." | Global Witness |

## Great Commission Foundation

Aside from the disputed latter section of Mark 16, a variation of the Great Commission mandate is contained in the other three Gospels and Acts (see figure 1.2).

Within the framework of the *missio dei*, incarnation, and the kingdom of God, the divine authorization for biblical church planting is the Great Commission. The apostolic Church was given the mandate to bear witness to Christ and his resurrection by making disciples of all nations. Though a disciple is made whenever a person places faith in Christ for salvation, discipling is a lifelong process. The best context for both making disciples and discipling—which includes baptism and teaching obedience (Matthew 28:19–20)—is the local community of disciples (i.e., the church).

## Biblical Paradigm

Luke recorded some of the details of church planting during Paul and Barnabas's first missionary journey. The majority of Acts 13–14 provides a glimpse of their paradigm. The team would enter into a city, preach the gospel, gather the believers together as new churches, and later appoint elders over those congregations. The latter part of Acts 14 records that after the two of them had planted churches in many cities, they backtracked, returning to those cities to appoint elders.

> When they had preached the gospel to that city and had made many disciples, they returned to Lystra and to Iconium and to Antioch, strengthening the souls of the disciples, encouraging them to continue in the faith, and saying that through many tribulations we must enter the kingdom of God. And when they had appointed elders for them in every church, with prayer and

> fasting they committed them to the Lord in whom they had believed. (Acts 14:21–23)

Following the appointment of the elders in all the churches, the team worked its way back to the Church in Antioch, which originally sent it on this missionary journey (Acts 13:1–4).

> **"I would argue strongly that church starters seek biblical-theological training because church planting is a deeply theological enterprise."**
>
> —Aubrey Malphurs, *Planting Growing Churches for the 21st Century*, 3rd ed. (Grand Rapids, MI: Baker Books, 2004), 27.

## Four Biblical Necessities

I am concerned that the Western Church has made church planting a very complex matter. It is not rocket science. Though large amounts of financial resources, highly trained and skilled leaders, and sophisticated strategies are not bad in themselves, they are not requirements for planting churches. In fact, in order to reach the more than four billion people on this planet who are not followers of Jesus, the Church is going to have to move away from complex paradigms that are not highly reproducible. If biblical church planting is evangelism that results in new churches, then church planting is a very simple means of making disciples of all nations. Hard work? Yes. Complex work? No.

So, if Acts 13–14 provides a glimpse of the paradigm used by the first missionary team, what was happening at the local level among the people in those different cities? Though the team did not visit Thessalonica on the first missionary journey, Paul's first epistle to the newly planted church in Thessalonica reveals the necessities for the birth of the church in that city.

> We give thanks to God always for all of you, constantly mentioning you in our prayers, remembering before our God and Father your work of faith and labor of love and steadfastness of hope in our Lord Jesus Christ. For we know, brothers loved by God, that he has chosen you, because our gospel came to you not only in word, but also in power and in the Holy Spirit and with full conviction. You know what kind of men we proved to be among you for your sake. And you became imitators of us and of the Lord, for you received the word in much affliction, with the joy of the Holy Spirit, so that you became an example to all the believers in Macedonia and in Achaia. For not only has the word of the Lord sounded forth from you in Macedonia and Achaia, but your faith in God has gone forth everywhere, so that we need not say anything. For they themselves report concerning us the kind of reception we had among you, and how you turned to God from idols to serve the living and true God, and to wait for his Son from heaven, whom he raised from the dead, Jesus who delivers us from the wrath to come. (1 Thessalonians 1:2–10)

Addressing this text, Charles Brock noted that contained within this passage are four necessities to plant churches among any people, in any place, at any time in history. These requirements are (1) **sowers**, (2) **seed**, (3) **soil**, and (4) **Spirit**.[5] Paul and his team represent the sowers. The gospel is the seed sowed in the hearts, or soil, of the Thessalonians. The Spirit is the Holy Spirit, who opens hearts to the gospel and brings about the birth of his churches.

Though church-planting methods and strategies will differ from people to people and place to place, these four necessities remain constant. Remove one of these and biblical church planting is impossible. If we add to these necessities, however, biblical church planting can still occur, but we may begin to move in the direction of approaches that are not highly reproducible.

## *Summary:*

1. There is no command in the Bible to plant churches.
2. It is in the process of making disciples that churches are planted.
3. Biblical church planting is evangelism that results in new churches.
4. Church planting is at the intersection of ecclesiology and missiology.
5. A theological framework for church planting should at least include *missio dei,* incarnation, and the kingdom of God.
6. A Great Commission theology supports the missionary practice of church planting.
7. The four necessities of church planting are (1) sowers, (2) seed, (3) soil, and (4) Spirit.

## *Reflection Questions:*

1. Do you agree or disagree that church planting is primarily about making disciples? Explain your answer.
2. Do you agree or disagree that contemporary church planters should begin by looking at the methods of Jesus when it comes to their missionary activities?
3. Are there other elements of a theological framework for church planting that should have been included in this chapter? If so, what are they?
4. What was your initial response to the statement that the Western Church has made church planting a complex matter?
5. Do you think there are more components to church planting than the four listed by Brock? If so, what do you think are biblical necessities in addition to these four?

## *Important Terms in This Chapter:*

- Biblical church planting
- Missiology
- Ecclesiology
- Sowers
- Seed
- Soil
- Spirit

Chapter 2

# ECCLESIOLOGY AND CHURCH PLANTING PART 1

**It's imperative that before we start a church we know what we're starting.**

—Aubrey Malphurs[1]

Each year my family takes a vacation, and like most families, we find ourselves packing until the last minute. Typically, we scramble to get our luggage packed, our car loaded, and all of our children's toys collected, with only moments to spare before we are supposed to be on the road. As we pull out of the driveway, our usual routine includes asking, "Did we forget something?" Next, we run through a mental checklist, marking off the items already packed that are deemed of the utmost importance. Despite this annual ritual, it is not unusual for us to find ourselves stopping somewhere down the road at a local store and purchasing forgotten items. If we would plan more efficiently for our trips, we could avoid some of these typical frustrations.

How we begin a journey affects not only the journey itself but also where we end up. There have been many times that I have found myself in a hotel in the evening, realizing that I have forgotten to pack my toothbrush or saline solution for my contacts. I have had to rush out late in the evening to a local convenience store to purchase these important items, usually paying three times more than what I normally would spend for such products.

Beginning well is part of the process of ending well. When it comes to church planting, missionaries must begin well by having a healthy understanding of the Church. Without establishing this proper foundation, church planters will find themselves frustrated on the journey and with many problems when they reach their destination.

> **"Before anything else, we start with the Bible to understand and build on the clear New Testament patterns of church planting."**
>
> —Ed Stetzer, *Planting Missional Churches* (Nashville, TN: Broadman and Holman Publishers, 2006), 37.

In this chapter, I will show the critical significance of ecclesiology in church planting. How church planters answer the questions, What is the church? and What are the functions of the church? will affect everything they do when planting churches. Charles Brock wrote, "I believe a perverted and tarnished view of what a church is constitutes one of the greatest hurdles faced by church planters."[2] A failure to understand what the church is will influence church-planting methods, strategies, and how church planters understand and misinster to the people.

## What Kinds of Churches Are We Planting?

Though there are many ways to plant churches, it is wise to plant contextualized churches. A **contextualized or indigenous church** springs from the soil and manifests many of the cultural traits and expressions of

## "The Church Is . . ."

Several years ago, Justice C. Anderson wrote the following paragraphs challenging some of our traditional language describing the local church.

> You say, "Let's go to church." Is the church some place to go? Another says, "My church believes such and such." Is the church an organization with bylaws? You give money "to the church"; then the church must be those who collect and spend the money! "I grew up in the church." What does that mean? Still another may insist, "The church ought to do something about it!" What is this church that he thinks should act? "At my church," opines another, "we have a great choir program." How can a church be *my* church? And is the church a place to have programs? "We go to Dr. So-and-So's church," states someone else. Is it really Dr. So-and-So's church? Other's argue, "The church keeps up the moral tone of the community." Is that the business of the church? "The best people in town belong to the church," we are told. Is the church, then, the society of the socially and morally acceptable?
>
> These commonplace sayings clearly demonstrate the multifarious meanings of the word *church.* Other popular concepts compound the problem of a precise definition. Without a doubt, many never get beyond the idea of the church as a building! Like the fifth-century barbarians who coined our English word *church*, the spatial concept prevails. The church is a place to pass by, get married in, or to have the preaching service. Others realize that the church is not merely a building but that it exists in the people and activities which go on in the building. To them the church is like a club, a fraternity, in which they can enjoy the company of some high type people. Dues are required to keep the buildings and activities properly maintained. Closely akin is the view that the church is a social agency with humanitarian ends, in other words, the religious arm of the United Way to prevent cruelty to human beings!
>
> Along with this, many consider the church to be a clinic where personal problems are solved; or put in another way, it is a type of religious physical fitness center where moral and spiritual jogging are prescribed to keep us religiously fit!
>
> Another common view of the church is that it consists of those who come weekly to hear a great preacher. A gifted orator gathers about him a loyal following who so love to hear him speak that they would not miss an opportunity to

hear him. Such "churches" tend to fade away rapidly when the dynamic personality moves away. Akin to this view is the idea that the church is a society to preserve the memory of Jesus. In other words, the church stands in the community as a monument to the past tradition of Jesus Christ and his mighty acts. Like the local museum, it perpetuates a great memory.

Now, how can all these be the church? Did Jesus have in mind buildings, clubs, officers, money collectors, and organizations when he said to his disciples, "I will build my church and the gates of hell shall not prevail against it" (Matthew 16:18, KJV)?

Taken from Justice C. Anderson, "The Nature of Churches," in *The Birth of Churches*, comp. Talmadge R. Amberson (Nashville, TN: Broadman Press, 1979), 48–50.

***Questions to Consider:***

1. Do our contemporary descriptions of the local church come from our traditions, the Scriptures, or both?
2. Do you agree or disagree with Anderson that such commonplace sayings regarding the local church are problematic?
3. What words or phrases, if any, do you need to change in order to be more biblical in your description of the local church?

the people themselves, rather than being a church that consists, primarily, of an outside culture imported onto the new believers.

For example, I grew up in southeastern Kentucky. Many of the churches there had a great appreciation for the use of a piano in the worship services. They also believed that a vital part of church life required a fellowship hall where the congregation periodically gathered for meals. Though the people in my hometown still favor these elements of church life, a piano and fellowship hall would probably be seen as an oddity in a church planted among a nomadic people group of Africa.

In the nineteenth century, missiologists Rufus Anderson and Henry Venn[3] discussed these matters and developed what became known as the

"**Three Selfs**" of indigenous churches: self-governing, self-supporting, and self-propagating. A **self-governing** church makes its own decisions. Though seeking the wisdom of others is helpful, there is no need to consult an outside body in all matters of church life. There is no governing official or authority overseeing the local congregation and mandating what that particular church will do or not do. For example, the local congregation is free to govern itself regarding the purchasing of property, appointing leaders, organizing its own order of service, and developing ministries.

**A self-supporting** church supports itself financially. If the congregation needs a new building, the congregation provides the money for such a structure. If it is necessary for the church to provide a full salary for the leaders, the church provides the income. A self-supporting church is not dependent on outside funds to meet the day-to-day financial requirements for ministry.

**A self-propagating** church is able to spread the gospel across its own local geographic area and throughout the world. Everything the local church needs in order to share the good news with others is already present among the members. No outside and separate authority (e.g., Western missionaries) is needed for the church to carry out the Great Commission.

> "True indigenous church principles are in reality New Testament church principles."
>
> —Melvin L. Hodges, *The Indigenous Church* (Springfield, MO: Gospel Publishing House, 1953), 58.

Though Venn and Anderson popularized the Three Selfs, over the years other **missiologists**—those who study the science and art of missions—have included other characteristics in the list. For example, a **self-identifying** church has its own identity as the local church in its area. To be considered a church, those who gather as a group must identify themselves as the local expression of the body of Christ. The group is not a mission, chapel, Bible study, or a preaching point. The group is not seen as a ministry of another congregation or a second campus. Self-identifying is the concept that the membership of a congregation has come together to clearly identify itself as the local church in its area.

Charles Brock, in his book *Indigenous Church Planting: A Practical Journey*, wrote about churches being **self-teaching** and **self-expressing**.[4] Self-teaching means that the individual members of the church family are able and willing to teach one another (Romans 15:14; 1 Corinthians 14:26, 31). For example, members can share with one another what the Lord reveals to them during their time in the Word.

Brock also noted that indigenous churches have the freedom to express themselves in a worship style according to the guidelines of the Scriptures. Therefore, churches in African contexts should have the freedom to express themselves through music with African instrumentation, rather than using a North American praise team. If a Nepalese congregation desires to sing psalms, hymns, and spiritual songs in accordance with its melodies, harmonies, and meters, then it should have the freedom to do so. If believers from a Muslim background want to use a preaching methodology that expects elders to sit on the floor while teaching the Scriptures, rather than standing in a pulpit area, then such freedom must be allowed. Some churches may expect their pastors to preach sermons in a monologue manner; other churches may find this insulting and expect sermons that involve dialogue with the people.

Self-expressing also includes the idea of the church being able to organize itself according to culturally appropriate patterns. For example, many Western churches operate with numerous committees in place and periodic business meetings. Such structures are not appropriate in other cultures of the world.

Indigenous churches should be **self-theologizing** as well. This means that they have the freedom to develop their own theologies regarding the unique cultural issues of their contexts. Self-theologizing is not the liberty to decide what parts of the Bible they will follow and what parts they will reject. The Scriptures establish the parameters whereby all theologies rise or fall. And though there is value and importance in church tradition and community wisdom, the Scriptures are paramount. No church has the freedom to tamper with, adjust, add to, or discard the teachings of the Scriptures. However, there are certain localized issues that impact churches but are not transcultural.

For example, churches in certain parts of Africa—particularly areas where there are large numbers of Muslim converts—struggle with the practice of polygamy. In the United Kingdom and in the United States, however, polygamy is not a widespread matter of ecclesiastical concern. Rarely would a systematic theologian address this topic for a Western audience, because the Church in the West is not being significantly affected by this issue. However, African churches need to have the freedom to allow the Holy Spirit to guide them in understanding how they should think about the issue of polygamy according to the Scriptures and how they should practice their faith in their contexts. So, a self-theologizing church, under the guidance of the Holy Spirit, is able to apply a biblically guided ethic to the local issues of the day.

## Do These "Selfs" Promote Self-Sufficiency?

It should not be assumed that these seven selfs advocate that indigenous churches be self-sufficient and isolated from other churches and from the empowering Holy Spirit. Though church planters should work toward planting autonomous churches, no church is an island unto itself. The Scriptures are clear that local churches are interdependent with other churches. Such interdependence includes healthy cooperation among churches for fellowship, accountability, and the propagation of the gospel.

Concerned that church planters would think that indigenous churches are to be self-sufficient, Brock emphasized that these selfs should be seen as "Christ-sustained" activities.[5] That is, only by the power of the Lord himself is the church able to live according to a kingdom ethic in the world. Therefore, these seven selfs only come about as the Lord gives the ability (Ephesians 2:10; cf. Philippians 1:6; Jude v. 24).

> "Christ is *building* his church so he commands believers to witness and work for its completion, now and in this age."
>
> —David J. Hesselgrave, *Paradigms in Conflict: 10 Key Questions in Christian Missions Today* (Grand Rapids, MI: Kregel Publications, 2005), 348, italics original.

## When Should a Church Be Indigenous?

If the church-planting team seeks to plant biblical churches, then local churches should be indigenous from the time they are planted. There is nothing that should keep them from manifesting the seven selfs from the very beginning. When the apostle Paul planted churches, they were considered churches from the very beginning. He did not establish a group of believers and then later, over time, gradually give them more and more freedom to become local churches.

Contemporary missionaries must realize and embrace this ecclesiology. From the moment the Holy Spirit gives birth to a local church, it is the local expression of the body of Christ. Of course, the church will mature in the faith over time. But on the day of the church's birth, it is a church in the biblical sense, with all the rights, privileges, and responsibilities appertaining to it. The church is not half a church today and a full church tomorrow, any more than a person is half a kingdom citizen today and a full kingdom citizen tomorrow.

> "St. Paul's churches were indigenous churches in the proper sense of the word; and I believe that the secret of their foundation lay in his recognition of the church as a local church . . . and in his profound belief and trust in the Holy Spirit indwelling his converts and the churches of which they were members, which enabled him to establish them at once with full authority."
>
> —Roland Allen, *Missionary Methods: St. Paul's or Ours* (Grand Rapids, MI: William B. Eerdmans Publishing Company, 1962), vii.

## What Are the Contemporary Ecclesiologies?

Stuart Murray, in his book *Church Planting: Laying Foundations*, was correct when he wrote, "An inadequate theological basis will not necessarily hinder short-term growth, or result in widespread heresy among newly planted churches, but it will limit the long-term impact of church planting, and may result in dangerous distortions in the way in which the mission of the church is understood."[6] In order to make any significant advancement for the kingdom, church planters must have a solid theological basis for their church-planting methods and strategies.

Church planting is a marathon and not a sprint. I once had the privilege of serving as an associate pastor with a church in central Indiana. I nicknamed the pastor "Marathon Man" because he loved to run and even completed several marathons, a task that I could not accomplish. He prepared himself for such a daunting task by training several months before the actual events. On the day of the races, he still had to pace himself if he wanted to finish. Of course, he could have treated the marathon as a sprint and left the starting line full throttle, beating the other contestants to the first mile marker; but he would have then been out of energy and would not have finished well.

The establishment of a healthy theological foundation for church planting is necessary if church planters desire to finish well. Short-term gains in the areas of numbers and dollars must not hijack the global mandate to make disciples of all nations. Church planters must pace themselves, and beginning with a healthy ecclesiology is the first step toward completing the marathon.

There are at least two contemporary ecclesiologies that are posing serious threats to the multiplication of churches across the globe—paternalistic ecclesiology and pragmatic ecclesiology. However, before addressing these two perspectives, it is necessary to discuss ideal types.

### Ideal Types

The concept of classifying social phenomena using ideal types was pioneered many years ago by the German sociologist Max Weber.[7] In an attempt to identify and understand various cultural constructs, such as religious or economic practices, Weber developed the tool of defining ideal types. These types exist as abstract concepts and are not found in the real world. They are helpful for educational purposes and as points of reference for comparisons with other types.

When we discuss the two problematic contemporary ecclesiologies that are influencing church-planting teams—the paternalistic ecclesiology and the pragmatic ecclesiology—these descriptions should be understood as ideal types, rather than pure examples that exist in reality. Despite the fact that such abstractions are not found in reality, many church planters are embracing ecclesiologies that closely resemble these types.

## Paternalistic Ecclesiology

**Paternalism** is the ideology that the beliefs and practices of one group should be forced onto another group in order to maintain control. This perspective creates a dependency of one group on another. One group is seen as superior while the other group is seen as inferior. Rather than the two groups being interdependently related and working together to accomplish a greater good, paternalism fosters an unhealthy codependency. Paternalism is much like the relationship between parents and their children in which parents make all the decisions for their children who are not capable of taking care of themselves.

Paternalism, as related to church planting, creates and maintains an indefinite parent-child relationship. Paternalism was a common practice in missionary work outside the West in the nineteenth through the early twentieth centuries. North American and European missionaries often applied the methods of the West to the cultures of the East, rather than using biblically informed, contextually relevant methods.

During this time in history, Western ethnocentrism ran high. Non-Western culture was rarely valued and was seen as savage and, at times, barbaric. Much missionary work not only involved taking the gospel to these peoples but simultaneously bringing them Western cultures. Rather than planting indigenous churches among the people, many churches were planted that reflected the Euro-American way of thought and life. The gospel and Western civilization were then understood as being intimately linked; therefore, conversion to Christ was viewed as conversion to Western culture. People viewed Christianity as *the white man's religion.*

As churches were planted, the Euro-American concept of the local church manifested itself. Church organization and structures, worship styles, teaching and preaching methods, leadership development, and theological education looked very similar to those elements found in the United States and Great Britain. Because nationals had not been trained in Western philosophies supporting such practices and models, and because few had the managerial and educational skills necessary to maintain such practices, the reality was that few of the national believers were capable of "doing" church the Western way. The result was that paternalism was necessary in order to make certain that the churches were maintaining the "proper" way.

As an ideal type, the **paternalistic ecclesiology** develops by the following process: First, the church planters ask the question, What are our cultural preferences for doing church the "right" way? Next, they decide, What is a good church model to support our understanding of this "right" way? And, finally, What is the biblical support for our determined model of church? (See figure 2.1.)

The church planters assume that since they have been believers for many years, they know what is the right way and the wrong way of doing church. This rationale, however, assumes too much. Church planters can become overconfident that they know what is healthy for churches in other cultures. And though experience is extremely important and wisdom gained over the years is invaluable, church planters must remember

Figure 2.1 **Paternalistic Ecclesiological Model**

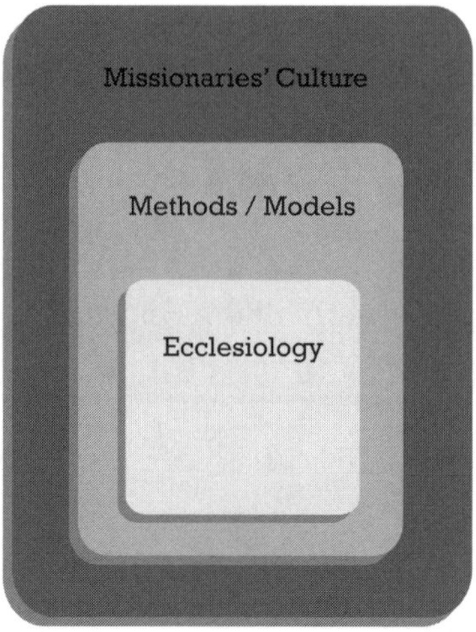

that it is impossible to plant the perfect church. In fact, there is no perfect church this side of heaven.

The greatest concern, however, with this ecclesiology is that it begins with the cultural preferences of the church planters, rather than beginning with the Scriptures. The paternalistic ecclesiology imposes the church planters' desired expression of church organization and structure onto the people.

For example, if the church planters believe that a praise team is the best approach (because a praise team worked well in their home church), then they will attempt to use such a paradigm with little regard for the people and their culture. If the church planters believe that age-graded Sunday school classes are the best approach to discipling (because their background included such a method), then they will attempt to impart age-graded Sunday school classes to the new believers, with little regard for the fact that the adults may be very resistant to having their children separated from them for any sort of spiritual training.

The final step in the paternalistic ecclesiological method takes the church planters to the Scriptures to find support for their preconceived notions about church-planting activities.

> "As the church proclaims the good news of the kingdom, people will come into the church and begin to experience the blessings of God's rule in their lives."
>
> —Wayne Grudem, *Systematic Theology: An Introduction to Biblical Doctrine* (Grand Rapids, MI: Zondervan Publishers, 1994), 864.

## Pragmatic Ecclesiology

The second ideal type of ecclesiology significantly influencing church planting today is **pragmatic ecclesiology**. Surely, Christians should be pragmatic to some degree. The church should desire to know what is working and what is not working to reach people with the gospel. Biblical stewardship demands that we ask practical questions such as, Why is the church growing rapidly among these people and not growing at all among those people?

Pragmatism, however, can be unhealthy if taken too far. Pragmatism is the ideology that supports a "whatever works" approach to church planting to the degree that the end justifies the means. Some forms of pragmatism assume that if churches are being planted, then God must be pleased and is pouring out his blessings—regardless of the methods used and the message being proclaimed.

A pragmatic ecclesiology is developed in the following fashion: First, church planters begin by asking the question, What works in planting churches? A pragmatic ecclesiology is typically being used when church planters begin their ministries by stating, "We are going to plant a

Figure 2.2 **Pragmatic Ecclesiological Model**

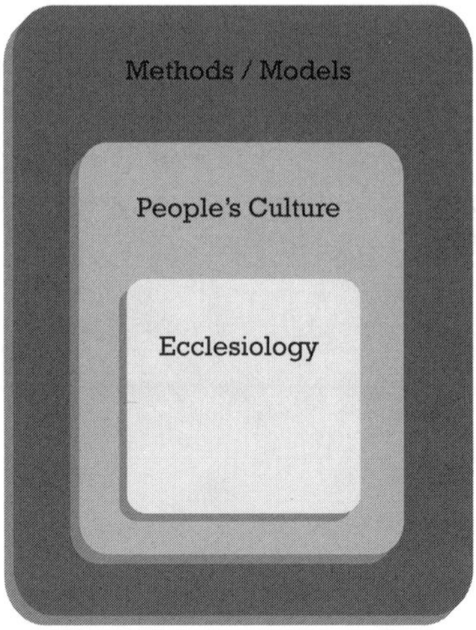

postmodern (or cell, or house) church, because Pastor X has seen it work well in his area." (See figure 2.2.)

Church planters advocating this ecclesiology find a model that is working in one location and attempt to make that model fit in the cultural context of the people they are called to reach. The focus is usually on finding models that attract a crowd.

Finally, these church planters would look for scriptures that support their particular, predetermined understanding of the Church.

The problem with this theological method of church planting is that "successful" models become the standard for understanding the church, usually without questioning the health of the church established. Such church planters spend more time grappling with how to make their model work than they do with seeking to contextualize biblical teachings.

## Biblical Ecclesiology

Tom Julien rightly observed, "Our problem is that we identify the local church by her cultural and historic expressions, more than by her biblical essence."[8] In order for church-planting teams to avoid the temptation of subscribing to unhealthy ecclesiologies, they need to heed the words of Julien and return to the Scriptures for a proper understanding of the church. Though this will be discussed more fully in chapter three, it is necessary to spend a moment commenting on the development of a **biblical ecclesiology** by church planters. Until they are able to answer questions such as, What is the church? and What are the functions of the church? the probability of adopting a paternalistic or pragmatic ecclesiology is very high.

Church planters must be aware of their own cultures because this has a dynamic effect on missionary work. John E. Apheh urged, "It is imperative that a cross-cultural church planter be able to understand what it means to be able to separate his culture from his message and communicate instead a contextualized message to his hearers."[9] Though no one can be culturally neutral—for everyone comes to the biblical text with a cultural bias—church planters must understand that the process of developing a biblical ecclesiology begins with allowing the Scriptures to speak for themselves. Church planters must seek to understand what is the **irreducible ecclesiological minimum,** or the basic essence of the church, for the church to be the church among any people.

> **"Lord, help us discern between those things that are merely *helpful* and those that are *essential*."**
>
> —George Patterson and Richard Scoggins, *Church Multiplication Guide, rev.* (Pasadena, CA: William Carey Library, 2002), 13, italics original.

It is this irreducible minimum that church planters must seek to translate to their target group. Anything less than this minimum fails to teach the new believers the doctrine of the church; and anything in addition to this minimum, though not necessarily wrong, possibly hinders the multiplication of indigenous churches.

Church planters must become students of the culture of the people—that is, understanding their worldviews, understanding the ways they do life. It is through this understanding that church planters develop reproducible methods and models. (See figure 2.3.)

I strongly recommend the study of church-planting techniques across the globe; however, these are culturally specific and, many times, are developed based on the strengths of the church planters and their gifts and passions.

Effective approaches should be studied and mined for their "golden nuggets" that are translatable from context to context. As church-planting teams sift the various models, they can then take those elements that will work well in their contexts and make the appropriate applications.

Figure 2.3 **Biblical Ecclesiological Model**

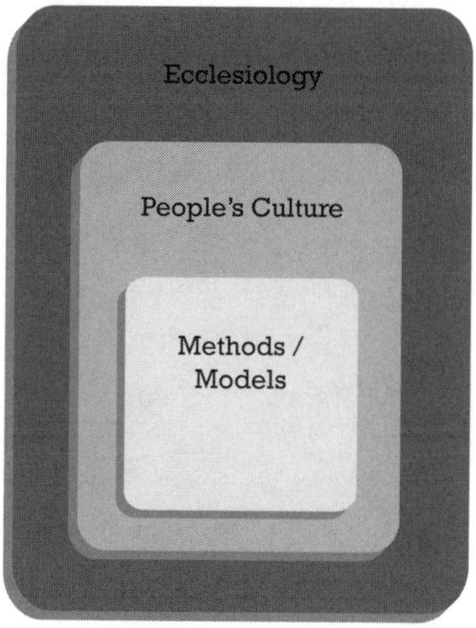


The result will be the development and use of culturally relevant church-planting methods.

## What Are the Implications of Ecclesiology for Church Planting?

I thoroughly enjoy the taste of coffee. In fact, I have been called a coffee snob. In addition to two drip-coffee makers at home, I also have a French press and an espresso machine. Even as I write this chapter, an iced mocha rests beside me on my desk. One day when I was attempting to make cappuccino, I noticed that my machine was not working. The beans were ground perfectly and enough water was in the reservoir. The power light was on and I could hear the water pump working, but no coffee was coming through the filter basket. After several minutes of significant frustration, I decided to reread the instructions. Then I discovered my problem: after I placed the water reservoir in the back of the machine, I had failed to press down the reservoir until it connected to the water pump. A *slight disconnect* made all the difference between having great cappuccino and me believing that I had another broken coffeemaker. (I have already worn out two other espresso machines.)

Though other chapters will address church-planting strategies, methods/models, and the multiplication of disciples and leaders, it is necessary at this point to stress that ecclesiology affects at least these three vital areas of church planting. I want you to see the connection between ecclesiology and these components. A disconnect at this point will lead to frustration, irritation, and numerous problems for church planters in the future.

## Church-Planting Strategies

Church planters who enter into ministry contexts with strategies that include the planting of only one church have a myopic understanding of the Great Commission. The apostle Paul greatly rejoiced when he heard that the church of Thessalonica was carrying the gospel well beyond itself into other regions (1 Thessalonians 1:8). Elsewhere the apostle revealed his desire to see the multiplication of the gospel across the world when he pleaded, "Finally, brothers, pray for us, that the word of the Lord may speed ahead and be honored, as happened among you" (2 Thessalonians 3:1).

"Church planting in any situation must make a high priority of the goal of reproduction—the multiplication of local churches throughout the land."

—Samuel D. Faircloth, *Church Planting for Reproduction* (Grand Rapids, MI: Baker Book House, 1991), 34.

Beginning with a biblical ecclesiology will position church planters to embrace strategies that are reproduction oriented. A healthy ecclesiology advocates that the church is to grow and multiply itself throughout the world. Missionaries who espouse a healthy doctrine of the Church enter into a context with the intention of planting churches that will multiply among a given people group or population segment.

## Church-Planting Methods/Models

A method is a way of doing something—a plan, a system, an approach. Applied to church planting, it is the system we use to plant churches. Models are the expressions of the church that come into existence by the use of particular methods. Church planters must understand that their ecclesiology will influence the methods they use and the resulting models.

For example, imagine two artists given the assignment to paint a picture of a building. After several hours of painting, the artists complete their tasks and reveal to us their masterpieces. Artist A painted a building in the form of a skyscraper. Artist B also completed the task accurately, but he painted a building in the form of a school. Though both artists accomplished the tasks correctly, their paintings were radically different. Their mental images of a building greatly influenced their final works of art.

Similarly, if church planters have a certain concept or model in mind when thinking of the local church, their methods will be toward the production of that particular understanding. Missionaries must use only methods that allow them to faithfully translate the gospel and what it means to be the local church into the context of the people.

The methods used to plant churches should be reproducible by the people themselves. If church-planting teams use complicated methods based on sophisticated training or Western culture, then the likelihood decreases for the gospel spreading from person to person and churches multiplying throughout a land. People reproduce what they know, and what they know is typically what they have personally experienced, seen, or heard. If the church planters are using methods that are difficult for the people to grasp, then the potential for reproduction diminishes.

## Multiplication of Disciples and Leaders

If global disciple making is the commission of the Church, then church planters must work for the multiplication of disciples and leaders who will in turn be a part of the multiplication of churches. Robert E. Logan correctly stated, "Any church multiplication movement that wants to multiply churches must also find a way to multiply leaders, for it will quickly run out of existing, ready-to-go leaders. Creating solid, reproducible methods for raising up indigenous leaders from the harvest will feed and sustain a church multiplication movement."[10] If global disciple making is the challenge set before the church-planting team, church planters fall woefully short of the mark when they embrace methods that are not conducive to such multiplication.

Now that we have addressed several issues related to the need for having a healthy ecclesiology, the next chapter will briefly address the essence and functions of the church.

### *Summary:*

1. How church planters answer the question, What is the church? influences their strategies, methods, and philosophies related to global disciple making.
2. Biblical church planting is evangelism that results in new churches.
3. The Bible is the starting point for the development of a biblical ecclesiology.
4. Church planters should work to plant indigenous/contextualized churches.

5. Indigenous churches are self-identifying, self-teaching, self-expressing, self-governing, self-propagating, self-supporting, and self-theologizing.
6. A paternalistic ecclesiology forces the church culture of the church planters onto the newly planted churches because it is believed that the church planters' culture is best.
7. A pragmatic ecclesiology assumes that a particular expression of the church is healthy and beneficial to all because it "works."
8. Ecclesiology particularly influences church-planting strategies, methods, and the multiplication of disciples and leaders.

## *Reflection Questions:*

1. What would an indigenous church look like in your area or culture?
2. Do you have a tendency to subscribe to a paternalistic ecclesiology or a pragmatic ecclesiology? If so, why? If so, what can you do to avoid this proclivity from interfering with your church-planting work?
3. Have you ever witnessed any examples of church planters manifesting characteristics of a paternalistic ecclesiology or a pragmatic ecclesiology? If so, why do you believe they approached church planting from such a perspective?
4. What is the C/church universal and local?

## *Important Terms in This Chapter:*

- Ecclesiology
- Biblical church planting
- Three Selfs
- Contextualized (indigenous) church
- Self-governing
- Self-supporting
- Self-teaching

- Self-expressing
- Self-identifying
- Self-propagating
- Missiologists
- Self-theologizing
- Paternalism
- Paternalistic ecclesiology
- Pragmatism
- Pragmatic ecclesiology
- Biblical ecclesiology
- Irreducible ecclesiological minimum

Chapter 3

# ECCLESIOLOGY AND CHURCH PLANTING PART 2

**Remembering that the church is a people should help us recognize what's important and what's not important.**

—Mark Dever[1]

Once when I was in New Brunswick, leading a church multiplication training conference for some Canadian church planters and pastors, I began a session by asking the participants to join me in a game of imagination. In this game I pretended to divide the participants into teams and assigned them the tasks of going throughout the city asking nonkingdom citizens to provide their responses to the question, What is church? After we took this imaginary trip, I asked everyone to speculate on what they believed would be the most common answers heard on the streets, and we made note of these responses. Then I guided the group to speculate on the responses they would anticipate receiving if they asked the same question to kingdom citizens. Again, we made note of these responses.

By this time, many of the participants had an idea where I was going with this activity. As we compared the probable answers from both groups, everyone realized that though there were some differences, the groups shared similar answers.

The final part of the exercise was the most poignant. I asked the crowd to look over the probable answers and offer biblical support for each of the responses. Though some of the anticipated responses from the believers had biblical support, many did not. When we examined both lists side by side, the group recognized that both unbelievers and believers comfortably identify the church in nonbiblical terms. On almost everyone's list was that *church* is a building, a worship service, or a place to go—all of which have no biblical support, since the church is not a place or event, but rather a people.

Church planters must keep in mind that the definition, function, and vitality of the local church do not come from financial resources, sophisticated structures and organization, numbers of people, or even a great preacher. Rather, the essence of the church comes from the citizens of the kingdom, indwelled and empowered by God, living according to a kingdom ethic that clearly establishes their relationship with God, each other, and the world. In this chapter, I hope to unpack this statement by addressing the definition and functions of the Church universal and local, as much as space will allow in this introductory book.

As mentioned in the previous chapter, the most critical issue in church planting today is an ecclesiological issue. Though we are part of local churches, we struggle to understand what the C/church is. Like barnacles that over time attach themselves to the hulls of ships, decades and even centuries of cultures and traditions of Church history can block our understanding of the biblical response to the question, What is the C/church? We must apply healthy, biblical hermeneutics (that is, the science and art of biblical interpretation) and come to a biblical response to this question. This is a challenging task, but an essential one. Though all of us are culturally biased, we must recognize our biases and, by God's grace, allow the Scriptures to define what we are to plant among the peoples of this world. Let us remember that our cultural expressions of the Church are not necessarily wrong, but they may interfere with making disciples of the four billion people on this planet.

## Defining the C/church

Though the majority of this chapter focuses on the New Testament, a healthy understanding of the C/church begins with a healthy understanding of the Old Testament. Though space will prevent me from returning to the Old Testament passages, church planters must recognize that much of the New Testament discussions of the C/church were founded on promises of God extending back to Genesis. This is especially true when we see in the New Testament the word ***ekklesia*** referring to the C/church. This word was used in the Greek translation of the Old Testament to refer to an assembly—particularly Israel as God's assembly in the wilderness.

The New Testament refers to the C/church in two general concepts. First, the Bible describes the Church as the universal group consisting of all the followers of Jesus, both living and dead. For example, in Colossians 1:17–18 Paul wrote, "He is before all things, and in him all things hold together. And he is the head of the body, the church." The words of Jesus also speak of the Church as a universal group of believers. In Matthew's Gospel he said, "And on this rock I will build my church" (Matthew 16:18). Clearly, in both of these passages, the immediate reference is not to a specific local congregation.

> **"We first need to understand what it means to be the church and then focus on what it means to do church."**
>
> —Thom S. Rainer and Daniel L. Akin, *Vibrant Church: Becoming a Healthy Church in the 21st Century* (Nashville, TN: LifeWay Press, 2008), 13.

Second, the Bible describes the church as being a local assembly of the followers of Jesus Christ. For example, throughout Acts 13–14 the missionary team was involved in planting local expressions of the body of Christ throughout various cities of the known world. Paul introduced many of his letters with words such as, "To the church of God that is in Corinth" (1 Corinthians 1:2) and "To the churches of Galatia" (Galatians 1:2) and "To the church of the Thessalonians" (1 Thessalonians 1:1).

Membership in the universal Church comes with the expectation that its members enter into the local expression of the body of Christ as well. It is through the local church that a person comes to understand and live out the Christian life as a kingdom citizen.

> **"The gospel is prior to the church and the church exists because of it. Therefore, if the church ever loses the gospel, it ceases to be a church."**
>
> —John S. Hammett, *Biblical Foundations for Baptist Churches: A Contemporary Ecclesiology* (Grand Rapids, MI: Kregel Publications, 2005), 73.

A local church is a group of baptized **kingdom citizens** in a particular geographical area who understand and identify themselves as the local expression of the body of Christ and agree to live together as the body of Christ according to the **kingdom ethic** provided in the Scriptures. In practical terms, such a group is guided by the Scriptures in how it is to live in relation to God, one another, and those who are not kingdom citizens. The New Testament ordinances of baptism and the Lord's Supper as well as other kingdom issues—such as worship, leadership, ministry to others, structure/organization, teaching and discipline, and evangelism and missionary work—are governed by this ethic, which involves love for God and neighbor (Matthew 22:37–40). George W. Peters accurately expressed the purposes of the Church when he wrote, "From the teaching of the New Testament it is easily perceived that the church operates in three relationships: *upward* to God in worship and glorification; *inward* to herself in edification, purification, education and discipline; *outward* to the world in evangelization and service ministries."[2]

## A Common Call

Entrance into the C/church begins with the work of God (Ephesians 2:8–9). Through the communication of the gospel (Romans 10:17), the Holy Spirit extends a call to those separated from God in their sinful state. Paul wrote, "Even as he chose us in him before the foundation of the world, that we should be holy and blameless before him" (Ephesians 1:4). Though the kingdom of God is not the same as the Church, God in his sovereignty continues to call out people to be citizens of his kingdom. This citizenship is primarily lived out in relationship with other citizens in a local kingdom community—also known as the local church.

> **"The gospel in all its multiple dimensions must be at the heart of church planting."**
>
> —Timothy J. Keller and J. Allen Thompson, *Church Planter Manual* (New York: Redeemer Presbyterian Church, 2002), 42.

## A Common Confession

Entrance into the kingdom of God, and thus entrance into the C/church, begins with the work of the Holy Spirit in the life of the unbeliever, resulting in a confession similar to that of Peter in Matthew 16. Jesus, speaking to his disciples, inquired about common understandings regarding his identity. After hearing the various misconceptions, he then confronted the disciples with the question, "Who do you say that I am?" (v. 15). Immediately, Peter responded with a declaration that is, in essence, the same confession all kingdom citizens have made throughout the ages: "You are the Christ, the Son of the living God" (v. 16).

Such a confession signifies that a person has repented of his or her sins and placed faith in the Lord Jesus. This confession is the key to entering the kingdom of God, thereby receiving eternal and abundant life (John 3:16; 10:10). It is on this confession that local churches have been planted and will continue to be planted across the globe.

## The Essence of the Church

In his article, "The Essence of the Church," Tom Julien discussed the fact that many church planters often define the local church in terms of their cultural preferences, which can lead to problems on the field. Julien admonished church-planting teams first to come to an agreement on what the local church is so they will know what they are planting.

> Our problem is that we identify the local church by her cultural and historic expression, more than by her biblical essence. To arrive at a clear definition of the local church we must make a distinction between the two. Sluggish thinking here will lead to differing assumptions in the church-planting team that will affect the basic principles of any church-planting ministry. The more focused we are on essence, the less attachment we will have to any particular cultural expression of the church. On the other hand, if the form or cultural expression of the church becomes our reference point, adapting to different cultural situations will create tension.
>
> The New Testament reveals the church both in her essence and expression. With regard to the essence of the church, this revelation is given in images and presented as fact; with respect to the cultural expression of the church, this revelation is given as example and is descriptive rather than prescriptive. . . .
>
> Let us come back to our original question, "What is a local church?" We have said that a local church is a visible manifestation of the biblical essence. Most of us, however, need something more concrete to work with. It is crucial that every church-planting team agree on a working definition, in concrete terms, that grows out of essence, and not expression. This definition must include those elements that

are indispensable to the identity of a church, and omit those that are not. This definition identifies the seed for church planting. Here is an attempt at such a definition. Members of every church-planting team need to be unified with respect to what they are planting even if it takes months of struggle to agree.

A local church is an organized body of baptized believers, led by a spiritually qualified shepherd, affirming their relationship to the Lord and to each other by regular observance of the Lord's Supper, committed to the authority of the Word of God, gathering regularly for worship and the study of the Word, and turned outward to the world in witness.

Taken from Tom Julien, "The Essence of the Church," *Evangelical Missions Quarterly* (April 1998): 148–49, 152.

***Questions to Consider:***

1. What do you think Julien meant by "If the form or cultural expression of the church becomes our reference point, adapting to different cultural situations will create tension"? Can you give an example of such tension?
2. Do you agree or disagree with Julien's definition of the local church?
3. Have you and your church-planting team taken the time to agree on a biblical definition of the local church? If not, why not? How do you know you are all on the same page when you talk about church planting?

## A Common Commitment

Closely connected to the common confession is a commitment on behalf of all of the members of the local church. Having been called out of darkness into the light through the confession of faith in Christ, believers are required to live according to the kingdom ethic that transcends the ethics of the world. This common commitment involves loving God completely (Matthew 22:37). Kingdom citizens are committed to the Creator of the universe and his lordship over their lives as a community and as individuals. Since they love him, they keep his commandments (John 14:15).

### A Common Community

The kingdom ethic that kingdom citizens are called to live requires not only a common commitment to God but also a common community or fellowship. Some have referred to this commitment to one another as a covenant. If anything can be said of the Jerusalem Church in the Book of Acts, it is clear that they had a commitment to one another. They were deeply involved in each other's lives, sharing what they had to meet needs (Acts 4:32–37; 6:1–6).

Church members are to carry each other's burdens (Galatians 6:2) and do good to all people, especially those who belong to the family of believers (Galatians 6:10). This commitment to community also involves being identified as the body of Christ in a particular geographical area. These men and women have intentionally agreed to come together to be the local expression of the universal Church.

### A Common Commission

The kingdom ethic demands that kingdom citizens respond to their neighbors (both local and global) with love. Though such love clearly involves serving them at their points of need, it also includes making disciples of their neighbors (Matthew 22:39; 28:19). In Matthew, Luke, John, and Acts, the Bible records a Great Commission mandate. This commission—though expressed in different words depending on the text—typically involves the Church going into the world and proclaiming the good news of Jesus Christ, baptizing new believers, and teaching them to obey the ways of the Lord in local churches. This commission involves kingdom citizens living according to the kingdom ethic so that those who are outside the kingdom of God will become kingdom citizens in other churches throughout the world.

> **"The church derives its being and essence from Christ."**
>
> —Everett Ferguson, *The Church of Christ: A Biblical Ecclesiology for Today* (Grand Rapids, MI: William B. Eerdmans Publishing Company, 1996), 133.

## Jesus' First Words

I am no auto mechanic, but I do realize that sometimes the small and rarely seen parts of the car are some of the most important. I remember when I had a belt replaced on my vehicle. Over time the heat and wear had caused the belt to crack and fray. The mechanic informed me if that single belt had broken, my vehicle would not have been able to move. I would have been stopped dead in my tracks. Such a small and uncomely part was vital to the working of the entire automobile.

An examination of Jesus' words referring to the C/church could cause some to assume that since Jesus used the word *ekklesia* only a few times in the Gospels (Matthew 16:18; 18:17), then we should immediately jump to the Epistles and gaze into the weightier discourses on the bride of Christ to truly understand the essence and practice of the Church. Such would be akin to me saying that I need to focus only on the more commonly observed parts of my automobile—to the neglect of the serpentine belt hidden under the hood and buried beneath other parts.

Now I realize that throughout Church history much ink and blood have been spilled over the interpretations of these passages, with a multitude of articles and books written addressing these texts. Therefore, some may say that in this section I have not done justice to these passages. At the risk of being misunderstood, I have included a brief discussion of them here. Church planters must understand Jesus' words in the Gospels in order to properly understand what they are to be planting.

## Matthew 16:13–19

This text, as we stated above, contains Peter's great kingdom confession that Jesus is the Christ. Following this declaration Jesus blessed Peter, noting that such knowledge had been divinely revealed. Then Jesus declared, "And I tell you, you are Peter, and on this rock I will build my church, and the gates of hell shall not prevail against it." Here Jesus taught that he himself will be the builder of his Church, it will grow, and not even the second most powerful force in the universe will be able to stop its expansion.

Jesus builds his Church as citizens of the kingdom of darkness become citizens of the kingdom of light. This element of the text teaches that being a part of the Church involves a relationship with King Jesus. While I believe the primary meaning behind Jesus' statement is that he promises to build his Church on this kingdom confession—which is ultimately based on his person and work as the Son of God—there is another important element found in this passage. Peter, along with the rest of the Twelve, was a part of establishing the foundation for the Church (Ephesians 2:20). Though I do not believe this passage offers a foundation for the origins and continuation of the papacy, other passages and the Book of Acts give evidence to the significance of Peter's work in the building of the Church.

> **"The universal church was the universal fellowship of believers who met visibly in local assemblies."**
>
> —Robert L. Saucy, *The Church in God's Program* (Chicago, IL: Moody Press, 1972), 17.

The second significant aspect of this text involves the matter of the keys of the kingdom and the notion of binding and loosing—again, a controversial passage, but important for church planters to understand. Simply put, this text reveals the authority given to the Church to carry out the work of the Great Commission on the earth. Jesus was communicating how the Church is to live in relation to those outside his kingdom. The keys convey authority and the ability to open the kingdom to others—using the gospel message—so that they may make the kingdom confession. What the Church does on earth has a dynamic and intimate relationship with the King in heaven.

## Matthew 18:15–20

This passage is known for advocating the importance of church discipline. However, I fear that many times church planters forget its context and, thereby, miss the important point that Jesus was making that the Church is about relationships with other kingdom citizens. The texts before and after this passage address relationships.

This passage addresses how the church is to relate to those who call themselves brothers and sisters yet fail to live like it. This discipline process leads up to the church speaking truth into the life of the erring individual, with the person being treated as a Gentile and tax collector if the words of the church go unheeded. In practical matters, the person is to be ostracized from the fellowship of the community. Though the church should continue to love and evangelize the person, he or she is no longer considered a kingdom citizen. If the person responds favorably in the process, the fellowship in the church is restored. If not, then the person remains outside the membership of the local church.

Once again, Jesus spoke of the binding and loosing, showing the dynamic and intimate relationship between the Church and the King. When this text is coupled with the promises of the Father hearing and granting the requests of his people in community with one another (v. 19) and Jesus' promise to be present when his people are in community with one another (v. 20), the truth about the Church becomes very clear. The Church involves intimate relationships with other kingdom citizens, and it is in the local assembly of those citizens that the Son is present. The King is greatly concerned with the health of the fellowship among kingdom citizens in the Church.

Specifically, these texts address the work of Christ and the building of his Church and how restoration should occur whenever someone in the church sins against another believer. Broadly speaking, however, from these two texts regarding Jesus' first words concerning the C/church, we learn that the C/church is about relationships. The passages help us to understand that life in the body of Christ is about *relationships* with God, *relationships* with other kingdom citizens, and *relationships* with those outside the kingdom—with these relationships being lived out according to the kingdom way of life. The birth, growth, and health of the C/church involve people relating to the Lord and one another according to biblical parameters.

Missionaries must not forget this fact. When church planting becomes focused on starting worship services, marketing, outreach programs, church models and structures, numbers, budgets, start-up costs, and children's programs, then the church-planting team has lost its focus on the kingdom ethic and must return to the Scriptures for proper reorientation toward its true purpose.

## Biblical Images

In addition to Jesus' words, the New Testament writers included numerous metaphors to provide us with a more robust picture of the Church. Below is a list of some of these terms.

- Family (Matthew 12:48–49; 1 Timothy 5:1–2)

- Body (1 Corinthians 12:20; Ephesians 1:22–23)
- Priests (1 Peter 2:9)
- Fellowship (1 John 1:7)
- Community (Acts 2:44; 4:34)
- Temple (1 Corinthians 3:16)
- Building (Ephesians 2:19–21)
- Bride (Ephesians 5:22–33; Revelation 21:9)
- Branches (John 15:5)
- Sheep (John 10:1–18)
- Salt (Matthew 5:13)
- Light (Matthew 5:14)

> **"Biblical theology is a mark of a healthy church."**
>
> —Thom S. Rainer and Daniel L. Akin, *Vibrant Church: Becoming a Healthy Church in the 21st Century* (Nashville, TN: LifeWay Press, 2008), 52.

It is important that church planters recognize what is included and what is not included in such a list. First, there is no reference to the C/church being a literal building. The closest the New Testament comes to such a description is with the word *temple* in Ephesians 2:19–21 and 1 Corinthians 3:16. These verses describe the C/church as a spiritual structure that Christ is building on himself and the work of the apostles and prophets; and the C/church is also something that the Holy Spirit indwells as he indwells kingdom citizens. Though the church is an assembly of people that physically meets together, there is nothing in these references defining the church by the worship service or a physical address, such as, "Church was at 11:00 AM" or "We went to church today." Neither is there any reference in the New Testament to the C/church being a denomination or a state-run organization.

The C/church is the work of God (Father, Son, and Holy Spirit) by his grace, mercy, love, and eternal plan. An examination of these images does reveal some very important aspects about the nature and function of the C/church. First, the C/church is dependent on something greater than itself: the King. The sheep need a shepherd. The branches need a vine. A bride must have a bridegroom. A building must have a cornerstone.

Second, the C/church is dependent on other kingdom citizens. A family requires more than one person. A fellowship and community must have healthy intimacy with one another for fellowship and community to exist. A healthy physical body requires all of its parts to work in harmony. When one part of the family, fellowship, community, or body suffers, all suffer.

Third, the C/church has a proper relationship to those outside the kingdom. Priests represent people to God and God to the people. Priests intercede on the behalf of others. Salt and light purify and counteract decay and darkness. Again, we see the principle of relationships with the King, other kingdom citizens, and those outside the kingdom being intimately connected to life in the body of Christ, particularly at the local level.

> "Rather, each local congregation is fully *ekklesia* in itself."
>
> —John S. Hammett, *Biblical Foundations for Baptist Churches: A Contemporary Ecclesiology* (Grand Rapids, MI: Kregel Publications, 2005), 30.

## A Covenant Community

There seems to be a growing trend these days for believers to quit attending their local churches while still considering themselves members of the universal Church. The Scriptures do not support such a position. The Bible assumes that all believers remain active members in local expressions of the covenant community. The local church ordinances help define this covenant relationship. Baptism is an initiatory rite and the Lord's Supper is an ongoing rite—with both serving as public declarations of the covenant relationship between Christ and his Church.

Life in the kingdom is meant to be carried out day by day at the local level. It is here that kingdom citizens are able to live out the kingdom ethic in accountability with one another. It is at this local level that the Church is able to rightly preach and teach the Scriptures, carry one another's burdens, hold one another accountable, love one another, encourage one another to good works, celebrate the ordinances of baptism and the Lord's Supper, fellowship, serve one another and their neighbors, and carry out the Great Commission.

At this point I would like to examine the local church from a different, yet biblical, angle. Many of us have grown to appreciate the use of different camera angles to show instant replays in the world of sports. This technique has changed the way people view and understand some of their favorite games. What is seen and assumed from one camera angle is sometimes understood better when examined using a different camera. In the paragraphs below I present a biblical perspective of the local church in categories of a "more than, less than" spectrum. I hope that this will assist you in viewing the local expression of the body of Christ from a different angle and lead you to a deeper understanding.

## More Organic, Less Institutional

An examination of passages addressing the C/church reveals an entity that is more defined by its organic nature and less by its institutional nature. Contrary to many Western notions, life in the kingdom is not about the church functioning in compartmentalized ways. Evangelism and discipleship are not programs. Worship does not only happen a couple of hours each week. Fellowship does not primarily take place in a large room referred to as a hall. The responsibilities for church membership are not diluted to, "Simply attend our meetings, agree with the pastors, and give a small amount of your money." Pastors/elders are not professional clergy who are paid to perform specialized activities. Obedience—and not the size of the congregation or the wealth and abilities of the members—is the measure of church health. Faith is not privatized; that is, church members do not march to the mantra: "What I do with my faith is between me and God and no one else." Rather, the local church is the people of God living as a family in relation to one another. Though it does have structure, order, leadership, and purpose, the church is not a business, bureaucracy, or corporation.

## More Simplicity, Less Structure

The vitality of the church is not related to complicated organization, but rather to the simple expression of the work of the Holy Spirit indwelling kingdom citizens in conjunction with the Scriptures and Spirit-appointed leaders (Acts 20:28). The preaching of the gospel message can be as faithfully and accurately communicated by the illiterate as it can be communicated by the greatest scholarly orator. The message is simple, and the means by which that message is communicated can be simple and still be powerful.

The church was never designed to take its essence and vitality from structures, programs, or organizations. It can be used in a mighty way for global disciple making even among the least organized and least bureaucratic communities. The church was never created to function as a large, impersonal machine.

## More Community, Less Acquaintances

Missionaries must recognize that the church is not a group of people connected by surface-level acquaintances. Rather, to be in the church means to be a part of an intimate community. We are brothers and sisters. Such appellations are not simply code words for a secret society. Believers are to bear one another's burdens (Galatians 6:2), love one another (John 13:34), confess sins to one another (James 5:16), and meet in order to encourage one another (Hebrews 10:25).

The church is to hold its members accountable for godly living and appropriately judge one another (1 Corinthians 5:12–13). As a spiritual family, what happens in the life of one member has ramifications for the other members (1 Corinthians 12).

## More Ministers, Less Minister

The Scriptures teach that every kingdom citizen is a minister; we are a royal priesthood (1 Peter 2:9). Church planters must understand that service in the body involves everyone ministering, not just the few people in top leadership. In no way, however, does this fact diminish the importance of the need for pastoral leadership. God has gifted some to be pastor-teachers for the equipping of the other believers in their individual ministries in the local church (Ephesians 4:11–12). In healthy churches all members are using their gifts and talents to minister to one another and the world (Romans 12:5–8).

Though newly planted churches should make intentional plans to have biblically qualified, Spirit-appointed elders and deacons to lead and serve as soon as possible, this structure does not have to be in place at the birth of the church. In the New Testament, local churches existed before the appointment of elders (Acts 14:23; Titus 1:5). Like the New Testament missionary teams, church planters must make certain that proper leaders are in place (1 Timothy 3:1–12; Titus 1:5–9). Biblical leadership is vital to the health of the church.

## More Participation, Less Passivity

Every kingdom citizen has something significant to contribute to the work of the body of Christ in his or her geographical location and throughout the world (Romans 12:3–8; 1 Corinthians 12–14). There is no New Testament concept of a pew sitter in the local church. Nor is there any biblical notion that someone can be a member of the body of Christ and only attend the worship gatherings. Being a part of the church means more than being a part of a crowd. Missionaries must grasp and teach the truth that passivity is not a part of kingdom life. Rather, kingdom life means bearing spiritual fruit and being discipled warriors in the ongoing spiritual battle.

### *Summary:*

1. The New Testament refers to a universal and a local expression of the body of Christ.
2. In the New Testament those who are part of the Church are also be part of a church.
3. It is very important for church planters to understand Jesus' teachings on the C/church as well as the biblical metaphors describing the C/church.
4. The church consists of kingdom citizens living in accordance with the kingdom ethic as described in the Scriptures.
5. The kingdom ethic involves the relationships between kingdom citizens with God, other kingdom citizens, and those outside the kingdom.
6. The church comes into existence as the Holy Spirit brings baptized believers together who understand and identify themselves as the local expression of the Church.

## *Reflection Questions:*

1. In conversations with others, do you describe the church in nonbiblical terms? If so, why? What are you communicating to others regarding the doctrine of the church?
2. Can you provide other biblical metaphors for the C/church not listed in this chapter?
3. Do you agree or disagree that the church is primarily about relationships? Explain your answer.
4. How does thinking about the church in terms of relationships and the kingdom ethic affect your thinking about church planting?

## *Important Terms in This Chapter:*

- *Ekklesia*
- Kingdom citizens
- Kingdom ethic

Chapter 4

# HOLY SPIRIT AND CHURCH PLANTING

**If we are to be in touch with God today, then, we must become acquainted with the Holy Spirit's activity.**
**—Millard J. Erickson[1]**

One recent day at my house a tragedy occurred. For some strange reason my Internet access was not working.

My modem was flashing like a Christmas tree, yet the message on my monitor clearly informed me that until the issue was corrected, there would be no surfing or e-mail for the day—most definitely a crisis!

After attempting to locate the problem, resetting the modem, unplugging and plugging in about five thousand cables, I finally decided to call the troubleshooting hot line. After a few moments on the phone, I had my problem diagnosed, and the prognosis looked good.

I was simply told to plug my telephone line into the phone jack.

Somehow (I'm thinking . . . the work of a fifteen-month-old, little boy) the phone cable became disconnected from the most basic yet vitally important element required for Internet service.

> "Missionary zeal is grounded in the nature and character of the Holy Ghost."
>
> —Roland Allen, *Missionary Principles* (Grand Rapids, MI: William B. Eerdmans Publishing Company, 1964), 55.

Though the Holy Spirit is not a force, but rather a person, church planters will find themselves impotent (much like my Web browser) when it comes to spiritual matters if they are not in close connection with the Spirit. Though every church planter I know would state that the Holy Spirit's role in the birth of churches is absolutely essential, there is little contemporary discussion regarding his role in this process. The purpose of this chapter is to fill a significant gap in the literature in an attempt to develop a biblical understanding of the Spirit in the advancement of the gospel. Consider the following.

Without the Holy Spirit:

- missionaries would not be called by God (Acts 13:2)
- missionaries would not be empowered for missions (Acts 1:8)
- missionaries would not be guided to receptive people (Acts 8:29; 16:6–7)
- missionaries would not have divine boldness for witness (Acts 4:13, 31)
- missionaries would not have the wisdom of God to speak clearly (John 16:13; 1 Corinthians 2:13)
- the conviction of sin, righteousness, and judgment would not happen (John 16:8)
- no one would be born again (John 3:5–8; 1 Corinthians 12:3)
- churches would not be birthed (1 Thessalonians 1:5–6)
- elders would not be appointed to oversee churches (Acts 20:28)

> "It is therefore indispensable that we should know what the Bible teaches concerning the Holy Ghost, both as to his nature and office."
>
> —Charles Hodge, *Systematic Theology,* vol. 1 (Grand Rapids, MI: William B. Eerdmans Publishing Company, n.d.), 523.

If the significance of the Holy Spirit is this important to church planting, then why is there a dearth of discussion surrounding the third person of the Trinity in many missiological circles?

## We Take the Holy Spirit for Granted

I remember when my wife and I were given a grandfather clock (which originally belonged to her grandfather) that chimed every fifteen minutes. For the first several weeks, every fifteen minutes we heard the clock. Over time, however, we grew so accustomed to the sound of the clock that we did not notice when it chimed. One day I was almost late for a meeting because I told myself that I needed to leave in fifteen minutes and that I would leave when I heard the clock. Since I was so used to hearing the chime, I blocked out the sound and failed to leave on time.

Unless we are daily dying to self and continually being filled with the Spirit (Ephesians 5:18), we run the risk of grieving the Spirit (Ephesians 4:30) and not "hearing" his voice and following his guidance. Our familiarity with the Spirit can lead to us taking him for granted. This real and present danger is devastating to church planters.

Those laboring in the trenches cannot simply assume that the Holy Spirit is going to always show up. I once recall driving down the road with a man who had planted several churches. As we passed a newly developed community of apartments, I recall him looking at those buildings and declaring with confidence, "I could easily plant a church in that community." Then I asked him, "How do you know the Holy Spirit will birth a church in that location?" He did not respond.

Church planters must not take the Spirit for granted and simply assume that they have a monopoly on him. Rather, wise are the missionaries who allow the Spirit to have a monopoly on them.

Church planting is more art than science, and, though there are normative workings of the Spirit, we must remember that we cannot accurately predict where he is coming from or where he is going. It is a mystery.

## We Are Afraid of Being Labeled "Charismatic"

I fear that some church planters have seen the extremism and abuse of the doctrine of the Holy Spirit and have reacted in a negative manner. Rather than returning to the Scriptures to guide their beliefs and practices, they have erred on the other side of the issue by practically denying the work of the Spirit in missionary activity. If we confess the Holy Spirit with our lips in church planting but deny him with our practice, we are simply missiological hypocrites. John V. Taylor observed, "But, while we piously repeat the traditional assertion that without the Holy Spirit we can get nowhere in the Christian mission, we seem to press on notwithstanding with our man-made programmes."[2]

## We Are Ignorant of the Biblical Teachings

Unfortunately, many missionaries have zeal without knowledge (Proverbs 19:2). They greatly desire to reach the world for Jesus but fail to understand Jesus because they relegate doctrine to the halls of theological academia. Since church planters are to baptize new believers in the name of the Holy Spirit (Matthew 28:19), it is of great importance to have a solid biblical understanding of him.

> "We cannot accept the teaching of the Acts, we cannot believe that the one thing of importance to our souls is to receive and to know the Spirit, without feeling ourselves driven to missionary action."
>
> —Roland Allen, *The Ministry of the Spirit: Selected Writings of Roland Allen* (Grand Rapids, MI: William B. Eerdmans Publishing Company, 1960), 61.

Another element contributing to our general ignorance of the missional nature of the Holy Spirit is the lack of theological articles on this subject. In preparing to write this chapter, I consulted a few highly acclaimed systematic theology books and, particularly, looked for discussions related to the missionary work of the Spirit. Unfortunately, I found very little. If our theologians are not addressing this matter, it is no wonder that the missionaries influenced by them are also not thinking along this line.

## What Is the Role of the Holy Spirit in Church Planting?

The Holy Spirit has a multifaceted role in the missionary activity of the Church. J. Terry Young was correct when he wrote, "Thus, any talk of planting churches must give careful attention to the subject of the role of the Spirit in bringing new churches to birth and maturity. The work of the Holy Spirit in the church is indispensable. Without him the church would have no life, certainly no vitality such as is needed to bring new churches to birth."[3]

Though entire books have been devoted to the topic of **pneumatology** (the doctrine of the Holy Spirit), the rest of this chapter will briefly describe twelve specific elements of the work of the Spirit in church planting.

## Empowering the Church

A search for the word *power* in the Scriptures reveals over two hundred occurrences, with many of these referring to the power of God. For example, God's powerful right hand shatters the enemy (Exodus 15:6). God gave Moses power to deliver the Israelites (Exodus 4:21). The Lord's power is not limited (Numbers 11:23). Several chapters in the Book of Job reveal the power of God through creation (Job 12; 23; 24; 26). The psalmist declared that the Lord has made known his power (Psalm 111:6). Nahum referred to God as being great in power (Nahum 1:3). It was the power of God that came on Mary that resulted in the miraculous conception (Luke 1:35). Jesus ministered in the power of the Spirit (Luke 4:14). The religious leaders of Jesus' day failed to understand the power of God (Mark 12:24). The power of God works to perform healings (Luke 5:17). Jesus gave power to his disciples to heal diseases and to cast out demons (Luke 9:1). Power came to the Church when the Holy Spirit arrived (Acts 1:8). The power of God enabled the Church to bear a mighty witness to the resurrection (Acts 4:33). On several occasions, Paul referred to the power of the Holy Spirit (Romans 15:13, 19; Ephesians 3:16; Galatians 4:29).

Even a cursory reading of the Scriptures reveals that the Spirit of God is **omnipotent** (all-powerful). He is not limited by anything in his creation and grants power to his people to accomplish more than they imagine or ask (Ephesians 3:20) related to his will and the expansion of his kingdom. Apart from the power of God that comes through abiding in his Son, the Church can do nothing for the kingdom (John 15:4), but those who believe in him are able to do amazing works (John 14:12).

## The True Missionary of Acts

Roland Allen (1868–1947) was an Anglican bishop who served for a short period of time as a missionary to China. He is best known for his writings about missionary methods and the natural growth of the Church. For Allen, the Holy Spirit was the reason for missionary zeal and Church growth. In the following excerpt from the conclusion of his work "Pentecost and the World," he summarized his perspective on the Holy Spirit and the practical results of such doctrine. For Allen, the true missionary is the Holy Spirit.

> In the preceding chapters I have tried to show that the coming of the Holy Spirit at Pentecost was the coming of a missionary Spirit; that the Spirit stirred in the hearts of the disciples of Christ a great desire to impart that which they had received; that He revealed to them the need of men for that which He alone could supply; that He enabled them to hand on to others that which they themselves had received; that He led them to reach out farther and farther into the Gentile world, breaking down every barrier of prejudice which might have hindered their witness, or prevented them from receiving into communion men the most remote from them in habits of thought and life. . . .
>
> If we believe in the Holy Spirit as He is revealed in the Acts, we must be missionaries. We cannot accept the teaching of the Acts, we cannot believe that the one thing of importance to our souls is to receive and to know the Spirit, without feeling ourselves driven to missionary action. We cannot believe that the Holy Spirit reveals our own need and the need of men without beginning to feel that need of men for Christ laid upon us as a serious call to action.
>
> We cannot believe that the Holy Spirit is given to us that those who so need Christ may be by us brought to find the one way of salvation for their souls and bodies in this world and in the world to come, without feeling impelled to action. We cannot believe that men everywhere, whatever their previous education or ignorance, whatever their civilization or barbarism, are capable of receiving Christ and His salvation, without being moved to take a world-wide view of our responsibility. We must embrace the world because Christ embraces the world, and Christ has come to us, and Christ in us embraces the world. Activity world-wide in its direction and intention and hope and object is inevitable for us unless we are ready to deny the Holy Spirit of Christ revealed in the Acts.

Taken from Roland Allen, "Pentecost and the World" in *The Ministry of the Spirit: Selected Writings of Roland Allen*, ed. David M. Paton (Grand Rapids, MI: William B. Eerdmans Publishing Company, 1960), 59, 61.

***Questions to Consider:***

1. Do you agree or disagree with Allen that the Holy Spirit is a "missionary Spirit"? Why?
2. Does the doctrine of the Holy Spirit require all disciples to be missionaries? Why or why not?
3. What did Allen believe about denying the Holy Spirit? Do you agree or disagree with him? Explain your answer.

## Calling the Missionaries

Throughout history God has called out his ambassadors to bear witness of his glory. He began in the garden by calling Eve to bear the seed that would crush the head of the serpent (Genesis 3:15) and would overcome the death brought about by the first Adam (Romans 5:14; 1 Corinthians 15:22). Abram was called to be a blessing to the nations (Genesis 12:2). Throughout the Old Testament, God continued to call people to special tasks: Noah, Ruth, David, Esther, Daniel, Isaiah, Jonah, and Malachi. The pattern is repeated in the New Testament with Mary, John the Baptist, the Twelve, the Seventy-two, Paul, Barnabas, Silas, Timothy, and John Mark—people called by God to labor for the fulfillment of salvation history.

## Sending the Missionaries

As mentioned above, Roland Allen referred to the Holy Spirit as a missionary Spirit and called the Church to truly understand and grasp the meaning and power of the Spirit as missionary. Though Allen died in 1947, the contemporary Church has yet to grasp the significance of this understanding of the nature of the Holy Spirit. Before Pentecost and the filling of the Spirit (Acts 2:1–4), Jesus' sending of the Twelve and Seventy-two (Luke 9; 10) foreshadowed a pattern that would continue through the work of the Holy Spirit. Probably, the clearest example of the Spirit sending missionaries to plant churches is in relation to the Church at Antioch (Acts 13:1–4). Luke noted that the Spirit not only called out Paul and Barnabas for specific missionary service but also sent them on their way.

## Working in the World

The nature of the Spirit is that he is constantly at work in the world. From creation (Genesis 1:2) until the end of the Book of Revelation (Revelation 22:17), the Spirit is constantly working out the will of God, especially related to the plan of salvation among the nations. Jesus taught the Twelve that the Spirit was working even when they were not on the scene, resulting in others reaping the harvest (John 4:34–38). Paul noted that though he and Apollos were at work, it was God who was causing the growth (1 Corinthians 3:7). Missionaries are wise to remember Tom Steffen's words, "The Holy Spirit was there prior to the arrival of the church planters, he is there during their stay, and he will remain after their departure."[4]

## Guiding Church Planters

Missionaries must rely on the guidance of the Spirit. It was the Spirit who led Paul and Silas to Philippi. On two occasions they attempted to travel to other areas, but the Spirit prevented them (Acts 16:6–7). Shortly after this interruption to the plans of the missionaries, Paul received the vision of the Macedonian man, and the team set sail for Philippi (Acts 16:9).

> **"Human instruments, apart from the Holy Spirit, cannot change dead hearts, obstinate wills, evil imaginations, perverted understandings, and biased judgments."**
>
> —J. B. Lawrence, *The Holy Spirit in Missions* (Atlanta, GA: Home Mission Board, 1966), 64.

## Preparing Persons of Peace

Though more will be said about receptivity and persons of peace in a later chapter, the **person of peace** is that individual who is the first one to come to faith in Christ through the love and service of the church-planting team. This person is significant to the dissemination of the gospel throughout the people group or population segment.

J. B. Lawrence wrote, "Missionaries would preach the gospel in vain to men who are dead in trespasses and in sins if the Holy Spirit did not quicken the perception of these men and make available to them the life-giving, redeeming gospel."[5] Wise church planters allow the Spirit to guide them to the people he is going to use to birth his church. It was through such guidance that the Spirit took Paul and Silas to the households of Lydia and the Philippian jailer and birthed the Philippian Church (Acts 16:14–15, 32–33).

## Providing Boldness, Peace, and Wisdom for Witness

Paul encouraged Timothy with these words, "For God gave us a spirit not of fear but of power and love and self-control" (2 Timothy 1:7; cf. Acts 7:55–56). When threatened, the early believers prayed for boldness to speak the word of the Lord. Luke noted this when he wrote, "And when they had prayed, the place in which they were gathered together was shaken, and they were all filled with the Holy Spirit and continued to speak the word of God with boldness" (Acts 4:31). It is also the Spirit who guides believers into all truth (John 16:13) and speaks through those who are brought to trial for their faith (Mark 13:11). It was the Spirit of Wisdom who spoke through Peter and John (Acts 4:13) and Stephen (Acts 6:10), confounding the religious leaders.

## Working through the Preaching of the Church Planters

All church planters are called to preach the gospel in the marketplace, among the highways and hedges, and in season and out of season (2 Timothy 4:2). Without the preaching of the gospel, disciples will not be made and churches will not be planted (Romans 10:14). Biblical church planting is evangelism that results in new churches. Paul recognized that his preaching was not with persuasive words, but rather with the Spirit's power (1 Corinthians 2:4; 1 Thessalonians 1:5; cf. 1 Peter 1:12).

## Convicting, Convincing, and Converting the Unregenerate

Since the message of the cross is foolishness to those who are perishing (1 Corinthians 1:18), the work of the Spirit is necessary for the salvation of sinners—convicting them of sin, convincing them of the righteousness and judgment of God, and converting their unbelief to faith (John 3:6; 16:8; Acts 16:14). Referring to the unbeliever, John Stott wrote, "Only the Holy Spirit can open his eyes, enlighten his darkness, liberate him from bondage, turn him to God and bring him out of death into life."[6]

> "[A] primary function of the Holy Spirit in the church is to lead it in missionary expansion, reaching people and planting churches."
>
> —J. Terry Young, "The Holy Spirit and the Birth of Churches," in *The Birth of Churches: A Biblical Basis for Church Planting*, compiler/contributor Talmadge R. Amberson, (Nashville, TN: Broadman Press, 1979), 167.

## Birthing and Gifting the Churches

Since churches come into existence as disciples are made, it is the Spirit who gives birth to local churches. He is the one who brings people to salvation and convinces them of the need to be the local expression of the body of Christ in their specific areas. Missionaries co-labor with him by preaching the Word and organizing the new believers, but credit must be given to the Spirit for his work. Young noted, "It seems to be a fair conclusion that one of the major works of the Holy Spirit in the New Testament age was that of planting new churches."[7] It was God who "opened a door of faith to the Gentiles" (Acts 14:27) that resulted in the planting of numerous churches during Paul's first missionary journey.

Also, new churches are gifted by the Spirit to be the body of Christ (1 Corinthians 12). Every church, regardless of age, consists of believers indwelled by the Spirit of God (Romans 5:5) and spiritually gifted to carry out the work of kingdom expansion.

## Appointing Elders over the Churches

Church planters have a tremendous responsibility of making sure new churches have biblical leaders overseeing the congregations. Paul and Barnabas appointed elders in the newly planted churches on their first missionary journey (Acts 14:23). Titus remained on Crete to appoint elders as Paul had instructed him (Titus 1:5). Though the apostle took the responsibility of appointing such leadership with much seriousness, he was also quick to point out that it was the Holy Spirit who actually was responsible for appointing the pastors (Acts 20:28).

## Protecting the New Churches until Glorification

Clearly, there were times when Paul had to leave a city because of persecution. Generally, he was willing to depart and plant churches elsewhere, while remaining connected to the new churches through letters and visits. Paul never saw this phasing out of the team from the scene as being irresponsible, but rather a necessity for healthy kingdom expansion. Even in light of the fact that he knew "fierce wolves" would come to attack the Church in Ephesus (Acts 20:29–30), he still wanted to travel on to Jerusalem in time for Pentecost (Acts 20:16).

How was Paul able to leave disciples who were recent converts to the faith? How was he able to leave the newly planted churches? Perhaps Allen said it best by referring to the apostle's faith in the Spirit.

> He believed in the Holy Ghost, not merely vaguely as a spiritual Power, but as a Person indwelling his converts. He believed therefore in his converts. He could trust them. He did not trust them because he believed in their natural virtue or intellectual sufficiency. If he had believed in that, his faith must have been sorely shaken. But he believed in the Holy Ghost in them. He believed that Christ was able and willing to keep that which he had committed to Him. He believed that He would perfect His Church, that He would stablish, strengthen, settle his converts. He believed, and acted as if he believed.
>
> It is that faith which we need today. We need to subordinate our methods, our systems, ourselves to that faith.[8]

Paul understood that the Spirit was able to "strengthen" the churches (Romans 16:25), and he would agree with Jude that the Spirit "is able to keep you from stumbling and to present you blameless before the presence of his glory with great joy" (Jude v. 24).

### *Summary:*

1. Without the Holy Spirit, churches would not be planted.
2. The Holy Spirit is a missionary Spirit.
3. There are at least three reasons for the neglect of a biblical understanding of the role of the Holy Spirit in missions.

4. The doctrine of the Holy Spirit is known as pneumatology.
5. There are at least twelve specific ways in which the Spirit works in the ministry of church planting.
6. Church planters must have a biblical understanding of the person and work of the Holy Spirit.

## *Reflection Questions:*

1. Do you agree or disagree with the reasons why the Western contemporary Church has not placed much emphasis on the role of the Holy Sprit in church planting? Are there other reasons you would add to the list?
2. Are there any contemporary church-planting practices that you believe grieve the Holy Spirit? Explain your thoughts?
3. Can you think of any additional ways in which the Holy Spirit is involved in church planting?
4. Is the Spirit calling you to serve as a missionary? What is he saying to you inwardly? What is your local church saying to you? Do you have a compelling desire to serve among a particular people group? If so, are you willing to share these thoughts and feelings with your pastor?

## *Important Terms in This Chapter:*

- Pneumatology
- Omnipotent
- Person of peace

Chapter 5

# PRAYER, SPIRITUAL WARFARE, AND CHURCH PLANTING

Prayer and missions are bosom companions.

—E. M. Bounds[1]

As I write this portion of the chapter, I am sitting in a hotel room in Atlanta, Georgia, looking out the window at the international airport where planes are taking off and landing every few seconds. This particular airport is one of the busiest in the world. From my vantage point, I can see the tower where the air traffic controllers provide guidance for the pilots and serve a critical role in the safety of the flights arriving and departing. I can see that if pilots neglect to communicate with the control tower, they are risking disaster.

Similarly, when missionaries neglect communication with their heavenly Father, they are risking disaster. As I write this chapter, I pray that the readers of this book will understand the essential role of prayer and the critical significance of spiritual warfare in missions. I hope that many of you will grow in appreciation of the primary place of prayer in your work.

*For you to be effective in church planting, prayer must precede your arrival on the field, saturate every step of the church-planting strategy, and continue for the new believers and churches after your team departs to plant other churches.* The permeation of prayer throughout the ministry is of paramount importance to *everything* the church-planting team does. Church planters must be people of prayer.

Though I will later address the two most important responsibilities of missionaries—evangelism and leadership development—it should be understood that even these great activities must be bathed in prayer. There are many things for a church-planting team to accomplish, and prayer must encompass all it does. If the team is too busy to spend significant amounts of time in communication with the Father, then it is simply too busy. One hero of the faith from Church history said that he had so much to do every day that he had to spend the first two hours of the day in prayer.

> "Evangelism is itself a spiritual battle, as we take the gospel of light into the kingdom of darkness."
>
> —Chuck Lawless, *Discipled Warriors* (Grand Rapids, MI: Kregel, 2002), 83.

As I look out my eighth-floor window across the interstate and over the tops of trees, I observe exciting things happening at the airport. What seems like a never-ending line of passenger planes are on the tarmac—some large and some small, some colorful and others plain. In the sky, planes are in formation to land, while others are taking off with great speed. Lights are flashing, and jet engines are roaring. With all this movement and excitement, it is easy to forget that these aircrafts will not take off and land safely without the air traffic controllers who sit atop a lonely tower.

Like the activity in the control tower, prayer may appear uncomely when examined against the excitement of evangelism, outreach events, and new worship services. In the excitement of the process of church planting, I pray that prayer would not become something that is done every now and then, but rather the vital piece of strategy upon which all the other pieces rest. Such a desire assumes the church planters are walking in the light "as he is in the light" (1 John 1:7). This intimate fellowship with the Father includes wearing the full armor of God so that church planters are able to stand against the schemes of the Evil One as they participate in the advancement of the kingdom (Ephesians 6:10–20). Prayer is to precede the battle, be maintained throughout the battle, and continue long after the battle. In other words, Christians are to "pray without ceasing" (1 Thessalonians 5:17).

> **"Church planting is actually strategic warfare and is similar to attempting to establish a beachhead in enemy territory."**
>
> —Fred Herron, *Expanding God's Kingdom through Church Planting* (New York: Writer's Showcase, 2003), 223.

## Apostolic Example

An examination of the biblical text reveals that both Jesus and the apostolic Church understood that a real spiritual battle was occurring between the kingdom of light and the kingdom of darkness. Throughout the New Testament, both Jesus and the Church reveal the priority given to prayer.

Luke reveals that Jesus was a man of prayer, even praying all night before the selection of the Twelve (Luke 6:12). He set the example as the great Apostle (Hebrews 3:1) and Intercessor (Hebrews 7:25) by praying for his disciples that the Father would keep them in the world and from the Evil One as they participated in the advancement of the kingdom (John 17:15).

Following the ascension, the filling of the Spirit and the explosive growth of the apostolic Church came about while the believers were continually devoting themselves to prayer (Acts 1:14). Such practice continued after the conversion of the multitude on the day of Pentecost (Acts 2:42), as the Lord continued to bring others to faith in Christ (Acts 2:47).

The apostles understood that a primary component of their ministries was prayer in conjunction with their evangelism (Acts 6:4). Paul prayed for the new churches on a regular basis. He told the Philippians that he prayed for them as he remembered them (Philippians 1:3–4). He reminded the Roman believers that he believed prayer was a means by which God worked to bring about the salvation of others (Romans 10:1).

In the New Testament, prayer was not a magical incantation that mystics wielded over God to manipulate him to accomplish their desires. Instead, prayer can be compared to breathing. Just as we naturally breathe as long as life is present, the disciples naturally communed with their Father. The apostles knew that the mission of the gospel is God's mission to be accomplished by his means. The battle is intense; therefore, an upright life that includes speaking and listening to the Commanding General is necessary for the multiplication of disciples, leaders, and churches throughout the world.

"We must pray for the Power, pray in the Spirit, pray at every phase and every turn of our witnessing."

—W. O. Carver, *Missions in the Plan of the Ages* (New York: Fleming H. Revell Company, 1909), 216–17.

## Spiritual Warfare

The life of the disciple is a life of constant spiritual warfare. Satan is constantly attempting to destroy the fellowship between believers and their Father. The Evil One is also working hard to steal the seed away from others to keep them from the kingdom (Luke 8:12). Rick Love warned, "Church planters need to be prepared to resist Satanic attacks that are *mental, moral* and *physical.*"[2] Satan knows exactly how to work with the world's system and with fallen flesh to maintain his ground and to hinder kingdom advancement. Missionaries, their families, and those they minister to will experience mental, moral, and physical attacks from the Evil One. Not only are such acts of opposition found in the Scriptures, but contemporary church planters, time and again, share stories of such warfare experienced on the field. This opposition can come in the form of temptation with issues such as laziness, lust, or an obsession with personal problems. At other times it manifests itself in the form of conflict in the home, physical illness, and expressions of demonic presence.

## The Need for Discipled Warriors

Someone once said that we do not fight for victory, but from victory. Even in light of Christ's work on the cross, missionaries continue to find themselves involved in various battles. In his book *Discipled Warriors,* Chuck Lawless called the Church to personal holiness through submission to the way of the Lord.[3] For it is only when church planters are grounded in their faith that they are wearing the full armor of God, ready for any spiritual opposition. Church planters cannot be warriors for battle and the advancement of the kingdom until they are solid disciples in the faith—living by God's truth, righteousness, and peace and walking by faith (Ephesians 6:10–18). There will be no resistance to the ways of the

Evil One (1 Peter 5:9) unless they are living according to God's Word and persevering in prayer (Ephesians 6:17–19).

> **"As those involved in starting new churches, we will do well to pray and pray and pray."**
>
> —Tom Nebel and Gary Rohrmayer, *Church Planting Landmines: Mistakes to Avoid in Years 2 Through 10* (St. Charles, IL: ChurchSmart Resources, 2005), 108.

## An Intercessory Team

Both Jesus and Paul addressed the importance of corporate prayer for the advancement of the kingdom. Jesus taught the importance of agreeing in prayer with other believers when he stated that intercession guaranteed that the Father would provide according to such praying (Matthew 18:18–20). While on mission with Jesus, the disciples were taught that some demons can only be cast out by prayer (Mark 9:29).

Paul knew the Corinthians' prayers were a significant part of his missionary work (2 Corinthians 1:11). Writing to the Philippian believers, he noted their prayers for him would be part of the process of his release from prison (Philippians 1:19). This conviction about the prayers of the saints working to deliver him from prison was also made known to Philemon, Apphia, and the church in Archippus's house (Philemon v. 22). A parallel can be found in the deliverance of Peter from prison as the Church fervently interceded on his behalf (Acts 12:5). Paul was not shy about telling the Colossian believers to devote themselves to prayer (Colossians 4:2), while specifically praying that the church-planting team would have opportunities to preach the gospel in a way that others would be able to hear and understand the message (Colossians 4:3–4).

E. M. Bounds once wrote, "The home church on her knees, fasting and praying, is the great base of spiritual supplies, the sinews of war, and the pledge of victory in this dire and final conflict. Financial resources are not the real sinews of war in this fight. Machinery in itself carries no power to break down heathen walls, open effectual doors and win heathen hearts to Christ. Prayer alone can do the deed."[4]

> **"We must have the intent to gather and plant churches whenever we engage in spiritual warfare. As we bind strongholds and release the people from their grip, it must be our intent to gather people into what will eventually become His church in that place."**
>
> —Bruce Carlton, *Acts 29* (n.p.: Radical Obedience Publishing, 2003), 85.

Church-planting teams must understand the power found in effective prayers of righteous people (James 5:16) and pray for the Lord to provide them with an intercessory team. H. Gerald Colbert reminded missionaries, "After confirming God's call, one of the first actions that a church planter needs to take is to enlist an intercessory prayer team as part of the total planting support system."[5] I once heard of a mission agency not sending any missionary to the field until he or she had developed an intercessory team of at least one hundred committed people. Church planters must not overlook the importance of taking the time for building an intercessory prayer team.

## Planter's Personal Prayer Life

One of my students who served with a church planter told me how impressed he was with one man's prayer life. Each week they would regularly gather to pray for at least a couple of hours for the unbelievers in the area. This student had realized that this commitment to prayer had been a vital component of the large number of people who came to faith in the community.

## One of the Biggest Challenges

Rick Love, in his work *Muslims, Magic and the Kingdom of God*, tackled the issue of spiritual warfare. In this brief excerpt, Love noted the lack of preparation that many missionaries have in this area before beginning their church-planting work.

> "Rick, I've got a solid background in theology. But my demonology is weak. Since coming to the field, though, I realized I need to rethink things. I read about Paul being thwarted by Satan, how much more could I?"
>
> This comment from one of my teammates is typical of many missionaries. Workers frequently cry, "I wasn't ready for this!" They have studied theology, Islamics and missiology, but they weren't prepared for the kind of spiritual warfare they faced when they reached the field. One of the biggest challenges we face is preparing people for spiritual warfare.

Taken from Rick Love, *Muslims, Magic and the Kingdom of God: Church Planting among Folk Muslims* (Pasadena, CA: William Carey Library, 2000), 149.

***Questions to Consider:***

1. How prepared are you for spiritual opposition on the mission field? How can you better prepare yourself? Your family? Your team?
2. What kind of spiritual warfare do you think Love was referring to when he wrote that "they weren't prepared for the kind of spiritual warfare they faced when they reached the field"?

Church planters must be men and women of prayer before their church-planting work. If they to not have a mature prayer life before they begin their work, then there is little likelihood they will be ready for the spiritual warfare encountered in the trenches of church planting. Potential missionaries lacking in this area should spend some time praying that the Lord would grow them in this area before they go to the field.

Though there are a multitude of matters for prayer that are significant to every church-planting team, the following are particular and ongoing issues that need to be prioritized. Prayer is needed for:

- guidance

- protection
- wisdom
- persons of peace
- receptive hearts
- words to speak
- the salvation of people
- the gospel to spread rapidly and with honor
- the new believers to grow in Christ and participate in the birth of churches
- the Holy Spirit to raise up elders

## Mobilizing an Intercessory Team

Paul recognized the need to remind and ask other believers to pray for him and his ministry. As he concluded his letter to the newly planted church in Thessalonica, he simply wrote, "Brothers, pray for us" (1 Thessalonians 5:25). After penning the majority of his great theological work to the believers in Rome, he requested that they "strive together" in prayer for him (Romans 15:30). Here he particularly asked them to pray for his deliverance from disobedient people in Judea and that his work in Jerusalem would be acceptable to the believers (Romans 15:31), so he could come to Rome (Romans 15:32). Paul also asked the Ephesians to pray for him so that he would have boldness and the words to share the gospel message with others (Ephesians 6:18–20).

Robert Logan and Jeannette Buller reminded church planters that "church planting is the frontline of ministry, so you can expect spiritual warfare. Mobilize intercessors who know you well and are ready to fight for you on a daily basis."[6] Their words of wisdom reveal the connections among church planting, spiritual warfare, and prayer. In another work, *The Church Planter's Toolkit*, Logan and Steve Ogne provided church planters with some simple guidelines for developing an intercessory team.

- Pray that God would provide the needed intercessors.
- Make a list of people who:
  - said they will pray for you
  - periodically call and ask for prayer requests
  - regularly ask if you have had answers to their prayers
  - are known to be people of prayer
  - have a natural connection with you
- Personally invite them to join your intercessory team for a specific period of time.
- Clarify your expectations for them and their expectations for you (e.g., how often they are to pray, how often you will provide them with updates).
- Communicate with them on a regular basis, informing them of answered prayers and new prayer requests.
- Pray for your intercessors, at least weekly, for God's protection over their lives.
- Personally contact your intercessors each year to see if they are still committed to serving as your intercessors or if they need to be released from their commitments.[7]

> "Our prayer must be the submission of ourselves to the Spirit and the bringing of ourselves into sympathy with the mind of the Spirit who is the Witness over and within the witnesses."
>
> —W. O. Carver, *Missions in the Plan of the Ages* (New York: Fleming H. Revell Company, 1909), 217.

## Do the Demons Know You?

In his work *Discipled Warriors,* Chuck Lawless reminded his readers that it is easy to become fascinated with having power over the demonic and forget about the significance of discipleship.

*Spiritual warfare isn't about naming demons; it's about so living a righteous life that our very life threatens the Enemy.* We needn't know the names of demons; what matters is that the demons know us because Christ lives in us. Christian obedience shakes hell more than any attempts to name the demons.

At the same time, conducting spiritual warfare by formula simply doesn't work. The sons of Sceva had heard that Jesus and Paul had power over the Enemy, and they tried to use those names in a formulaic way. They recited the words but lacked the power.

Some people approach spiritual warfare with a formula, claiming the name of Jesus over the demons, assuming that just reciting the name *Jesus* will ensure victory. That didn't work so well for the sons of Sceva. Others use model prayers to overcome demons for every sin they face. Still other people established routines for confronting and removing demonic influences. Spiritual warfare is not about learning a formula to overcome the Enemy; it is instead about *living a life* that gives the Enemy no place to get a foothold. Obedience, rather than ritual, overcomes the Enemy.

Here's my concern: Many people are enamored of the power and excitement of spiritual warfare, but leaders aren't often calling them first to holiness and obedient living. They are trying to be warriors without first being discipled. Acts 19 shows us clearly that that position is dangerous. To take on the Enemy without wearing the armor of God is foolish indeed.

Taken from Chuck Lawless, *Discipled Warriors* (Grand Rapids, MI: Kregel, 2002), 214–15, italics original.

***Questions to Consider:***

1. Do you agree or disagree that spiritual warfare has more to do with righteous living than gaining special knowledge about demons or formulas to control them? Explain.
2. Read Acts 19:11–17. Do you believe that contemporary church planters still encounter physical manifestations of demons? Explain your answer.
3. What would the apostle Paul have done differently than the Jewish exorcists of Acts 19?
4. Why do you think the evil spirit did not fear the Jewish exorcists?
5. Do you think the demons know and fear you?

## Prayer and Church-Planting Movements

The multiplication of disciples, leaders, and churches is connected to the prayers of the righteous on behalf of the lost. Prayer has played a major part in the birth of all the confirmed global church-planting movements. As David Garrison reminded us, "Extraordinary prayer lays a firm foundation for a Church Planting Movement."[8] An excellent prayer life is something that a church planter must nurture for the sake of his or her own growth in the faith and the expansion of the kingdom.

Paul recognized this connection between prayer and the rapid dissemination of the gospel when he wrote to the newly planted church in Thessalonica, "Finally, brothers, pray for us, that the word of the Lord may speed ahead and be honored, as happened among you" (2 Thessalonians 3:1). Also, after the resolution over the dispute between the widows regarding the food distribution in Jerusalem—when the apostles were able to return to preaching and prayer (Acts 6:4)—Luke noted, "And the word of God continued to increase, and the number of the disciples multiplied greatly in Jerusalem, and a great many of the priests became obedient to the faith" (Acts 6:7). There has always been an intimate connection between rapid kingdom advancement and intentional fervent prayer.

### *Summary:*

1. Prayer must be a significant component of every aspect of the church-planting strategy.
2. Church planters must not underestimate the importance of prayer and the dangerous reality of spiritual warfare.
3. Both Jesus and the apostolic Church modeled prayer and understood its intimate connection to the expansion of the kingdom.
4. Satanic attacks are mental, moral, and physical and are heavily directed toward missionaries and their families.

5. A firm grounding in the faith is what enables church planters to put on the full armor of God.
6. A mature personal prayer life is necessary before entering into the ministry of church planting.
7. Following the example of the apostle Paul, contemporary church planters must recognize the importance of intercessors and ask for their prayer support.
8. The rapid expansion of the kingdom has always been interconnected with fervent prayer.

## *Reflection Questions:*

1. How much priority is given to prayer in your overall church-planting strategy?
2. To whom will you be accountable for your prayer life while on the field?
3. How will you and your team involve others in praying for the church-planting ministry?
4. Who on your team will constantly update your intercessors regarding answered prayers and new requests? How will this person remain in contact with them (e.g., e-mail, letters, telephone calls, etc.)?
5. On the following scale, rate the health of your prayer life:
   Poor ➤ Fair ➤ Good ➤ Excellent
6. Why did you score yourself the way you did? What can you do to mature in your prayer life before moving to the field?
7. Do you need to ask God to give you a strong desire to be a man or woman of prayer for the sake of the kingdom? If so, will you do that now?

## *Important Terms in This Chapter:*

- Spiritual warfare
- Discipled warriors
- Intercessory team

Chapter 6

# EVANGELISM AND CHURCH PLANTING

**Jesus intended for the disciples to produce his likeness in and through the church being gathered out of the world.**

—Robert E. Coleman[1]

A few years ago North American television audiences were introduced to a new game show, *The Weakest Link.* Contestants would compete against one another to avoid being labeled "the weakest link" and thereby lose the game. That phrase, *the weakest link*, has been around for some time. It is a metaphor describing a chain composed of a series of interlocking links, with the chain strength dependent on all of the links. The chain is only as strong as the weakest link in the series.

*Biblical church planting is evangelism that results in new churches.* There are many ways to plant churches among the multitudes of the peoples of the world, but the biblical model is that new churches come into existence as people come out of the kingdom of darkness and into the kingdom of light. The irony is that much church planting today, especially throughout North America, substitutes other matters for evangelism. With many church-planting teams, evangelism is the weakest link in their church-planting strategies. Many default to gathering believers together to the neglect of evangelism. This transfer-growth form of church planting must stop if we are ever going to be able to make disciples of the over four billion people on planet Earth.[2]

Gary Rohrmayer noted that "evangelism entropy" is a common problem in the lives of church planters. When left to itself, personal evangelism tends to move to disorder. He warned, "If church planters are not disciplined in networking and spending time with unchurched people, they can end up starting a church for the churched instead of a church to reach the community."[3] Within this chapter I hope to address the relationship of evangelism to church planting, with the hope of establishing principles to assist church planters in overcoming evangelism entropy.

> **"In the New Testament it is very evident that evangelism was not a special activity to be undertaken at a prescribed time, such as a once-a-year crusade or a once-a-week visitation effort, but it was the constant overflow of individual and corporate experiences and knowledge of Christ."**
>
> —D. James Kennedy, *Evangelism Explosion*, 4th ed. (Wheaton, IL: Tyndale House Publishers, 1996), 4.

## Defining Evangelism

Throughout the twentieth century, the Church struggled to define evangelism. Some groups, such as the World Council of Churches, wanted to define evangelism as being related to maintaining a Christian presence throughout the world. A nonconversionist theology drove much of their missionary practices. Good and important deeds—such as helping the poor and oppressed, encouraging Christians, taking a stand for social issues, and other relief efforts—defined their evangelistic practices. Such groups moved so far from a biblical understanding of evangelism that Harvey T. Hoekstra, a member of the World Council of Churches, made a call to return to the Great Commission by titling his 1979 publication *The World Council of Churches and the Demise of Evangelism*.[4]

Not all groups, however, succumbed to the gods of this age and lost a missional theology that understood the relationship of proclaiming the gospel and making disciples of all nations. In 1974, under the influence of the Billy Graham Evangelistic Association, the Lausanne Congress on World Evangelization developed the following explanation of the nature of evangelism that has significantly influenced church planters since that time:

> To evangelize is to spread the good news that Jesus Christ died for our sins and was raised from the dead according to the Scriptures, and that as the reigning Lord he now offers the forgiveness of sins and the liberating gifts of the Spirit to all who repent and believe. Our Christian presence in the world is indispensable to evangelism, and so is that kind of dialogue whose purpose is to listen sensitively in order to understand. But evangelism itself is the proclamation of the historical, biblical Christ as Savior and Lord, with a view to persuading people to come to him personally and so be reconciled to God. In issuing the gospel invitation we have no liberty to conceal the cost of discipleship. Jesus still calls all who would follow him to deny themselves, take up their cross, and identify themselves with his new community. The results of evangelism include obedience to Christ, incorporation into his Church and responsible service in the world. (1 Corinthians 15:3, 4; Acts 2:32–39; John 20:21; 1 Corinthians. 1:23; 2 Corinthians. 4:5; 5:11, 20; Luke 14:25–33; Mark 8:34; Acts 2:40, 47; Mark 10:43–45)[5]

Simply put, **evangelism** is the sharing of the good news of Jesus Christ that includes challenging people to repent of their sins and place their faith in him for life, both eternal and abundant. Church planters are to follow the example of the apostle Paul, who testified "both to Jews and to Greeks of repentance toward God and of faith in our Lord Jesus Christ" (Acts 20:21). When doing the work of an evangelist, John R. W. Stott correctly wrote, "Our goal is indeed 'so to present Christ Jesus in the power of the Holy Spirit' that men may be persuaded to come to him in penitence."[6]

## Misconceptions about Evangelism

Alvin Reid, in his book *Introduction to Evangelism*, noted that there are at least four common misconceptions about evangelism.[7] These four erroneous approaches are discussed below. Church planters must work diligently to avoid these misconceptions and not teach them to others.

**Mute Approach.** This misconception is the view that evangelism is accomplished simply by living a good moral life before unbelievers. Rather than verbally sharing the gospel, which is biblically required (Romans 10:14), the individual simply let's his or her light shine before others. It should be remembered that though Jesus lived a life without sin before others (Hebrews 4:15), he still verbally proclaimed the good news (Mark 1:14–15).

> **"A scriptural doctrine of evangelism should be the controlling element in any practice of evangelism."**
>
> —Will Metzger, *Tell the Truth: The Whole Gospel, to the Whole Person, by Whole People*, 2nd ed. (Downers Grove, IL: InterVarsity Press, 1984), 15.

**Scalp-Hunting Approach.** This misunderstanding is the belief that evangelism can be defined by stealing believers from other churches or that evangelism ends with making converts. These definitions divorce evangelism from the Great Commission. Evangelism is not only about making converts but also about desiring those new believers to grow in grace and knowledge of the Lord Jesus Christ (2 Peter 3:18).

**Professional-Fisherman Approach.** This error advocates that evangelism is reserved for the professional. It is the belief that ministers are paid to do evangelism and ordinary Christians are not capable of such a task. Of course, the Scriptures require that all followers of Jesus be involved in evangelism, not just the specialists (Acts 1:8; 1 Peter 3:15–16; 2 Timothy 4:2). Church planters must be careful to empower and encourage all believers to share the gospel, rather than accommodate this fallacy within their church-planting strategies.

**Cop-out Approach.** This misconception defines evangelism as anything the church does. For example, inviting someone to a Bible study or a Christian concert is seen as evangelism. Visiting the sick or giving a cup of cold water to someone is considered evangelism. When everything becomes evangelism, usually evangelism is not occurring. Though invitations to events and serving others should be a part of an evangelistic strategy, in and of themselves, they are not evangelism.

## Understanding and Sharing the Gospel

Since evangelism is about sharing the gospel, it is necessary to address briefly the components of this message church planters proclaim. J. I. Packer's words are a reminder of the power of the gospel: "They must be told of Christ before they can trust Him, and they must trust Him before they can be saved by Him. Salvation depends on faith, and faith on knowing the gospel. God's way of saving sinners is to bring them to faith through bringing them into contact with the gospel."[8]

The **gospel** is the good news about Jesus Christ. It is the story of how a holy God redeems people in their fallen state by his grace through their repentance and faith (Ephesians 2:8–9). It is about the death, burial, and resurrection of Christ as Lord. Wayne Grudem noted that there are at least three elements of the gospel call that must be extended to others: (1) an explanation of the facts concerning salvation, (2) an invitation to respond to Christ in repentance and faith, and (3) a promise of forgiveness and eternal life.[9]

**Explanation of the Facts concerning Salvation.** In order for someone to come to faith in Jesus, he or she must have a general knowledge of Christ and his salvation. Grudem noted that this knowledge must include these facts:

- All have sinned (Romans 3:23).
- Death is the penalty for sin (Romans 6:23).
- Jesus died to pay the penalty for people's sins (Romans 5:8).

Though Grudem did not mention the holiness of God and the resurrection in this section of his book, we must include those facts in our preaching of the gospel (1 Corinthians 15:14).

**Invitation to Respond to Christ in Repentance and Faith.** Just as Jesus extended a call to others (Matthew 11:28–30), church planters must call others to repentance and faith (Luke 13:3; Acts 3:19; 20:21). Repentance is the turning from sin, and faith (i.e., belief) is the turning toward Jesus for the forgiveness of sin. Repentance and faith are two sides of the same coin. To repent is to confess Christ as Lord (Romans 10:9). One cannot exist without the other. Whenever someone truly forsakes sin, he or she receives Christ.

**A Promise of Forgiveness and Eternal Life.** Though there are many facets of the gospel message (e.g., it is a gospel of peace, hope, immortality), the primary promise of the good news is that Christ's salvation provides forgiveness of sins and eternal life (which includes abundant life now). John 3:16 is a great reminder of this truth that we must proclaim.

> **"There are, in fact, two motives that should spur us constantly to evangelize. The first is love to God and concern for His glory; the second is love to man and concern for his welfare."**
>
> —J. I. Packer, *Evangelism and the Sovereignty of God* (Downers Grove, IL: InterVarsity Press, 1961), 73.

## Eight Principles of Biblical Evangelism[10]

How did the first-century believers share the good news of Jesus in their circles of influence? Though many books have been written on this topic, I have come to understand that there were at least eight principles that guided their methods. These principles are discussed below.

### They Proclaimed an Exclusive Gospel

The message of Jesus and the apostolic Church was not just another message (1 Corinthians 1:23). It was good news—an exclusive type of good news. Salvation was found in no one other than Christ, and people had to place explicit faith in him (Acts 4:12). Jesus was seen as the only way to the Father (John 14:6). Repentance toward God and faith in the Lord Jesus were proclaimed to Jew and Gentile (Acts 20:21). This gospel was proclaimed to those following the Jewish religious ways (John 3) and Samaritan faith traditions (John 4; Acts 8). It was also proclaimed to the philosophers, to the extremely religious (Acts 17), and to the God fearers (Acts 10). It was news of love, hope, freedom, healing, deliverance, reconciliation, and forgiveness. It was a message of God incarnating himself among people, dying as atonement for the sins of the world, and resurrecting from the dead (1 Corinthians 15:1–4).

## They Were Intentional in Sharing the Gospel

Evangelism did not just happen by coincidence. They were intentional in their efforts. Evangelism was not a backup plan in case the other good deeds of the Church did not work. John recorded, "And he had to pass through Samaria" (John 4:4). Though it is easy to miss the gravity of these words, it should be remembered that common prejudice of the day emphasized that no decent, right-minded Jew would ever travel through Samaria when traveling from Judea to Galilee. Rather than journey through that region, Jewish people would circumvent the entire area. Jesus, however, intentionally entered into this area and encountered the Samaritan woman. She and other people from her village became believers (John 4:39–42). Following this encounter, Jesus left the area. So, apparently, the primary reason Jesus traveled through Samaria was to reach these people with the gospel.

> **"For however expressed, whether as the Messiah of Old Testament expectation, as Lord over the demonic powers or whatever other category of interpretation was employed, the early preachers of the good news had one subject and one only, Jesus."**
>
> —Michael Green, *Evangelism in the Early Church* (Grand Rapids, MI: William B. Eerdmans Publishing Company, 1970), 51.

## They Were Spirit Led

It has been said that the Book of Acts should actually be titled *The Acts of the Holy Spirit*. From the very beginning (Acts 1:8), he was the one who enabled the Church to witness effectively throughout the world. He was the one who provided boldness to share the gospel (Acts 4:31). He worked through the apostles to perform signs and wonders (Acts 2:43). He called out missionaries (Acts 13:1–3).

Following a great awaking in a Samaritan city (Acts 8:4–8), Philip received word from an "angel of the Lord" (Acts 8:26) to go to a southbound road leading from Jerusalem to Gaza and await further instructions. Upon Philip's arrival, the Spirit told him to go up to the chariot of the Ethiopian, who was ready to come to faith (Acts 8:29). Also, the Spirit led Peter to evangelize the household of Cornelius (Acts 10:19–20).

## They Understood the Importance of Culture

Jesus and the apostolic Church knew about the value of culture in the communication of the gospel. For example, in Paul's Mars' Hill address, he began his message by stating what would have been a compliment to the Athenians—that they were very religious people (Acts 17:22). Continuing, he then decided to connect with his Athenian hearers, not with a passage from the Old Testament, but rather quoted freely from their own poets (Acts 17:28–29). Later, in his defense before Agrippa, Paul made certain to conduct himself as any proper orator would have before such a statesman—by stretching out his hand before proceeding to speak (Acts 26:1). Being aware of the various cultures of their audiences allowed the early evangelists to connect with the people and gain a hearing.

## They Were Flexible in the Context

Closely related to their understanding of the value of culture was the fact that the methods and gospel presentations of Jesus and the apostolic Church varied from situation to situation. Jesus did not speak to Zacchaeus as he did to Nicodemus. Paul did not present himself in the same manner to Agrippa as he did to Lydia (Acts 16). Jesus' encounter with the Gerasene demoniac required a different approach than how he engaged the Samaritan woman. Though the gospel message did not change (Acts 20:21), the contexts required different methods of engagement and communication.

## They Began with Felt Needs

In many evangelistic encounters, Jesus and the apostolic Church began with the people's felt needs at the moment. Since Nicodemus believed that his genealogical account was sufficient to earn God's favor, Jesus spoke of being "born again" (John 3:3). The Samaritan woman was not concerned with her heritage, but rather getting water from a well; Jesus used this concern as an opportunity to speak of "living water" (John 4:10). Philip did not begin by instructing the Ethiopian about Adam and Eve, but rather started answering the man's questions about a passage. (Acts 8:35).

## They Spoke the Truth in Love

Though Jesus could have spent much time speaking about the evils of adultery and fornication to the Samaritan woman, he acknowledged her wickedness and continued in the conversation (John 4:17–18). Jesus could have scolded and severely rebuked Zacchaeus for having wicked business practices (Luke 19:7). He decided instead to stay at his house, bring salvation (Luke 19:9), and continue his reputation as a friend of tax collectors and sinners (Luke 7:34). Jesus and the apostolic Church never denied wickedness. They always called people to repentance out of love (Mark 10:21), even when they spoke to the self-righteous.

> "If we want to be biblically accurate we must insist that the essence of evangelism lies in the faithful proclamation of the gospel."
>
> —John R. W. Stott, *Christian Mission in the Modern World* (Downers Grove, IL: InterVarsity Press, 1975), 40.

### They Were Post-Conversion Oriented

Though evangelism is the first step of the Great Commission, the mandate to the Church includes making disciples (Matthew 28:19). The New Testament was not written to provide its readers with every detail of the historic events. Sometimes I wonder what happened to those first-century people who were evangelized but not mentioned again in the Scriptures. Despite this silence, Jesus and the apostolic Church were concerned with what occurred in the lives of people after they came to faith.

For example, after the Gerasene demoniac was converted, he begged Jesus to allow him to get into the boat and accompany him. Rather than agreeing to the man's plea, Jesus immediately called the man to obedience and to bear fruit for the kingdom. Jesus sent him back into his region to proclaim the works of God (Mark 5:19). The result? The man obeyed and everyone marveled (Mark 5:20). Also, Philip baptized the Ethiopian, who was eager to take this step of obedient faith (Acts 8:36–39).

Church planting was (and still is) a major part of fulfilling the Great Commission. A reading of the Book of Acts and the Epistles reveals that the new believers were gathered together in new churches. Paul followed up with the new believers through visits, letters, and messengers.

## Evangelism: Only the Beginning

Evangelism (i.e., making disciples) is the tip of the Great Commission iceberg. The rest of the mandate includes baptism and teaching obedience to those newly made disciples. Church planters cannot be satisfied with people making a profession of faith, but rather must work to make certain their church-planting strategies include those new believers becoming fruit-bearing disciples in new churches. Though the Great Commission begins with evangelism, it does not end with it. The sanctification process in the life of a follower of Jesus is a lifetime work. Church planters must keep this important fact in mind and make certain that their missionary practices reflect this theological truth.

## Doing the Work of an Evangelist

Besides prayer, the two primary tasks of missionaries are evangelism and leadership development. Though evangelism is activity number one, I am amazed at how much missionary work is not related to evangelism. Church planters will spend enormous amounts of time devoted to administrative tasks and meetings with believers, rather than working to minister to and connect with unbelievers.

In many cultures of the world, evangelism is a slow and progressive task. I have known of church planters who labor for years among certain peoples without seeing anyone profess faith in Christ. If a church-planting team comes from a Western culture that prizes production and abhors the inefficient use of time, it is no wonder that many church planters begin well by doing evangelism, but then shift to doing nonevangelistic tasks that produce measurable results. On any given day, it is often more satisfying to our egos (and supervisors) to have completed a task that has a visible outcome than to spend an entire day sharing the gospel and see no one make a profession of faith.

Many church, parachurch, and denominational funding agencies work to detract church planters from this initial priority. In almost all situations in which church planters are held accountable to those funding their ministries, a periodic report of the work's progress is required. Such reporting generally asks for an account of tasks accomplished (e.g., visits, gospel presentations, converts). Though such reporting is necessary and wise, it becomes problematic when funding is attached to production. Though church planters are called to evangelism, it is the work of the Holy Spirit that brings people to faith and repentance (Ephesians 2:8–9). This work of the Spirit is a mystery and cannot be predicted. Unfortunately, however, missionaries are usually rewarded by the number of people they have gathered together, even if that number mostly consists of believers from other churches, rather than from the biblically faithful, contextually relevant evangelism they are doing.

## Church Planters: Don't Evangelize Everyone

It is often a discouraging reality for the church-planting team to enter into a new area and see the large numbers of unbelievers. "How do we share the gospel with all of these people?" may be the initial question asked. However, in his book, *Focus: The Power of People Group Thinking* (Monrovia, CA: MARC, 1989, p. 25), John D. Robb challenged church planters to avoid asking such questions when he wrote:

> Instead of trying to reach every individual in our target group ourselves, outsiders can establish a cross-cultural beachhead by ministering in-depth to some. We then trust the Holy Spirit to use the resulting believers, who as cultural insiders can help their own people more effectively than we ever could.
>
> This is particularly important for those people groups still unreached by the spread of the gospel, since perhaps 80 percent of non-Christians are separated by language and cultural barriers from churches and agencies that could reach them.

***Questions to Consider:***

1. Do you agree or disagree that instead of attempting to evangelize everyone in their communities, church planters should work through those who come to faith out of the harvest fields in those communities?
2. Though Robb referred to cross-cultural church-planting work, do you believe the principle has any application to church-planting contexts where there are few cross-cultural dynamics involved? Explain.

## Evangelism at All Stages of the Strategy

Though church planters may be working with national believers in their areas, serving as advocates for their people group or population segment, and partnering with other churches to assist in the work, nothing is to detract from the missionaries doing the work of evangelism (2 Timothy 4:5). Evangelism should be included in all of the stages of their strategies. From the time the team arrives on the field to the time of its departure when elders have been appointed over the congregations, evangelism is always to be a significant part of its work. Though the team on the front end will do the majority of the evangelism, it will become less involved in the task as more and more people from the harvest return to labor in the harvest fields. The new believers must increase in this area, while the team must decrease.

## Persons of Peace: A Vital Key to Evangelizing a People

It is not the task, desire, or goal of missionaries to evangelize an entire city, people group, or population segment by themselves. Rather, the church planters are to reach the initial converts and then work with them and through them to share the gospel across their social networks. When planting churches, the missionary is functioning as an apostle (Ephesians 4:11), with the purpose of equipping others to do the work of the ministry (Ephesians 4:12). These initial believers are referred to as **persons of peace** who take the gospel to people and places where the missionaries could never go.

In 1955 Donald A. McGavran began the contemporary Church Growth Movement with the publication of his book *The Bridges of God: A Study in the Strategy of Missions.*[11] In this work McGavran advocated the idea that the gospel was designed by God to travel naturally across the social networks (i.e., bridges) of family, friends, and acquaintances that God has sovereignly established in people's lives. Later, some came to refer to these networks as a person's ***oikos,*** taken from the Greek word for *household.*[12] The principle, however, remained the same. Rather than extracting new believers from their social environments and forcing them to abandon their cultures and embrace Western cultural expressions of Christianity, missionaries should equip, empower, and release new believers back into their communities and work with them in evangelism that results in new churches. Such persons of peace are a vital key to making disciples of all nations.

## *Summary:*

1. Evangelism is the sharing of the good news of how the Holy God of the universe provides salvation and abundant life to sinners through the sacrifice of Jesus Christ.
2. Several misconceptions exist about evangelism.
3. The gospel is the good news about Jesus Christ.
4. There are at least eight biblical principles for evangelism.
5. Evangelism is only the first component of the Great Commission, not all of it.
6. One of the most important tasks of missionaries is doing evangelism.
7. Though church planters will change roles as their work progresses, evangelism is to be a part of every role.
8. Church planters are to work with the persons of peace to reach a population with the gospel.

## *Reflection Questions:*

1. When you share the gospel, do you share all the information mentioned under the heading "Understanding and Sharing the Gospel" at the beginning of this chapter? Why or why not?
2. As a church planter, aside from prayer, is evangelism a priority throughout your week? If not, what are you doing that takes the place of evangelism? Do you need to spend more time in

evangelism?

3. Of the biblical principles related to evangelism, are any lacking from your personal evangelism?
4. Are you and your team strategizing to work with persons of peace? If not, why not?

### *Important Terms in This Chapter:*

- Evangelism
- Gospel
- Persons of peace
- *Oikos*

Chapter 7

# DISCIPLESHIP AND CHURCH PLANTING

**The ultimate goal of Jesus for his disciples was that *his life be reproduced in them and through them into the lives of others.***

—Robert E. Coleman[1]

It is amazing how much difference a little mistake can make. As I write this section, there is a great amount of construction work taking place on my seminary's campus. Along with any building formation comes the participation of many individuals. Architects, engineers, masons, carpenters, and many others all have to work together to complete the task successfully. Imagine the problems that would arise if those drawing up the blueprints gave an incorrect measurement of fifteen feet when in reality it should have been five feet. Or consider the dilemma if the brick masons did not lay the brick with great precision. A slight margin of error with the first brick could easily cause an entire wall to become the next Leaning Tower of Pisa!

Or, for another example, consider e-mail. I prefer brief addresses. Why? Because the more characters that exist, the greater the likelihood that I will mistype the address. With one incorrect stroke of the key, my important message would not arrive at the proper destination. Small problems can interrupt the desired result.

On a similar note, poor discipleship training in the lives of new believers will interrupt the spread of the gospel across a people group or population segment. What happens in the life of the church at the level of the individual disciple affects the health of the leaders raised up, the churches planted, and the movements started. While Charles Brock was speaking about church planting, I once heard him say, "What you want in the end, put in at the beginning." These are profound words and relate to every level of the church multiplication process, especially to the issue of discipleship. What church planters instill in the lives of the new believers will shape the entire church multiplication process for generations to come. Missionaries are part of the process of contending earnestly "for the faith that was once for all delivered to the saints" (Jude v. 3). The gravity of such responsibility is not to cause missionaries to freeze with fear, but rather it should cause missionaries to fully rely on the Spirit and remember to pray without ceasing as they make disciples of all nations.

## What Is a Disciple?

A disciple is a follower, one who is devoted to the leadership of someone else. In kingdom terms, a disciple is a follower of Jesus, a Christian (literally, "a little Christ"). The one who loves Jesus is the one who will keep his commandments (John 14:15). The Church's marching orders involve making disciples of all nations (Matthew 28:19). As church planters preach the good news, the Lord of the harvest will draw people to himself (John 12:32; Acts 16:14). A disciple is the most basic element in the local church. Without followers of Jesus, there is no church.

# What Is Discipleship?

Discipleship is "followership." Simply put, discipleship is growing as a kingdom citizen by living according to the kingdom ethic (i.e., the ways of the Lord). Discipleship involves the teaching of biblical doctrine; however, it is not simply the communication of doctrine. The greatest commandment (Mark 12:30) includes not only loving God with our minds but also is more holistic, including our hearts (emotions) and strengths (actions). The Western Church has, for the most part, defined the fulfillment of the Great Commission as making converts, with discipleship consisting solely of imparting knowledge to the new disciple. In the West we have come to believe that if we are giving disciples the right facts about God, then our task is complete. The greatest commandment and Great Commission contradict such practice. Rather, the Church is to teach obedience (Matthew 28:20).

Discipleship is a process. The Bible describes this process as sanctification, or growth in Christ. It begins with a person's decision to follow Jesus (i.e., conversion, or justification). It continues throughout the believer's life in this world (i.e., sanctification). It concludes when the individual is face-to-face with Jesus (i.e., glorification).

Discipleship is also a part of leadership development. Again, unfortunately, in the West we have dichotomized discipleship from leadership development. Biblically, however, developing as a leader in the church means growing as a disciple. Leadership apart from discipleship is dangerous to the body of Christ and will result in leaders who are likely to fail miserably with the local church.

> "Disciples who are shepherds-in-training should begin at once to train others, passing on what they receive from their trainer."
>
> —Patrick O'Connor, *Reproducible Pastoral Training: Church Planting Guidelines from the Teachings of George Patterson* (Pasadena, CA: William Carey Library, 2006), 60.

# Where Is Discipleship Learned?

Though spiritual growth does happen apart from the local church, discipleship is learned primarily in community with other kingdom citizens in kingdom communities, or local churches. In the New Testament there is a reason why believers were baptized shortly after their conversion and churches were planted quickly. Growth in Christ happens as brothers and sisters are accountable to each other. Rather than attempting to mature a group of believers and then establish them as a church, the apostle Paul planted churches first and then taught the new believers to obey all that Christ commanded. Following the instruction of Jesus, Paul made disciples, baptized them, and *then* taught obedience in the context of newly planted kingdom communities. Church planting can be rapid; obedience to the commands of Christ is a lifelong journey.

Over the years I have become convinced that there are at least four structures in the life of the church that assist believers in their maturity. Rarely are all four in place in the early days of new churches. Over time, however, church growth usually brings these elements to fruition. Healthy growth occurs at the following levels: corporate, small group, micro group, and individual. Church planters who instill within the church a healthy understanding of growth in Christ at these levels prepare the new congregations for the development of these culturally translatable structures.

## Corporate Component

The corporate aspect of the local church is the time when the church gathers to encourage one another (Hebrews 10:24–25) and celebrate the resurrection of the Lord. Such a time of corporate worship, in most cultures, includes singing, the Lord's Supper, studying the Scriptures, prayer, fellowship, and maybe food. During this corporate gathering of the entire church, growth in faith should occur in the lives of the members.

## Small-Group Component

In many house churches, the small-group component also serves as the corporate component. However, the small-group component of the local church is that group which allows for a degree of ongoing accountability and fellowship that rarely occurs in the corporate, larger meetings. Some churches refer to their small groups as community groups, cell groups, fellowship groups, Bible study groups, or Sunday school classes.

## Micro-Group Component

The micro-group level is a gathering of two or three individuals to encourage each other in the ways of the Lord. The best contemporary example of this component was developed by Neil Cole to be used in church-planting contexts. "Life Transformation Groups" are weekly gatherings of two or three same-gendered individuals for Scripture reading, confession, accountability questions, and prayer for unbelievers.[2] Over the years, I have noticed that there is a degree of accountability that occurs at the micro-group level that is rarely carried out at the small-group or corporate levels. For example, believers tend to share more of their struggles in a group of two or three same-gendered people, unlike when they are in a mixed-gendered group of ten or twelve people.

> "Evangelism, discipleship, and leadership development, although usually discussed separately, are all part of the same continuous whole."
>
> —Robert E. Logan and Tara Miller, *From Followers to Leaders* (St. Charles, IL: ChurchSmart Resources, 2007), 57.

## Obedience-Oriented Discipleship

The following excerpt is taken from the writings of missionary and seminary professor George Patterson. Here Patterson shared his approach to discipleship training.

> In Honduras we find that when we baptize repentant believers immediately, without giving them long doctrinal courses first, we can follow up the great majority and we teach them obedience from the very beginning. They are saved to obey the Lord Jesus Christ in love, and we don't put a large emphasis on doctrine. The doctrine comes! They will learn all their life. This is the error of the American missionary. He manufactures Christians through an intellectual process. He just blindly assumes that if they learn the right doctrine, and believe correctly, and have the right interpretation of Scripture, that this is the way that we make them into Christians. NO! That's not the way we make disciples. It has little to do with the brain, but it has much to do with the heart and the soul.
>
> Make obedient disciples. Then you will see churches multiply. If you just get intellectual decisions, they may believe right, they may know all the dispensations and the covenants, and they may know this and that, but what do you have? Are they multiplying churches? Are they fulfilling the Great Commission of Christ? Are they actually doing what Christ ordered?

Taken from George Patterson, "The Spontaneous Multiplication of the Church," in *Perspectives on the World Christian Movement: A Reader*, eds. Ralph D. Winter and Steven C. Hawthorne (Pasadena, CA: William Carey Library, 1981), 610.

***Questions to Consider:***

1. Do you agree or disagree with Patterson that it is best not to place a great degree of emphasis on doctrine at first? Explain your answer.
2. Is it possible to teach obedience and large amounts of doctrine as church planters? Explain.
3. Can you provide examples of missionaries or churches that believe that correct knowledge automatically leads to obedience? Do you agree or disagree with Patterson's observation of North American missionaries?

### Individual Component

The individual component is the smallest level in the local church where discipleship occurs. It is here that individuals grow in their walks with the Lord as they have daily personal devotion times, worship, share the gospel with others, fast and pray, give money to kingdom causes, and serve others. Church planters must instill healthy structures of spiritual disciplines within the individual lives of new believers. The discipleship that occurs at the individual level will affect the micro groups, small groups, and the corporate levels of the newly planted churches.

Since the church is made up of individuals, the church will mature over time. Just as the individual disciples will grow in their sanctification, the church will grow spiritually as well. Just as no church planter expects a new believer to be as spiritually mature as someone who has been a disciple for ten years, neither should church planters expect newly planted churches to be like churches that have been established for ten years. *The sanctification of the church is not the sanctification of a corporation, business, organization, or social club, but rather of people.* The discipleship process for newly planted churches will not end on this side of heaven. Therefore, healthy doctrine and practice must be a priority from the very beginning, but church planters' expectations must be tempered primarily by the Scriptures and not their church life from back home that consisted of a mature congregation.

## What Constitutes Effective Discipleship?

There are at least three aspects of healthy discipleship that church planters must work to make certain are a part of their discipling processes and will be instilled in the hearts of the new churches. These three aspects are discussed below.

## Knowledge with Application

First, church planters must be teaching sound doctrine to the people as well as the application of such information to their daily lives. The apostle Paul spent a great amount of time exhorting Timothy and Titus to make certain that sound doctrine was a part of the churches in their respective areas (1 Timothy 4:6, 16; 6:1–4; 2 Timothy 4:3; Titus 1:9; 2:1, 7).

## Involvement in Fruit-Bearing Ministry

Believers—regardless of age, gender, calling, or education—are to be bearing fruit in their lives for the kingdom (Matthew 7:17–18; John 15:5). People need to be taught how to live as disciples. Every believer has a ministry and is a minister, but believers also need church planters to teach them how to be faithful with such a great trust. Church planters teach others that they have been endowed with spiritual gifts for the building up of the body of Christ. Such hands-on ministry in their day-to-day lives is part of the way whereby the Spirit works out the sanctification process in the lives of the believers and churches. Involvement in kingdom activities is part of the discipleship process. As a new believer learns how to follow the Lord in the real world, he or she grows as a disciple.

## Accountability with Other Believers

The kingdom ethic is to be lived out in community with other kingdom citizens. It is no wonder the writer of Hebrews encouraged his readers to urge one another on to good works (Hebrews 10:24) and that Paul noted that we are to bear one another's burdens (Galatians 6:2). Discipleship has always been designed to take place in the company of other believers. Church planters must make certain to teach that there is no room in the body of Christ for the ideology of independence and isolation, often expressed as, "What happens in my life is simply between me and God and no one else!" On the contrary, what happens in the life of any believer, even when no one else is watching, affects the entire church. The church is to judge itself (1 Corinthians 5:12–13).

## What Are Some Guidelines for Teaching Discipleship?

It is important for church planters to know how to begin the process of teaching new kingdom citizens how to live according to the kingdom ethic. Some may even feel overwhelmed regarding what to do after a new believer's conversion. The following paragraphs outline six guidelines to assist you in knowing where and how to begin discipling others in your context.

### Set the Example

Unfortunately, in much of North American Christianity, discipleship is mostly defined in terms of providing new believers with Bible knowledge. The Scriptures, however, reveal a different picture of the elements involved in discipleship training. Clearly, right doctrine must be communicated, but there is more to the Great Commission than orthodoxy (right belief). Orthopraxy (right practice) is a must.

The apostle Paul spoke of this on numerous occasions when he pointed to his life as a model for the new churches to follow. Though the apostle was quick to note that he had not obtained his heavenly reward (Philippians 3:12–16) and was not without sin (Romans 7:14–25), he had no problem teaching new believers that they should imitate his ways in both orthodoxy and orthopraxy:

- "Brothers, join in imitating me, and keep your eyes on those who walk according to the example you have in us." (Philippians 3:17)
- "Be imitators of me, as I am of Christ." (1 Corinthians 11:1)

- "Now we command you, brothers, in the name of our Lord Jesus Christ, that you keep away from any brother who is walking in idleness and not in accord with the tradition that you received from us. For you yourselves know how you ought to imitate us, because we were not idle when we were with you, nor did we eat anyone's bread without paying for it, but with toil and labor we worked night and day, that we might not be a burden to any of you. It was not because we do not have that right, but to give you in ourselves an example to imitate." (2 Thessalonians 3:6–9)

Paul also exhorted other church planters who worked with him to establish a healthy example for the new churches in Ephesus and on Crete. He wrote:

- "Let no one despise you for your youth, but set the believers an example in speech, in conduct, in love, in faith, in purity." (1 Timothy 4:12)
- "Show yourself in all respects to be a model of good works, and in your teaching show integrity, dignity, and sound speech that cannot be condemned, so that an opponent may be put to shame, having nothing evil to say about us." (Titus 2:7–8)

Contemporary church planters must make certain they are leading lifestyles that can be reproduced by new believers. Today's church planters would do well to remember the example set by the apostle Paul to the Thessalonians to impart *both* the gospel and their very lives (1 Thessalonians 2:8).

## Keep It Simple

Church planters must work diligently to keep the discipling process simple; this is the biblical way. Keeping it simple means they are responsible for teaching biblical depth. It must be remembered that the same apostle Paul who practiced teaching the whole purpose of God (Acts 20:27) was the same individual who desired that the Word of God would spread rapidly (2 Thessalonians 3:1) and who planted churches rapidly. Contemporary church planters must not forget this aspect of Paul's ministry. An irony in the kingdom is that the deep teachings of the faith are not mysteries that only a few scholarly individuals know, but rather they are simple enough to be grasped by every Spirit-filled believer and passed on to other Spirit-filled believers.

> **"The need of the hour is a return to the kind of evangelism which majors in people winning other people to Christ and building those they have won into disciples who can win and build others."**
>
> —Robert E. Coleman, *The Master Plan of Evangelism*, 30th anniversary edition (Grand Rapids, MI: Fleming H. Revell, 1993), 173–74.

Church planters who have been trained in Bible colleges and seminaries have to work diligently to make certain they express themselves in ordinary speech and do not allow their highly detailed knowledge to get in the way of teaching others simple obedience. Neil Cole reminded us that the discipling process is like passing a "light" baton.

> Imagine if the relays at the Olympic track and field event required that each runner pass a lead baton instead of aluminum! The relays might still be entertaining to watch, but not for the right reasons. We watch the Olympics to witness athleticism, grace and skill, not slapstick comedy. I'm confident that the times would not drop but the baton would.
>
> This is how our churches have approached discipleship in recent days. We most often fail to see multiplication occur because the baton we try to pass is too much. The disciple-making baton

> is so complicated and laden with unnecessary encumbrances that the work does not get passed on to the next runner, but rather is dropped. We must simplify the process so that it can easily be passed on without sacrificing the essential components that change lives.[3]

Church planters must communicate the depths of the Scriptures in simple ways that the people in their contexts can grasp.

## Begin at the Individual Level

There is a real temptation for church planters to concentrate their efforts on discipleship at the corporate level *first*, hoping it to trickle down to the individual level. Sometimes the use of such a model stems from having seen this approach modeled in their churches back home, which have been in existence for decades.

Such a temptation must be overcome. Though it is not glamorous to spend more time with a few individuals as opposed to a crowd, it is necessary for healthy church growth. Church planters who attempt to begin their work by trying to disciple a crowd of people will, generally, end up with a church that consists mostly of people with nominal levels of commitment. The kingdom ethic, however, demands that the church consist of a membership that is sold out to the Lord.

Since the most basic unit of the local church is the individual, church planters should begin the discipleship process at the individual level. There are several reasons for this. First, this way best follows the pattern established by Jesus. Our Lord did not come to organize groups of people, but to make disciples. Though he taught the crowds, he spent more time teaching a few disciples. Second, it is easier to reproduce a disciple rather than a corporate worship gathering. Since one of the primary responsibilities of church planters is the multiplication of disciples, they need to be working to assist believers in spreading the good news in their circles of influence. Third, it is difficult to establish maturity at the corporate level and expect it to be transferred to the individual level if a healthy understanding of discipleship does not already exist at the individual level.

## Teach Obedience

Teaching obedience does not require complex paradigms, diagrams, and charts. It does not require advanced degrees. The purposes of God stated in the Scriptures are understandable to those who come to faith in him. Rich and poor, the academic and the unschooled, literates and illiterates are all capable of growing as disciples by obeying Christ's commands in the Bible. In Matthew's account of the Great Commission, the command is to make disciples which includes baptizing them and teaching them to obey (Matthew 28:20). The church is responsible for teaching obedience.

> "Once people have been converted, it is imperative that they feel themselves to be a part of the divine family, that they faithfully gather with other members of the family, and that they regularly participate in the activities of the family."
>
> —David J. Hesselgrave, *Planting Churches Cross-Culturally: North America and Beyond*, 2nd ed. (Grand Rapids, MI: Baker Academic, 2000), 192.

I have heard of some church planters who wait for new believers to apply one principle to their lives before teaching them a second principle. There is much to commend this simple pattern—it communicates high expectations to the disciples, it allows for the church planters to model obedience, and it is faithful to the Scriptures.

Another value to this obedience-oriented paradigm of discipleship training is that it avoids the Western notion that teachers are to provide people only with knowledge, tell them to apply it to their lives, and then move on to the next lesson. In most of the small groups and churches that I have been a part of over the years, seldom have I ever had anyone ask me, "So, J. D., tell me how you applied last week's Bible study to your life, marriage, job, and family before we move on to the next lesson." If church planters do not expect their people to mature in obedience, they will not plant healthy churches. They may plant churches that love the Lord with their minds but fail to love him with all their hearts, souls, and strengths.

Effective church planters will work to disciple others by teaching them how to obey the knowledge they receive from the Scriptures. Orthodoxy (right belief) must be accompanied by orthopraxy (right practice). It is not possible to have orthopraxy apart from orthodoxy; and orthodoxy robbed of orthopraxy is not orthodoxy. Church planters must teach doctrine to new believers and hold them accountable for it. New believers are to be both hearers and doers of the Word of God (James 1:22), and church planters must teach them the significance of obedience by modeling it before them and teaching them to hold each other accountable.

## Teach Healthy Disciplines as Soon as Possible

I once watched a television program about a particular bird that was raised in captivity and never knew its mother. The scientists who nurtured the animal did all they could to imitate the mother bird, even using bird puppets to feed it. When the time came to reintroduce the creature to the wild, many artificial means were required for the transition. The bird required a proper model to follow regarding survival and could not have successfully returned to the wild without the scientists' great efforts and interventions.

Similarly, church planters have the responsibility of nurturing new believers and modeling for them lives of obedient Christians. They are also responsible for instilling survival techniques in the form of healthy spiritual disciplines within the new believers and churches as well. Charles Brock, president of Church Growth International, served for over twenty years as a church planter in the Philippines. While working with new believers, he developed a discipleship training tool entitled *I Have Been Born Again, What Next?*[4] The value of this resource is that it is studied in community with other new believers and leads them on a journey of developing spiritual disciplines in their lives. At the conclusion of this study, the church planters challenge group members to ask themselves if they believe the Spirit is leading them to become a church in their community. The topics addressed in this simple resource include:

- a new nature
- a new power: the Holy Spirit
- a new guide: the Bible
- a new privilege: prayer
- a new hope
- new relationships
- a new understanding of baptism
- a new family: the Church
- a new reminder: the Lord's Supper
- a new opportunity: tithing
- a new responsibility

In addition to these topics, I would include teachings related to spiritual warfare and fasting. The discipleship process is a lifelong journey that begins with spiritual birth. There are many things that can be taught to new believers, and missionaries will need to make adjustments according to their contexts and convictions. But, for now, this list is a good place to begin.

## Return Them to the Field Immediately

Since the Holy Spirit is a missionary Spirit, it is no wonder that whenever someone comes to faith in Christ, he or she generally has a great amount of zeal to share this new good news with others. In the Scriptures there are many examples of this type of evangelism. Andrew found Simon and brought him to Jesus (John 1:40–42). Philip located Nathanael and shared the Messiah with him (John 1:45). The Samaritan woman returned to her village with the news of the Savior (John 4:28–29). On several occasions, I have either witnessed or heard of new believers sharing their faith with family and friends soon after their conversion. It is very important that church planters realize that new believers need to be encouraged to share their faith with others immediately.

As soon as I have the privilege of seeing someone come to faith in Jesus, I ask him or her, "Who do you know who needs to hear this message of good news?" Upon finding out the name of a person, I challenge the new kingdom citizen to share this message with that person within the following twenty-four hours. I then say that I'll be praying for them both and promise to follow up later in the week.

Church planters must hold others accountable for evangelism. The longer new believers are not involved in personal evangelism, the easier it is for them to remain in disobedience in this area of their lives. If church planters begin with the expectation that a disciple is an intentional witness, then they are teaching new believers the significance of obedience to the Great Commission from the beginning.

### *Summary:*

1. A disciple is a follower of Jesus Christ.
2. Discipleship begins at conversion and continues throughout a person's lifetime.
3. Discipleship and leadership development cannot be separated.

4. Church planters must follow the biblical paradigm of discipleship by keeping the process simple.
5. Church planters must remember that growth in Christ occurs best in the context of community, with such community being new churches.
6. To disciple new believers effectively, church planters must provide knowledge with application, hands-on involvement in ministry, and accountability.
7. Church planters must set the example of what is a healthy disciple.
8. New believers need to be exposed to some basic teachings and develop some healthy spiritual disciplines soon after they come to faith.
9. Church planters must return new disciples to the field immediately to share the good news with their family, friends, and acquaintances.

## *Reflection Questions:*

1. In your own life, how has the example of believers (both good examples and bad examples) affected your growth in the faith?
2. How has your biblical knowledge, involvement in ministry activities, and accountability with other believers affected your growth in the faith?
3. As a missionary, do you have any concerns about telling the new churches you plant, "Imitate me as I imitate Christ"? Explain your answer. Are there things in your life that you need to address now before you go to the field?
4. How will you teach obedience to new believers so that they will do likewise in the new churches?

## *Important Terms in This Chapter:*

- Disciple

- Discipleship
- Obedience-oriented discipleship

Chapter 8

# LEADERSHIP DEVELOPMENT AND CHURCH PLANTING

But in many ways the selection and training of leaders are most important aspects of church planting because these individuals will not only manage church affairs, they will model the faith for good or ill.

—David J. Hesselgrave[1]

In chapter six I mentioned that the two primary responsibilities for all church planters are evangelism and leadership development. In this chapter we will address this second significant task of the missionary. Everything does not rise or fall on leadership, but it surely comes very close.

## One Important Question All Church Planters Should Ask

Surprising, shocking, and absurd comments generally remain in the minds of most people for a long time. I have often used this technique to communicate to church planters the importance of developing leaders. I like to ask them the following question: "What is the most important question that I should always be asking myself?" After allowing them a moment or two to make suggestions, I respond with this answer: "As a church planter, you should always be asking yourself the question, If I was walking down the street and was struck by lightning and died, what would happen to the newly planted churches?" Now, clearly, this is not a pleasant thought, but that is the point. By asking the question in an absurd manner, I hope it will stick with church planters long after they leave the room (or close this book).

If the church-planting team is doing a good job of developing leaders, the new church would be shaken by the removal of the team, but their vitality would continue. They would still be self-governing, self-propagating, self-supporting, self-teaching, self-expressing, self-identifying, and self-theologizing. One of the greatest temptations facing church planters is that of control. Many fear that unless they are in control of everything, the new believers will not be able to function correctly as a church. However, it is only when church planters are out of control that the Holy Spirit can be in control.

## Our Goal concerning Leadership Development

Though there are different types of leaders in the church, leadership development is about a process of leading someone to faith in Christ and equipping that person to become a fruit-bearing disciple who begins to reach others with the gospel. The multiplication of churches requires the multiplication of leaders and disciples. Robert E. Logan and Neil Cole reminded church planters that they should work "to raise up leaders *for* the harvest and *from* the harvest through a more effective and reproducible process of leadership development within local churches, resulting in church multiplication movements."[2] The phrase "reproducible process" is vital to the multiplication of churches. If leaders are not being multiplied, churches cannot be multiplied in an effective and healthy manner.

> "Effective church planters develop strong leaders."
>
> —Fred Herron, *Expanding God's Kingdom through Church Planting* (New York: Writer's Showcase, 2003), 207.

## Leadership: The Bottleneck of Church Multiplication

Upon examination of church-planting movements across the globe where there is a large number of conversions and churches being planted in a short period of time, one of the major concerns of missiologists and missionaries is that of having enough trained leaders to pastor those churches. Unfortunately, I have heard some missionaries say that the number of conversions needs to slow down since they are not able to raise up leaders fast enough. Such a situation is not healthy when the Lord is blessing the Church with such growth that we would dare want the Lord of the harvest to stop the process of making disciples so that pastors can be raised up to shepherd the new churches.

Rapid church growth and leadership development are not mutually exclusive. They go hand in hand and must work together. Granted, major problems arise when leaders are not being trained in proportion to the conversion growth that is occurring. Such a bottleneck in the growth of the Church is not a problem with the Holy Spirit's working, but rather a blessing to be worked through by the missionaries. Just as many church planters carry with them poor understandings of the requirements for a local church to exist, many also have numerous extrabiblical expectations for church leaders. Such requirements slow down the leadership development process and, thereby, create the bottleneck of Church growth.

Rapid church multiplication can occur in conjunction with the multiplication of church leaders. It should be noted that the same apostle who desired to see the rapid dissemination of the gospel (2 Thessalonians 3:1)—and only spent three years with the Church in Ephesus (Acts 20), his longest time in any location on record—is the same man who advocated that right doctrine be embraced by church leaders and taught to the churches (2 Timothy 2:2, 15).

## Biblical Evidence for Leadership Development

Even a cursory glance at the New Testament examples of leadership development reveals very simple paradigms for quickly raising up leaders. Logan and Cole reminded church planters that Jesus began by reaching the Twelve from the harvest field *first* and then developed them as leaders to return to the harvest fields to reach others.[3] A brief examination of the approach to leadership development used by Jesus reveals the following: (1) he modeled the desired tasks, (2) he taught the concepts for knowledge attainment, (3) he sent them out for on-the-job training, (4) he continued to teach and correct them following their field-based training, (5) he empowered them to raise up other leaders from the harvest, and (6) he removed himself so the Twelve could accomplish more than he could.

Paul took a similar approach to leadership development. Several times throughout his letters, Paul noted that others should imitate him as he imitated Jesus (Philippians 3:17; 1 Corinthians 11:1; 2 Thessalonians 3:6–9). His model could easily be followed by the newly planted churches (1 Thessalonians 1:6–7).

There were times when Paul intentionally phased himself out of a particular community, leaving behind Timothy or Titus for a season to train leaders in the churches (2 Timothy 2:2; Titus 1:5). He also exhorted both of these men to manifest healthy examples to those believers in Ephesus and Crete (1 Timothy 4:12; Titus 2:7–8).

## Two Simple Models for Multiplying Leaders

Two highly reproducible models of leadership development are the "Model, Assist, Watch, Leave" (M.A.W.L.) approach and what I will call the "I/You" approach. The former was addressed in David Garrison's book *Church Planting Movements: How God Is Redeeming a Lost World.* The latter paradigm is referenced in Robert E. Logan and Tara Miller's book, *From Followers to Leaders.*

It should be noted that the amount of time required to work through each of these paradigms is going to vary from context to context. There is no set time for either approach. Here is the art of leadership development. Church planters cannot assume that everyone will respond the same way in the leadership development process. Some leaders will mature faster than others.

> **"Any church multiplication movement that wants to multiply churches must also find a way to multiply leaders, for it will quickly run out of existing, ready-to-go leaders."**
>
> —Robert E. Logan, *Be Fruitful and Multiply: Embracing God's Heart for Church Multiplication* (St. Charles, IL: ChurchSmart Resources, 2006), 33.

### M.A.W.L. Approach

Following the "Model, Assist, Watch, Leave" paradigm, church planters would model preaching and leading in worship, for example, in a manner that is contextually relevant and reproducible. After a period of modeling, the church planters would begin assisting the emerging leaders in these tasks. At this point, these new believers are no longer observing, but rather participating in acts of leadership. After the missionaries have spent some time assisting the new leaders, the roles change again. This time the missionaries are watching, evaluating, correcting, and encouraging these individuals as they take on all of the responsibilities. Finally, the missionaries phase out their roles, leaving the trained leaders to guide the church themselves.

## I/You Approach

This paradigm also allows for a time of modeling, assisting, watching, and leaving but is staged differently from the M.A.W.L. approach. The I/You model is staged as follows:

- Stage 1: I do the task and you watch me.
- Stage 2: I do the task and you assist me.
- Stage 3: You do the task and I assist you.
- Stage 4: You do the task and I watch you.
- Stage 5: You do the task and someone else watches you.[4]

For example, if a missionary attempts to train someone in personal evangelism skills, this model would play out as follows. The church planter takes the person along with him as he shares his faith in the marketplace. This continues for some time until the church planter begins to have the individual assist him in the work by initiating the conversation with an unbeliever or by sharing his testimony at a proper moment. After a period of time, the church planter does less and less of the evangelism as the trainee takes on more and more of the responsibility. The fourth stage begins when the church planter only observes, evaluates, and encourages the individual during and after the witnessing encounters. Finally, the trainee becomes a trainer by finding someone else to begin stage one of the model with, and the church planter finds another trainee.

"A significant part of the church planter's job is to provide a healthy environment for leaders to grow within the emerging church."

—Glen Schneiders, "Developing the Leadership Culture," in *Church Planting from the Ground Up*, ed. Tom Jones (Joplin, MO: College Press Publishing Company, 2004), 297.

## Direct versus Indirect Leadership

Though there are many styles of leadership, Charles Brock designated two major categories: direct and indirect. **Direct leadership** is a top-down approach. It involves the leader being in control most of the time and the people around the leader tending to be more passive. **Indirect leadership**, however, allows for the leader to mentor, coach, and guide others. Rather than telling others what to do and how to do it, someone using the indirect style teaches people what to do and assists them in developing the skills and abilities necessary to accomplish the tasks for themselves.

Different situations call for different styles of leadership. Sometimes missionaries will have to take a direct approach. Since church planters are to be involved in leadership multiplication, however, the indirect style should generally take priority. Such an approach helps foster an atmosphere of ownership by the people, since the indirect style emphasizes empowering others.

## Remembering Brother Ravi

In the following excerpt, Daniel Sinclair reflected on his experience of seeing God raise up elders in newly planted churches. Here he specifically commented on encountering Brother Ravi.

> I remember one day when I was invited by a friend from a sister agency to participate in a fellowship meeting of new believers. I knew some of the believers; I didn't know others. We fellowshipped together and prayed for each other. Then it was announced that Brother Ravi was going to lead us in a study in Galatians. Ravi, who had come to faith only about three months earlier, did a fantastic job! It was such a clear example to me of how Christ gives gifts to His new churches, as we are promised in Ephesians 4:11–12, and how this brother's gift of teaching—though not yet refined—was unmistakable. It is such an encouragement when you see plainly that the new church isn't going to need you for very long, as Christ through His Spirit is going to take care of them and make them what He wants them to be. . . .
>
> In most cases, good church planters will want to exit as soon as it is feasible. That means that as early as possible they want to put responsibilities into the hands of the local believers. This requires a process of training, delegation, review, and further equipping. And throughout that process the local believers will both fail and succeed—with ups and downs, with good motives and bad—and through all this they will grow up in Christ and develop their gifts.
>
> We have called the period between the time when you first have one or more believers willing to serve and the eventual appointment of elders an *incubation period*. How long should that last? I am personally in favor of it being as short as possible.

Taken from Daniel Sinclair, *A Vision of the Possible: Pioneer Church Planting in Teams* (Colorado Springs, CO: Authentic Media, 2005), 196, 197, italics original.

***Questions to Consider:***

1. Does the thought of Brother Ravi being able to teach from Galatians shortly after his conversion cause you any concern? Explain.
2. Why do you think Sinclair found encouragement in the fact the church would not need the church planters for a long period of time?
3. Do you agree or disagree with Sinclair that the incubation period should be as short as possible? Explain.

## Giving Them Freedom but Not Free Rein

Giving priority to an indirect style of leadership development does not mean that the church planters sit idly by and allow everyone to do what is right in his or her own eyes. Rather, leadership development is mainly an art. As parents encourage their children, church planters want the people they serve to grow and experience more and more of the abundant life in Christ. Freedom must be given, including the freedom to make mistakes. However, *freedom* and *free rein* are not the same things. Healthy parameters must be established that allow for people to make mistakes, while keeping them from harming themselves or the churches.

I once recall training some youth workers. In an attempt to equip and develop them as leaders, I intentionally double booked myself on the day of a large annual youth rally. Since I knew they had observed and assisted me in youth ministry, I knew they were ready to work together and lead our group of teenagers to the event. After the look of shock and horror faded from their faces, they decided to take on this task—after all it was only one day.

Well, as you may have guessed, the next day I did not have to debrief these workers. They debriefed me! "You'll never guess what those kids did in public!" they exclaimed almost simultaneously. "She was sitting in the wrong seat and being disruptive!" vented another. Though I had to address their comments and concerns, in the end, I greatly encouraged them in their leadership abilities. They matured tremendously as leaders by "wrestlin' teenagers" all day. Among many other things, they learned how to function better as a team, the logistics of taking such a trip, what forms of communication to use with teenagers, and the challenges and blessings of such ministry.

Could I have done a better job than those youth workers? Absolutely. But that was not the point. The point was to develop them as leaders. I provided them enough freedom that they would probably make some mistakes (and they did), but not so much freedom that they would destroy the youth ministry or themselves (or a kid).

At times an unhealthy aspect of our egos raises its ugly head. We know that raising up leaders takes time; but we become impatient. We believe that no one else can do a better job than we can, and we want it done correctly the first time. But when it comes to developing other leaders, time and patience and humility are required.

> "Teach new leaders in a way that they can imitate at once, for your teaching style must be kept reproducible."
>
> —Patrick O'Connor, *Reproducible Pastoral Training: Church Planting Guidelines from the Teachings of George Patterson* (Pasadena, CA: William Carey Library, 2006), 73

## The Simple Aspect of Leadership

One common definition for leadership is influence. According to this concept, a leader is someone who is able to positively or negatively affect someone else. In the general sense, a kingdom leader is someone who is influencing others either to come to faith in Christ or to grow in their faith in Christ.

If someone knows at least one thing, then that person is able to lead others in that direction. For example, if Clarence just started having a daily devotional time with the Lord last month, he already knows enough to teach a new believer how to begin such a daily practice. Church planters must remember that general leadership is not something so complicated that only a few are able to do it. And it is imperative that missionaries begin by teaching and modeling this simple aspect of leadership to the new believers.

Church planters must assume that every new believer is a leader in some capacity. Parents can be taught to *lead* their children. Husbands can be taught to *lead* their families. All believers can be taught to share the gospel, so that they may experience the blessing of *leading* someone else to Jesus.

## Appointing Elders

The appointment of the first elders in a local church is a major milestone in the life of that church and in the overall church multiplication strategy. Though clearly there is no set timeline to be followed as to when elders are to be appointed, I believe it is best to do it as soon as possible, rather than delay the matter. At the conclusion of the first missionary journey, Paul and Barnabas returned to the churches they had just planted, and Luke recorded that they "appointed elders for them in every church, with prayer and fasting they committed them to the Lord in whom they had believed" (Acts 14:21–23).

> **"Surely if the pattern of Jesus at this point means anything at all, it teaches that the first duty of a church leadership is to see to it that a foundation is laid in the beginning on which can be built an effective and continuing evangelistic ministry to the multitudes."**
>
> —Robert E. Coleman, *The Master Plan of Evangelism*, 30th anniversary edition (Grand Rapids, MI: Fleming H. Revell, 1993), 36.

There are some important principles found in Paul's missionary work that contemporary church planters must learn and apply to their own ministries. First, Paul clearly established the general parameters for the qualifications for elders (1 Timothy 3:1–7; Titus 1:5–9). Second, though the leaders from the Church in Jerusalem would have probably been more mature in the faith and qualified to serve, he had no problem appointing elders selected from among the new churches. Third, Paul manifested a missionary faith in the sanctifying power of the Lord that allowed him to commend the new churches to God (Acts 20:32). Fourth, though Paul was not a permanent fixture attached to the new churches and their leaders, he continued the relationships by visiting (Acts 20:17), by writing letters (e.g., 1 and 2 Thessalonians, Philippians), by leaving team members behind to assist for a season (Titus 1:5), and by sending others (Philippians 2:19, 25).

The church-planting team should ask itself and the church, Who are the men of the church who meet the biblical parameters, are clearly walking in the light (1 John 1:6–7), are willing to make the time commitment, and are willing to be taught how to serve as elders? In many new churches, such men may already be recognized by the churches as leaders.

Daniel Sinclair offered five excellent recommendations to assist church planters in the process of appointing elders in new churches.[5] I have inserted some of my own comments in brackets where I believe the new churches need to be more involved in the process or where additional helpful information can be found.

1. After instilling a healthy biblical ecclesiology, teach the entire church about the importance of elders in leading, teaching, and shepherding the church. Remind them that your role as an apostolic messenger will change over time and that the elders will become more and more involved in teaching and leading.
2. Begin to change your role to where you spend more and more time mentoring and developing potential elders. Remember 2 Timothy 2:2, and look for faith-filled, available, and teachable people.
3. Establish elder candidates and begin discussing these men with

the rest of the body. [When such men are identified and agree to move in the direction of becoming elders, I would advocate asking the church to prayerfully consider whether or not these men should be appointed to these roles.]

4. Begin working with these elder candidates to become the elders of the church. [Some resources that may help you in equipping these men are (1) Dick Scoggins's *Leadership Training Guide,* available at www.dickscoggins.com, and (2) Alexander Strauch's *Biblical Eldership: An Urgent Call to Restore Biblical Church Leadership,* revised and expanded (Littleton, CO: Lewis and Roth Publishers, 1995).]
5. Especially in pioneer and hostile environments, church planters must speak candidly about suffering and persecution. Elders should know the possibilities and the biblical responses to such opposition.
6. [This sixth point is my inclusion to a basic appointment process for elders: Whenever the Holy Spirit makes it clear that such men are to be the elders of the church, the missionaries and the churches should have a time, once again, to prayerfully consider these leaders. After the men's lives and doctrines have been examined, the churches should make the final decision as to whether or not these men should become their elders. Such a decision-making process teaches the churches to be self-governing as the Spirit leads them to their pastors (Acts 20:28).]

## Increasing and Decreasing

Just as Jesus eventually raised up a handful of leaders, empowered them, released them, and returned to heaven, and just as the apostle Paul worked diligently to make certain that elders were appointed in the new churches he planted, contemporary church planters should also go through planned role changes in their ministries to make sure that they are increasing the leadership roles of others while decreasing their own roles.

I once noticed a building that was being constructed. After the steel skeleton had taken shape, scaffolds were erected around the hollow framework. For some time these scaffolds remained in place until the building's construction was complete. In a very similar way, the church-planting team is to exist much like a scaffold.[6] The team is there to plant the church and work with the church to appoint the first elders. Following this time, the missionaries repeat this process with other churches they establish, and as the new churches continue to grow, they possibly network the new churches together.

> "Missionaries holding a high view of a church know that it can do God's work, so they help churches raise up their own leaders, relying on the gifts that the Lord gives the flock to do its ministry."
>
> —Patrick O'Connor, *Reproducible Pastoral Training: Church Planting Guidelines from the Teachings of George Patterson* (Pasadena, CA: William Carey Library, 2006), 331.

## Phase-out Strategy

In his book *Passing the Baton: Church Planting That Empowers*, Tom Steffen popularized the concept of "phase-out." In essence, this aspect of the church planting involves the team intentionally strategizing for planned role changes so that indigenous leadership is developed to oversee the churches. Such an element in a church multiplication strategy does not involve abandoning the new churches and severing the relationships; but rather, as Steffen noted, "responsible phase-out begins with a *strategy of closure* for the overall people group, and for each subculture within that community."[7]

His approach to the changing roles of the church planters consists of six phases.

- **Phase 1: Learners.** This phase begins before the team arrives on the field and continues throughout the team's departure.
- **Phase 2: Evangelists.** This phase begins shortly after the team arrives, but their role as evangelists diminishes as the new believers begin to take on more evangelistic responsibilities.
- **Phase 3: Teachers.** As the team begins to see people come to faith, they will spend more and more of their time as teachers. However, like evangelists, their role as teachers will diminish as the new believers begin to take on more teaching responsibilities.
- **Phase 4: Resident Advisors.** Over time the church planters become coaches to the new churches. Here the church planters are providing counsel and guidance while continuing to live among the people, but the churches are self-governing.
- **Phase 5: Itinerant Advisors.** As the new churches and their leaders continue to mature in the faith, the church planters engage in planned absences. It is during this phase that the missionaries continue to assist with tough decisions, but are periodically absent and are not involved in the daily activities of the churches.
- **Phase 6: Absent Advisors.** During this last phase, the missionaries are involved in other church-planting activities elsewhere, but remain in fellowship with the newly planted churches. Though their focus involves another ministry, they continue the relationships and pray for the new churches.[8]

## Postscript: A Note to Those Who Plant-and-Pastor

A common missionary paradigm found throughout the world, especially in Western contexts, is that of plant-and-pastor. This is most prevalent in the United States and Canada. Almost every church-planting book, assessment, conference, training manual, and class that is designed for a U.S. or Canadian audience is founded on the concept that the church planters will become the pastors of the new churches. Though more is said regarding this paradigm in a later chapter, I felt it was necessary to mention the relevance of planned role changes to this approach.

Even if church planters begin as missionaries and then transition to being pastors, a variation of the phase-out concept is critical to them as well. First, leadership development must remain a part of such church-planting strategies. Though the church planters will begin the work by doing most of the ministry themselves, they will want to see people come to faith and mature in their gifts to build the body of Christ. Such growth will require the new believers to take on more responsibilities, causing the church planters to empower and release others. Second, the church planters will become involved in raising up elders to serve alongside them. Third, as the newly planted churches become more established, the church planters/pastors will have to increasingly involve themselves with daily church maintenance while raising up leaders to be sent out for missionary activity.

### *Summary:*

1. Church planters should always be asking themselves what would happen to the new believers and churches if something tragic happened to the church-planting team.
2. Poor leadership development hinders church health and multiplication.

3. Church planters must embrace simple and highly reproducible models for leadership development.
4. Church planters must be willing to allow new believers to grow and mature as leaders. This process will involve making mistakes.
5. It is extremely important that church planters raise up and appoint elders over the new churches.
6. A phase-out component in a church-planting strategy allows the church planters to progress through planned role changes as the church and its pastors mature.
7. Church planters embracing a plant-and-pastor model must learn to apply variations of phase-out to their work in order to develop effective and mature leaders.

### *Reflection Questions:*

1. Do you agree with the goal of leadership development as noted by Logan and Cole? Explain your response.
2. Is your leadership style preference more direct or indirect? What strengths and limitations does your preference bring to the mission field?
3. As a church-planting team, take some time to think through Steffen's six phases for phasing out of your context. How do you see yourself and the team functioning at each phase? Be as descriptive as possible.
4. Is phase-out a part of your church multiplication strategy? Why or why not?
5. Are you following the paradigm of planting-and-pastoring? If so, why did you select this approach? As the church planter/pastor, how will you raise up leaders in the church?

### *Important Terms in This Chapter:*

- Leadership

- Leader
- M.A.W.L. model
- I/You model
- Direct leadership
- Indirect leadership
- Phase-out
- Plant-and-pastor

Section II

# DISCOVERING MISSIOLOGICAL PRINCIPLES

While discovering church planting, it is important that you understand some fundamental principles of missions. Since church planting is missionary work in action, this section covers some of the principles that I believe are important for you to know now. Chapters nine and ten address the importance and principles of strategy development for global church multiplication. Chapter eleven covers the topic of receptivity and church planting. Unless called by the Lord to work in apathetic or hard-soil areas, missionaries should seek to work in areas that are the most receptive to the gospel. It is here that church-planting teams are more likely to see the rapid multiplication of disciples, leaders, and churches. Chapter twelve provides an overview of the principle of contextualization. Here you will come to understand how to know your people linguistically, geographically, demographically, historically, culturally, politically, and spiritually. Chapters thirteen and fourteen focus on the principle of the mother church and church planting, as well as how established churches can get involved in such missionary activities. Finally, chapter fifteen addresses the much-neglected yet incredibly important principle of church-planting teams.

Chapter 9

# STRATEGY AND CHURCH PLANTING PART 1

**Why missionary strategy? Because with it we all will be more effective instruments in the hands of the Lord of the harvest.**

**—C. Peter Wagner[1]**

The concept of strategy development is critical to the overall work of the advancement of the Church. Despite this significance, there are few books addressing this matter, making it ripe for more research and writing. Among the limited resources a few of the best works include the following: Edward R. Dayton and David A. Fraser, *Planning Strategies for World Evangelization* (Grand Rapids, MI: William B. Eerdmans Publishing Company, 1980); C. Peter Wagner, *Frontiers in Missionary Strategy* (Chicago, IL: Moody Press, 1971) and *Strategies for Church Growth: Tools for Effective Mission and Evangelism* (Ventura, CA: Regal, 1989); Aubrey Malphurs, *Advanced Strategic Planning: A New Model for Church and Ministry Leaders,* 2nd ed. (Grand Rapids, MI: Baker Books, 2005); and *Strategy 2000: Churches Making Disciples for the Next Millennium* (Grand Rapids, MI: Kregel Publications, 1996). For an outstanding study of the history of missionary strategy, I direct you to R. Pierce Beaver's article "The History of Mission Strategy," *Southwestern Journal of Theology* 12 (Spring 1970): 7–28.

When I examine the North American context, I find three matters of concern related to general strategy development. I should add, these concerns are not necessarily limited to North America. First, our strategies generally are based on a limited vision. The focus is on planting a church rather than saturating a people group or population segment with the gospel and several churches. Many church planters tend to be myopic in their visions.

Sometimes I hear church planters say they have a vision to plant a "church-planting church." Though this sounds like a great vision, it often translates into planting a church here and another there, every few years. Or, rarely, I hear, "We will plant a church every year." This seems like a fantastic vision; however, with several billion people in the world without Christ, one church planting another church per year will not even scratch the surface of lostness in the world. Such visions are too small.

A second matter of concern regarding many church-planting strategies is that the methods used are not highly reproducible by the people who are reached with the gospel. What is modeled to the new believers and churches are paradigms that only highly trained teams can reproduce. If God called out missionaries from those new churches, few to none would be able to plant churches—having only witnessed that one particular model. We must acknowledge the reality that most church-planting paradigms in North America are not going to reach the over 200,000,000 nonkingdom citizens, let alone the billions outside of this continent.

A final matter of concern is that of rigid strategies. Contexts are made of people who are social beings, and social beings are in a state of constant change. Church-planting strategies that are not adaptable to shifting contexts end up failing as the winds of change blow.

This chapter is written in light of these concerns. However, before we continue, it is necessary to begin with a definition of strategy.

## Defining Strategy

Strategy is a military term that addresses the maneuvers that work together to overcome the enemy. Merriam-Webster defines it as "the science and art of employing the political, economic, psychological, and military forces of a nation or group of nations to afford the maximum support to adopted policies in peace or war."[2] Missiologists have adopted this same word to describe the science and art of advancing the gospel into the Enemy's territory, resulting in kingdom expansion.

So, what is strategy as related to the growth of the Church? C. Peter Wagner defined strategy as "the chosen means to accomplish a predetermined goal."[3] Aubrey Malphurs noted that a strategy is "the process that determines how you will accomplish the mission of the ministry."[4] In the highly practical resource *The Church Planter's Toolkit*, Robert E. Logan and Steven L. Ogne commented that strategy is that process which translates vision into reality.[5] Therefore, in light of these definitions, I have chosen to define **strategy** as *a prayerfully discerned, Spirit-guided process of preparation, development, implementation, and evaluation of the necessary steps involved in biblical church planting.*

> "Because missions must begin with the wishes of the sovereign God yet function within the context of a social situation, strategy is defined as *the practical working out of the will of God within a cultural context.*"
>
> —Gailyn Van Rheenen, *Missions: Biblical Foundations and Contemporary Strategies* (Grand Rapids, MI: Zondervan, 1996), 140, italics original.

## Prayerful Discernment

As noted in a previous chapter, prayer must come before, during, and after the church-planting work. It is a critical part to the life and ministry of the Church. Wilbert R. Shenk reminded us that "strategic planning ought to begin and end with the prayer 'Your will be done.'"[6] Strategies void of seeking the face of the Lord are strategies that are doomed to failure.

## Spirit-Guided Process

Also alluded to in a previous chapter, healthy strategic planning is based on the conviction that the Spirit is the critical component in each of the steps of developing church-planting strategies. It must be remembered that "the heart of man plans his way, but the LORD establishes his steps" (Proverbs 16:9). It is in the process of developing and implementing the strategy that the Spirit provides guidance (Acts 16:6–10). Strategic planning is not a one-step event in time, but rather a journey. It involves many details and trial and error.

## Preparation

This component of the process involves prayer, people group and community research (see chapter twelve on contextualization), development of an end vision and goals, and an understanding of the church-planting team's values, mission, and purpose.

## Development

The development component involves planning the action steps of how the team will move from where it is to where it believes the Spirit desires it to go in the process of church planting.

### Implementation

Strategic planning is a practical activity. It cannot be accomplished in a classroom or laboratory. There must be the implementation of the action steps. All of the research, planning, and dreaming must be applied to the context.

### Evaluation

In light of their goals and the Spirit's leading, church planters must constantly be evaluating the overall progress of the work. Biblical stewardship demands healthy checkups from time to time and the necessary adjustments that follow.

> **"Therefore, a thorough understanding of missionary goals is the first step toward the formulation of an effective strategy."**
>
> —C. Peter Wagner, *Frontiers in Missionary Strategy* (Chicago, IL: Moody Press, 1971), 17.

## Benefits of a Strategy

According to Logan and Ogne, many church planters have vision but fail to have an effective strategy.[7] By nature, church planters tend to be "big picture" people. They usually have the end vision in mind but fail to work backward and think through all the necessary steps to move from where they are presently to that vision becoming a reality.

Though challenging work, the benefits of strategic planning far outweigh any limitations to the developmental process. Consider some of the advantages to having a strategy as noted by Dayton and Fraser:

- It challenges us to seek God's will.
- It helps us anticipate the future.

- It assists us in communicating with others on our team so everyone will be on the same page.
- It provides us with a sense of direction and cohesion.
- It guides us in knowing what we will *not* do.[8]

## Does One Size Fit All?

The following excerpt from Dayton and Fraser's work, *Planning Strategies for World Evangelization,* shows the authors' perspectives that church planters should not assume that there is one strategic approach to reaching the world. Rather, the authors argue for a standard approach to guide missionaries in the strategic-thinking process.

> It is our conviction that *both* the differences and the commonness of humans must be respected in any successful approach to strategy. The people who need to be reached by the gospel are found in groups that are significantly different in terms of language, cultural traits, felt needs, life-style, modal personality, and responsiveness. In seeking an effective and meaningful hearing for the gospel, the evangelist must tailor a strategy for reaching the unreached on the basis of the particular attributes of the specific group which needs the gospel. What role the evangelist will play, what gifts and special methods need to be employed, how many Christian workers and what resources will be required all depend upon the nature of the particular group. . . .
>
> So important is this in our thinking that we could call this approach a people-centered strategy. While we believe there is a role and a place for standard solutions (they work well in cultures that share certain similar traits and where social change is slow), they have a very limited role and place in our day and age. We are convinced that there is no single, universal strategy that can be applied to all the unreached peoples of our world, or even a majority of them. . . .
>
> Consequently, we reject standard solutions for unstandard peoples. They do not work, and worse, they often do more harm than good. . . .
>
> But we are convinced that *there is a standard approach which can be used to devise strategies which will be effective for each remaining unreached group.* It is the approach that is based upon serious consideration of the cultural and

contextual differences that make each people unique, and upon a problem-solving method that provides a way of understanding how that uniqueness can become part of an evangelistic strategy. In short, it is based on the conviction that God has a unique strategy for each unique people. To discover that strategy we need to respect the particularity of a people and to utilize a series of basic questions which provide the information necessary for us to make decisions about the strategy that might best communicate the gospel.

Taken from Edward R. Dayton and David A. Fraser, *Planning Strategies for World Evangelization* (Grand Rapids, MI: William B. Eerdmans Publishing Company, 1980), 116–117, italics original.

***Questions to Consider:***

1. Do you agree or disagree that the differences and the similarities of people have to be taken into consideration when developing strategies? Explain.
2. Do you agree or disagree with the authors that there is no universal strategy to be applied to all peoples? Explain.
3. What do you think are some of the necessary questions that need to be asked when developing church multiplication strategies?

## Contemporary Objections to Strategy

Before describing the important elements of healthy church multiplication strategies, it is necessary to list some of the reasons why there is opposition to such planning today in certain circles.

### Strategic Planning Attempts to Replace God's Sovereignty

A variation of this objection was thoroughly addressed and rebutted by William Carey in the eighteenth century.[9] It is the objection that if God is going to reach the world, then he will do it in his way and in his timing. He is in control, and we should not make any necessary attempts to be a part of that rule. Basil Clutterbuck was correct when he wrote, "At the heart of Christian obedience and Christian enterprise, lies this paradox: God is the supreme Strategist, and it is He who does His work in the world; yet He does not do it without us. He uses us as His workmen; He also calls us to intelligent planning under His own direction."[10]

## Strategic Planning Hinders the Spirit

It can be argued that the development of strategies hinders the work of the Holy Spirit by creating rigid structures. This objection wrongly assumes there is no freedom of the Spirit with such planning. Healthy strategies, however, are flexible and are not written in stone. They are not developed in a laboratory apart from the context.

I once invited a former student to speak about his church-planting work. When he had finished addressing the class, I asked him what would be his one piece of advice for church planters. He quickly stated, "Here's what you need to do. You need to make sure that you take the nice, neat strategy that you compile into an attractive binder, hold it high over your head, and throw it into the garbage can! When you get to the field, everything begins to change, and your strategy has to adjust accordingly."

Though his comment was hyperbolic—for I know he was not opposed to developing strategies—his point was well made. We make strategies as the Spirit guides, but also must allow for his continual guidance in the field. Dayton was absolutely correct that "planning strategies for evangelization is no substitute for the powerful presence and action of the Holy Spirit!"[11]

> **"It is of urgent necessity that mission strategy and method be subjected to theological critique."**
>
> —Wilbert R. Shenk, *Changing Frontiers of Missions* (Maryknoll, NY: Orbis Books, 1999), 113.

## Strategic Planning Is Pragmatism

Granted, it is possible to use unbiblical strategies to plant churches. Unfortunately, many churches have been planted that compromise the gospel and other essential doctrines. Healthy strategy development is not pragmatism. It is pragmatic, however, because all Christians are to be pragmatic. We are commanded to *make* disciples; therefore, we need to know *what works* to accomplish this goal. Donald A. McGavran commented, "Church growth seldom comes without bold plans for it."[12] The Church is not to accomplish church planting through *any* means but must accomplish this task through *some* means.

## Strategic Planning Requires Accountability

Though those who oppose planning never voice this objection, nevertheless, I suppose, it remains in the back of their minds. The truth of strategic planning is that it demands accountability. If a church-planting team makes plans to take the gospel to 200,000 people in its population segment in three years, then at the end of three years someone must ask the question, Did you meet your goal? Strategic planning will not allow the Church to sit passively and be a poor steward of its resources. Biblical church-planting strategies hold missionaries responsible.

## Strategic Planning Interrupts Laziness

Another objection no missionaries would vocalize is that they refuse to make plans because of personal laziness. Strategic planning is challenging work. It requires much prayer, research, goal setting, action steps, trial and error, and constant evaluation. Those who take the development of church-planting strategies seriously are not slothful people.

## Biblical Foundations for Strategy

Before addressing the principles involved in the development of church multiplication strategies (see chapter ten), it is vitally important to begin by examining the scriptural support for such a practice. Since there is clearly no step-by-step approach delineated in the Bible related to global disciple making, some—such as Michael Green—believe that no strategy existed for the apostolic Church: "There does not seem to have been anything very remarkable about the strategy and tactics of the early Christian mission. Indeed, it is doubtful if they had one. I do not believe they set out with any blueprint. They had an unquenchable conviction that Jesus was the key to life and death, happiness and purpose, and they simply could not keep quiet about him. The spirit of Jesus within them drove them into mission."[13]

Though I agree with Green that there was no formal strategy, as we might define one today, the apostolic Church did have a commission and a plan to fulfill that commission (Acts 1:8). It has been advocated for many years that there was a particular pattern to the work of the apostle Paul.[14] He would enter a city, evangelize the people, gather them into congregations, appoint elders over the churches, and follow up accordingly (e.g., Acts 13–14). His goal of making disciples through church planting specifically took place through a variety of means.

> **"As Toynbee says, there is a danger in using an archaic strategy and imagining that because it worked in the past it will do so indefinitely."**
>
> —Gilbert Baker, "Principles of Missionary Strategy—I," *Church Quarterly Review* 157 (October–December 1956): 478.

He primarily ministered in urban environments of significant political, economic, educational, and religious influence. If a synagogue existed, he began preaching in that location. He worked to plant churches through evangelism. If a people group was unreceptive to the gospel, he would go to those who were receptive (Acts 18:6–7). He wrote letters to the new churches, visited, or delegated follow-up matters to others (e.g., Timothy, Titus). He even accomplished these tasks to such a degree that he was able to speak of his work being completed in a region (Romans 15:18–25).

Despite the fact that the apostolic Church did not sit around in the upper room with a whiteboard and sticky notes, mapping out an approach to plant churches throughout Asia Minor, there was a plan with a variety of methods to make disciples of all nations through planting churches.[15]

The Bible does offer numerous examples of plans: God had a plan for the tabernacle that Moses received on the mountain (Exodus 26:30). God spoke to Moses about his plans that he desired to carry out regarding the inhabitants of the Promised Land (Numbers 33:56). David gave Solomon the detailed plan for the construction of the temple (1 Chronicles 28:11–12). Isaiah noted that God makes plans that cannot be interrupted (Isaiah 14:24–27). Jeremiah wrote that God made plans against Edom (Jeremiah 49:20). Peter spoke of the predetermined plan of God in relation to Jesus (Acts 2:22–23). Paul noted that Jesus came at the right moment in God's plan (Galatians 4:4). And though not all will be saved, it is God's plan for all to hear and understand the gospel (John 3:16; 1 Timothy 2:3–4; 2 Peter 3:9).

In conjunction with such examples, there are also guidelines and warnings that must be followed in making plans for the future. Wisdom is needed; a person of understanding can draw out a plan in the heart (Proverbs 20:5). Jesus recognized that planning was a natural part of life when he mentioned calculating the cost of building a tower or entering into war (Luke 14:28). However, future plans should include the will of God, since there is no guarantee for a tomorrow (James 4:13–16).

Apart from God, the natural plans of people lead to foolishness (Proverbs 26:12) and death (Proverbs 16:25). Even the apostle Paul's strategy to preach in Asia and Bithynia was interrupted by the Holy Spirit, who had different plans (Acts 16:6–7).

Another important issue related to planning is that of defining success. Church planters must be careful not to define success in secular terms. Missionary success is associated with faithfulness to the calling and wise stewardship in relation to Great Commission obedience, rather than being solely focused on the numbers of baptisms and churches planted. Missionaries and their supervisors would be wise to remember this important distinction.

### *Summary:*

1. Missionaries cannot operate on the strategic philosophy of "Ready! . . . Fire! . . . Aim!" but rather that of "Ready! . . . Aim! . . . Fire!" Unfortunately, many individuals and churches approach the billions of unbelievers in a very haphazard manner without a Matthew 28:19/Revelation 7:9 vision, significant goals, and intentional action steps.
2. Healthy strategies are flexible and adaptable to the leading of the Spirit.
3. Strategic planning is both a science and an art that involves specific and abundant prayer.
4. A team significantly benefits from having a strategy.
5. Common objections to strategic planning are not justified in light of biblical, theological, and missiological reflection.

### *Reflection Questions:*

1. When it comes to strategic planning, which statement best represents your attitude: "Forget about it! God's in control!" or "I plan every detail to the nth degree because it will work out as I

plan it!" What would be an expression that you believe represents a healthy perspective on strategic planning for church multiplication?

2. Can you list some benefits not mentioned in this chapter to having a church multiplication strategy?
3. Of all the objections to developing strategies, which do you think is the most common one that you will face from others? From yourself?

### *Important Term in This Chapter:*

- Strategy

Chapter 10

# STRATEGY AND CHURCH PLANTING PART 2

**It is better to put an imperfect plan into operation than to carry on splendid church and mission work while waiting for the perfect plan to appear.**

**—Donald A. McGavran[1]**

Now that we have covered some of the important aspects of the foundations for strategic planning and some of the objections commonly found among missionaries, we need to spend this chapter examining some of the principles and steps involved in strategic development. As noted in the last chapter, entire books have been written about the topic of strategy development. It is my hope that this chapter will not only introduce you to this topic but also assist you and your church-planting team in developing your church multiplication strategies.

## Principles of Strategy Development

There are at least five important principles for developing strategies that should guide the planning work of church planters. Since there are many distractions that can interfere with strategic development, it is critical that church planters ground their strategies on the right principles. Beginning with a healthy foundation assists in making certain the team is moving in the proper direction.

### Biblically Based

All healthy strategies are biblically based. Hugo Culpepper once commented, "To be effective, strategy must have solid biblical and theological foundations."[2] Without grounding the strategy in the Scriptures, church planters run the risk of deviating from what the Lord expects from his Church.

### Stewardship Oriented

A second guiding principle for strategy development is that of wise stewardship. As stewards of the mysteries of God, church planters must be found trustworthy (1 Corinthians 4:2). The use of money, time, and people in church-planting strategies must be considered with great care, because the Lord expects believers to be wise stewards of their resources for making disciples of all nations (Luke 12:42–48; 19:11–27). The question must be asked, In light of the billions of unbelievers in the world, is this strategy a wise strategy advocating a healthy use of the provided assets?

### Contextually Relevant

Strategies that fail to be contextually relevant reflect a lack of biblical support and poor stewardship. Strategies must facilitate the connection between the people and the gospel. Such strategies will also include a process of moving people from a conversion experience to being the body of Christ in that local context.

## Structurally Adaptable

Flexibility is a key principle in strategy development. Church-planting strategies must not be too rigid, or they will break when change arrives. There is much science to strategic planning; however, strategies must allow for adjustment so church planting can occur.

> **"We must not commit the blasphemy of conceiving missionary strategy as something man-centered and man-controlled. It is Christ who builds His Church, not we; the strategy of all true evangelism is His, not ours."**
>
> —Basil Clutterbuck, "World Missionary Strategy," *London Quarterly and Holborn Review* 182 (January 1957): 30.

## Reproducible

Because global disciple making is the command the Church follows, wise church planters must always be asking themselves the question, Will this strategy assist in the multiplication of disciples throughout the world? Because methods are the means for applying the strategies to the real world, those methods must be highly reproducible. Though all methods are reproducible to a degree, some are more difficult to replicate than others. George Patterson's question must be asked: "What is the shortest possible route to plant a church that will spark a spontaneous movement to Christ?"[3] A simple and highly reproducible method is usually the answer.

## ABCs of Strategy Development

Though there is no single approach to developing church multiplication strategies, the rest of this chapter provides some helpful parameters for this process. In the paragraphs below I have outlined these parameters in three steps. (For a visual overview see figure 10.1.) The first step, "Apply the Strategic Filter," helps church planters to stay focused on what is important in their work. It establishes a framework for keeping their strategies within biblical boundaries for kingdom advancement. The second step, "Basic Questions Are Asked," raises some of the most important questions that church planters must answer in the process of developing healthy strategies. Finally, the third step, "Consider the Action Steps," simply challenges church planters to think through how they will apply their knowledge to the field.

Figure 10.1 illustrates the ABCs of Strategy Development.

### Step 1: Apply the Strategic Filter

Filters are used in everyday life to strain out matter that might adversely affect the end product. Chefs use filters to prevent large particles of vegetables from entering into their sauces. Painters use filters to remove small particles from their paints that will hinder the beauty of their finished works. Whenever I have the oil changed in my car, the mechanic always shows me the car's air filter and encourages me to keep a clean one in place. The strategic filter advocated in this chapter is a biblically and missiologically based framework to assist in the initial stages of strategy development. The application of such a filter will assist in screening out many of the elements that hinder church planters from developing effective multiplication strategies.

**Begin with God's Calling.** Dayton and Fraser wrote, "And if the world is to be evangelized, if every person in the world is to have an

Figure 10.1 **The ABCs of Strategy Development**

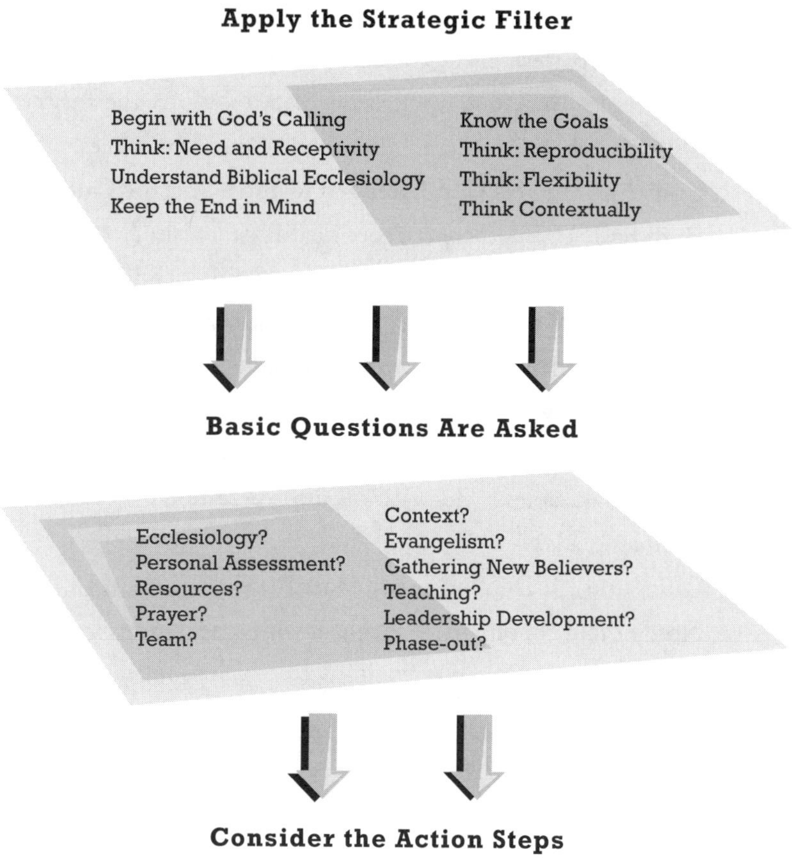


opportunity to know Jesus Christ as Lord and Savior, then cross-cultural missionaries need to understand the people to whom they are called, to uncover God's strategies and plans for reaching these people, and to sense that God is setting them aside to be about his business in a particular part of the world."[4] It is necessary to begin all strategic development with the call of God. Here are some guidelines to consider when beginning the strategy development process:

- **Guideline #1: Assume the Great Commission.** The general call for all believers is to "make disciples of all nations" (Matthew 28:19). Intentionally making disciples is to be the normative pattern of the Church any time, any place, among any people. Therefore, where is the place to begin? The answer is simply, wherever there are people who are not disciples.
- **Guideline #2: Has God Extended to You a Specific Call to Hard Soil?** Unless there is a specific call for a team to work among an apathetic or resistant people and the sending church has confirmed that call (Acts 13:1–3), then the team should move to Guideline #3. The call to be a Jeremiah or an Ezekiel and labor for years in a resistant field is a legitimate and valid calling, but not normative. The Church is commanded to "make disciples," which carries the expectation of seeing disciples made.
- **Guideline #3: Determine the Most Receptive and Most Needy Field.** In order to be faithful with available resources, church planters should prayerfully locate the peoples and areas where receptivity is high and need is great. Dayton and Fraser noted that understanding a peoples' receptivity level to the gospel is "basic within a strategy for evangelization."[5] Even the apostle Paul, who took the gospel to the Jews first, would turn his attention to the more receptive Gentiles upon encountering hard soil (Acts 18:6–7).

**Think: Receptivity *and* Need.** The world is a big place, and with several *billion* people who are not believers, the initial question is, Where do we begin planting a church? Some missiologists, such as Wagner, believe that need is not a good starting point for strategy development because it does not distinguish between "those needy non-Christians who are receptive to the gospel and those who are not."[6] Though there is much weight to his argument, I advocate that missionaries must think in terms of *both* receptivity and need in order to determine priority in missionary work. The Receptivity-Need Analysis Guideline (see figure 10.2) challenges church planters to see peoples as fitting into one of four general categories.

Figure 10.2 **Receptivity-Need Analysis Guideline**

| NEED \ RECEPTIVITY | **High** | **Low** |
|---|---|---|
| **High** | **A** Priority 1 | **B** Priority 2 |
| **Low** | **C** Priority 3 | **D** Priority 4 |

The degree of need among a people for new churches should be determined by, at least, two criteria. First, what is the overall percentage of the population that is evangelical? Because evangelicals by definition are followers of Jesus and believe that a born-again (regenerative) experience is necessary for salvation, then using the evangelical population as a benchmark is the best guarantee in determining the percentage of the population who are not followers of Jesus.[7] Second, are there a reasonable number of churches among the people group/population segment that can effectively minister to all of the peoples? What constitutes "effectively minister" is up for debate and, many times, arbitrarily defined.

Though definitions also differ, some missiologists have attempted to develop a description of what constitutes a "reached" or "unreached" group. According to Dayton and Fraser, "Observation and research has shown that when approximately 10 or 20 percent of the people within a group have accepted an idea or a new religion, they have the ability to evangelize the rest of the group."[8] The Discipling A Whole Nation (DAWN) Movement advocates at least one intentionally evangelistic church per 400–600 people in rural areas and one such church for every 1,000–1,500 people in the cities.[9]

**Understand Biblical Ecclesiology.** The most critical issue in church planting relates to the church planters' ecclesiology. How they answer the question, What is the Church (universal and local)? will affect *everything* they do in their missionary work. A clear understanding of the Scriptures' teaching on the local church will guide the development of the strategy and the methods they implement to accomplish the vision.

**Keep the End in Mind.** Church-planting strategy begins with the end in mind—with the end *not* being the planting of a church. A missional theology that supports church planting is not a theology that desires to see the planting of a church as the end result, but rather the transformation of a society by the gospel in the political, educational, legal, athletic, entertainment, military, economic, and familial realms. If the end is to see citizens of the kingdom of darkness become citizens of the kingdom of light, then church-planting strategies must begin with this end vision; all that church planters "put in at the beginning" will work toward accomplishing or detracting from making disciples of all nations.

David Garrison challenged strategists to begin by asking the **WIGTAKE** question, "What Is It Going to Take" to see this people group or population segment saturated with the gospel and a multitude of churches come into existence?[10] Whether the team is working among a French-speaking community in Quebec, a nomadic people in the Middle

## Working the Ripe and Green Fields

Missiologist C. Peter Wagner once gave an illustration regarding the use of missionary personnel in receptive and nonreceptive areas. Consider the following scenario taken from his chapter "The Fourth Dimension of Missions: Strategy" in *Perspectives on the World Christian Movement: A Reader*, eds. Ralph D. Winter and Steven C. Hawthorne (Pasadena, CA: William Carey Library, 1981), 578, italics original:

> Suppose, for example, that you owned an apple orchard. In field A, a worker could harvest five bushels in an hour. In field B, it would take him five hours to harvest just one bushel. In field C, he couldn't harvest anything because the apples are all still green. If you had thirty workers today, where would you send them? I think I would send twenty-nine of them to field A so as not to lose the fruit there. I would send the other one to do what he could in field B and also keep his eye on field C. His job would be to let me know when those fields were ripe so I could redeploy the personnel.
>
> Parallel situations arise time after time in missionary work. Some peoples are ready to be harvested today, some are not yet ready. These "unresponsive peoples" should not be neglected—someone should be there who is expert enough to tell when they are becoming ripe for the gospel. In one sense you need the very finest workers in the unresponsive fields but no one who takes strategy seriously would advocate a massive labor force in green fields. Jesus wouldn't. He does not tell us to pray for more laborers to go to green fields or to fallow fields. The laborers are needed for the *ripe harvest* fields.

***Questions to Consider:***

1. Do you agree or disagree with Wagner's use of the missionaries?
2. Where would you send the thirty missionaries?
3. In what field would you and your team prefer to work?
4. Is your present ministry context like field A, B, or C?
5. Are you serving where the Lord has called you to serve?

East, a Japanese arts community in Tokyo, or an inner-city Mexican community in Los Angeles, the team must prayerfully ask the Lord the WIGTAKE question.

Garrison offered some questions to assist in the development of the end vision:

- What is God's vision for this people, this city, or this community?
- How many churches will it take to reach these people, to reach this city, to reach this community?
- What will those churches look like as they come into existence? As they're being planted as indigenous churches from the very beginning, what will they look like?
- Where will their leaders come from?
- What will these leaders need to know?
- How will these leaders get the training they need?
- How long will this training take?
- How many leaders and churches are there now?
- How rapidly are new leaders being trained and new churches being planted as of the present moment?
- At the current rate, how long will it take to produce the number of churches that you believe is needed to fulfill that God-given vision for that people, that city, that community?[11]

**Know the Goals.** After the conceptualization of the end vision, the goals necessary to achieve that end vision must be articulated. What are the necessary goals to accomplish the multiplication of churches throughout the people group? Having clear, concise, and measurable goals allows the team to put feet on its strategy.

**Think: Reproducibility.** Church-planting strategies that are developed with the world in mind (macro) must begin at the local (micro) level. All that goes into supporting the strategy must work to multiply disciples, leaders, and churches. Generally, there is a negative association between the complexity of the methods used and the potential for people to use those methods to plant other churches. Simple contextualized methods are easier for indigenous leaders to reproduce when God calls them to plant other churches.

> **"The more we evangelize and the more disciples we make, the more churches will be multiplied and grow and this is why, in planning strategies, we aim for church growth."**
>
> —C. Peter Wagner, *Strategies for Church Growth: Tools for Effective Mission and Evangelism* (Ventura, CA: Regal Books, 1989), 55.

**Think: Flexibility.** The need for church planters to allow their strategies to be flexible and adaptable is best illustrated by the events leading to the birth of the Philippian Church.

> And they went through the region of Phrygia and Galatia, having been forbidden by the Holy Spirit to speak the word in Asia. And when they had come up to Mysia, they attempted to go into Bithynia, but the Spirit of Jesus did not allow them. So, passing by Mysia, they went down to Troas. And a vision appeared to Paul in the night: a man of Macedonia was standing there, urging him and saying, "Come over to Macedonia and help us." And when Paul had seen the vision, immediately we sought to go on into Macedonia, concluding that God had called us to preach the gospel to them. (Acts 16:6–10)

After spending several days in the city of Philippi, Paul and his team shared the gospel with Lydia, her household, the jailer, and his household, which resulted in the birth of the church. Had Paul not been flexible and sensitive to the leading of the Spirit, he and his team would not have gone to Macedonia. It was through the application of his strategy to enter Asia and Mysia that the Spirit guided him to Philippi. It was in the *process* of going into all the world that the Spirit was able to guide the team to his desired location.

**Think Contextually.** Dayton and Fraser advocate that understanding the people is "the single most important element in planning strategies for evangelism."[12] A healthy understanding of the people geographically, historically, politically, demographically, culturally, linguistically, and spiritually will greatly assist in developing a strategy that is relevant to the context.

The need to keep the context in mind will help alleviate the temptation to clone strategies from teams that were successful in other contexts. Wagner's words assist in illustrating this important point.

> Many choices have to be made in planning strategy. When you have discovered an appropriate strategy for one situation you cannot assume it will always work in another situation, although some strategies can be transferred, if the goal and circumstances are nearly identical. For example, certain situations in a baseball game indicate that the best strategy is clearly for the batter to bunt, and almost invariably a bunt will be attempted. But change the circumstances slightly and the decision on whether to bunt becomes more difficult. Likewise, some evangelistic methods may work very well in a given situation, but they may be next to useless when circumstances are different.[13]

> "Effective strategy grows out of theological and social science considerations."
>
> —Gailyn Van Rheenen, *Missions: Biblical Foundations and Contemporary Strategies* (Grand Rapids, MI: Zondervan, 1996), 139.

## Step 2: Basic Questions Are Asked

After the church-planting team has applied the strategic filter, the next step in the process of strategy development is simply asking basic questions. The following is a list of several questions that need to be considered according to specific categories.

**Ecclesiology.** What is your understanding of the church? How do you understand the church biblically, theologically, and missiologically? What about the organization that makes up the church?

**Personal Assessment**. What is your motive for planting churches? What is your calling? What is your vision from God? Why are you working to plant a church in this particular community? What is your plan for your family as related to church planting? How will the members of the team hold each other accountable for maintaining the spiritual disciplines privately and corporately?

**Resources.** What resources (people, time, money, etc.) do you have for church planting? How do you plan to use those resources over the next two or three years?

**Prayer.** Have you recruited intercessors to pray for you, the ministry, your team, and your family? What element does prayer play in the overall strategy that you have? (See chapter five.)

**Team.** What is your plan for working through the local church to find and develop team members? How involved in the church-planting work will your sending church be? What are the responsibilities and expectations of the sending church? What responsibilities and expectations are placed on the team members? (See chapter fifteen.)

**Context.** What are the geographical, demographical, cultural, spiritual, historical, linguistic, and political characteristics of the people? How well do you know the people from firsthand experience and not just from literary research and discussions with other missionaries? (See chapter twelve.)

**Evangelism.** What is your approach to evangelizing the people? How will you connect with the people? How do you plan to locate the persons of peace? How do you think the people will respond to you and your ministry to them? Where will baptisms occur? Who will be responsible for conducting those baptisms? (See chapter six.)

**Gathering New Believers.** What will be your approach to gathering the new believers together in regular meetings with one another? What will be your approach to lead them in the process of understanding and covenanting together to be the church in that area? How will you teach them what it means to be and function as a church? What do you anticipate will occur during those early gatherings of new believers? In what location do you think those believers meet?

**Teaching.** How will you teach them to observe all that Christ commanded? How are you going to train those new believers to multiply disciples, leaders, and churches? What will be the role of men and women in the teaching process? What will be the expectations for fathers and mothers to one another, as well as to their families? How will you teach and model high expectations for the new believers? (See chapter seven.)

**Leadership Development.** What will be your approach to raising up leaders from the new believers? How much of your leadership training will be classroom oriented? How much of your leadership training will be on the job? Will your leadership style be more direct or indirect? (See chapter eight.)

**Phase-out.** How will the team prepare the new congregation for its departure? How long do you anticipate it will take for the team to arrive on the field, plant the church, and appoint elders over the new church? Is phase-out a part of your overall strategy? If not, why not? (See chapter eight.)

## Step 3: Consider the Action Steps

The action steps for one church-planting team will differ from those of another team. What is necessary to plant churches among the Punjabi of Vancouver may not be necessary to reach a segment of the cowboy subculture in North Carolina. Reaching Turkish immigrants in Western Europe will require different steps from reaching Japanese engineers in Brazil. The steps involved in multiplying churches in Havana will likely differ from the required work in Mexico City. The process of applying the strategic filter (Step 1) and asking good questions (Step 2) are the more scientific side of strategic development; considering and implementing the action steps (Step 3) is more of the artistic side of the work. This step cannot be taught through a textbook or in a classroom. It is here that the team must prayerfully put hand to the plow and take to the field. Experience is necessary.

### *Summary:*

1. Global disciple-making strategies are biblically based, stewardship oriented, contextually relevant, and structurally adaptable, and they advocate highly reproducible methods.
2. The ABCs of Strategy Development are (1) Apply the strategic filter, (2) Basic questions are asked, and (3) Consider the action steps.

### *Reflection Questions:*

1. Do you agree or disagree with the ABCs of Strategic Development? Why?

2. Do you agree or disagree that the Receptivity-Need Analysis Guideline is a good tool to determine priority? Why?
3. Are there any dangers of labeling some fields a higher priority than other fields? If so, describe those dangers.
4. Is the transformation of societies through global disciple making too grandiose a vision for individual church planters? Explain.

### *Important Terms in This Chapter:*

- ABCs of Strategic Development
- Receptivity-Need Analysis Guideline
- Strategic filter
- WIGTAKE question

Chapter 11

# RECEPTIVITY AND CHURCH PLANTING

**The receptivity or responsiveness of individuals waxes and wanes. No person is equally ready at all times to follow "the Way."**

—Donald A. McGavran[1]

During my time as a college student, I was regularly involved in sharing the gospel with other students on campus. Whether the method involved a late-night discussion outside my dorm room with a neighbor across the hallway, a cold-call visit that included placing a gospel tract in the hands of a stranger, or a conversation with a classmate over dinner, one thing was certain: some people decided to follow Jesus, others were curious yet apathetic, and some were hostile to the truth. Though I did not realize it at the time, I was experiencing what missiologists refer to as the principle of receptivity.

Though God extends calls to church-planting teams to certain areas and peoples, an initial question to ask is, Where should we begin in our church-planting activities? For example, if a team receives a calling to a major city such as Miami, Moscow, Sao Paulo, or Morocco, upon arrival it will quickly realize that such areas contain large numbers of different population segments. Knowing where to begin immediately becomes a critical question. Or maybe such a team is called to work among the African American population of Baltimore. Once again, upon arrival the team would soon discover that of the 60 percent of the population that claims to be African American, not all Baltimore African Americans are alike. Much diversity exists, including varying levels of receptivity to the gospel among the demographic segment.

**Receptivity** is the term used to describe an individual's or group's response to the gospel. Those with a positive response are said to be more receptive to the gospel; those who are more apathetic or resistant to the gospel reveal lower levels of receptivity. The planter should also keep in mind that some of the more receptive peoples may be those with the least evangelical presence.

The sovereign work of the Holy Spirit in the regenerative act of making disciples and planting churches is a mystery (John 3:8). As noted in chapter four, it is the Spirit who stirs the hearts of individuals and groups, drawing them to the Father. Though this mysterious work of the Spirit cannot be explained, somehow he works in conjunction with the sinful hearts of people and their contexts to raise receptivity levels. As church planters make disciples of all nations, they should, generally, be looking to see where receptivity is highest—for there it is obvious that the Spirit is at work.

"An essential task is to discern receptivity and—when this is seen—to adjust methods, institutions, and personnel until the receptive are becoming Christians and reaching out to win their fellows to eternal life."

—Donald A. McGavran, *Understanding Church Growth* (Grand Rapids, MI: William B. Eerdmans Publishing Company, 1970), 232.

The principle of receptivity advocates that individuals and groups are like different fields. In agricultural terms, some fields are easy to farm and produce a great harvest of crops, while other fields are difficult and yield few, if any, crops. In figure 11.1 below, Field A represents a group of people hostile to the gospel message, who would prefer that church planters not enter their area. Whereas Field C represents a group of people highly receptive to the truth. In fact, such a field is typically asking the same question as that of the Philippian jailer, "What must I do to be saved?" (Acts 16:30). On the other hand, Field B, in general, has an apathetic attitude toward the gospel that is typically expressed by such statements as, "Jesus may be good for you, but not for me. I'm doing just fine on my own."

The way in which the gospel is presented also affects receptivity. Are the church planters sharing the gospel in a contextually appropriate way that is faithful to the Scriptures? Confusing, cold, angry, impersonal, false gospels, and irrelevant methods all impact how the message is received. Our methods of evangelism must not create barriers between people and the gospel. The cross should be the only stumbling block, not our attitudes or methods (1 Corinthians 1:23).

Figure 11.1

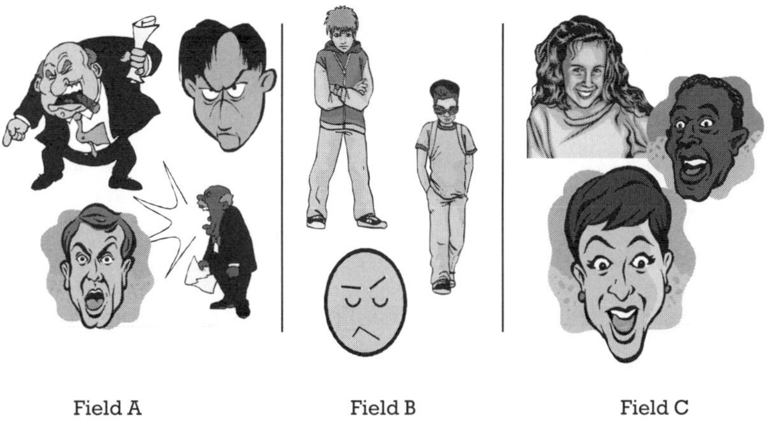

## Abuses of the Principle

Before continuing, I must note that the principle of receptivity can be abused. Problems arise whenever the principle is used to justify withholding the gospel from a people because they do not manifest a high level of receptivity. This practice is not only an example of disobedience to the Great Commission but is also strategically unwise, for the only way to know if a people such as Field A is becoming more receptive is to share the gospel with them. Just as Donald A. McGavran noted years ago that "no one should conclude that if receptivity is low, the Church should withdraw mission,"[2] contemporary church planters must not neglect any field.

> "The most common missionary error is to deploy an excessive number of workers in fields where the harvest is not yet ripe; while at the same time in the ripened harvest fields, fruit is being lost because of lack of workers."
>
> —C. Peter Wagner, *Frontiers in Missionary Strategy* (Chicago: IL: Moody Press, 1971), 44

## The Importance of Receptivity to Church Planters

The principle of receptivity is important to church planters for a variety of reasons. All of the following statements should be taken into consideration as your team seeks to understand and prayerfully apply this principle to the work.

### It Follows the Biblical Example

As already noted, there are several biblical passages that address the principle of receptivity as related to missionary practice. Jesus departed regions when the people did not wish to hear his message (Mark 5:17–18; John 8:59). He instructed the Twelve and the Seventy-two to depart from those towns in which the people were resistant (Matthew 10:14; Luke 9:5; 10:10–11).

The apostolic Church allowed this principle to influence its practice. When Paul and Barnabas experienced significant resistance from the Jews in Antioch in Pisidia, they turned their attention to the more receptive Gentiles (Acts 13:46–52) and eventually "shook off the dust from their feet" (v. 51) and departed for Iconium. After arriving in Iconium, they received a mixed reception and eventually fled to Lystra and Derbe to preach the gospel (Acts 14:1–7). After planting the Philippian Church, Paul and Silas departed the city at the request of the magistrates (Acts 16:38-40). When the Jews opposed Paul in Corinth, he "shook out his garments" in protest and turned his attention to the Gentiles (Acts 18:1–11).

## The Time Is Short

Three eschatological realities should cause church planters to apply the principle of receptivity to their ministries. First, the church planters themselves are not guaranteed tomorrow. James offered a clear reminder that our lives are a vapor (James 4:14). Church planters must make the most of their opportunities to serve the Lord in this life. Second, and closely related to the first, is the fact that there is no guarantee that unbelievers will have another opportunity to hear the gospel. Life is short, and church planters need to strategize in accordance with God's sovereignty and life's brevity. Third, the imminent return of Christ should lead missionaries to work to disseminate the gospel as quickly *and* as faithfully as possible (Mark 13:10).

## It Results in Rapid Church Growth

Of the three representative fields in figure 11.1, Field C is the most likely to first witness the birth of disciples and churches. Though Field B may experience a substantial number of conversions and new churches after several years, Field C will grow the fastest and result in the most churches in a much shorter period of time. There is a positive correlation between the receptivity level of the people and the number of churches planted.

## Our Resources Are Limited

Church planting involves biblical stewardship. I know of no church planters who have unlimited amounts of time, money, and people to assist in the missionary work. In fact, most church planters I know are under significant constraints of finances and time. The fact of limited resources should cause church planters to strategically look for the most receptive peoples to the gospel, for it is among such people that church planters are most likely to see results. Our Lord demands that we be faithful and wise stewards of the resources he entrusts to us (Matthew 25:14–30; Luke 19:11–27).

> "One thing is clear, receptivity wanes as often as it waxes. Like the tide, it comes in and goes out. Unlike the tide, no one can guarantee when it goes out that it will soon come back again."
>
> —Donald A. McGavran, *Understanding Church Growth* (Grand Rapids, MI: William B. Eerdmans Publishing Company, 1970), 218.

## Wisdom Tells Us to Make the Best Decisions

The Book of Proverbs is a book about wisdom. In it we learn that wisdom is to be sought after as someone would search for silver or hidden treasures (Proverbs 2:4). Even God attributes the creation of the world and heaven to wisdom (Proverbs 3:19). If the Lord of the universe has wisdom as a necessary component of his character, how much more do church planters need wisdom as they seek to carry out the will of God on the earth? Even if God's calling was not involved in missionary activity and there was no biblical example to follow and time was not limited and church growth was not an issue and unlimited resources were available to church planters, wisdom would still dictate beginning among the people most receptive to the gospel.

## Person of Peace

When approaching the people the church planters are called to serve, an initial step is *not* for the team to decide how they are going to personally evangelize *all* of these people. Rather, they should reach a few people who will then become equipped (Ephesians 4:11–12) to reach their friends, families, and acquaintances (see figure 11.2). Examples of

Figure 11.2 **Person of Peace Theory**

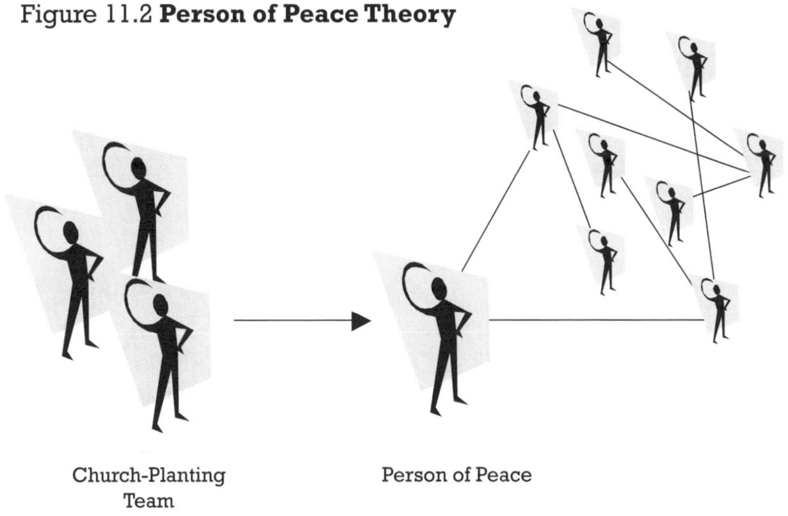

this approach are found in the New Testament. The Samaritan woman was the key person in reaching her community (John 4:28–30, 39–42). The formerly demon-possessed man of the Gerasenes was significant in bringing glory to God throughout the Decapolis region (Mark 5:18–20). Cornelius gathered together his family and friends to hear the gospel (Acts 10:24). Lydia was instrumental in seeing the conversion of her household (Acts 16:15). The Philippian jailer's household came to faith as a result of his connection with Paul and Silas (Acts 16:30–34). Crispus and his household became believers through Paul's preaching (Acts 18:8). As we have mentioned before, missiologists refer to such an individual as a **person of peace**.

Drawing from Jesus' instructions to the Seventy-two to stay with a "son of peace" (Luke 10:5–6) as they went preaching the gospel, contemporary missionaries have sought to identify those initial people who, through their relationships and influence, serve as a bridge on which the gospel is able to travel into the people group or population segment. Since church planters, generally, have few or no relationships with the people they are called to serve, persons of peace provide the gateway into their communities.

Writing of this concept, Robert E. Logan and Neil Cole observed, "When God is at work in starting a new church, He often lays the foundation within a 'person of peace.' This person can be the first domino in a chain reaction among a pocket of people. A person of peace is typically

- responsive to the message you bring
- relationally connected to all in the pocket of people
- renowned in reputation"[3]

> "Who are the most receptive people? I believe there are two broad categories: People in transition and people under tension."
>
> —Rick Warren, *The Purpose-Driven Church: Growth without Compromising Your Message and Mission* (Grand Rapids, MI: Zondervan Publishing House, 1995), 182.

# Using the P.A.W. Approach

In order to find persons of peace, I often encourage teams to use the P.A.W. approach: Pray, Act, and Watch. Though this paradigm is not a linear model—but rather all three aspects, at times, are happening simultaneously—for the sake of explanation, I will address each aspect individually.

## Pray

As already mentioned several times, prayer is a critical component of any missionary work. Before teams enter the field, they should already be spending significant amounts of time in prayer. After the team arrives, it should be praying that the Lord would open hearts to the gospel, asking for "Lydias," who will be the initial believers to form the new churches (Acts 16:11–15) and influence their communities.

## Act

As the team prays, it must get out into the community among the people. Churches are not planted in offices. The team must love and serve the community. It must connect with people relationally while sharing the gospel among the highways and hedges. As the team acts with humility and connects with the people, the Lord will provide opportunities for the good news to be proclaimed. There are multitudes of ways a team can be active: Bible studies, service projects, sports camps, having neighbors over for dinner, cookouts, block parties, street evangelism, door-to-door visitation, meeting families at parks, or simply connecting with people in restaurants and coffee shops.

## "But What about William Carey?"

When addressing the matter of receptivity, someone usually raises the question, "But what about William Carey?" meaning that Carey served for many years as a missionary before seeing converts. Though Carey is the most popular illustration, Church history contains other similar examples. When the gospel first enters a context in which the people have had little or no understanding of it or into areas that have had poor examples of the faith, the field is usually unreceptive.

In the excerpt below, missiologist C. Peter Wagner commented on the fact that though there are some who experience calls to resistant peoples, such callings should not be seen as the norm.

> Generally speaking, the Holy Spirit will lead those who are willing to work into the harvest fields which are already white. At times, however, He may lead otherwise. Prophets such as Ezekiel and Isaiah were required to bring the message to a resistant people. Other prophets, such as Jonah, were sent to receptive peoples. We should regard the predetermined failure of Isaiah as an unusual leading of God, however.
>
> This is not the norm. Since God is not willing that any should perish, He delights in leading His servants out to peoples who have been prepared for the gospel and who will turn to Jesus Christ in abundance.

Taken from C. Peter Wagner, *Frontiers in Missionary Strategy* (Chicago, IL: Moody Press, 1971), 47.

***Questions to Consider:***

1. Do you agree or disagree with Wagner that the Spirit normally leads church planters to receptive people? Why?
2. Has your calling placed you in a more receptive or less receptive field?
3. Would you be willing to spend your entire life working in a similar field as Isaiah? Explain.

## Watch

While sharing the good news with contextually relevant methods, the team should watch where the Spirit of God is working. For example, though Paul normally began his work in the synagogues, his strategy in

Philippi deviated from the norm, possibly because no synagogue existed. After spending "some days" in the city (Acts 16:12), the missionaries finally located a place of prayer by a river. It was at this location that people were engaged in the spiritual activity of seeking God. Realizing that the opportunity to speak to the women gathered there was not by chance, Paul shared the gospel, which resulted in the first believers in Philippi (Acts 16:14).

Arguing that the fields are "ripe for harvest," Logan and Cole encouraged church planters, "Open your eyes to find the fields" containing "good soil."[4] As church planters use the P.A.W. approach to finding persons of peace, it is not difficult to see God already at work among the fields of this world. According to Logan and Cole, such receptive peoples tend to fall into six categories:

- Bad people make good soil; there is a lot of fertilizer in their lives (Luke 5:32).
- Those in poverty are often good, receptive soil (James 2:5).
- Young people are often more receptive than older (Matthew 18:3).
- Those searching for God in the occult or other religions can actually be more open than you think (Matthew 7:7).
- The uneducated and the powerless are often good soil (1 Corinthians 1:27).
- Those deemed insignificant and discriminated against (1 Corinthians 1:28-29).[5]

### *Summary:*

1. The principle of receptivity is not a principle that advocates withholding the gospel from resistant peoples.
2. Generally, missionary practice should be to occupy resistant fields lightly, until such fields become more receptive.

3. The principle of receptivity is important to church planters because it follows the biblical example, time is short, the result is rapid church growth, resources are limited, and wisdom demands the best decision making.
4. The person of peace is an individual receptive to the message of the gospel and a significant person to the dissemination of the gospel throughout a community.
5. The P.A.W. approach is one simple approach to locating persons of peace.

### *Reflection Questions:*

1. Do you agree or disagree with the notion of occupying resistant soils lightly with church planters? Explain.
2. Are you and your church-planting team approaching a community with the desire to reach the persons of peace, equip them, and send them into their communities; or do you desire to reach all of the community on your own as a team?
3. Following the P.A.W. approach in your context, what are fifteen ways you and your team can *act* to connect with the people and share the gospel?
4. Who are the people groups and population segments in your context that you believe are the most receptive to the gospel? Are you and your team working among those people? If not, why not?

### *Important Terms in This Chapter:*

- Receptivity
- Person of peace
- P.A.W. approach

Chapter 12

# CONTEXTUALIZATION AND CHURCH PLANTING

**The message of the gospel must not only be expressed in the categories and world view of the local culture, it must also fill them with biblical substance and so revolutionize them.**

—Paul G. Hiebert[1]

My all-time favorite television show is *The Beverly Hillbillies.* I don't know if being a Kentuckian has anything to do with my interest in this program. Regardless, every episode of this program from days gone by is about one theme: communication breakdown.

The story behind each episode is about a poor, uneducated family—the Clampetts—from the mountains of Tennessee that discovered oil on its property, became very wealthy, and moved to Beverly Hills, California, one of the world's most exquisite and elite communities. Though the Clampetts find themselves living in a mansion in their new location, their worldview and language still reflect the ways of the mountains of Tennessee. In each episode of the classic comedy, the Clampetts constantly encounter communication problems with their California neighbors. To the Clampetts, the swimming pool is a cement pond. A billiard table is a dining table with strange holes in it. Every time they hear the doorbell ring, it is taken as a sign that someone will soon be knocking on their front door. A kangaroo is an overgrown jackrabbit that should be shot so Granny can make rabbit stew for supper.

From a missiological perspective, *The Beverly Hillbillies* offers church planters a glimpse into the world of contextualization issues. How do you effectively communicate the gospel and plant churches among people when the communication is always breaking down and when the team is looked at as if it is as strange as the Clampett family?

## Defining Contextualization

**Contextualization** is simply the attempt to effectively communicate the gospel and the kingdom ethic to others in such a way that they may understand and place their faith in Christ and become fruit-bearing disciples in local churches. Contextualization, as related to church planting, addresses two particular areas. First, it is connected to how the church planters communicate the gospel. Second, it is related to how the church planters teach obedience to the new believers. Though both areas are related to communication, the first is primarily concerned with the missionaries being receptor oriented (making certain that the people understand the gospel); and the second is primarily concerned with the cultural flavor the church takes as the new kingdom citizens live out the kingdom ethic in their communities.

## No Gospel Blimps in Church Planting

Over the past several years, I have shown scores of students *The Gospel Blimp.* This movie, based on the book of the same title by Joseph Bayly, is a humorous satire about a group of white, middle-class, suburban

Christians living in North America in the 1960s. Out of their desire to reach their neighbors with the gospel, they decide that the best way is to purchase a blimp and fly it over their town, playing gospel music over loudspeakers and dropping tracts on people's yards. After months of "evangelizing" their community and numerous citizen complaints, one couple comes to faith in Christ. Excited to find out what element of their strategy was used by the Lord, they ask the new believers about the process of their conversions. Much to their chagrin, the blimp was not the significant factor involved, but rather, their conversions came about through another couple getting to know them, ministering to their needs, and effectively sharing the truth of the good news in a culturally appropriate manner.

> "Missionary contextualization that is authentically and effectively Christian and evangelical does not begin with knowledge of linguistics, communications theory, and cultural anthropology. It begins with a commitment to an inerrant and authoritative Word of God in the autographs of Old Testament and New Testament Scripture."
>
> —David J. Hesselgrave, *Paradigms in Conflict: 10 Key Questions in Christian Missions Today* (Grand Rapids, MI: Kregel, 2005), 274.

David J. Hesselgrave and Edward Rommen eloquently wrote that "Christian contextualization can be thought of as the attempt to communicate the message of the person, works, Word, and will of God in a way that is faithful to God's revelation, especially as it is put forth in the teachings of Holy Scripture, and that is meaningful to the respondents in their respective cultural and existential contexts."[2] The gospel needs to be understood in a meaningful way. This is the challenge of contextualization: The church planters have their own cultures, they are preaching a gospel that is of a first-century Middle Eastern culture, and they are preaching to contemporary audiences with their own cultures. For the team to be able to communicate in a meaningful way, it must have an accurate understanding of itself, the historical gospel of the Scriptures, as well as the people it is called to serve.

## The Flavor of the Church

The ice-cream giant Baskin-Robbins used to promote its sweet concoctions with the boast of having thirty-one flavors. Even if someone did not know all of those flavors, the chances were very good that he or she could find a flavor of ice cream to enjoy. Baskin-Robbins offered more than vanilla, chocolate, and strawberry.

Though the motivation for planting local churches should not primarily come from the marketing concept behind Baskin-Robbins, the notion of variety is a necessary, and biblical, reality. Since churches are made of people and those people have their own cultures, contextualized church planting will result in local churches reflecting the cultures of those new kingdom citizens.

> **"Biblically faithful contextualization results in churches that can more easily multiply and saturate a sub-culture with the saving gospel of Christ and transforming communities of faith."**
>
> —Dan Morgan, "Contextualization Challenges: Three Major Issues Facing the Church Planter" (unpublished paper).

There are at least three factors that affect the flavor of new churches. The first and most important is the biblical parameters. The Scriptures establish an irreducible minimum that is necessary for a local church to be the church any time, any place, and among any people on the planet. The second factor is that of the culture(s) of the people. Their worldviews, music styles, dress, communication methods, structures, and organizations shape the local church. The kingdom ethic, however, gives precedence to the Scriptures. This ethic dictates that the culture(s) of the people bows to the lordship of Christ whenever the people's culture(s) conflicts with the Scriptures.

These two factors are the most important elements that should give a new church its flavor. However, there is a third factor that flavors the new church—the cultures of the church planters. No church-planting team can be culturally neutral, nor can it put its culture on hold while planting churches. Just as the apostle Paul told many churches to imitate him (1 Corinthians 11:1), contemporary church planters should lead lifestyles that can be imitated regarding faith and practice.

Church planters should work to avoid importing too many of their cultural preferences onto the new churches. Prayerful discernment must be used in all that they do. Like impressionable children, the new believers are always watching and learning from the missionaries. Church planters must avoid contemporary versions of colonialism by teaching the people to obey the ways of the Lord while allowing the Holy Spirit to shape the flavor of the church in its context.

The missionaries' cultures will most strongly influence the first generations of churches. Over time, such foreign cultural stamps should diminish. Like a photocopy of a photocopy of a photocopy, there is a diminishing return on the clarity of details of the original print. Church planters must work to avoid translating their cultural preferences to the people, leaving as light of an impression as possible. However, the missionaries should leave a strong biblical impression, teaching the new believers how to study the Scriptures, rely on each other, and be guided by the Holy Spirit.

## Biblical Examples of Contextualization

Two significant biblical examples of contextualization in action are the incarnation of Christ and Paul's willingness to become all things to all people. As noted in chapter one, when the Son of God took on flesh (Galatians 4:4) and made his dwelling among people (John 1:14), God demonstrated the importance of contextualization to missions. By walking the streets of the first-century people, eating their food, enjoying their company, and suffering with them, he was contextualizing the good news. As he spoke their language and understood their cultures, he showed the necessity of culturally sensitive communication of the hope of salvation.

Later the apostle Paul would write about his willingness to become all things to all people so that he could reach some with the good news (1 Corinthians 9). To the Jew, he would become a Jew; to the Gentile, he would become a Gentile. Paul wanted to know how best to communicate the message so that disciples would be made and they would be taught to obey all that Christ commanded. He would speak to those with a Hebraic worldview by beginning with references to the Old Testament (Acts 13:16–41). He would communicate to the Grecian mind by starting with elements from their culture (Acts 17:16–34).

> "The message must be tailored or contextualized in such a way as to remain faithful to the biblical text while understandable in and relevant to the receptor's context."
>
> —Stan Guthrie, *Missions in the Third Millennium: 21 Key Trends for the 21st Century*, revised and expanded (Colorado Springs, CO: Paternoster Press, 2000), 129.

## Remembering What Kinds of Churches We Are Planting

In chapter two we reviewed how church planters must work to establish contextualized, or indigenous, churches. As you recall, such churches are shaped primarily by the cultures of the peoples, rather than the cultures of the missionaries. These churches spring from the soil, manifesting the cultural expressions and traits of the people, couched within the biblical parameters. We also noted that such churches are to be self-governing, self-supporting, self-propagating, self-teaching, self-identifying, self-expressing, and self-theologizing from the moment of their births. Though these congregations will mature in the faith, they do not start as half churches today and become full churches tomorrow.

## Understanding the People

In order to be effective at contextualization, missionaries must be students of the people they are called to serve. This approach requires a missionary to always be a learner and a servant to all. My anthropologist friend Bryan Galloway once gave me a signed copy of one of his books on discovering worldviews with the following statement: "Enjoy and get to know them first!" When couched in terms of a Great Commission theology, such words are important for the missionary to apply to his or her context. Having an understanding of a people is vital to the other strategic aspects of church multiplication. Such understanding affects how a church-planting team approaches a context, communicates the gospel, begins teaching obedience, and organizes the churches.

In his book *The Purpose-Driven Church,* Rick Warren advocated knowing the people geographically, demographically, culturally, and spiritually.[3] Though I want to address these four areas, I believe there are at least three additional areas worthy of understanding. We also need to understand a people historically, politically, and linguistically as well.

### Geographically

The geographical location of a community or a people within a community affects its ways of life. In North America, for example, regional differences are widespread. Maritimers differ from Midwesterners, and Southern Appalachians are not like New Englanders.

## The Flavor of the Faithful

Using a story written by his daughter Lyndi, Phil Parshall shared the following story about the challenges of contextualization in a Muslim environment. As you read the following account, consider the perspective of the unbeliever in your context.

> Akbar was tempted to go inside this foreign church, and see for himself what was going on. His wife would probably get mad at him if he did. Slowly, he walked toward the gate, noticing the barbed wire running along the top of the high walls which was put there to keep out the beggar kids. Then he looked up at the cross standing tall on the top of the building. How awful! The cross! What a symbol of hatred that represented to Akbar. It reminded him of the grotesque stories he had learned in school about the Crusades—how his Muslim ancestors had been killed by cross-carrying Crusaders. . . .
>
> Akbar reached down to unbuckle his sandals. But he noticed that there were hardly any shoes outside compared to the number of people inside. How repulsive! In a mosque no one is allowed to wear shoes. He pulled off his sandals, added them to the small pile, and then walked in the door. . . .
>
> On the front row, sitting all together, was the missionary's family—the husband, wife, and two daughters. Akbar was amazed to see them all together. . . . He hoped no one else would be offended like he was. . . .
>
> His eyes fell on a picture on the wall. It was of a man who looked nice enough, with long hair and a beard, but then, slowly he read the words under the picture: "Jesus Christ." He couldn't believe it! No Muslim would have a picture of a prophet hanging on a wall! It was totally forbidden. . . . He found a seat and sat down. Picking up one of the books, he saw that it was thick and nicely bound. He opened it and tried to read it, but he couldn't really understand the words. One word he saw was "Bible." This was the Christian's holy book. Did they just let it lay around where it could get messed up? Didn't they care if someone dropped it or touched it with dirty hands?
>
> He looked up and saw the missionary's children running around. In a mosque children wouldn't be allowed to be a

nuisance. The children were playing with the same type of book he had in his hands—the Bible. Didn't the missionaries care if their children showed disrespect to a holy book?

Akbar saw flowers by the pump organ and wondered if they were for decoration, or if they were an offering to the Jesus man. . . .

Looking at the missionary's wife, he saw that she wore a sleeveless long dress. Even the high class women in the town didn't wear sleeveless blouses with their saris. It was indecent! He noticed she didn't have any way to cover her head when she prayed. . . .

Just then, the evangelist stood up in the front and began to talk. He welcomed everyone, then gave some announcements. Then he told them to turn to page 30 in a song book. Were they going to sing? Sure enough, a man got up and went to the pump organ and began to play. It was very strange to him as Muslims only chant their songs.

Akbar reached for the only other book he saw and found the page. He couldn't read well enough to follow along too well, so he just listened. The tunes were totally foreign. He could tell everyone was having trouble singing the song. He liked chanting much better. . . .

Again, the missionary got up and began to speak. Akbar listened for a while but at the word "Jesus," he could no longer listen. As a Muslim, he only saw Jesus as a good prophet that lived long ago—not as the "Son of God." How repulsive to think of God having relations with Mary and having a son whom they named Jesus.

Taken from Phil Parshall, *Muslim Evangelism: Contemporary Approaches to Contextualization* (Colorado Springs, CO: Authentic Publishing, 2003), 63–67.

***Questions to Consider:***

1. Why was Akbar so offended by this church?
2. Were any of the preferences and practices of the church sinful?
3. Do you think the culture of this congregation will help or hinder evangelization and discipleship in this Muslim context? Why?
4. Are there elements in the Muslim context that this church could embrace without compromising the truth of the Scriptures? If so, describe those elements.
5. What would a worship gathering among your people group or population segment look like? Describe the music style? Preaching style? Order? Other activities?

I once observed this in the city of Indianapolis, where the phrase *wrong side of the tracks* became a reality to me. There is a section of the west side of the city in which the community north of the railroad tracks has middle- and upper-middle-class neighborhoods. The homes are attractive and have well-manicured lawns. The shopping district has a large mall with numerous brand-name stores. There are some good parks and nice restaurants as well. However, across the railroad tracks, the community has lower-income housing. The shopping district has several old buildings, many of which have bars over the windows and doors. There are adult book stores, old buildings in need of repair, and poorer quality restaurants.

Similarly, in many other cities, immigrants congregate in ethnic enclaves referred to by such names as "Chinatown," "Little Vietnam," or "Little Havana." In the Majority World, squatter communities on the perimeters of many urban environments are separated from the rest of the city. Roads, rivers, mountains, and valleys often separate communities from one another.

Understanding the geography assists church planters in identifying the natural and man-made barriers that may hinder their work. For example, if a team chose to work on the west side of Indianapolis, the chances would be slim of effectively reaching people on both sides of the tracks through a single ministry or Bible study. Since the two communities are radically separate, it would be better for the team to begin serving both communities separately, doing different outreaches based on the different contexts.

## Demographically

Demographics are the human statistics of the country. Many governments have the means for researching and knowing the factual information about their people. To understand a people demographically, the church-planting team must ask questions such as:

- What types of people live here?
- What are their ages?
- What are their marital statuses?
- What are their income levels?
- What are their educational levels?
- What are their occupations?
- Is the community growing or declining? At what rate?
- Which ethnic groups are living in the area?
- What are the sizes of those ethnic groups?
- What is the crime rate in this community?
- What types of crimes are the most prevalent?

The practical outworking of such knowledge can be seen in the following examples. Suppose the church-planting team approaches a population segment with plans to begin ministering to the children there, only to discover that few of the families in the area have children. Or suppose a team wanted to begin a Bible study in an ethnic enclave of a city, only to discover that few of the residents were literate. The Bible study could continue, but the way it would be conducted would have to differ radically from a method used among the highly educated.

## Culturally

When the church-planting team examines a people group's or population segment's culture, it is basically gaining an understanding of the worldview(s) of those people. Understanding culture requires the gathering of knowledge related to the people's beliefs, social structures, knowledge, and behaviors. Some questions to consider during this process of research include:

- What is the general lifestyle of the people?
- What is their general mindset?
- What are their interests? Their values?

- What are the hurts of the people?
- What causes them the most fear? The most joy?
- What are their dreams for the future?
- What are their major material possessions?
- What value do they place on family? On work?

Understanding a people's culture provides the team a window into the hearts of those people. Since actions stem from the desires of the heart, cultural understanding is vitally important to church planting. Cultural discernment allows the team to get a better grasp on the needs of the community and to speak insightfully into the lives of the people.

## Spiritually

An understanding of the religious commitments of the people is also necessary. When researching the spiritual culture, church planters are seeking to find answers to questions such as:

- What is the spiritual climate of the people (e.g., highly devout, agnostic, apathetic, etc.)?
- What are the religious traditions and rituals (e.g., forms and meanings)?
- What types of religious buildings, shrines, etc. exist in the community?
- What are the sizes of the different religious groups in the area?
- Are there merchants in the area that sell religious books, paraphernalia, icons, spells, etc.?
- What Christian ministries are currently active among the people?
- Are there any religious groups networking together—especially churches, denominations, and parachurch organizations?
- What is the percentage of evangelicals among the people?
- How many evangelical churches are in the community?

An example of doing spiritual research could bc thc following: A church-planting team, while driving through a small Midwestern U.S. town, notices that, though the population of the community is small in number, there is a large, elaborate Hindu temple on the outskirts of the town. Seeing such a building, the team rightly concludes that there must be a fairly large Hindu population in the community and/or within a couple-hours' drive of the temple.

Another example could be this scenario: When prayer walking through an isolated mountain village in Brazil, a team notices that at least three-quarters of the homes in the community have an outdoor statue of Mary or a Catholic saint. The team realizes that Catholicism has a strong presence in the village, even though the church planters do not observe any Catholic worship facility.

## Historically

The history of a people greatly influences their present realities for good or evil. The abuse of the Native Americans at the hands of the Europeans over three hundred years ago still hinders missionary work among these original North Americans to this day. Twenty years of a dictatorship over a people shapes the ways they think and live in relation to authority. Economic depressions, food shortages, diseases, lack of education, and a multitude of other historical factors weigh heavily on the worldviews and manners of the present generation.

Early in the twentieth century, the North Korean capitol, Pyongyang, experienced a great revival. However, following the Korean War in the 1950s, North Korean Christians were forced to go underground and remain there to this day. Church planters must become students of the history of their people and countries. A failure to know the history of the people and their community is a sure way to misunderstand why those people think and live as they do.

## Politically

Though many missionaries do not enjoy spending their time involved in politics, it is very important that they are familiar with the political perspectives of the people they are called to serve. Are the people Democrats, Republicans, socialists, conservatives, liberals, or anarchists? The kingdom of the Evil One is strongly driven by power and money, and politics is tightly connected to both of these concepts. In certain parts of the world, political differences separate individuals and communities to such a degree that it is a futile task for church planters to attempt to gather the differing groups together for an evangelistic Bible study or other outreach event.

> **"Contextualization must mean the communication of the gospel in ways the people understand, but that also challenge them individually and corporately to turn from their evil ways."**
>
> —Paul G. Hiebert, *Anthropological Insights for Missionaries* (Grand Rapids, MI: Baker Book House, 1985), 185.

## Linguistically

Not only should missionaries learn the language of the people, but they must be familiar with the colloquialisms, slang, and street talk. Studying European French is absolutely necessary if a team is going to work among Parisians. However, if the team is going to work among the Quebecois (French-speaking Canadians), it will need to spend a significant amount of time learning the variations of the language found in Quebec. Church planters should learn European Spanish if they are working in Madrid, but the Guatemalan variation (and possibly some of the many Mayan dialects) should be learned when serving in Guatemala City.

Meaning and worldview are tightly connected to the language spoken by the people. Language provides a window into the hearts of the speakers. In many nations it is common to find bilingual and trilingual people. The *lingua franca* of the country is necessary for them to function in the marketplaces, schools, and businesses. However, the heart language of the people is what many speak when they discuss issues related to spiritual matters. Missionaries must learn the heart language of the people in order to be knowledgeable about their worldviews and to effectively communicate the gospel.

## Sources of Information

My second favorite television show of all time is *The Andy Griffith Show*. This classic comedy of the 1960s is about a small-town sheriff who is able to maintain law and order in his community without carrying a gun. One particular episode has a missiological lesson for church planters.

One day in the town of Mayberry, a stranger arrives well dressed and with briefcase and suitcase in hand. He asks the local barber for the location of the hotel where he decides to stay for a few days. No one in this small community knows anything about the stranger, and so the gossip mill begins churning. "Is he a spy or a Communist?" some ask. "Could he be with the FBI?" others inquire. What makes this unknown character even more puzzling is that he knows very personal details about the lives of many of the residents of Mayberry. In fact, he knows about their pasts and even the names of many of their children.

Though this stranger is very friendly and cordial to the people, his knowledge of their lives begins to greatly trouble them. By the end of the episode, the sheriff and the people corner this foreigner and demand that he tell them how he knows such details about them. Of course, the man apologizes for scaring the people and gives them an explanation: "When I was in the military, I bunked with one of your residents. He would tell story after story about his wonderful town of Mayberry and the friendly people there. After hearing his tales, I decided that I would one day visit this charming place. So, after I got out of the service, I decided to subscribe to your newspaper. For the past five years, I have been reading it from cover to cover, learning everything I could about Mayberry and its people."

The missiological point was well made. Thanks, Andy!

Unless a team is working among a remote people on whom little cultural and sociological research has been done, there is no excuse for church planters to be ignorant of their people's geography, demographics, culture, spirituality, history, politics, and language *before they arrive on the field.*

The natural question that follows is, Where can I find such information about the people I am called to serve? Especially in Western contexts and throughout many urban locales across the world, there are numerous resources that can guide the research process. The following list is a starting point:

- Internet
- Neighborhood associations
- Police
- Universities/colleges
- Seminaries
- Chamber of commerce
- Mayor's office
- Historical society
- Realtors
- Embassies
- School superintendents
- Newspapers
- Books
- Local magazines
- Gatekeepers in the community
- Missionaries
- Historians
- Libraries

- Churches
- Parachurch organizations
- Mission agencies
- Denominational offices
- Census data
- Marketing/demographic firms
- Online radio stations

## The Best Source of Information

Wise church planters do not spend all their time in research departments, obtaining a superfluous amount of information about the people. Rather, they should be good stewards of their time and resources and keep two guidelines in mind. First, they will do necessary—but not excessive—research before going to the field. Missionaries are not attempting to write the next book about the people, but rather to begin the learning process that will best prepare them for the field.

Second, church-planting teams must remember that *the best source of information about the people is the people themselves*. Therefore, it is absolutely necessary that teams hit the streets, neighborhoods, and marketplaces and spend time meeting the people. Remember, churches are not planted in the office, but rather among the people. And the learning process will continue as long as the teams are in the field.

### *Summary:*

1. Contextualization is critical to church planting.
2. Contextualization involves communicating in such a way that effective understanding occurs.
3. Contextualization, as related to church planting, specifically deals with communicating the gospel and the cultural expressions of the life of the local church.

4. There are several biblical examples of contextualization.
5. Contextualization is not about cloning a church in the cultural image of another church.
6. Contextualization is not about importing the cultural preferences of the church planters into the newly planted churches.
7. Indigenous churches are characterized by at least seven "selfs."
8. Churches should be planted as indigenous churches from the very beginning.
9. It is important that church planters know their people geographically, demographically, culturally, spiritually, historically, politically, and linguistically.
10. The people themselves are the best source of information; so church planters must spend time with the people.

## *Reflection Questions:*

1. Can you think of any examples of churches that were planted but were not contextualized among the people? What, if any, problems arose within those churches?
2. Do you believe that a church can and should manifest the seven "selfs" from the time of its birth? Explain your answer. If yes, what will that manifestation look like in your church-planting context?
3. Considering the people you are called to serve, what are the characteristics of a typical individual? A typical family? Can you briefly describe them geographically, demographically, culturally, spiritually, historically, politically, and linguistically?

## *Important Term in This Chapter:*

- Contextualization

Chapter 13

# THE MOTHER CHURCH AND CHURCH PLANTING PART 1

For pastors and other leaders truly committed to the church growth imperative of the Great Commission, church planting is not an option.

—Thom S. Rainer[1]

Having three young children makes my house an exciting environment. It is fascinating to watch how children depend on their parents and how they do not enjoy being separated from them. Soon after my wife and I converted our basement into a playroom, there was a time when our oldest children would not venture downstairs alone. And my youngest is presently at the stage of experiencing separation anxiety whenever I leave him alone in a room.

I remember from my own childhood being separated from my mother in a department store. I had wandered off into the toy section, when moments later I realized that my mother was not nearby. I walked around the aisles, displays, and the circular hanging racks of clothes, but my search for her was to no avail.

Soon I began to question if she was still in the building. Despite the fact that I knew she would never leave me, my feelings of loneliness and insecurity began to intensify. After wandering for what seemed to be an eternity, I finally located her and was extremely relieved and comforted by her presence. Needless to say, I did not venture off again during that shopping trip.

Many U.S. and Canadian church planters today feel very much like children who have been separated from their parents. Many feel as if the Church has given up on them. They look around and see other churches across North America that have no desire to assist in church planting yet have resources (e.g., people, finances, buildings) that could be used for missions. While serving in the trenches, they hope to be supported and encouraged as the Church advances throughout the Enemy's territory; but in reality, the Church, many times, abandons them on the frontlines.

There are exceptions to this norm. Though many U.S. and Canadian churches will not get involved in domestic missions, ironically, some of those very churches will participate in supporting church planters who leave for other parts of the globe. Though their foreign mission efforts are to be greatly commended, it is long overdue for churches to realize that North America is a huge mission field.

Though there are many principles in this and the next chapter that can be applied to non-Western churches, I am primarily writing to the body of Christ in the United States and Canada because I am the most familiar with the churches in these countries. Also, I write to these Western churches because they have an enormous amount of resources to assist in partnering with domestic missionaries in their own lands.

In this chapter, I will address several issues related to the connection between established churches and church planting. First, I will discuss the need for such churches to be involved in church planting. Second, I will reveal the vital connection between church planting and the growth of the church. Third, I will offer several reasons why churches should be involved in domestic church planting. In the next chapter, I will list several ways in which established churches can become involved in church planting.

Very few U.S. and Canadian churches are mother churches, that is, those birthing new churches on a regular basis. For example, in my denomination—the Southern Baptist Convention—which is known for its passion for evangelism and missions, it is estimated that less than 5 percent of all of our churches are involved in church planting.[2] Though I have not studied churches among other denominations in detail, particularly outside of the United States and Canada, my guess is that the majority of them in Western contexts have little or no involvement in similar missionary labors.

## Don't Forget about the Other Wing of the Plane

Though I do not fly as much as some people, I do use the airlines several times each year. I am very thankful that every time I board a plane that I do not have to wonder if there are two wings on the craft. It goes without saying that before an airline boards passengers and sends the plane down the runway, there are at least two wings on the craft. No one would dare think of attempting flight without two wings!

*Many Western churches, however, have been attempting flight with only one wing on the airplane.* Church planting is the other wing that has been missing for some time.

When it comes to the growth of the church, many pastors view church planting as a detriment. "Larger is better," is the typical rationalization. Church culture awards and praises pastors for the size of their congregations, not the number of missionaries they send to plant churches across the street or across the country. Just as all airplanes must have two wings, the church must be growing by enlarging its present membership as well as by sending out church-planting teams.

> "I believe that you measure the health or strength of a church by its *sending* capacity rather than its *seating* capacity."
>
> —Rick Warren, *The Purpose-Driven Church* (Grand Rapids, MI: Zondervan, 1995), 32, italics original.

Since the 1970s when the Church Growth Movement began to impact North American churches, the emphasis has been on growth that enlarges individual congregations and has failed to stress the importance of church multiplication.[3] In light of this distorted understanding of church growth missiology, we must remember the movement originated in the mission field outside of North America with an emphasis on multiplying congregations in the various people groups throughout the world. Donald McGavran, the father of the movement once wrote, "Thus today's paramount task, opportunity, and imperative in missions is to multiply churches in the increasing numbers of receptive peoples of the earth."[4] The Church needs to return to its roots and recapture the vision for church multiplication in North America and beyond.

## How Do Churches Grow?

Church growth theorists note that there are four main types of growth: expansion, internal, extension, and bridging. **Expansion growth** results from three sources—a congregation leading people to Christ, believers transferring their church memberships from one congregation to another, and children being born to members of the congregation. The second type of growth is **internal growth**. This can come from several sources, such as increasing spiritual maturity among a church's members and from expanding the campus and/or facilities of the church. Building an educational space or adding on to a parking lot is a type of internal growth. It is usually these two types of growth (expansion and internal) that most North American churches consider when they hear the words *church growth*.

The remaining two types of church growth are directly related to church planting. The first type is **extension growth**. This occurs in a culture similar to that of the mother church. For example, a young, middle-class African American congregation experiences extension growth when it decides to plant a church among other young, middle-class African Americans. The other type of church-planting growth is **bridging growth**, which occurs among a slightly, or even radically different, culture from that of the mother church. For example, a middle-class Anglo congregation participates in bridging growth when it plants a church among migrant Mexicans or lower-income, first-generation Asians.

These latter two types of growth—extension and bridging—are just as legitimate as expansion growth; however, many churches and denominations do not reward or recognize those who practice them. The words of a church planter from Kansas support this statement: "The biggest obstacle to new work many times is the existing pastors in the area. Everyone wants to grow a big church and feels threatened by new works that might take prospects or members. We as a denomination lift up, write up, and light up the big church pastor to the point that many of our best wouldn't consider starting a new work. And existing pastors keep striving to get to the top for the limelight."[5]

One Evangelical Free church planter echoed similar thoughts. He wrote, "I believe many church leaders are living in the 'bigger is better' syndrome. This affects the willingness of a church sending off 25, 50, or 100 or more people to be a great starting core of a successful church plant."[6] Until church leaders are convinced that the greatest need of the hour is both extension growth and bridging growth, churches will always have a limited kingdom vision.

## Why Be Involved in Church Planting?

At the time of this writing, my daughters are five and almost three years of age. They are learning the art of questioning everything. "Why this?" and "Why that?" are currently common expressions around our home. Asking the *why* question is a means of learning. Though some may find it frustrating, I welcome it.

It is only natural for any established church to ask the why question when thinking about church planting. Aubrey Malphurs was correct when he wrote, "For a growing, maturing planted church or an established church to start a daughter church, it must think carefully about its reasons for desiring to start another church."[7] Though in this chapter I will not address the common objections to such missionary activity (see chapter twenty-one), I will note here that churches should be involved in this ministry because of the several sources of evidence:

- Biblical evidence
- Traditional evidence
- Demographic evidence
- Cultural evidence
- Denominational evidence
- Evangelistic evidence
- Religious evidence
- Economic evidence[8]

### Biblical Evidence

The most common biblical example of a church involved in planting other churches is the Antioch Church (cf. Acts 13–28). Malphurs noted the connection between this church and church planting: "What's important to observe here is how the early churches such as the one at Antioch understood the Great Commission mandate. Jesus said, 'Make disciples!' The Antioch church accomplished this through sending out two missionary church planters who started a number of daughter churches in Asia Minor, Macedonia, and Achaia. What better way to spread the gospel than to plant a number of significant churches in the areas targeted for evangelism."[9]

Though I have already referenced the biblical evidence for church planting, I will restate here that churches should be involved in church planting because it is a pattern clearly followed by the New Testament Church. In Matthew 28 and Acts 1, Jesus commanded his followers to go and make disciples throughout the entire world. As they went on mission, they were to baptize and teach. The Book of Acts shows how Jesus' commands to his followers played out. Because of the faithfulness of the early disciples, churches were planted in Jerusalem, Antioch, Philippi, Rome, Colossae, Berea, Corinth, Laodicea, Thessalonica, Ephesus, Sardis, Philadelphia, Pergamum, Thyatira, Smyrna, and numerous other cities scattered throughout the Roman Empire.

> **"Churches obey the last command of Christ when they plant a new church to evangelize an unreached area."**
>
> —Elmer Towns and Douglas Porter, *Churches That Multiply* (Kansas City, MO: Beacon Hill Press, 2003), 22

## Traditional Evidence

Because of a long chain of church planters, the gospel finally arrived on the shores of North America; churches were planted, and centuries later you and I came to follow Christ. Churches that are planting churches

## Swimming Upstream

In his excellent work *The Ripple Church: Multiply Your Ministry by Parenting New Churches,* Phil Stevenson challenged pastors to lead their churches to begin new works. Though it is greatly needed and rewarding work, he added that it is like swimming upstream.

> You've seen the image a thousand times. A rock tossed into a pod. The rock makes a splash. Ripples emanate from the point of impact, spreading across the surface of the water until they reach the other shore. We call it the ripple effect.
>
> In that same way, a new generation of churches is creating a ripple effect across the country. Led by men and women of vision, these congregations are extending their influence out from the center, into their communities and across their regions.
>
> How?
>
> A few courageous leaders have done what few in the twenty-first century church are willing to do. They have turned their focus outward, planting new churches rather than simply gathering more people into existing ones. These ripple churches have become points of impact for a movement that is spreading around the world.
>
> But it hasn't been easy. By choosing influence over influx, ripple churches have sacrificed their own comfort and security in order to bring forth the next generation of Christians. They have abandoned contemporary notions of success in order to bring about Kingdom growth. They have been willing to swim against the stream of popular culture.
>
> Is it worth it?
>
> Nimbus Dam is located roughly fifteen miles east of downtown Sacramento, California, a short jaunt up the Highway 50 corridor toward the south shore of Lake Tahoe. Nimbus Dam controls the water flow of the American River as it makes its way west toward the Sacramento River and, ultimately, to the Pacific Ocean.
>
> The river's current can be brisk, especially in the fall, when an extraordinary event occurs. That's when salmon make their way east from the ocean, swimming against the west-flowing current. The fish head upriver in order to spawn. The journey requires tremendous energy, and many salmon die along the way. But they complete this trip, swimming against the flow, in order to reproduce. If they don't, their species will not survive.

The salmon could, I suppose, live out their lives downstream. It would be more comfortable, with no current to fight and no risk. Upstream is unknown to them. To swim upstream demands an effort they may not be able to muster. Yet these creatures seem to know that something exists upstream that can be found nowhere else: the opportunity to create a new generation.

In fact, the salmon that make their way against the current each fall are themselves the product of a preceding generation's effort. Their predecessors expended the energy to swim against the tide so they could create new life. This year yet another generation of salmon will make that same journey. The cycle of growth continues.

Today, the church desperately needs a new generation of leaders that is willing to swim against the current. Too many of us enjoy the relative calm of downstream life. We convince ourselves that gathering more people around us in a single church will ensure the existence of the species. It won't. A large school of salmon swimming comfortably in the warm ocean will not survive indefinitely. Those salmon must fight their way upstream to create new life. Similarly, we must sacrifice our time, energy, and money if we are to create new congregations. The survival of the church depends on it.

This will never be easy. In the current of church culture, bigger is considered better. We measure ourselves by buildings, bodies, and budgets, and the bottom line is weekly worship attendance. In this climate, the idea of planting new churches out of existing ones raises a few eyebrows. Therefore leaders who participate in the church planting movement must swim against popular opinion.

They must be willing to abandon commonly held notions about achievement and success. To stay downstream is much easier. Yet as Zig Ziglar noted, even a dead fish can swim downstream. The kind of multiplication that will ensure the future of the church can never happen in the downstream culture. We need to swim against the tide.

So the challenge for today's church leaders is twofold. First, we must realize the need to propagate the gospel by multiplying congregations, and then we must sacrifice in order to do so. That will mean resisting the temptation to merely grow larger as a congregation, and that will require faith.

We risk much by swimming upstream. It's always easier to stay where we are—complacent and comfortable. We need leaders who have the God-given faith to move forward in spite of fear and uncertainty. By doing so, we will lay the foundation for an entire new generation of believers. Lives will be transformed. The church will be revolutionized. The entire world will be changed.

Will you accept this challenge? Will you move beyond the small circle of your own comfort and begin the ripple that will affect your community and your world? I saw a television advertisement that touted its product this way: "It began with a drop that caused a ripple, which caused a wave, which caused the whole world to stand up and take notice." One drop makes a difference. One leader can begin a great movement. One ripple can change the world.

Will it begin with you?

Taken from Phil Stevenson, *The Ripple Church: Multiply Your Ministry by Parenting New Churches* (Indianapolis, IN: Wesleyan Publishing House, 2004), 15–17.

***Questions to Consider:***

1. Should churches turn their focus outward, "rather than simply gathering more people into existing ones"?
2. Does the contemporary church need a new generation of leaders "willing to swim against the current"?
3. Do you have any fears of accepting Stevenson's challenge to swim upstream and plant churches?
4. What, if anything, is preventing you from leading your church to plant other churches?

are standing on the shoulders of the faithful who have sacrificed and gone before us so that centuries later we could hear the good news and come to serve the Lord. The church that says, "Yes, we will plant churches!" is the church that says to the world, "We will not allow centuries of Church history to stop with us. We will not allow the faithfulness and sacrifice of our brothers and sisters to end with us. We will look beyond ourselves (if the Lord tarries) to a future generation that will need this same gospel!"

## Demographic Evidence

As of 2007 the estimated population of the United States was over 300 million and Canada was over 33 million. Consider the following statistics: It is estimated that the unchurched populations of the United States and Canada are 195,000,000 and 24,000,000, respectively. From the mid-1980s to the mid-1990s, the population in the United States increased 11.4 percent, but the overall Church membership declined 9.5 percent.[10] According to David T. Olson, in the United States, on average, 4,000 new churches are started every year, but 3,700 church cease to exist at the end of any given year.[11] That's nearly 71 churches per week that cease to exist. According to his estimates, an additional 2900 churches are needed each year simply for the Church to keep up with population growth.[12]

> **"Church planting is a normal and natural function for a church. If it does not take on this task, it has become rootbound."**
>
> —Jack Redford, *Planting New Churches* (Nashville, TN: Broadman Press, 1978), 23.

## Cultural Evidence

Through immigration the United States is now 13 percent foreign born and Canada is 20 percent foreign born.[13] Without going into too much detail showing the ethnic diversity among those countries, we should note that 28 percent of all Canadians originated from the British Isles, 23 percent are of French origin, 15 percent are from other European countries, and 2 percent are Amerindian,[14] not to mention those of numerous Asian, African, and Arab backgrounds. Though 77 percent of the United States is considered white and 13 percent is considered black, there are also large populations of Hispanics, Asians, Africans, and Arabs.[15] Though these statistics help paint a picture of the ethnic landscape, they do not tell us about vast cultural differences found within any given ethnic group. These numbers tell us nothing regarding the ways people communicate, learn, organize themselves into groups, or interact with one another—all very important elements to understand in relation to church planting.

No church can reach everyone in its community. Churches tend to reach people from the same or slightly different culture from themselves. Culture is a powerful force affecting the way people interact and see the world. The United States and Canada are two of the most culturally diverse countries on the planet. Instead of looking at our cities as black or white or rich or poor, we need to see the great diversity that is before us.

For example, I grew up in a small Kentucky town, and my wife grew up in one of the larger cities within the same state. I grew up hearing nonseminary-trained preachers in small country churches who clearly used nonpolished preaching styles, to say the least. My wife was never exposed to this type of preaching. Whenever I hear an "unpolished" country preacher on the radio, I am able to understand clearly the message preached; however, my wife has a difficult time even understanding the words because the communication style is foreign to her cultural upbringing.

> **"Consequently, a church can know that it's time to become a parent by the very fact that it's a church, regardless of whether it's growing, stagnant, or dying."**
>
> —Aubrey Malphurs, *Planting Growing Churches*, 3rd ed (Grand Rapids, MI: Baker Books, 2004), 256.

## Denominational Evidence

Denominations that do not plant churches today will cease to exist tomorrow. According to Olson, for a denomination to keep up with population growth, it needs to plant at least one new church for every fifty established churches.[16]

As of 2008 the United States was approximately 26 percent evangelical,[17] yet Olson noted on any given weekend in 2005 only 9.1 percent of the evangelical population attended a church worship service. According to the website of the Evangelical Fellowship of Canada, in 2003 only 12 percent of Canadians were evangelically aligned Protestants, with another 7 percent evangelically aligned Catholics.[18] As with the United States, I assume the actual number of evangelicals is even smaller than those numbers. Referencing the website ReligiousTolerance.org, *On Mission* magazine noted that the percentage of Christians in Canada is in "relatively rapid decline."[19] I have heard of reports from western Canada that tell of towns with populations as high as one thousand without a single church of any kind. Over 80 percent of Southern Baptist churches in the United States are either plateaued or declining. Church planting is a way to change the present denominational realities.

Historically, Methodists and Baptists have experienced the importance of church planting (see chapters seventeen and eighteen). In the early days of the United States, it was both the Methodist circuit rider and the Baptist farmer-preacher who pioneered the land and planted churches. Such missionary efforts propelled those groups to become the largest U.S. Protestant denominations in the nineteenth and twentieth centuries.

## Evangelistic Evidence

Missiologist C. Peter Wagner wrote that the "single-most effective evangelistic methodology under heaven is planting new churches."[20] While this statement is not always true, nevertheless, church planting has the potential to be a very effective evangelistic method. Various studies have shown that younger churches tend to have higher baptismal rates than older churches. An article in *Christianity Today* once cited Bruce McNicol as reporting that among evangelical churches, those under three years in age reach, on average, ten people for Christ for every one hundred members in a given year. Churches that are between three years old and fifteen years old will reach five people per year. Churches over fifteen years old will reach three people per year. According to the article, "90 percent of all churches reach their peak in attendance, outreach, and giving by their twelfth birthday."[21] In a study of Anglo churches from 1987 to 1989, it was discovered that the new churches baptized thirteen people for every one hundred members compared to established Anglo churches that baptized three people for every one hundred members.[22] In another study, it was noted that churches ten years old or older average 2.5 baptisms per year per one huindred members and that churches ten years old or younger average 10.8 baptisms per year per one hundred members.[23]

> **"Many say they plan to birth a new church, but few actually do it. Since it is the nature of the Church to grow and multiply, then something needs to change from the inside out. Often, the problem is in the genetic coding of the church."**
>
> —Robert E. Logan and Neil Cole, *Beyond Church Planting* (St. Charles, IL: ChurchSmart Resources, 2005), 7.

## Religious Evidence

The countries of the world contain a very diverse religious landscape. Such is most definitely the case in the United States and Canada, and the Church's growth is not doing so well. Many cults and other world religions are growing at a very rapid rate. Malphurs noted in his book on church planting that the Mormons have tripled in size between 1965 and 2001 in the United States and that the Jehovah's Witnesses did likewise in Canada.[24] Christianity grew by only 5 percent from 1990 to 2000 in the United States, and compare this statistic with the following growth rates:

- Nonreligious/Secular: 110% increase
- Islam: 109% increase
- Buddhism: 170% increase
- Hinduism: 237% increase
- Unitarian/Universalist: 25% increase
- Native American: 119% increase
- Baha'i: 200% increase
- New Age: 240% increase
- Sikhism: 338% increase
- Scientology: 22% increase
- Taoism: 74% increase
- Deism: 717% increase[25]

## Economic Evidence

Though some church-planting methods are very expensive, a costly endeavor is not necessarily required. If church-planting teams allow the Scriptures to provide the definition of church (see chapters two and three), then very few financial resources are needed to plant churches. Biblical church planting can be one of the most inexpensive evangelistic ministries of established churches.

### *Summary:*

1. The New Testament model is for churches to plant churches as they fulfill the Great Commission.
2. Church planting has been the missing wing in the growth of U.S. and Canadian churches.
3. Churches grow through expansion growth, internal growth,

extension growth, and bridging growth.

4. According to Donald McGavran, the paramount task for the Church is the multiplication of churches among the peoples of the world.
5. The biblical, traditional, demographic, cultural, denominational, evangelistic, religious, and economic evidence all point to the need for established churches to plant churches.

### *Reflection Questions:*

1. What are your thoughts regarding the statement that many Western churches have been "attempting flight with only one wing on the airplane"? Do you agree or disagree? Why?
2. Are you surprised that church growth involves more than expansion growth and internal growth? What do you think the people of your church believe about how churches grow?
3. Is your church open to extension and bridging growth? If so, among what people group, population segment, or geographical location should it start working?
4. Do you agree or disagree with the evidence presented regarding why churches should become mother churches? Why do you hold such views?

### *Important Terms in This Chapter:*

- Mother churches
- Expansion growth
- Internal growth
- Extension growth
- Bridging growth

Chapter 14

# THE MOTHER CHURCH AND CHURCH PLANTING PART 2

Next to God, the existing church is the greatest resource for church planting.

—Rodney A. Harrison[1]

I am always delighted when local churches get involved in church planting in North America. Such churches realize that the Great Commission mandate for them as kingdom citizens extends not only to the ends of the earth but also across the street. The role of the mother church in such missionary activity is vitally important. Though there are many ways to plant churches, it is my conviction that the best and most healthy way is for the local church to become significantly involved in such missionary labors. This is clearly a biblical model.

In the 1970s there was a television commercial advertising instant iced tea. As the commercial rolled, a man stood on the edge of a swimming pool with a glass of iced tea in hand. He raised the glass to his lips, leaned backward, and took the Nestea plunge into the swimming pool.

I was reminded of this commercial as I was thinking about how many churches fear that becoming involved in church planting is like taking such a backward, out-of-control plunge into the deep end of some "church planting swimming pool." However, this fear is not well founded.

Whenever I do consultations with established churches regarding church planting, one of their first questions is, How do we get involved? Some time ago I wrote two articles in an attempt to answer this question. The first was originally published in the *Journal of the American Society for Church Growth*, and part of this work is found in the remaining portion of this chapter.[2] An abbreviated version was later published in *SBC Life-Journal of the Southern Baptist Convention.*[3] Both of these articles can be located in the Articles section of my website at www.northamericanmissions.org.

> **"Among the Kekchi people . . . if a church didn't reproduce itself after six months it was considered an unhealthy church."**
>
> —David Garrison, *Church Planting Movements: How God Is Redeeming a Lost World* (Midlothian, VA: WIGTAKE Resources, 2004), 195.

## Levels of Involvement

The first thing churches should understand is that there is a multitude of ways to be involved in church planting. The following discussion suggests different levels of commitment but is definitely not an exhaustive list. Many churches do not consider themselves capable of being involved in church planting because they tend to think of involvement at just one level—usually a level believed to be out of reach. My recommendation to churches considering church planting is that they should begin anywhere, anytime.

One level of involvement is for churches to partner in order to plant a church. This type of partnership allows for varying degrees of involvement. I have heard of some partnerships in which one of the churches agreed to carry most of the weight in the joint endeavor.

Some churches become involved by using an **outside church planter**—an individual who is not originally from the congregation. The congregation or a denominational source will, sometimes, financially support this individual so the church planter can work full time. Sometimes the mother church will send out some people to work with the church planter in the mission work.

Some churches will get involved by sending out their own **church-planting team** with their own leaders. This type of involvement requires a deeper level of commitment. This level of involvement is clearly a biblical route. Regardless of the church's level of involvement, the following are ten different activities, along with practical application points, in which mother churches can participate in church planting.

## Calling Out the Missionaries

It was within the context of the local church that Saul and Barnabas were set aside for missionary work. Luke wrote, "In the church at Antioch there were prophets and teachers . . . While they were worshiping the Lord and fasting, the Holy Spirit said, 'Set apart for me Barnabas and Saul for the work to which I have called them'" (Acts 13:1–2 NIV).

Established churches need to recognize the significance of this passage. There is a direct connection between the responsibility of the local church and the sending of church planters.

**Practical Help.** There are numerous ways that local churches can be involved in calling out missionaries; however, the leadership of the church *must* take the initiative. An atmosphere needs to be created that encourages the belief that "our church expects members of this congregation to be sent out as missionaries in our Jerusalem, Judea, Samaria, and to the ends of the earth!" The leaders of the church need to pray regularly for a healthy atmosphere that fosters the biblical understanding of calling out and sending out church planters. Staff members need to teach and talk about these matters. Church periodicals need to reflect this church-planting enthusiasm. For example, the church could add to its newsletter or worship bulletin a brief story profiling a church-planting team working within the geographical proximity.

One of the most important and most practical means for creating a healthy atmosphere among the believers is the use of the pulpit. The pastors who regularly minister from the pulpit with the Scriptures bear the majority of this responsibility. The people need to know that the Scriptures clearly teach that church planting is a healthy and natural expression of a missional church. Ed Stetzer noted, "The vision must come from the *pulpit*, because presenting the vision through preaching signals to the church that, of all the many important matters the pastor could have preached, the church planting vision has taken precedence."[4]

## Prayer Support

One of the most important things a church can do for its church planters is pray for them on a regular basis. The apostle Paul recognized the importance of having other churches pray for him: "And also [pray] for me, that words may be given to me in opening my mouth boldly to proclaim the mystery of the gospel, for which I am an ambassador in chains, that I may declare it boldly, as I ought to speak" (Ephesians 6:19–20).

> **"An obedient church has an inherent, God-given power to multiply, just as all other living things that God created."**
>
> —George Patterson and Richard Scoggins, *Church Multiplication Guide*, revised ed. (Pasadena, CA: William Carey Library, 2002), 12.

**Practical Help.** Every week churches should consider devoting a portion of the worship service to a time of prayer for the church-planting team. For example, at the time of this writing—though our church is just over eighteen months old—we have had the blessing of sending out two church-planting teams to Cleveland and New Orleans. During every worship gathering, our lead pastor has someone guide the congregation in a time of prayer for these two teams, their families, and their work. Also, churches can encourage different Sunday school classes or small groups to pray for the needs of church planters. Groups could gather for a meal in someone's home and conclude with a time of prayer for specific concerns stated by the church-planting team. Weekly prayer meetings could revolve around a time of prayer for the work. Instead of meeting in a building for a prayer meeting, churches could prayer walk through different communities in which a church-planting team is working; or they could meet in the home of one of the church planters for a night of prayer. Church leaders should encourage the church-planting team to recruit intercessors for its ministry.

## Encouragement and a Body of Identity

Church planting can be a lonely endeavor, especially when the team is working in a pioneer area where few strong relationships with other believers exist. Many times the team consists of one family sent by the Lord to an area where it is miles from home and Christian fellowship.

Established churches need to offer encouragement to church planters and their families on a regular basis. Church planting can be some of the most discouraging and frustrating work in ministry. Churches need to remind their church planters that they are available for them and will minister to them in both good times and bad times.

On different occasions the apostle Paul returned from his missionary journeys to the Church in Antioch, from which he was originally sent out

(Acts 14:26; 18:22). If anyone needs encouragement and the opportunity to connect with other believers, it is church planters.

They also need a place to call home; they need to be able to identify with an established body. If asked by people in a community if they are with a church, the team should be able to respond in the affirmative with a specific congregation. In many contexts this affirmation will lend credibility to the ministry.

**Practical Help.** Established church leaders must understand that their work with church planters is an extension of their own ministries and not a distraction or a hindrance to such ministries. The following are some ideas for encouraging and connecting with church planters:

- Encourage church members to have a meal or coffee with the church-planting team/family every couple of weeks.
- Allow the church planters to preach for you and have a significant role in leading the congregation in worship and/or study.
- Encourage members to "adopt" the church-planting family(ies) and begin helping them adjust to a new life and new location.

> "North America is filled with pastors and churches that aren't willing to sponsor daughter churches and to make the sacrifices necessary to support a new church start. It will require thousands of churches willing to sponsor church plants to reverse the self-destruction of North American culture."
>
> —Ed Stetzer, *Planting Missional Churches* (Nashville, TN: Broadman and Holman Publishers, 2006), 322.

## Pastoral Mentoring and Accountability

Just as the team members need to have close connections with a local congregation, they also need pastoring. But who pastors the church planters? Seldom is this question asked, because it is assumed that missionaries are not in need of pastoral ministry. This erroneous assumption leads to the belief that church planters are on a higher spiritual plane than other church members.

Church planters need someone who will walk with them during both the good days and bad days of their ministries. They need mentors who can serve as compassionate encouragers, while remaining firm challengers. They need individuals with whom they can share ideas, evangelistic strategies, family concerns, and frustrations.

Church-planting teams need to be held accountable for their stewardship with the opportunities the Lord has provided. When a team is in a new location miles from close friends, temptations abound. For example, unless the church planters are making wise use of their time each day, it is easy to be busy doing good things, but actually accomplishing very little. They need to be held accountable for nurturing healthy relationships with their families and for having personal devotional time. They need to be held accountable for implementing their church-planting strategies and accomplishing the milestones they have established.

**Practical Help.** Pastors should consider making it a priority to pastor the missionaries. They can easily offer their ministries to them. It is easy to be a Barnabas! Weekly e-mails can be sent to church planters, inquiring how they are doing. Pastors should consider having a bimonthly lunch meeting with them. By showing interest in their work, established churches can easily hold church planters accountable.

> "Starting new congregations is the fastest way to fulfill the Great Commission."
>
> —Rick Warren, *The Purpose-Driven Church* (Grand Rapids, MI: Zondervan, 1995), 180.

## Training

Like most ministers, church planters desire ongoing training. Though many churches may not be able to directly provide the desired training for church planters, within most denominations there are individuals who are skilled in various areas of ministry in general and church planting in particular. Also, there are many parachurch organizations that provide ongoing training for church planters. Church planters need times of refreshing. Being on the frontlines is draining, and opportunities for practical training can sometimes serve as a breath of fresh air.

**Practical Help.** Pastors should consider inviting church planters (and paying their expenses) to attend conferences and training events that they normally attend. Though the material covered may not be directly applicable to the present missionary work, nevertheless, it may provide training that will be useful in the future. Another idea is to start a monthly book club with the missionaries. Each month a different book can be selected for discussion.

## Resources and Financial Support

Many churches do not become involved in church planting because they believe they do not have any resources to support such work. I think, however, this excuse represents a rare exception, rather than the norm.

I was recently conducting a seminar on becoming a church-planting church when I asked the participants how much money was needed to plant a church. After taking a moment to think, one man responded, "About $110,000 if you want to do it right." Following his response, many of the participants remained silent; others raised their eyebrows in shock. I responded with the following question, "What is your definition of 'right'?" He did not have a clear answer.

Our understanding of the church will affect our thoughts concerning the use of resources in church planting. Most churches do not believe they can help in the area of finances because the church itself owns a very costly piece of property and a building and after ten years is still paying off the debt. They reason like this: "Since we have all this 'stuff,' and we are a church, therefore, to be involved in church planting means that other churches must have the same 'stuff'; and we can barely afford our possessions." Churches should not assume that what they own is necessary for a church to be planted.

> **"But we reproduce in kind. Christians should multiply converts. Churches should multiply congregations."**
>
> —Ralph Moore, *Starting a New Church: The Church Planter's Guide to Success* (Ventura, CA: Regal Books, 2002), 256.

**Practical Help.** Churches have a multitude of resources to use for church planting. For example, I challenge churches to do the following:

- Be willing to allow a church-planting team to use your photocopier, office space, computers, and office supplies.
- Share your building space with the new church. Allow them to use the worship areas, classrooms, nursery, and even storage space.
- Assist them in obtaining bulk-mail permits and tax-exemption numbers.
- Send members from your church to serve as temporary workers to help out until the church is planted. Encourage these members to make a time commitment (e.g., one year) to serve on the team. Following their commitment, they will return to the mother church.
- Send members to help plant the church and remain with the new church indefinitely.
- Send youth groups to do short-term mission trips with the missionaries.

- Consider a special quarterly offering for the church-planting work.
- Give a percentage of your overall missions/evangelism budget to the church-planting work.
- Enlist certain Sunday school classes to sponsor the church-planting work. The classes can participate in hands-on work with the church planters, and they can give special offerings to the work.

## Constant Recognition of the Missionaries

People are quick to forget. Rick Warren, in his book *The Purpose-Driven Church*, commented that he had to recast the church's vision and purpose every twenty-six days because people forget even the important things.[5] The church-planting team needs to be constantly brought to the minds of the church members. I have been in several situations in which the leadership was in agreement with a particular ministry, but because it failed to communicate regularly the significance of the ministry, the rest of the church soon forgot the ministry existed. Even if the church leaders are supportive of the church-planting work, the rest of the church needs to be supportive of the work as well. One of the ways to keep up their support is simply, on a regular basis, to remind the church members of the church-planting ministry in which they participate.

### Some Benefits of Being a Mother Church

In their work, *Spin-off Churches: How One Church Successfully Plants Another*, authors Rodney Harrison, Tom Cheyney, and Don Overstreet provided the following list of the benefits to the established church when it is involved in church planting.

> At least thirteen things (the "lucky thirteen") happen within sponsoring churches when those churches become actively

involved in planting new churches:

1. Sponsoring keeps the church fresh and alive to its mission and vision and challenges the church's faith.
2. Sponsoring reminds the church of the challenge to pray for the lost.
3. Sponsoring enables the church to welcome other people into the kingdom that it would not otherwise have assimilated.
4. Sponsoring creates a climate open to birthing a variety of need-meeting groups within the sending church.
5. Sponsoring provides evangelistic vitality and activity.
6. Sponsoring encourages the discovery and development of new and latent leaders.
7. Sponsoring encourages coaching, mentoring, and apprenticeship in ministry while providing a renewed understanding of how we are all part of a team effort.
8. Sponsoring provides an occasion for church members to get to know missionaries personally.
9. Sponsoring builds on the past and insures the future.
10. Sponsoring minimizes the tendency toward a self-centered ministry.
11. Sponsoring provides an education in missions and serves as a stimulus for young people's dedication to Christian service.
12. Sponsoring provides a visible proof that God is still working through people and that some are responding to his commission to go out and evangelize.
13. Sponsoring provides a new opportunity for personal involvement in missions.

Taken from Rodney Harrison, Tom Cheyney, and Don Overstreet, *Spin-off Churches: How One Church Successfully Plants Another* (Nashville, TN: B&H Academic, 2008), 65–66.

***Questions to Consider:***

1. Which of the above thirteen benefits appeal to you the most?
2. Can you think of some other benefits that church planting would bring to the health of your church?

**Practical Help.** In a church where I used to serve, I would invite the church's church planter to come and give a testimony during the morning worship service. In the church where I currently serve, the lead pastor periodically encourages our church planters to send brief, high-quality videos to be shown during our worship gatherings. Be creative in finding ways to keep the church consciously aware of the lives of the church planters and the overall progress of their work. The following are some suggestions that you may desire to implement in your situation:

- Do a "Church-Planting Update" section in your newsletter.
- Have the church planters regularly post information regarding the work on your church's website. You could even create a special link on your site entitled "A Day in the Trenches" and allow each of the church planters to daily post a synopsis of what he or she did that particular day.
- Allow the church planters on a periodic basis to assist in leading in the church's worship time or Bible study time. Numerous opportunities are available, such as preaching, leading in prayer, or sharing a testimony of what took place the previous week.
- Have a regular time of prayer for the church planters during the worship service.
- Periodically create and show a video shadowing the church planters as they go through any given week.
- Host special, yet informal, dinners for the church that have the families of the church planters as the guests of honor.

## Remaining Flexible

Church planting by definition is cross-cultural work. Even if the church planters are working among people of a similar ethnicity, they are crossing cultures and confronting various worldviews. There is always a necessity to contextualize the gospel for a new culture.

Contextualization is easier said than done. In conjunction with the work of the Holy Spirit, church planters are required to use many methods to communicate the truth of Christ. It is very likely that the methods used by mother churches to reach the members of their own congregations are not the methods that will be used by their church planters.

> **"In order for a congregation to develop a strategy for planting churches, that congregation—or at least its principal leaders—must have assumed evangelistic responsibility for a significant geographical area."**
>
> —Charles Chaney, *Church Planting at the End of the Twentieth Century*, revised ed. (Wheaton, IL: Tyndale House Publishers, 1991), 123.

From the vantage point of many mother churches, church planters appear to do strange things. Though churches must hold church planters accountable for their ministries, as long as they are faithful to the Scriptures and not conveying a shallow understanding of what it means to be a disciple of Christ, much flexibility should be permitted for them to reach their people.

The missionaries are the ones in the trenches and have a first-hand grasp of the situation. Many times it is easy for mother churches in different contexts to demand that church planters follow particular methods. This noncontextualized guidance easily results in frustration for the church-planting team as well as little or no church growth. Several years ago Jack Redford commented, "Many times the sponsoring church wants to force the issues for the mission, making decisions and demanding action before the mission is ready. Rather than force these issues, the sponsor should provide opportunities for the new chapel to develop the issues on its own. This, however, takes time, effort, and patience. Again, like the parent and child, the sponsor should allow the 'child' to express its feelings and then deal realistically and honestly with them rather than squelching creativity and maturation."[6]

**Practical Help.** Allowing the church-planting team much flexibility does not mean that mother churches do not offer guidance, accountability, encouragement, or support. Providing a healthy environment in which the church-planting team—guided by the Holy Spirit—can be creative in its methods not only helps the team but also can reveal to declining or plateaued churches the need to change methodologies when necessary. If the pastors of the mother church are supportive of the peculiar methods of the church-planting team, then the potential increases for the whole church to be more accepting as well. The chances are good that if the leadership is excited about what the missionaries are doing, the church will catch that excitement.

## Establishing Clear Expectations

"Whenever there are two or three gathered in His name, there is bound to be a disagreement," so says the old adage. Misunderstandings will come; it is a fact. What is important is how misunderstandings are addressed. Mother churches and church-planting teams need to have clear expectations for the partnership.

Though there are many areas of these partnerships that need to be addressed, the following are of the utmost importance: (1) roles of the mother church and the church-planting team, (2) use of mother church's facilities and office supplies, (3) finances, and (4) involvement of the members of the mother church in the actual church-planting work. Each of these areas can quickly become points of tension and frustration and manipulated by the Evil One if they are not discussed early in the church-planting work.

**Practical Help.** Churches should consider using the resource *Mother or Partner: Church Commitment Profile.*[7] This small booklet written by Paul Becker attempts to answer two questions: What are we going to do for the church planter and the new church? and What are we not going to do for the church planter and the new church?

If it is culturally appropriate, I encourage churches and church planters to write out the overall agreement as a **covenant of understanding**. By putting things in writing both parties are able to have a tangible resource regarding the parameters of the partnership. If an official, written document is inappropriate, then oral communication should be done in the presence of several witnesses who are significant leaders in the community.

## Recognizing Their Legitimacy

Church planters and the newly planted churches are extremely significant to the kingdom. They are legitimate in the body and not some subpar group of believers who just do not have everything together yet.

Throughout the Scriptures those planting the churches were seen as a vital component of fulfilling the Great Commission. The teams, which were willing to give up the comfort of familiarity to venture into unknown territory to plant churches, were held in high esteem among the brothers and sisters. Church planters should still be held in high esteem among the mother churches. Pastors must discourage any referencing of the church planters as *hopefully arriving* at a point of significant ministry; church-planting efforts are valuable from the beginning.

Pastors should not refer to a newly planted church as a "**mission church**," because such a label communicates something less than a church. Historically speaking, this terminology has been very popular. Often, when a mother church was involved in planting another congregation, the daughter church, at least for a season, was labeled as "our mission." The problem is that if the daughter church is a church, then, biblically speaking, it should be labeled as a church. Period. Regardless of what the governmental, denominational, or cultural policies are for officially defining a church, mother churches must be bold enough to scripturally define when a mission becomes a church.

> **"Many of our faithful people are more than ready to move into reproducing their church; but let's face it, they can only go as far as the pastor's passion and support for the project will allow."**
>
> —Jim Henry, "Casting a Vision for Reproduction of Your Church," in *Reaching a Nation through Church Planting*, compiler Richard H. Harris (Alpharetta, GA: North American Mission Board, 2003), 84.

**Practical Help.** Mother churches are better prepared to properly understand their church-planting work after they spend time journeying through certain books of the Bible. Acts, 1 and 2 Corinthians, Ephesians, Philippians, and 1 Thessalonians should be studied while attempting to address two questions: When did the church plants become churches? and What were the attitudes of the existing churches toward those who planted churches? Churches may want to consider reading Elmer Towns and Douglas Porter's book *Churches That Multiply: A Bible Study on Church Planting* (Kansas City, MO: Beacon Hill Press, 2003) or *Creating Communities of the Kingdom: New Testament Models of Church Planting* (Scottdale, PA; Waterloo ON: Herald Press, 1988) by David W. Shenk and Ervin R. Stutzman.

## A Word to Church Leaders

Pastors, you are the most important individuals in the process of churches planting churches. If you have not caught the vision to plant other churches, then the chances are very good that your congregation will never plant other churches. The following are some things to consider related to you as an individual.

First, a vision from God is a must. This vision must be received, embraced, and owned by the pastoral leadership. Second, you need to have a biblical understanding of the nature and purpose of the local church, not necessarily a Western-culture understanding of the church. Third, a healthy understanding of the Holy Spirit is essential. You must believe that the Spirit is able to regenerate individuals and sanctify congregations. Remember, the apostle Paul was able to entrust newly planted churches to the Holy Spirit and their leadership (Acts 20:32).

The fourth item for consideration is related to your security in who you are as a pastor. If you are insecure in your ministry, it will be difficult to lead a church-planting church. Insecurity breeds the fear of losing control. (Remember, for God to be in control, we must be out of control.) Church planting is messy work, and you should expect the unexpected. Insecurity creates a dependency mentality among the congregants and hinders church multiplication. Insecurity creates a fear that the church-planting team/church planter might do a better job than what I have done. Insecurity creates selfishness: "If we send out resources—money, leaders, programs, and excitement—there will be less for us." Insecurity results in a myopic kingdom vision. Only repentance and God's grace can heal us of the sin of insecurity.

Ralph Moore's exhortation is appropriate to note in the conclusion of this chapter: "Every mature organism is capable of reproducing itself. Some do it many times. But most congregations will never do this in their lifetimes. The reason is that pastors think the fruit of their ministry stops with making converts. Most think of multiplying the number of Christians in their community. But we reproduce in kind. Christians should multiply converts. Churches should multiply churches."[8]

The lack of established churches involved in church planting should be a major concern for all believers. For most churches, being "on mission," especially in North America, is simply rhetoric. Church planters are in need of our support on a variety of levels. It is time for more churches to become mothers, instead of remaining on birth control.

### *Summary:*

1. Churches that have never been involved in church planting do not have to plunge into the deep end of the pool at first. There are numerous ways a church can become involved in church planting.
2. The pastors/elders are the most important people in the church when it comes to leading a church to plant other churches.
3. Pastors/elders must have a vision for seeing their church become a mother church.
4. Many pastors/elders will have to overcome the sin of turfism and insecurity before leading their churches to plant other churches.

### *Reflection Questions:*

1. Is your church already participating in church planting? If so, what is its level of involvement?
2. What can your church do in the next three months to assist in church planting in North America and beyond?
3. Are you willing to lead your church in becoming significantly involved in planting churches? If so, what steps will you take in the next twelve months to move in this direction? If you are not willing, please explain your reason.
4. Are there issues in your heart that you need to address before leading your church to become a mother church? If so, what are those issues? Will you deal with them right now?

### *Important Terms in This Chapter:*

- Outside church planter
- Church-planting team
- Covenant of understanding
- Mission church

Chapter 15

# TEAMS AND CHURCH PLANTING

**Churches planted by an effective ministry team tend to be stronger, and their future tends to be more secure.**

**—Elmer Towns and Douglas Porter[1]**

The icon of U.S. history is that of the lonesome, rugged pioneer working to do all that he can to serve the common good of helpless individuals. This rugged individualism appeared in popular culture, and I grew up hearing songs that hailed Davey Crockett as the "King of the Wild Frontier" and the lonesome, six-foot-six-inch-tall, 245-pound miner named "Big Bad John," who experienced a Pyrrhic victory while saving coal miners at the sacrifice of his own life. Our television sets spoke of a hero from another planet who came to earth to fight for "truth, justice, and the American way." This Superman was "faster than a speeding bullet, more powerful than a locomotive, able to leap tall buildings in a single bound," yet functioned as a loner attempting to masquerade as the mild-mannered Clark Kent.

But for me, the true solitary hero who modeled the individualistic way of life was the man who was trademarked by his "fiery horse with a speed of light, a cloud of dust," and his hearty "Hi-yo, Silver!" With the clarion call of Rossini's *William Tell* overture, we quickly gathered around our television sets with great anticipation, waiting to find out what would happen to "the daring and resourceful masked rider of the plains" who "led the fight for law and order in the early West." This hero was so popular that even today people describe solitary individuals as "lone rangers." (Of course, it must be remembered that even the Lone Ranger worked with his faithful Indian companion, Tonto.)

Though the lonesome leader is an icon of U.S. pop culture, such a model must not represent church-planting teams. When contrasting missionaries who leave North America with those remaining in North America, it is not surprising to find that the former are leaving as church-planting teams (or arriving in another country with the strategy to join an already-existing team); whereas, for many North American missionaries, the lone ranger paradigm still takes an unfortunate precedence.

> "For us teams are like a basketball team where all the members are pooling their abilities and working in a coordinated effort to see a cluster of reproducing churches. They are not like a track team where each one does his or her own thing hoping that of all the individuals laboring in different fields with little cooperation, one or two churches might be planted."
>
> —Dick Scoggins, *Building Effective Church Planting Teams* (unpublished manuscript available at www.dickscoggins.com).

This chapter makes the argument that church-planting teams should be the normative model for global church planting. After examining the biblical evidence of church-planting teams, I will address some of their strengths and limitations. This chapter concludes with a discussion of eight personal qualities essential for every team member and the importance of developing a team covenant.

## Teams: The Apostolic Example

The Bible is filled with examples of teams working together to accomplish a task for the kingdom of God. Noah worked with his sons to build the ark. Moses and Aaron led the Israelites into the Promised Land. Nehemiah knew that he could not rebuild the walls of Jerusalem by himself, and so he worked with a large group of people. Even in the creation accounts, God reflected his tri-unity with reference to the Spirit hovering over the face of the deep (Genesis 1:2), the declaration of "let us" create man in our image (Genesis 1:26), the preincarnate Word (John 1:1–3), and Paul's reference to the Son's creative acts (Colossians 1:15–17).

After modeling preaching, healing, and casting out demons, Jesus on two occasions sent out teams to repeat his example. Beginning with the Twelve (Luke 9:1–6) and shortly thereafter with the Seventy-two (Luke 10:1–12), he commissioned teams of disciples to advance the kingdom of God. No one was to go alone.

It is not surprising that just as the Father, Son, and Holy Spirit eternally work in community as a healthy team, the saints throughout the ages would reflect such a paradigm when working toward kingdom goals. Working as a team is a divine characteristic and must be a component of any missionary endeavor.

An examination of the Book of Acts reveals that the apostolic Church continued the team paradigm as modeled by Jesus. David W. Shenk and Ervin R. Stutzman observed that such cooperation was typical. They commented, "Nevertheless, it is also true that when the believers reached out through church planting, the Acts record suggests that the ministry was always carried forward by a team. They apparently never commissioned a missionary to go alone into a new region to plant churches. A noteworthy example is the commissioning of Paul and Barnabas, accompanied by John Mark, as missionaries to the Gentiles. These men were commissioned by the church in Antioch to plant churches among people who had never heard the gospel."[2]

## Strengths of a Team

As explained above, the team approach follows the apostolic pattern. Aside from this biblical support, there are many other benefits from working as a team. I have outlined several of these strengths in the paragraphs below.

**Shared Leadership.** A team approach to church planting allows for a sharing of the responsibilities for the missionary work. Shared leadership keeps the weight of the church-planting task from overwhelming one individual. Though in all likelihood there will be a team leader—a first among equals—everyone is involved in a significant leadership role to some degree.

**Accountability.** Teamwork fosters accountability. When church planters work side by side, it is easier for them to hold each other accountable regarding their walks with the Lord, their relationships with their spouses and children, and their faithfulness to the church-planting tasks. Without accountability, missionaries can become wasteful with their time and unwise with their schedules.

**Encouragement.** Though church planters are guaranteed a multitude of blessings from their work, church planting can be extremely discouraging. A team can create a healthy atmosphere for support, especially for the difficult days.

**Diversity.** A team makes room for a diversity of gifts and talents. Instead of one person attempting to accomplish all the necessary tasks, a team allows for a variety of people—and their gifts and talents—to accomplish those tasks. A team of varying abilities can accomplish more for the kingdom than any individual working alone. The sum is greater than its individual parts. The limitations of one team member are compensated by the strengths of another.

> "Churches planted by a team of workers will be stronger than those planted by a single church planter simply because of the broader range of gifts represented by the ministry of a team."
>
> —Ben A. Sawatsky, "A Church Planting Strategy: For World Class Cities," *Urban Mission* 3, no. 3 (November 1985): 10.

**Strength in Numbers.** Church planting can be a very lonely ministry. A team provides support for the journey and protection against opposition from the physical and spiritual realms. There is power in numbers.

**A Functional Body of Christ.** In situations where church planters are miles away from other churches they can fellowship and worship with, the team can temporarily function as the church. Though not a local church, the team allows for all the families involved to function as the body of Christ gathered for mutual edification. But it is unwise and unhealthy for church planters to minister for months and years without any interaction with a local congregation.

**Pastoral Care.** Greg Livingstone noted that a healthy church-planting team offers pastoral care to itself "so that each member will remain fit for serving God."[3] Each team member is looking after the welfare of the others. If one member of the team suffers, all the team suffers.

**A Training Ground.** Livingstone also stated that a team can provide opportunities for the newer members to grow as church planters.[4] By allowing for such flexibility, the team serves as a place for equipping and multiplying new church planters.

**A Faster Evangelistic Growth Potential.** Roger S. Greenway observed that since more laborers are available for evangelism, the growth potential increases.[5] Generally, there is a correlation between the amount of preaching and the number of disciples made. For example, a team with five individuals doing the work of evangelists is more likely to see a faster harvest for the kingdom than for a single missionary working alone.

**Wisdom in Numbers.** Greenway also astutely noted that wise decision making for the day-to-day activities are best accomplished by a group close to the ministry context.[6] Several church planters working together can provide the counsel needed for the significant atypical decisions that periodically arise on the mission field.

**Model of Church for the New Believers.** Another strength that Greenway discerned is that the team can model healthy body life for the new believers: "The team represents a microcosm of the Body of Christ more vividly and effectively than do one or two missionaries working alone."[7] Missionaries are constantly under the careful scrutiny of the people they serve. Their words and actions model how followers of Christ are supposed to live in community with one another as the body of Christ.

## Limitations of a Team

Though the biblical evidence supports a team approach, wise missionaries must also be aware of the limitations of teams. Without a proper understanding of the limitations, church planters may be tempted to assume that as long as they form a team, their work will be accomplished without many difficulties. It is important that missionaries keep their expectations tempered by reality.

**Length of Time to Make Decisions.** One or even two church planters can typically make quick decisions with little or no planning.

However, with a team, decision making takes longer. Time is needed for everyone to process the issues of discussion and come to necessary conclusions for action. If there are several individuals on a team—especially a team with several members serving in a bivocational or tentmaking capacity—it may be difficult to coordinate the schedules of all of the team members for the necessary meetings.

> "Rather than looking for 'super apostles' who can do all the work by themselves, the churches and agencies should be looking for those who can make a significant contribution to a team church planting effort."
>
> —Greg Livingstone, *Planting Churches in Muslim Cities: A Team Approach* (Grand Rapids, MI: Baker Books, 1993), 75.

**Inevitability of Conflict.** One thing is certain about church-planting teams: conflict will occur. Even the apostle Paul was not immune to conflict. He and Barnabas argued over John Mark so sharply that they parted ways for the sake of the kingdom (Acts 15:36–41).

Conflict, though usually not enjoyable, can be a sign of health and enhance the team's spiritual growth when managed correctly. Effective teams recognize that conflict will occur and develop a protocol for conflict resolution so that members can respond in a godly manner when differences arise.

**Potential to Become Inwardly Focused.** Teams need to stay focused on the task at hand; otherwise, the church–planting team may become a church instead of planting a contextualized church among the people. Especially in areas where the people are not very receptive to the gospel, the team may settle for enjoying life together and building up one another.

## Teams: Scaffolds or Buildings?

In the 1800s missionaries to China and missiologist John Nevius once referred to missionaries as "scaffolds" to be removed when the "building" was established. The building that Nevius referred to was a metaphor for the Church planted among a people. At the end of the twentieth century, Dick Scoggins addressed this matter of the church-planting team serving as a scaffold. Referencing missiologist George Patterson, Scoggins made the following observations:

> George Patterson has likened a church planting team to a scaffold which surrounds the structure which is being built: the church. Care must be taken to be sure that the scaffolding is in good shape so that the job can be accomplished. But there is a danger of spending so much time and effort on the scaffolding that the job of building the church is missed. Never lose sight of the goal that the scaffold must be dismantled and removed from the building.
>
> Indeed, a major problem is that some teams spend so much time among themselves they end up becoming a church themselves instead of a temporary means to plant the church. For instance one team I visited had begun to set up a Sunday School for their kids, have a regular preaching service, had even begun looking for buildings to meet in! They were hoping to invite nationals to visit and use this as a preaching point. I pointed out that beginning with this model, the nationals would not be satisfied until they had something similar which likely would be many years away since the skills of the team were far beyond what new believers would gain, not to mention that homiletic tools like commentaries which the church planters took for granted were not even existent in the Muslim country!
>
> After a while they could see that they were setting up a church of which they would have to be a part for the foreseeable future. This may be a way of planting a church, but is not suitable for a church planting team whose authority is *temporary*, and whose ministry must be *itinerant*. And such a church is not likely to reproduce at any rate.
>
> When something like this happens, purpose, function and lines of authority between church and team often become muddled and confused. The church and the team get in each other's way, or become so antagonistic that they can no longer cooperate. A spirit of co-laboring turns into a spirit of competing. If a team is going to fulfill its mandate, and let the

church fulfill hers, the team must carefully distinguish its own mandate from the mandate of the church.

Taken from Dick Scoggins, *Building Effective Church Planting Teams* (unpublished manuscript at www.dickscoggins.com), 11, italics original.

***Questions to Consider:***

1. Do you agree with Nevius, Patterson, and Scoggins that teams should exist temporarily until the church is planted? If not, why not?
2. Scoggins's story takes place in a Muslim country; do you believe that the metaphor of temporary scaffolds can be applied to North America? Why or why not?
3. What do you believe is meant by "Care must be taken to be sure that the scaffolding is in good shape"?

## *The Barnabas Factors*

In my book *The Barnabas Factors: Eight Essential Practices of Church Planting Team Members*, I examined Barnabas's life and ministry as a model for character and personal qualities that should be present in all church planters.[8] I once knew a church planter who was so eager to get people on his team that he would recruit anyone who was breathing and interested! This is a strategy for disaster when it comes to team development. When few people are willing to serve on church-planting teams, there is a real temptation to settle for anyone willing to serve—believing that you can work out the possible rough edges later. Another strong temptation presently facing church planters is to recruit others based on their talent and passion. Though a person may make a significant contribution to the work through the use of a dynamic skill, such gains may be short lived if the person fails to manifest the Barnabas Factors in his or her life.

Team development should begin by applying the Barnabas Factors as a screen for potential members. Before receiving an invitation to join your team, a potential member should have a proven history of manifesting eight significant practices:

- Walks with the Lord
- Maintains an outstanding character
- Serves the local church
- Remains faithful to the call
- Shares the gospel regularly
- Raises up leaders
- Encourages others with speech and actions
- Responds appropriately to conflict

## Covenant of Team Understandings

By far, the best resource to date on developing church-planting teams is Dick Scoggins's unpublished book, *Building Effective Church Planting Teams*. Scoggins, who has had years of experience working with church-planting teams in North America and across the globe, has written this highly practical resource and made it available at his website.[9]

> **"The time has never been better for wide scale implementation of team strategies in the urban world."**
>
> —Roger S. Greenway, "The 'Team' Approach to Urban Church Planting," *Urban Mission* 4 (March 1987): 5.

In this work Scoggins strongly admonished church planters to develop a covenant before serving together as a team. It is in the process of developing a written covenant that the team is able to address very important matters they probably would not consider until they are on the field and facing the challenges of the ministry. By wrestling through certain issues and questions before they get to the field—before the times of conflict arise—the team will be better prepared to address the critical issues it will face. Such a process helps facilitate a healthy team and assists in preventing the team from shipwreck against the rocks of disaster. Scoggins encouraged team leaders to take the lead and develop this document "which will enable potential team members to understand how your team will function."[10] The following questions are adapted from his list of questions to include in a Covenant of Team Understandings (COTU).

- Summarize briefly (a sentence or two): Where are you going? What is your specific target (people group, socioeconomic segment, city, etc.)? Are there any nonnegotiables in your strategy?
- What are some ways you will be able to get employment for your team members?
- Who makes lifestyle decisions? Where to live? Apartment? House? As single families or as a team? What does a person have to agree to before he or she leaves for the field?
- For those who are financially supported, how is the support level set? What does this level include? Does it include ministry expenses or just personal family needs? Will there be any funds pooled for team ministry? An emergency fund?
- How are decisions made?
- How is conflict to be resolved? What recourse is there if the conflict is with the team leader (put yourself in their shoes)?
- What if someone determines that he or she should not be there after arriving? What is the exit procedure? How soon can he or she leave? Is there a probation period?
- If your COTU deals with cross-cultural church planting, will a team member be expected to learn a language?
- What skills are expected of someone joining the team? How does a person really know that he or she is ready to go?

- What about theological issues? Are there any theological nonnegotiables, such as charismatic leanings, etc.? What kind of person would be most comfortable on this team?
- What happens if the team leader feels called to another area and leaves behind a remnant of the team?
- What provisions are there for sickness, emergencies, vacations, and leaves of absence?
- To whom is the team leader accountable? How do your sending churches fit into your team's effort? Who is responsible for seeing that the work is kept in high profile in the sending church? What kind of coaching or mentoring are you going to get from outside the team?
- Are there any restrictions on the team for the first year (visits home, vacation, training in other places)?
- How do you envision team life? Will the team meet for worship? Prayer? Training? Socially? How often? Will there be different roles for men and women? Will you accept single women on the team?
- How will shepherding roles be set up? What if you have problems in your family? In whom will you confide? Will there be discipling of younger members by older ones? If your wife is a member of the team with you, who is responsible to shepherd her? In what areas?
- What sort of reporting procedure will be followed (to the home church, other agencies, etc.)?[11]

### *Summary:*

1. The lone ranger approach to missionary work is unwise.
2. The overwhelming biblical evidence points to the need for a team approach to church planting.
3. The strengths for using church-planting teams strongly outweigh

the limitations for such teams.

4. Team leaders should begin by looking for potential team members who clearly manifest a history of the Barnabas Factors in their lives.
5. A Covenant of Team Understandings is an essential component for healthy church-planting teams. Team leaders should develop such a guideline and use it when considering potential team members.

### *Reflection Questions:*

1. Are you the type of person who would more likely be a lone ranger or a team member when it comes to church planting? Explain your answer.
2. Can you think of some other strengths and/or limitations of church-planting teams not mentioned in this chapter?
3. Have you ever served on a church-planting team? If so, do you think it was a healthy or unhealthy team? Explain your conclusion.
4. Using the scale below, how would you rate your potential team members according to how you believe they manifest each of the eight Barnabas Factors?

   Low                Medium                High
   1 • 2 • 3 • 4 • 5 • 6 • 7 • 8 • 9 • 10

5. Using Scoggins's Covenant of Team Understandings as a guideline, develop such a tool for your personal church-planting work. Is there anything that Scoggins failed to include in his work that you believe is significant to a healthy team?

### *Important Terms in This Chapter:*

- Church-planting team
- Scaffold
- Barnabas Factors
- Covenant of Team Understandings

Section III

# DISCOVERING HISTORICAL PARADIGMS

Contemporary church planters must be students of Church history. We need to learn from our brothers and sisters of yesteryear as they labored to carry the gospel across the globe. Though this section is not representative of the two thousand years of Church history—for there is much to learn from many other epochs and groups—it does focus on three particular groups that were significantly involved in the advancement of the kingdom. Chapter sixteen examines the early Moravians and their missionary endeavors to some of the most neglected and remote parts of the world. Chapter seventeen turns our attention to the early North American frontier as we get a glimpse of the labors of the Methodists in the New World. Chapter eighteen keeps us on the frontier and informs us of the work of the Baptists as they moved westward.

Chapter 16

# EARLY MORAVIANS AND CHURCH PLANTING

On January 1, 1900, the united membership of the four provinces of the Moravian Church was 38,280. The *Diaspora* societies on the Continent of Europe embraced about 70,000 in their connection. The membership of the congregations gathered from among the heathen was 96,380.

—J. Taylor Hamilton[1]

Ruth A. Tucker referred to the Moravian Church as "one of the most remarkable missionary churches in Christian history."[2] In the eighteenth century when few were thinking about missionary activities, the Moravians were going to the most remote places on the globe and working among some of the most resistant and neglected people. The story of the Moravians and their church-planting activities throughout the world is a story of perseverance, simple evangelical faith, and methods that influenced generations of missionaries. When a Moravian was once asked what it was like to be a Moravian, he responded, "To be a Moravian and to further Christ's global cause are identical."[3] This chapter will introduce you to the Moravians: what they believed about missions, where they did missions in the 1700s, 1800s, and 1900s, and how they planted churches.

## Who Were the Moravians?

The Moravians trace their origins to the 1400s to a group known as the *Unitas Fratrum*, or the Brethren. The Brethren were followers of John Hus, who was burned at the stake for his Protestant views. After Hus's death his followers became a scattered and persecuted group.

By the early 1700s some of these Brethren and other Protestant groups found refuge on the Saxony estate of **Count Ludwig von Zinzendorf**. This estate was known as **Herrnhut** ("Lord's Watch"), and this group of believers came to be called the Moravians. Zinzendorf provided leadership to this group. He was strongly influenced by Pietism, a movement that drew from the works of Philip Jacob Spener and advocated a very simple evangelical way of life and belief. Though Zinzendorf was a well-educated man, he was not an academic but was a gifted missions organizer and missionary thinker.

> "The Moravians were the first Protestants to put into practice the idea that evangelizing the lost is the duty of the whole church, not just of a missionary society or a few individuals."
>
> —Kenneth B. Mulholland, "Moravians, Puritans, and the Modern Missionary Movement," *Bibliotheca Sacra* 156 (April–June 1999): 222.

## Where Did the Moravians Serve as Missionaries?

One of the unique elements about the Moravians was their burden to do missions. Though other Protestants had been involved in missionary activity, the Moravians were the first Protestants to recognize that the task of church planting and missionary work is the responsibility of the church and not the work of governments through their colonization activities.[4]

An examination of a map of the Moravian missionary locations reveals an amazing global vision and their willingness to travel to remote points, using the primitive means of transportation of their day. It was not unusual for Moravian missionaries to spend months traveling by foot from point A to point B and then get on a boat and travel for another several weeks. Upon arriving on another continent, they would spend another several months traveling by train, foot, or beast of burden. For most of the missionaries, just getting to the field of the people God had called them to serve was a great sacrifice and dangerous task.

## Early Moravian Dates and Locations of Missionary Service

1732: Virgin Islands, St. Thomas, Danish West Indies
1733: Greenland
1734–1736: St. Croix, Danish West Indies
1734: Northern Scandanavia
1734 & 1738: Georgia
1735: Surinam & South America
1736: The Gold Coast, Africa
1737: South Africa
1738: Amsterdam, Holland
1739: Algeria, Africa
1740: Eastern and Midwestern United States
1740: Ceylon and Romania
1740: Constantinople
1747: Persia
1752: Egypt & Abyssinia
1754: Jamaica
1756: Antigua
1759–1795: East Indies, Nicobar Islands, and Tranquebar
1765: Barbados
1771: Labrador

1777: St. Kitts
1787: Taboga
1815–1822: Serving among the Kalmuck Tartars
1849: Honduras & Nicaragua
1855: Magdala
1859–1861: Cabo Gracias a Dios
1860: Wanuta-Haulouver in Ephrata
1864: Tasbapauni in Bethany
1871: Kukalaya and Quamwatla
1875: Karata
1884: Yulu
1885: Alaska
1886: Little Sandy Bay & Twappi
1890: California
1890: Trinidad
1891: Tanzania
1893: Dakura
1895: Edmonton, Canada
1903: Karawala
1907: Sangsangta
1907: Santo Domingo
1923: Musawas
1927: Bilwi Puerto Cabezas
1938: Bonanza
1938: La Luz

Taken from James Weingarth, *You Are My Witnesses* (n.p.: Inter-Provincial Women's Board of the Moravian Church, 1981), 27, 31, 81, 89–90; Ruth A. Tucker, *From Jerusalem to Irian Jaya,* 2nd ed. (Grand Rapids, MI: Zondervan, 1983, 2004), 102.

By the end of 1760 more than two hundred Moravians had been sent as missionaries. Some sixty-six missionaries, including their wives, had seen more than four thousand conversions. Four-fifths of those were in the West Indies.[5] Tucker noted, "Their all-consuming purpose was to spread the gospel to the ends of the earth, a passion that was evident in their proportion of missionaries to lay people, by some estimates a ratio of 1 to 60."[6] According to Colin A. Grant, the Moravian community sent no less than 2,158 missionaries across the globe.[7]

## How Did They Plant Churches?

In what has been called Zinzendorf's "first contribution to the Science of Foreign Missions," the count instructed some of his earliest missionaries with three principles. After studying the limitations of the missionary methods used by Egede in Greenland, Zinzendorf admonished:

> You are not to aim at the conversion of whole nations: you must simply look for seekers after the truth who, like the Ethiopian eunuch, seem ready to welcome the Gospel. Second, you must go straight to the point and tell them about the life and death of Christ. Third, you must not stand aloof from the heathen, but humble yourself, mix with them, treat them as Brethren, and pray with them and for them. . . . And how is it that missionaries have failed in the past? They have failed because, instead of preaching Christ, they have given lectures on theology.[8]

In an ironic fashion Zinzendorf had no desire to extend the membership of the Moravian Church. Though churches were planted, Moravian missionaries focused little efforts on church planting. Hutton wrote, "Other missionaries toiled conscientiously for their respective native lands and for their respective State Churches; Zinzendorf toiled for the glory of God alone; and in his instructions to the missionaries he made that point abundantly clear. 'You must not,' he said emphatically, 'try to establish native churches; you must not enroll your converts as members of the Moravian Church; you must be content to enroll them as Christians.'"[9]

According to Gustav Warneck, "The instructions to missionaries were very simple, and the missionary methods were of a purely spiritual kind. The baptized were organized into congregations altogether after the model of those at home, and these were diligently visited on the part of the missionary directorate, which formed an integral part of the [governing board of the Moravian church]."[10]

So the major limitation of the Moravians' missionary work was that, while they focused on making disciples, they did not focus on planting churches but merely connected the disciples with already-established churches. Therefore, the natural question arises, Why include this chapter in a book on church planting? Though the Moravians' missionary strategy fell short in this particular area, their church-planting work was very significant in the methods used and in the conversion growth they experienced. We will discuss below twelve of their noteworthy methods of planting churches across the globe.

## Mission Stations

As Moravians would leave Herrnhut and travel to the field they were called to, they would begin by establishing their places of residence. Missionaries would practice communal living wherever they were located in the world.[11] Much of what they did was reflective of the model they had been exposed to at Herrnhut. For example, in one area of Greenland, the first work established there was actually named New Herrnhut. David A. Schattschneider noted, "Settlement congregations were organized as self-contained, self-supporting towns that were expected to be centers of outreach."[12]

> **"Many of the missionaries have been quite simple people, peasants and artisans; their aim has been to live the Gospel, and so to commend it to those who have never heard it."**
>
> —Stephen Neill, *A History of Christian Missions* (London: Penguin Books, 1964), 237.

## Team Approach

A second significant component of the missionary methods of the Moravians was that they went as teams throughout the world. No one went alone. This pattern follows the biblical example and allows for the camaraderie necessary to endure the numerous dangers and times of isolation confronted in global travel.

## Areas of Need

The Moravians traveled to pioneer areas. Zinzendorf encouraged missionaries to go to the neglected peoples. It was not uncommon for missionaries to work among the marginalized. In fact, the first missionaries sent out went to the Caribbean and worked among the slaves. Others ventured into Greenland and worked among the indigenous population in that remote country as well.

Reflecting on the history of the Moravian Church, Stephen Neill wrote, "The Moravians have tended to go to the most remote, unfavourable, and neglected parts of the surface of the earth."[13] Places such as Surinam, America, Labrador, and parts of Russia were pioneer areas for their Protestant evangelical work.

> **"In harmony with Zinzendorf's original purpose, the service of Moravian missions has been to a great extent among primitive races and in out-of-the-way places."**
>
> —Philip Henry Lotz, *Founders of Christian Movements* (New York: Association Press, 1941), 48.

## Focusing on Receptive Peoples

Moravians focused their work among the receptive people, and many times among the outcasts. In some cases, despite this intention, missionaries would labor for many years before seeing anyone come to faith.

Zinzendorf believed that the Holy Spirit is the only true missionary.[14] The role of the individual is that of being in the hands of the Holy Spirit and working according to the Spirit's guidance. Another closely related and important concept in his missiological views was that of "firstfruits." He encouraged his missionaries to work among receptive people. Believing that the Holy Spirit prepares hearts—as in the biblical accounts of the Ethiopian eunuch and Cornelius—Zinzendorf taught his missionaries to take hope in the fact that the Spirit of God is at work long before the arrival of the missionaries. Zinzendorf promoted the idea of being encouraged by the firstfruits—the first individuals who come to faith in Christ—rather than being discouraged until large numbers come to faith.

## Keeping It Simple

Zinzendorf encouraged the missionaries to preach a very simple message of Jesus Christ. As noted in an article in *Christian History*, "Zinzendorf assumed the heathen already knew about God, but needed to know of the Savior, particularly his wounds on the cross."[15] He expected his missionaries to preach to the hearts of people and did not encourage philosophical arguments, but rather a straightforward preaching of Christ, his death, resurrection, and the hope he provides. Zinzendorf held to an exclusive message of salvation—that apart from Christ there is no salvation.

## Long-Term Perspective

It was not unheard of or uncommon for missionaries to spend their entire lives working among a particular people in a particular area. Many would make great sacrifices—including prison sentences, the loss of health, and the loss of life—to preach the gospel to people in pioneer areas. For example, it was five years into the work before the Moravian missionaries saw the first convert in Greenland. Initial attempts in Labrador resulted in the deaths of the missionaries.

## Cultural Acquisition and Language Learning

The missionaries immersed themselves in the cultures of the people and sought to learn their languages. They wanted to know how best to communicate the gospel message, and so language learning was, in many cases, done upon arrival. Their incarnational approach to missions led Karl-Wilhelm Westmeier to conclude that among the work done in North America, the missionaries so adapted to Native American ways that at times they were taken to be natives themselves.[16]

## Bible Translations

The Moravians had strong convictions about the significance of the Scriptures. Many of the missionaries sought to understand the languages in the field so that they could translate the Scriptures for the people.

## Missionary Zeal

Great zeal for the Lord in the lives of the Moravians was the powerful force that drove them to leave the comfort of Herrnhut and travel across the globe. J. C. S. Mason also noted that among historians "key reasons for the Moravians' exceptional zeal for service abroad was the extent to which the missions were always an integral part of the whole Church. . . . From the very beginning Zinzendorf ensured that the whole community at Herrnhut participated in decisions which led to the launch of the missions and his successors followed similar practices when general synods were held."[17]

## Priority of Prayer

The Moravians were known for a prayer meeting that lasted for one hundred years. Individuals of the Herrnhut community set aside an hour a day, around the clock, for one hundred years to pray for the missionary laborers of the people.

## Sheep Stealing Not Allowed

As the Moravians went about their missionary activities, no sheep stealing was to be permitted. The aim of the Moravian Church was simply to "win souls for the Lamb."[18] They did not seek to extract believers out of other churches, but rather saw their efforts as a part of the process of bringing the firstfruits into the kingdom. Though they also worked in parts of the world to congregationalize unchurched German Lutherans, Schattschneider stated, "Under no circumstances were the missionaries to proselytize from other Christian groups."[19]

> **"The Moravians not only approved but also expected and regulated self-support on the part of their missionaries."**
>
> —William J. Danker, *Profit for the Lord: Economic Activities in Moravian Missions and the Basel Mission Trading Company* (Grand Rapids, MI: William B. Eerdmans Publishing Company, 1971). 32.

In other words, the focus of the missionary task was on conversion growth. Though the Moravians became a denomination unto themselves, Zinzendorf's plan was never for the Moravians to be a separate denomination, but rather to come alongside other denominations in existence (particularly that of the Lutheran and Anglican Churches) and work to reform the church already in existence. Zinzendorf had a kingdom vision, rather than a desire for denominational expansion.

## Tentmaking Expected

Though Moravian leadership eventually challenged the church at home to support the missionaries and evangelists sent out, the early missionaries went out as tentmakers.[20] Self-support was seen as the expectation of all the missionaries who went out across the globe. Working as potters or merchants or other artisans, the Moravian missionaries supported themselves and their missionary works by the labor of their own hands.

William J. Danker, in his book *Profit for the Lord*, examined the tentmaking practices of the Moravian Church. According to Danker, "The most important contribution of the Moravians was their emphasis that every Christian is a missionary and should witness through his daily vocation. It was their tentmaking platforms that greatly facilitated the dissemination of the gospel. The Brethern selected crafts rather than agriculture because these would give them greater mobility for the missions of the Lamb. And the Moravians matched their artisan missionaries to appropriate fields. This was one reason for their overall success."[21]

## Missionaries as the Norm, Not the Exception

The Moravians saw missions as the normative life of a follower of Christ. So typical was the practice of sending missionaries that Colin A. Grant cited historian A. C. Thompson as writing, "So fully is the duty of evangelizing the heathen lodged in current thought that the fact of anyone entering personally upon that work never creates surprise. . . . It is not regarded as a thing that calls for widespread heralding, as if something marvelous or even unusual were in hand."[22]

## What Was Their Influence on Other Church Planters?

The early Moravian missionary model greatly influenced future generations of church planters. At that time in history, there was no other Protestant model to follow. Tucker noted, "Catholic religious orders were involved in mission enterprises throughout the world, but they were seen as extensions of a powerful religious bureaucracy headquartered in Rome. The Moravians, on the other hand, were more like an independent agency, and the missionaries sent out were sometimes married couples with families. The Moravians, with their mission posts scattered around the world, set an example through trial and error of how actual mission work could be carried out, and their writings were invaluable sources for new agencies that were emerging."[23]

> **"The contribution of the Moravians, beginning half a century before Carey, was to produce a shift of emphasis of missionary awareness within Protestantism."**
>
> —David A. Schattschneider, "William Carey, Modern Mission, and the Moravian Influence," *International Bulletin of Missionary Research* 22 (January 1998): 8.

Though the influence of the Church stretched far and wide, it impacted two individuals probably more than anyone else: William Carey and John Wesley. It was through the friendship and witness of Moravians that John and Charles Wesley were converted.[24] Mulholland noted that Wesley visited Herrnhut to examine their work and then used the Moravians as a model for Methodism, especially adopting Zinzendorf's words as his famous motto: "The world is my parish."[25]

### *Summary:*

1. The Moravians were one of the most significant missionary forces in Church history.
2. Zinzendorf led a small group of Moravians to carry the gospel to some of the most remote places on earth.
3. The Moravians proclaimed a simple gospel message and applied many effective missionary principles to their work.
4. The Moravians did little church planting, but rather saw themselves as working to assist established churches throughout the world, especially the Lutheran and Anglican Churches.
5. The Moravians advocated a mission-station approach to missions.

### *Reflection Questions:*

1. What are the three most important things you learned from this chapter that you can apply to your church-planting activities?
2. Why do you think the Moravians were able to accomplish so much in spreading the gospel with few material resources, little training, and during a time before the technological and scientific advancements of the twenty-first century?

### *Important Terms in This Chapter:*

- Count Ludwig von Zinzendorf
- Herrnhut
- Firstfruits
- Tentmaking

Chapter 17

# METHODIST CHURCH PLANTING ON THE NORTH AMERICAN FRONTIER

**Before the war there were only 4,921 Methodists in America; yet at the end of his life Asbury counted 212,000 of them, mostly recent converts.**

—Martin E. Marty[1]

The beginnings of the Methodist Church extend back to eighteenth-century England with the work of John and Charles Wesley and George Whitefield. All three men were deeply committed to the Anglican Church but were concerned with the lack of zeal and passion for holiness that seemed to be prevalent among its members. After forming a small student organization at Oxford known as the Holy Club in 1737, they soon found themselves leading a renewal movement within the Church. Though **John Wesley** is credited as the father of the global denomination known as the Methodists, throughout his life he never desired to break away from the Anglican Church, but rather work from within to bring reformation.

The witness of the Moravians was instrumental in bringing about Wesley's conversion. During a visit to Herrnhut, he was greatly influenced by their model of life and ministry. Also, the leadership of Whitefield prompted Wesley to use the method of field preaching to spread the gospel among the people of England and Wales. Wesley realized that this unconventional practice could be used for the glory of God; and it would later be used by the Methodists in North America.

By 1739 Wesley had started two Methodist congregations. As a part of this renewal movement he began riding a circuit, making frequent stops to preach to anyone who would listen. These evangelistic messages quickly resulted in many people coming to faith in Christ. Since Wesley did not advocate breaking away from the Church of England, he encouraged these new believers to participate in the local churches' worship and Communion services as well as in weekly, small accountability groups. Along the circuit, Wesley organized new believers into these small groups, or classes, complete with their own lay leaders. According to William Warren Sweet, it was the class meetings and lay preaching that significantly contributed to the growth of Methodism in Great Britain and later in North America.[2] Such classes met each week to hold each member accountable for growth in holiness.

The Methodists were among the migrants moving to the New World. In conjunction with their presence and a growing burden to take the gospel to those living across the ocean, Wesley soon extended a call for individuals to go to the American colonies to preach. Richard Boardman and Joseph Pilmoor were the first English Methodists to go specifically to preach the gospel, thirty years after the first Methodist congregations were planted in England.[3] Though their work marked the official beginning of Methodism in North America, Irish Methodist immigrants were already present in the new land.[4]

Shortly after **Francis Asbury**'s arrival in America in 1771, he began to use the same circuit-riding methodology pioneered by Wesley in England. Riders were sent on preaching circuits, organizing new believers into classes and grouping classes in a particular geographical region into societies. Again, not wishing to separate from the Church of England, Asbury encouraged the new believers to attend regular services with a church in the area, if one was present.

> "Here lies the secret of [Asbury's] greatness—his life was marked by unbroken commitment to and communion with God."
>
> —John T. Wilkinson, "Francis Asbury: 1745–1816," *The London Quarterly and Holborn Review* (July 1966): 217.

The numbers of Methodists grew rapidly in the American colonies and Canada—so much so, that the Church of England was not able to provide enough ordained ministers to serve the people, particularly with the ordinances. Though Wesley was originally opposed to ordaining Methodist clergy, he finally realized that the Church of England was not going to assist the Americans. Coming to believe his ordination was sufficient to ordain others, he provided a means whereby Asbury could be ordained and begin serving as the superintendent (later to be called *bishop*) of the Methodists in America. During the Christmas Conference in Baltimore, Maryland, in 1784, Asbury began serving in this role and led the newly formed Methodist Episcopal Church in America to incredible growth along the frontier.

## Methodist Expansion in Frontier America

By the time of Wesley's death in 1791, the Methodists numbered 79,000 in England and 40,000 in America. By 1957, however, there were 40 million Methodists across the globe.[5] Even a cursory glance at American Church history quickly reveals the rapid growth of the Methodist Church. When Asbury began his work in America, it was estimated that there were approximately 600 American Methodists, but by the time of his death in 1816, there was a well-organized Church with well over 200,000 members.[6] The ratio of American Methodists to the population had grown so quickly that the Methodists were described as the "fastest growing denomination in America."[7]

## Methodist Convictions

There were several Methodist beliefs that helped facilitate the rapid multiplication of churches. As Sweet noted, "The whole organization of Methodism was missionary in purpose with no line of demarcation between missions and evangelism."[8] First, the Methodists believed in preaching a simple gospel message. Methodist preachers focused on clear gospel presentations that could easily be understood by pioneer peoples.

> "God's blessing upon the evangelistic zeal of the itinerant lay preachers soon made Methodism the most influential Protestant force in the United States."
>
> —Paulus Scharpff, *History of Evangelism*, trans. Helga Bender Henry (Grand Rapids, MI: William B. Eerdmans Publishing Company, 1966), 98.

Second, even after the formation of the **Methodist Episcopal Church in America** in 1784, they maintained highly reproducible and simple structures. Local classes and societies were easily formed, and laypeople led such groups in the absence of the circuit preacher.

Third, they believed in the apostolic nature of the missionary. Asbury, as well as the circuit riders under his leadership, functioned in an apostolic role. These men were constantly taking the gospel to the public arenas, beginning new groups of Methodists, and appointing leaders.

Fourth, personal holiness was a significant factor in the lives and work of the Methodists. They believed their fellowship with the Lord was paramount in their lives and ministries. And out of their strong relationship with the Father flowed their zeal and ability to reach others.

## Missionary Methods

Of the different denominations working across the American frontier, the Methodists are one group that allows us easily to discern their missionary methods. Asbury, having been trained under the methodology of Wesley in Great Britain, quickly became discouraged upon arriving in America when he noticed that Methodists were remaining in the cities and not developing circuits. Out of frustration and need, Asbury's organizational genius became forever etched in Church history when he began to apply Wesley's methods to the burgeoning frontier.

**Circuit Riders.** Sweet observed in his monumental *Religion on the American Frontier 1783–1840: The Methodists* that "more than any other single factor, 'itineracy' was responsible for the rapid spread of Methodism throughout the United States in the frontier period."[9] These men enlarged their preaching circuits, thus enlarging the Church, as the frontier boundary was pushed westward. Where settlers were found, there the Methodist circuit riders followed. Circuits generally took weeks to travel, with the average having fifteen to twenty-five preaching points where the riders would stop and proclaim the gospel.[10]

**Camp Meetings.** After attending his first camp meeting in 1800, Asbury recognized that such gatherings for several days of worship and preaching could be used effectively by the Methodists. Though the Church never officially mandated such revival gatherings, for about one hundred years thereafter, such scheduled meetings were used by many circuit riders.[11] Hundreds, sometimes thousands, of people would travel for miles to camp and attend such services to hear the preaching of the gospel.

> **"Asbury was convinced that preachers should go where the gospel was most needed."**
>
> —Mark A. Noll, *A History of Christianity in the United States and Canada* (Grand Rapids, MI: William B. Eerdmans Publishing Company, 1992), 171.

**Class Meetings.** Though the system of class meetings was birthed out of the Methodists' attempt to gather money to pay off debts to build buildings for public preaching, it soon became a way to provide pastoral care to the people.[12] Charles Edward White described the components of this system.

> A Methodist society included all the Methodists in an area. It was divided into groups, or classes, of 12. The people met each week to study the Bible, pray, and report on the state of their souls. Each class had a leader who reported to the preacher in charge of the society. . . .
>
> Because the leaders knew each class member intimately, they could tailor their words to each individual need. The frequent meetings meant that wrong attitudes could be stopped before they developed into sinful actions. In this context of frequent, personal, and loving contact, church discipline became a powerful redemptive force.[13]

This approach of gathering together in small groups across the frontier was a system that required little preparation and was easily adapted to

## Preachers of Poverty

Peter Cartwright was one of the most famous Methodist circuit riders. This colorful character was most instrumental in the planting of many Methodist churches across the American frontier. The following excerpt from his journal reveals the life of poverty that most circuit riders experienced.

> I think I received about forty dollars this year; but many of our preachers did not receive half that amount. These were hard times in those Western wilds; *many*, very *many*, pious and useful preachers were literally starved into a location. I do not mean that they were starved for want of food; for although it was rough, yet the preachers generally got enough to eat. But they did not generally receive in a whole year money enough to get them a suit of clothes; and if people, and preachers too, had not dressed in home-spun clothing, and the good sisters had not made and presented their preachers with clothing, they generally must retire from itinerant life, and go to work and clothe themselves.
>
> Money was very scarce in the country at this early day, but some of the best men God ever made, breasted the storms, endured poverty, and triumphantly planted Methodism in this Western world.

Taken from Peter Cartwright, *Autobiography of Peter Cartwright*, Introduction by Charles L. Wallis (Nashville, TN: Abingdon Press, 1984), 74, italics original.

***Questions to Consider:***

1. Do you believe there was a connection between living this lifestyle of poverty and the rapid planting of Methodist churches across the frontier? Explain.
2. Can you list any contemporary examples of preachers living a life of poverty who are seeing the rapid growth of the Church as a result of their sacrifices?
3. What comforts are you willing to sacrifice to spread the gospel and plant churches?

the American context. The class meetings allowed for ongoing accountability, fellowship, and encouragement, especially in light of the fact that it would generally be several weeks before the circuit-riding preacher could return to meet with the believers.

## Evaluation of Methodist History

The Lord used the early Methodist Church in a powerful way to spread the gospel and multiply churches across the American frontier. There is much to learn from Methodist history that can assist church planters today, regardless of their geographical locations or people groups. Though there are many golden nuggets of truth to gather from our Methodist brothers and sisters of yesteryear, the following are five significant elements that composed their work in the eighteenth and nineteenth centuries.

### Abundant Gospel Sowing

Methodist preaching was directed to the heart. Sermons were filled with calls for repentance and faith in the Lord Jesus. Reflecting on their preaching, Ben Witherington wrote, "The circuit rider knew that every sermon had to be 'preached for a verdict' and every camp meeting had to be treated as a golden opportunity to reach the people for Christ. . . . When one is convinced that but for *this* one sermon or *this* one camp meeting, souls are on the way to hell, it tends to make one take the task at hand very seriously."[14] These preachers not only expected to see the Lord bring people to salvation but also knew that preaching the gospel was necessary for the rapid growth of the Church. Methodist preaching appealed to the freedom of the will to follow Christ. The notion that all people were equal before God and could come to him appealed to the free-spirited, individualistic people of the frontier.[15]

Preaching was typically outside the confines of a comfortable environment. Methodist preachers were always in the highways and hedges, proclaiming the gospel. Asbury is known to have preached in a multitude of places, including homes, barns, taverns, courthouses, prisons, and at public executions.[16] Wherever people were located, there Methodists preached the gospel. They did not wait for the people to come to them, but rather they went to the people.

> "Its preachers were all missionaries. Every one of them 'was an extensionist,' enlarging his field of operations in every possible direction, opening a new preaching place at this point and that, his circuit in this manner growing steadily, until it had to be divided."
>
> —Ezra Squier Tipple, *Francis Asbury: The Prophet of the Long Road* (New York: The Methodist Book Concern, 1916), 191.

## Evangelistic Zeal

Like a wildfire that could not be extinguished, the evangelistic zeal of the early Methodist preachers drove their labors across the American frontier. Despite persecution, sickness, bad weather, hunger, and other dangers facing a lone man on horseback on the frontier, the zeal for the Lord was great among these believers. Their gratitude for salvation and passion to please the Lord and see another person enter into the kingdom motivated them to preach in the highways and byways of the young country.

## Contextualization

Apart from Asbury, many of the circuit riders were Americans.[17] Though Asbury imported the Wesleyan model from Great Britain, he connected it to the people. With people coming to faith who were later sent back to the harvest field as circuit riders, they did not have a steep learning curve regarding understanding the culture and language of the people scattered across the frontier. These preachers knew the people they ministered to because they were of the people.

Peter Cartwright compared the irrelevant and ineffective preaching of the "young missionaries" from the East Coast sent to evangelize the frontier with their "old manuscript sermons, that had been preached, or written, perhaps a hundred years before," with the effective work of the Methodists. He commented, "The great mass of our Western people wanted a preacher that could mount a stump, a block, or old log, or stand in the bed of a wagon, and without note or manuscript, quote, expound, and apply the word of God to the hearts and consciences of the people."[18]

> **"The denomination grew, not because it was well organized, but because its preachers were well endowed with holy energy and an unction from on high."**
>
> —Ezra Squier Tipple, *Francis Asbury: The Prophet of the Long Road* (New York: The Methodist Book Concern, 1916), 184.

## Sacrifice

The call to be a circuit rider was a call to great sacrifice. Many circuit riders, including Asbury, never married. Such a lifestyle was so difficult that half of the Methodist circuit riders died before the age of thirty-three.[19] It is well known that Asbury traveled approximately 300,000 miles on horseback or carriage during his lifetime. Such men were willing to risk safety, comfort, convenience, pleasures, and their very lives to see the gospel spread rapidly and churches multiplied across the frontier.

## Simple Organization

Though the Methodist Episcopal Church in America did have Asbury as a bishop—who assumed the responsibility for the Methodists in America—the Methodist system allowed for classes to be started and grow with ease. It was streamlined, easily adaptable to the context, and expanded without much difficulty. In many cases, a circuit rider would come into a new community only to discover that the local Methodist farmer was already gathering his neighbors into his cabin for weekly preaching services. The simple organization of the class system allowed for growth without a great deal of oversight by the circuit rider. The local lay leadership was responsible for the people under its care.

Though the circuit riders did receive an annual income, it was only a bare minimum; all circuit riders, including Asbury, received the same amount.[20] There were no educational requirements for Methodist preachers, like those required by the Presbyterians of the day. Early Methodist circuit-riding candidates were scrutinized according to the four questions: (1) Is this man truly converted? (2) Does he know and follow the Methodist rules? (3) Does he do a good job preaching? and (4) Does he have a horse?[21]

## Reflection on Why the Growth Slowed

Some scholars who have examined the birth, growth, and decline of Methodism have commented on the fact that the rapid growth of the Church began to slow when the Church transitioned from the apostolic work of the circuit rider to focus more on the established ministry of the pastorate. Colin Brummitt Goodykuntz observed: "The itinerant preacher riding the circuit continued to be the principal missionary agency of this Church, but it was noticeable, however, as time passed that there was a growing tendency for the circuit riders to become settled pastors; furthermore, as Methodism grew in strength and popularity it lost some of its early fervor. Bishops sounded the warning against these changes and declared that Methodism would lose its power unless it retained the methods and institutions under which it had made such rapid progress."[22]

Though the established church must focus on healthy pastoral ministries, it is not to do so to the detriment of the apostolic work of the church. The shifting from a missional mode to a maintenance mode is commonplace among new churches and denominations. However, both wings of an airplane are required for proper flight; both a pastoral emphasis and an apostolic zeal are necessary for healthy kingdom churches.

## Summary:

1. Within a short period of time, Methodists became the largest denomination in America, growing mainly through conversion growth.
2. Francis Asbury's leadership in adopting Wesley's model was instrumental in planting Methodist churches across the frontier.
3. Circuit-riding preachers, camp meetings, and the class system were important methods in the work.
4. The Methodists' zeal for evangelism, proper contextualization, willingness to make significant sacrifices, and simple organization all contributed to the rapid planting of churches.

## *Reflection Questions:*

1. What aspects of the Methodist work on the American frontier can be applied to church planting in your context?
2. Why do you believe the circuit riders had such a great zeal for evangelism?
3. Do you agree with some scholars who believe that one of the causative agents leading to the decline in Methodism was the move from an apostolic to a pastoral emphasis? If so, what could have been done to prevent such stagnation?

## *Important Terms in This Chapter:*

- John Wesley
- Francis Asbury
- Methodist Episcopal Church in America
- Circuit riders
- Camp meetings
- Class meetings

Chapter 18

# BAPTIST CHURCH PLANTING ON THE NORTH AMERICAN FRONTIER

Baptists achieved an unprecedented growth. By 1844 the total membership was 720,046 with 9,386 churches and 6,364 ministers. This represented an increase of 360 per cent in thirty years, whereas the population of the United States had increased only 140 per cent in that period of time.

—Robert G. Torbet[1]

It has been said that the westward movement of settlers across the frontier of the United States in the 1700s and 1800s was a Baptist movement.[2] Today Baptist church buildings are located across all fifty states. How did the Baptists begin as a small and, at times, a persecuted sect to become the largest Protestant denomination in the United States within such a short period of time?[3] It is the purpose of this chapter to take a look at the eighteenth and nineteenth centuries to find answers to this question.

The literature concerning the Baptists on the American frontier during this time contains little detailed information regarding the methods used to plant churches. For example, it is common to find historians and sociologists recording scant descriptions addressing frontier church planting, leaving out the details important for our study: "They rented a school-room, and commenced teaching; while for want of better accommodations, they occupied the same room on the Sabbath and on Wednesday evening for preaching. In February, they constituted a small church. In April, they baptized several candidates, for the first time."[4] However, despite these limitations, there is sufficient information available to piece together a picture of the various methods used by those Baptists.

## Overarching Factors

Before examining these methods, it is necessary to understand the overarching factors contributing to church planting on the frontier. These spiritual, contextual, and institutional factors worked together for the growth of the Baptist churches.

> "Baptist farmer-preachers came with the people because they *were* the people."
>
> —Roger Finke and Rodney Stark, *The Churching of America, 1776–1990: Winners and Losers in Our Religious Economy* (New Brunswick, NJ: Rutgers University Press, 1992), 79, italics original.

### Migration

As a missiologist, I would like to write that all the Baptist growth across the frontier was an organized missional matter resulting from a strategic approach to take the gospel to the frontier and that the number of churches multiplied throughout the West from intentional evangelistic efforts. However, such a romantic notion of yesteryear would not be accurate. Though the rise of mission societies contributed to organized missionary activity, much of the initial Baptist work across the frontier occurred as the Lord worked primarily through the economy of the day.

The major factor drawing many pioneers away from the east and toward the west was economics. Baptists, including preachers, were no exception to this norm, as H. Leon McBeth observed: "The mass migration through the Cumberland Gap in the late 1770s included a number of Baptists, many of them Separates from Virginia. . . . As migration increased, Baptist churches sprang up rapidly. By 1790 at least 43 Baptist churches existed in Kentucky, with 3,209 members."[5]

Many of the churches planted across the frontier were planted because Baptists were moving westward in search of land and a better way of life. Though not all Baptists traveled westward planting churches as the result of quality-of-life issues, many did.

## Awakening

The First Great Awakening that swept through America in the 1730s and 1740s fueled the growth of the Baptists. In fact, McBeth wrote that the Awakening was the "Matterhorn" of the 1700s for the Baptists.[6] A great evangelistic zeal permeated the churches that resulted in much conversion growth. Many pastors ventured out on evangelistic preaching tours and planted churches.

## Farmer-Preacher

Frontier church planters were far from being understood as professional ministers. It was possibly William Sweet who first described the typical Baptist frontier church planter as the "farmer-preacher," noting that he was the one who was responsible for almost all of the Baptist work on the frontier until the formation of the Baptist Home Mission Society in 1832.[7] According to Sweet, "The typical Baptist preacher of the early frontier came from the ranks of the people, among whom he lived and to whom he preached. He was a farmer and worked on his land five or six days each week, except when he was called upon to hold week-day meetings or funerals. He preached on Sunday and not infrequently during the week. He generally was without much education, for not only was there little opportunity for him to obtain an education, but there was a deep-seated prejudice against educated and salaried preachers."[8]

Though committed to the Lord, preaching his good news, and planting churches, the farmer-preacher was a simple man who primarily lived and worked among the people he served. Describing John Taylor, a pioneer Baptist, Chester Raymond Young commented that he "lived out his calling as a man of the cloth and as a tiller of the soil."[9]

The ministry of the farmer-preacher was an incarnational ministry and appropriately contextualized in every way. The Baptists were able to experience such tremendous growth on the frontier partly because the farmer-preacher was from the people and of the people. For a description of the nature of these men, see the insert "Keeping It Real with the People."

## Baptist Beliefs

Entire books have been written addressing Baptist theology. Beside these books is a second listing of books that reveals the theological differences among Baptist groups throughout Church history. At the risk of being reductionistic, and since this chapter is not primarily about Baptist theology, it is necessary for me to briefly list the general distinctives of a Bapitst church. Since theology drives and supports church growth methodology, it is important to understand, at least generally, the convictions behind the expansion of the Baptists across the American frontier.

## Keeping It Real with the People

In their book, *The Churching of America, 1776–1990*, sociologists Roger Finke and Rodney Stark attempt to explain the rapid growth of the pioneer Baptists and Methodists. The following excerpt is an excellent summary contrasting the nature of the Baptist and Methodist ministers with those of the more-established denominations of the time.

> The organizational forms used by the Baptists and the Methodists were quite different, but their clergy were nearly interchangeable. In both denominations, ministers primarily came from the ranks of the common folk and to a very important extent, remained common folk. Unlike the Congregational, Presbyterian, and Episcopalian ministers, who typically were of genteel origin and were highly trained and well educated, the Baptist and Methodist clergy were of the people. They had little education, received little if any pay, spoke in the vernacular, and preached from the heart.
>
> The local preacher for either of the upstart sects was a neighbor, friend, or relative of many of the people he served. Although this may have meant that the clergy held the same prejudices as did their flocks—and thus hampered the prophetic role of religion—it fostered a close relationship between the minister and the people in the pews. The minister shared the wants, needs, and desires of the people, and he made every effort possible to share the same religion too.

Taken from Roger Finke and Rodney Stark, *The Churching of America, 1776–1990: Winners and Losers in Our Religious Economy* (New Brunswick, NJ: Rutgers University Press, 1992), 75–76.

***Questions to Consider:***

1. What are the advantages and disadvantages of ministers coming "from the ranks of the common folk"?
2. Finke and Stark pointed out that early Baptists remained with the common folk. What do you believe are the things that transition ministers away from the common folk?
3. What are the advantages of theological education and having paid ministers? Are there any disadvantages?
4. What can we learn from the description of the pioneer Baptists that we can apply to a twenty-first-century context?

Borrowing from R. Stanton Norman's work, *The Baptist Way: Distinctives of a Baptist Church*, here are the typical Baptist beliefs:

- Biblical authority: The Bible is the revelation of God to mankind and is the source of guidance for both belief and practice on both the personal level and local church level.
- Lordship of Jesus Christ: Christ is the head of the Church, and his followers are to submit to his rule over their lives.
- Regenerate church membership: All true members of the Church are to have a personal conversion experience to Christ (i.e., be born again).
- Church discipline: The local church is to teach and correct its members according to the Bible.
- Congregational polity: The local church governs itself (i.e., congregational government that views all regenerate members as priests) as guided by the Bible, the Holy Spirit, and its leaders.
- Universal Church and local church: The universal Church contains the followers of Jesus throughout history and the contemporary world; the local church is the autonomous, local expression of the universal Church whereby its members are united together by a covenant in the Lord.
- Church leaders: Each local expression of the universal Church has its own servant leaders of pastor(s)/elder(s) and deacons.
- Ordinances: Baptism by immersion, following conversion (i.e., believer's baptism), and the Lord's Supper (i.e., Communion) are the two ordinances of the church.
- Religious freedom: People are free to practice their faith without government interference.[10]

## Baptist Church Growth on the Frontier

Baptist church growth in the 1700s and 1800s was incredible. Though different scholars record slightly different statistics, the general trend of significant growth is evident. Robert G. Gardner's work on Baptist history reveals that in 1740 Baptists numbered 3,142 members with 60 churches. However, by 1790 they had grown to 67,857 members and 987 churches.[11] J. H. Spencer recorded that by 1790, there were 65,233 Baptists in America with 927 churches.[12] Roger Finke and Rodney Stark recorded that the Baptists claimed to have numbered 65,345 members by 1790, but swelled to 172,972 members by 1810.[13] Commenting on thirty years of growth from 1814 to 1844, Robert G. Torbet wrote that Baptists grew by 360 percent, achieving a membership of 720,046 with 9,385 churches.[14] Such church growth outstripped the population growth of the United States during this same period, which was 140 percent.

> **"The evangelical groups such as Methodists and Baptists gained more converts on the frontier and enlarged their membership in the West more than the more formal and conservative churches because they met the needs of the people they served and were more truly adapted to the character of the people in the more primitive parts of our country."**
>
> —Spencer Bidwell King Jr., "The Baptist Role in Winning the West," *Baptist History and Heritage* 6, no. 3 (July 1971): 145.

Though such overall numbers can be helpful in discerning Baptist growth, more specific information is helpful as well. Spencer noted that by 1790 the population of the state of Kentucky was 73,677, with Baptists numbering 3,105 among 42 churches. Statistically speaking, this means there was approximately 1 Baptist for every 24 Kentuckians.[15] On another note, the Sandy Creek Church planted in North Carolina in

1755 began with 16 members. Within three years, the church had grown to 606 members.[16]

> **"In 1700 Baptists had only a few scattered churches in America; by 1800 they had become the largest denomination in the land."**
>
> —H. Leon McBeth, *The Baptist History: Four Centuries of Baptist Witness* (Nashville, TN: Broadman Press, 1987), 152.

## Church-Planting Methods

An examination of the historical accounts found in primary and secondary writings reveals a number of different church-planting methods used by the Baptists. It should be stated that not all of these methods began with evangelism. However, for the most part, those planting the churches were very evangelistic and led congregations in evangelism. An examination of the statistics in the previous section reveals that the Baptists grew substantially through conversion growth.

### Mother Churches

There were numerous churches planted on the frontier that quickly became mother churches, working to plant other congregations. Some of the first Baptists who settled in North Carolina were involved in planting several churches. One account tells of William Sojourner moving from Virginia with several others in 1742. They settled on Kehukee Creek in Halifax, where they planted a church. Within ten years this congregation became the mother of sixteen other churches.[17] Severns Valley Church in Elizabethtown, Kentucky, constituted in 1781, was involved in planting so many churches that historian J. H. Spencer wrote, "Old Severns Valley is the mother of a multitude."[18]

Though the story is told time and again in various locations, perhaps the most famous example of a mother church is Sandy Creek Church in North Carolina. Eighteenth-century historian Morgan Edwards noted, "Sandy Creek church is the mother of all the Separate-baptists. From this Zion went forth the word, and great was the company of them who published it: it, in 17 years, has spread branches westward as far as the great river Mississippi; southward as far as Georgia; eastward to the sea and Chesopeck bay; and northward to the waters of Potowmack; it, in 17 years, is become mother, grand-mother, and great grandmother to 42 churches, from which sprang 125 ministers."[19]

There were two significant ways in which mother congregations gave birth to daughter churches: "hiving off" and "arms and branches."

## Hiving Off

C. Peter Wagner suggested that "hiving off" occurs when a group of believers from a mother church harmoniously and intentionally separates from that church to begin another congregation in a different location.[20] For example, in 1795 Stamping Ground Church of Scott County, Kentucky, hived off Great Crossing Church with thirty-five members. It began meeting in a local home and constituted as a church in September 1795.[21]

## Arms and Branches

Until certain churches constituted as independent congregations, separate from their mother churches, they remained an arm of the parent church. For example, Sandy Creek Church in North Carolina would establish "arms" whenever a man was not ready for ordination but was licensed as a preacher.[22] These arm congregations remained under the care of the mother churches until they developed a separate identity.

In 1762 Ezekiel Hunter made evangelistic trips to Lockwood's Folly in North Carolina, where he baptized some people and planted a church in that location. Since this congregation was without a pastor, Hunter organized this church as a "branch" of the New River church. Three years later Hunter planted another church that established two branch congregations—one at White Swamp in Bladen County and the other at Livingston's Creek in Brunswick.[23]

> **"Not only was the time favorable, but the Baptists had within themselves qualities and ideals which gave impetus to their progress."**
>
> —Robert G. Torbet, *A History of the Baptists*, 3rd ed. (Valley Forge, PA: Judson Press, 1963), 244.

## Traveling Churches

As Baptists migrated westward, history records that churches migrated together from the east to the west, replanting themselves on the frontier with their original pastors. Two examples of this method include Gilberts Creek Church and Providence Church, both from Virginia and replanted in Kentucky. Commenting on Gilberts Creek, Baptist pioneer John Taylor recorded that in 1781 "they were a church as they came along. And where they settled down on Gilberts Creek in Lincoln County, they were an organized church at once."[24]

## Colonialization

The term describing this method was used by C. Peter Wagner in his book *Church Planting for a Greater Harvest.*[25] Though similar to the traveling church method, colonialization requires people to move, resettle, and *then gather* together as a new church in the new location. The story of Sandy Creek Church is one example of this method and its missional impact on the surrounding area: "Soon after arriving, the little group of new settlers was organized into a church which took the name Sandy Creek, and Stearns was appointed the pastor. Stearns, Marshall and Joseph Reed, another preacher in the Sandy Creek church, were soon engaged in evangelizing throughout a wide territory. The Sandy Creek church grew from sixteen members to six hundred six; and other churches were formed. New converts at Abbott's Creek, thirty miles away, were formed into a church and Marshall was ordained as its pastor."[26]

## Nonprofessional Church Planters

Many Baptists were involved in church planting who had not been theologically educated. Many churches were planted by men from among the churches who sensed God's leadership in this area of life and had manifested gifts of exhortation as confirmed by their congregations. It was not unheard of for a group of Baptists to begin gathering for study, encouragement, and worship without a designated elder or elders. Though some groups remained without pastoral leadership for a few years, Baptists usually were quick to recognize the need to make official designations of themselves as churches with their own pastors. It was also common practice for a congregation to form and later call one of its members to serve as the pastor.

In 1788–1789 a group of settlers from New Jersey arrived in Ohio. Several of them had been members of the Baptist church at Scotch Plains in Essex County. Sweet described the beginnings of the new church in Ohio: "Among these settlers were several outstanding leaders, chief of whom were Judge Goforth and General John Gano of New York, and, although they had no minister at this early period, they began at once to hold divine worship, the leaders taking turns in conducting the service. The next year, 1790, the Reverend Stephen Gano, pastor of the First Baptist Church of Providence, Rhode Island, visited the settlement and organized a church, at the same time baptizing three converts. This was the first Baptist church in the Northwest Territory."[27]

> "With the exception of the anti-mission Baptists, the frontier churches were eager to evangelize."
>
> —Robert G. Torbet, *A History of the Baptists*, 3rd ed. (Valley Forge, PA: Judson Press, 1963), 358.

## Missional Pastors

It was common for pastors of established churches on the frontier to be involved in church planting. Some pastors were periodically sent out on itinerant evangelistic trips into other communities for several weeks to preach and plant churches. Pastor Hezekiah Smith spent several weeks each year in the pioneer areas, preaching the gospel and planting churches.[28] These missional pastors were significant in beginning many new works across the frontier. John Whitaker, the planter and first pastor of Bear Grass Church in Kentucky, assisted in constituting most of the early churches planted within fifty miles of Louisville.[29]

## Plant and Pastor

Many Baptist churches were started by individuals who would immediately become the pastors of those churches. Joseph Bledsoe planted and became the first pastor of Wilderness Church in Spottsylvania County, Virginia, in 1778.[30] In 1781, on the same day, Severns Valley Church in Elizabethtown, Kentucky, constituted and ordained John Gerrard as its first pastor.[31]

## Gather the Scattered

As Baptists migrated westward in search of land and a better way of life, many soon found themselves isolated from other Baptists and from fellowship. Some men began to gather these scattered Baptists into churches across the frontier. Spencer poetically described the work of such leaders.

> Marshall, Craig, Cave, Smith, Barnett, Whitaker and Lynn had been tried in the relentless fires of persecution and purified as silver. Inured to hardships and dangers, they had lost the sense of earthly fear, and were prepared to surmount every difficulty, that they might gather into folds Christ's scattered sheep, and feed them with the bread of life. They were traversing the wilderness in search of the straying lambs, and calling them together to partake again of the heavenly feast of love and fellowship, which they had so sweetly enjoyed in the now far away churches of their native land.[32]

The origins of Bear Grass Church in Kentucky where John Whitaker planted and pastored for many years is another example of the gathering of the scattered Baptists.

> In this large diocese John Whitaker labored alone, save when some preacher came from afar to assist him. One of his preaching points was about six miles east of Louisville. Here he collected the scattered Baptists from the surrounding settlements, and, in January, 1784, with the aid of James Smith, solemnly constituted them a church, under the style of the Baptist church on Bear Grass.
>
> Bear Grass was not only the first, but for a period of more than eight years, the only church in Jefferson County, or within thirty miles of Louisville.[33]

### Associations

As the number of Baptist churches across the frontier increased, usually those churches would gather together to form associations for fellowship, accountability, encouragement, cooperation, and evangelism. According to McBeth, such associations partnered together to plant other churches, noting that by the 1760s the Philadelphia Association employed an "evangelist at large" who traveled to needy areas functioning as a church planter.[34]

> "Frontier preachers generally supported themselves with some help from their congregations. This assistance was more often in goods and labor (e.g. help with harvest) than in cash. There was a widespread Baptist opposition to salaried clergy at the time."
>
> —Jeffrey Wayne Taylor, "Daniel Parker (1781–1844): Frontier Baptist Warrior for the Old Way," *Baptist History and Heritage* 32, no. 2 (April 1997): 60.

## What We Can Learn

A critical reflection on the work of the frontier Baptists reveals several important matters for contemporary missionaries. First, Baptists have always been a "people of the Book." Their high view of the Bible served as a foundation for taking the gospel to others. Though they did not appear to have a highly delineated theology of evangelism and missions, they sought to be obedient to the Lord's plan in taking the gospel to all the world.

Second, Baptists used a highly contextualized approach to their ministries. Their ministers held many sociocultural commonalities with the people they preached to and pastored. The gospel usually travels the fastest when the missionary does not have to cross significant cultural barriers. Baptist preachers lived, worked, played, and traveled with the people they served. Such preachers were of one heart and mind with the people.

Third, and closely related to the previous point, Baptists kept church and ministry simple compared to other denominations at the time. For example, the Congregationalists, Presbyterians, and Episcopalians required sophisticated organizational structures that operated with high overhead, and they educated their ministers to a level of expertise that focused on realities far removed from the needs of the frontier people. The Baptists (and Methodists), however, were able to move quickly with the gospel and plant churches because their ecclesiology did not require those complicated expectations of what constituted "legitimate" churches and ministers.[35] Also, these simpler Baptist methods were more in keeping with the culture of the frontier, which was less formal and structured than the towns and cities of the east.

Fourth, Baptists maintained the ecclesiological perspective that the local church—while interdependent with other Baptist churches—was fully autonomous. Under the leadership of the Holy Spirit, Baptists believed that the local church should be self-governing. This congregational form of church government appealed to the frontier demography and allowed Baptists to make local and quick decisions about ministry issues. Rather than wait for direction from a bishop or presbyter who lived miles away in another state, Baptists had everything they needed for carrying out the ministry through the local churches in their communities.

### *Summary:*

1. Though they began with few in number, Baptists quickly became the largest denomination in the United States.
2. Migration, the First Great Awakening, and the farmer-preacher were three significant means that the Lord used to rapidly multiply Baptist churches across the frontier.
3. The typical farmer-preacher was a man from among the people he served.

4. There were several church-planting methods used by Baptists on the American frontier.
5. A biblical foundation, evangelistic zeal, simple ecclesiology, and healthy contextualization are four principles that guided the multiplication of Baptist churches.

### *Reflection Questions:*

1. Do you believe that such church multiplication can still happen today? Do you believe that it can happen in Western countries? Explain.
2. Which of the methods (if any) used on the frontier would be appropriate for your context? Why?
3. Do you think it was a healthy approach for some Baptists on the frontier to begin churches with people who were already believers, rather than by evangelism that led to new churches? Explain. What are the limitations (if any) of starting with believers?

### *Important Terms in This Chapter:*

- Farmer-preacher
- Hiving off
- Arms and branches
- Traveling churches
- Colonialization

Section IV

# DISCOVERING CONTEMPORARY ISSUES

In this final section you will discover some contemporary matters related to global church planting. Obviously, there are other issues that need to be addressed by twenty-first-century church planters, but space limitations required that I only mention a few. However, these few are very significant in the lives of church planters. Chapter nineteen raises the issue of the blessings and stressors on the church-planting family. Chapter twenty categorizes a few common church-planting models and provides a framework to evaluate contemporary models. All church planters will face objections to their ministries. Therefore, chapter twenty-one lists and responds to the most common objections and will assist you in being better prepared in responding to others. Chapter twenty-two addresses the global phenomenon of urbanization. The majority of the world's population lives in cities, and, unfortunately, the Church has not done very well in reaching it. In no way does the inclusion of this chapter diminish the importance of church planting in rural contexts, where the need is still great. However, the challenge of the world's cities is such a pressing matter today that a specific chapter is warranted. Chapter twenty-three introduces you to the importance of tentmaking as a significant strategy for global disciple making. Chapter twenty-four attempts to respond to the question, What are church planters? Here I discuss the place of the missionaries who plant and pastor churches and the apostolic missionaries who raise up pastors from the harvest. While the former is the predominate model in the United States, the need of the hour is for the latter model to be the norm, especially in Western contexts. This book concludes with a chapter devoted to church-planting movements. This ubiquitous concept permeates the minds and hearts of most church planters. In this chapter, I address some general information related to such movements while discussing their possibilities in the West.

Chapter 19

# FAMILY MATTERS AND CHURCH PLANTING

**If the family isn't behind the vision, then God is telling the prospective church planter that the time for planting a church isn't right.**

**—Aubrey Malphurs[1]**

Several years ago I did an informal study to identify the most critical issues facing North American church planters. A survey of 190 church planters representing thirteen different churches, parachurch organizations, and denominations revealed that these families were feeling stress from the ministry.[2] Shortly after that study, I decided to begin raising the matter to the attention of church planters and their families before they enter the field. Since the time of that study, I have been pleased to notice that other churches and denominations have been attempting to address family matters related to church-planting work.

Having worked with and equipped scores of church planters over the last decade, I have been concerned with the fact that some church-planting husbands tend to be so focused on the ministry that they neglect their wives and children in the process. What also troubles me is that in some North American contexts, the family is not seen as a part of the missionary team, but rather as a secondary importance to the work. However, outside of the North American context a different picture exists. The family is generally identified, trained, equipped, and sent to serve as a missionary family by churches and mission agencies. This represents a much more holistic understanding of the family and its relationship to missionary activities.

In this chapter I hope to raise several issues related to the family and global church planting. Families serving the Lord in all areas of ministry will be subject to intense spiritual warfare. But those families serving in the trenches in the domain of the kingdom of darkness will experience an even greater amount of opposition. If the Evil One can tear down the family, he will destroy the church-planting work.

> "Church planting is the hardest thing that I have ever done. The only thing that keeps me going is knowing that I am doing exactly what God wants me to do and I am in the exact place He wants me to be."
>
> —Ellie from Port St. Lucie, Florida, in *My Husband Wants to Be a Church Planter: So What Will That Make Me?* comps. and eds. John M. Bailey and Sherri Jachelski (Alpharetta, GA: North American Mission Board, 2007), 28.

## General Considerations

Before heading to the field as missionaries, future church planters should spend significant time in extended conversations with church-planting families, listening to the good, the bad, and the ugly about life on the field. Rather than blindly entering into the church-planting trenches, families need to seek the wisdom of those who have gone before them in such kingdom endeavors. As much as possible, I have included in this chapter several comments from church-planting families addressing a variety of matters.

## The Highs and Lows

I hate roller coasters. Period. I recently went to an amusement park with my family and rode a "kiddie" roller coaster with my oldest daughter. Though I did not reveal my feelings to her, I felt very nervous. As soon as we sat down on the seat, I had flashbacks to my childhood when I rode Space Mountain at Walt Disney World. I cannot adequately describe that horrible experience! The up-and-down, jolting rides on these torture devices are experiences that I can easily do without. Let me ride It's a Small World, and I'll be fine . . . assuming I don't get seasick.

Church planting is like a spiritual roller-coaster ride. An examination of the apostle Paul's letters reveals great elation coupled with the immense disappointment and concern regarding the new churches. I have heard contemporary church planters note that the spiritual highs and lows are both incredible and frequent. One church planter shared with my students that the highs were some of the greatest highs he had ever experienced in his walk with the Lord; but he quickly followed up with, "And the lows are some of the greatest lows that I have ever experienced in my faith."

The family entering into church-planting ministry must realize that the ups and downs will soon become a reality for them. When boarding the roller-coaster ride of church planting, they need to make certain that everyone fastens their seat belts.

## Top Struggles for Wives

Few research findings have been published addressing the interpersonal issues regarding church-planting families. More research needs to be conducted and disseminated to assist those preparing for the mission field. In an attempt to better prepare church-planting families, my mission agency—the North American Mission Board of the Southern Baptist Convention—conducted an extensive survey of church-planting wives in the United States and Canada and used the findings as the basis for the book *My Husband Wants to Be a Church Planter: So What Will That Make Me?*[3] This incredibly valuable resource provides a glimpse into family life, especially how this missionary work affects wives.

> **"Before starting, the couple must discuss the financial pressures and spiritual strength necessary to endure difficulty in this task or there will be conflict in the marriage."**
>
> —Church planter in Georgia.

Using an online survey and telephone interviews, the researchers were able to identify the ten most commonly occurring areas of struggle for wives. After compiling this list, a second online poll was conducted of church-planting wives, asking them to rank (with 1 being the highest and 10 being the lowest) the issues they struggled with the most. The following is the list of struggles, ranked from the greatest to the least.

1. Personal finances
2. Feeling overwhelmed with needs/responsibilities
3. Time management/priorities
4. Boundaries between home life and church life
5. Effect of church plant on the family
6. Lack of time with husband
7. Loneliness/isolation
8. Lack of emotional/spiritual support from local churches
9. Criticism/rejection from individuals
10. Understanding your role as the wife of a church planter[4]

Families preparing for the field, especially in the United States and Canada, need to discuss these issues among themselves, their church-planting teams, partnering churches, and supervisors. The findings from these church-planting wives can provide guidance for future missionaries to the field.

## The Blessings

The blessings of being a church-planting family are too numerous to mention. Though the challenges are great, the study by the North American Mission Board noted that 85 percent of the church-planting wives surveyed believed that church planting had a positive effect on their children.[5] Children have the opportunity to be involved in kingdom advancement in such a way that they would generally not be allowed in many established ministries. Church planters typically have flexible schedules to meet the needs of the context. Many families enjoy freedom from the time constraints of a 9-to-5 job. The family is able to be involved in seeing people come out of the kingdom of darkness and begin to grow in the faith. Dave Smith noted, "In church planting, you set the culture. So make it as family friendly as possible."[6] Since biblical church planting is evangelism that results in new churches, church planters and their families can avoid all the traditional expectations placed on ministers by longtime church members, because most new believers do not have such assumptions.

> "I remember how alone, helpless, and weary I felt at times in the early days. But, hindsight is a reminder that the Lord has been faithful from the beginning and will see us to the end."
>
> —Francis Hale, quoted in Arnell ArnTessoni, *Gentle Plantings: A Personal Journal for Church Planters' Wives* (Concordville, PA: The Church Planter's Network, 2001), 71.

## Personal Considerations

In addition to the general considerations, it is important that you take some time to think through some personal matters. As you read through the rest of this chapter, prayerfully consider how these issues apply to your family. Use these concepts as starting points for conversations with your family to prepare everyone for working effectively together in the harvest field you have been called to by God.

### Don't Neglect Your Personal Time with God

You might think that advanced theological education automatically causes seminary students to spend significant amounts of time alone with God and his Word. Unfortunately, many times the opposite situation is the case. Students can easily attend church-planting classes, spend a great amount of time studying theology, missiology, and methods, but never spend any time on their faces before God. This terrible neglect often translates to the mission field. Church planters get so caught up in making great sacrifices for God that they fail to maintain a daily quiet time in the Scriptures and in prayer. We easily forget that the Lord would rather have obedience than sacrifice (1 Samuel 15:22). Church planters who neglect their daily times alone with God eventually see the negative effects of this omission in their personal lives and, naturally, their families.

### Home Life Does Not Have to Be Perfect . . . Just Next to Perfect

The church-planting family follows in the footsteps of the apostle Paul when he wrote to the Corinthians, "Be imitators of me, as I am of Christ" (1 Corinthians 11:1). Even though Paul was very transparent and willing to admit his shortcomings (Romans 7:14–25; Philippians 3:12–14), he also recognized that as a church planter he *was* the model of the Christian life to the people.

## A Tragic Ending

Debbie Millman has been involved in church planting for many years. In her writing "Where Does the Church End and Our Home Begin," she shared the unfortunate story of a couple who began their work with great passion, but lost their marriage in the end.

> Early in our ministry, my husband and I knew a couple who planted a church. They put everything they had into it. The church met in their home for the first year. Eventually, they started meeting in a local school, but the pastor's office was still at the house. His cell phone and pager were always on just in case anything might come up. (And a lot came up!) He barely took a day off. The family income was used to finance many aspects of the church. His wife worked full-time, served as the church secretary, and directed the children's ministry. Their hearts for lost people were as big as Texas, so they gave it their all. She felt neglected. He went into a deep depression. Today, our friends are divorced.

Taken from Debbie Millman, "Where Does the Church End and Our Home Begin," in *My Husband Wants to Be a Church Planter: So What Will That Make Me?* comps. and eds. John M. Bailey and Sherri Jachelski (Alpharetta, GA: North American Mission Board, 2007), 73.

***Questions to Consider:***

1. What was your initial reaction to Millman's brief account?
2. At what point does zeal and sacrifice for kingdom advancement become problematic?
3. Though some issues cannot be known before entering the field, what are some boundaries that you and your family need to establish before beginning your missionary work?
4. What do you think this couple should have done differently to help avoid such a tragic ending? If you are married, what does your spouse think this couple should have done differently? Do your responses differ? If so, why?

No, missionaries should not wait until their family life is perfect before they hit the field. But, like Paul, they should be transparent and reveal certain struggles in order to better equip others. However, missionaries must not go into the thick of the battle with deep and significant problems that will surface when the marriage comes under the pressure of spiritual warfare and the daily challenges of the ministry. Church-planting families are models to others. Joyce Jackson, who has been involved in church planting for several years, was correct when she warned, "A healthy marriage matters in a church plant; it is one of the critical factors that will determine the survivability of a new work. Those who attempt a new work with unresolved marital issues only add to their problems. Remember, even a healthy marriage will experience stress resulting from the unique pressures of church planting."[7]

## If Your Family Falls, the Church-Planting Work Falls Even Harder

A Vineyard church planter once told me, "Burning out for Jesus stinks, especially when it is not just the church planters who burn out but their wife and kids, too. . . . My wife and kids come before my ministry and always will. After God, they are my highest priority. The people who plant with me need to see this demonstrated." Missionaries everywhere need to heed such counsel.

> **"Rather, success should be measured by the well-being of the whole family in the midst of effective participation in the Great Commission."**
>
> —Tom Steffen and Lois McKinney Douglas, *Encountering Missionary Life and Work: Preparing for Intercultural Ministry* (Grand Rapids, MI: Baker Academic, 2008), 276.

It is always a tragedy when a marriage ends. Not only is it a sin against a holy God, but the future ramifications of such sin will affect many people for years to come. When the marriage of a leader in the

Church is severely strained or ends, however, the ripple effect of negative consequences is even greater. Church planters must realize that if their family falls apart on the mission field, the shockwaves of detriment to the church-planting work will be devastating not only to the immediate ministry but also to the new believers, their family members, unbelievers in their social networks, and the general community at large. The collapse of a family will hinder the faith of the individuals and families in the church. "If the gospel is not able to keep the marriage of such spiritual giants together," many will incorrectly assume, "then there is little hope for any of us." The credibility and witness of the church-planting team and the new church in the community will be decimated if the family in leadership breaks apart.

> "Relational stress on families is great. Church planters often move into areas where they have no relational support networks."
>
> —Church Planter in Washington State, U.S.A.

## Take Days of Rest and Be with Your Family

Church planters are some of the most devoted and hardest-working servants in the kingdom. We should praise God for their commitments to the Lord and his Great Commission. However, such zeal unchecked by God's Word and accountability easily devolves into workaholism. The command of the Sabbath also applies to church planters (Exodus 20:8–11). Many church planters learn obedience to this command the hard way. Lindsay Rohr shared her shortcomings: "At first, we worked so hard we didn't take a day off for weeks at a time. After about a year, we started falling apart. . . . God knows us better than we know ourselves."[8] A weekly day of rest with the family is critical to a healthy walk with the Lord and a healthy family.

In addition to a day of rest, church planters should make time for extended periods of rest. Joel Rainey's humorous, yet poignant, comments remind church planters to avoid his mistake and take regular vacation times: "The first year of our church plant, I took a grand total of four days vacation. My family suffered for it, and in the end, the church didn't benefit either. That was by-far the most bone-headed thing I ever did during my time as a church planter, and I did a lot of bone-headed stuff!"[9]

This ministry is intense and weighs on the family so much that extended periods of time away are necessary. It should be remembered that even during the flurry of ministry activities Jesus removed himself and his disciples to spend time alone for prayer and rest (Mark 1:32–35; 6:30–32).

> **"After watching many shipwreck their families in the name of church planting, I decided that if I was going to err, it would be on the side of investing too much, not too little, in those closest to me."**
>
> —Dave Smith, "Faith and Family," in *Church Planting from the Ground Up*, ed. Tom Jones (Joplin, MO: College Press Publishing Company, 2004), 151.

## Develop a Family Strategy

I once heard a church planter in the state of Washington comment on the need to think about strategy related to the family. In his e-mail to me he warned, "The planter must at all costs take care of his/her family. Church planting can be the worst thing that could ever happen to a family. A planter must have as much of a plan for nurturing his family as he does for growing a church. It's a shame that planters can be the very ones who turn those closest to themselves away from God."

After hearing from this church planter, I began encouraging church-planting teams to make certain that they have a plan for nurturing their families. This plan could include things such as using the dinner table as a time to share about what the Lord did in each other's lives throughout the day and having a daily time to pray for the unbelievers in the community. Such a strategy should also include a plan to involve the entire family in significant roles in the ministry.

### *Summary:*

1. The stress of church planting on the family is one of the most critical issues facing church planters in the United States and Canada.
2. Before going to the field, it is very important for families to talk with other missionaries about life on the field.
3. The church-planting ministry involves many spiritual highs and lows.
4. There are numerous blessings that come with being a church-planting family.
5. Maintaining a personal, daily quiet time with the Lord and setting a healthy example as a family are requirements for effective ministry.
6. Church planters must take time to rest.
7. It is necessary for church planters to have a strategy for nurturing their families in the process.

### *Reflection Questions:*

1. Are both you and your spouse in agreement that God is calling your family to serve as church planters?
2. Who are the seasoned missionary families that your family can speak with before your work begins?
3. Are there unresolved issues in your marriage that you and your spouse need to work through before going to the field?

4. What excites and concerns you about responding faithfully to God's calling on your life to be a missionary? How does your spouse respond to this question? How do your children respond to this question?
5. Are you and your family already maintaining an individual, daily devotional time with the Lord? How will you hold yourselves accountable to this spiritual discipline while on the field?
6. Are you a workaholic, and do you neglect your family? Do you fail to rest each week? If yes, will you repent of these sins now?
7. What do you need to include in your family strategy to nurture your family so everyone will continue to grow in faith and be used by the Lord in the church-planting endeavor?

### *Important Term in This Chapter:*

- Family strategy

Chapter 20

# MODELS AND CHURCH PLANTING

**Every church planting model brings its own strengths and weaknesses to the church planting arena.**

**—Tom Steffen[1]**

When church planters begin to consider their work, they confront the issue of church models. Over the years I have had church planters approach me, asking the question, What model should I use? Or, more commonly, I hear them say that they are going to plant a cell church, a cowboy church, a postmodern church, a house church, and so on. Such initial questions and statements concern me because they generally reveal that the missionaries are trying to decide on a model or have already decided what model will work best among people they have *yet* to meet.

Neil Cole's description of church models and structures being analogous to water pipes is an excellent place for us to begin when thinking about church-planting models.

> Of course, there are good pipes and better pipes. Rusty pipes can pollute the otherwise fresh water of heaven. Some pipes have a

> greater capacity and longer lifespan than others, but essentially pipes are pipes, and all pipes serve the same function. Once you taste the pure, clean, and refreshing Water of Life, you'll never thirst again. How sad it is if you give the glory for this to pipes rather than the Spring of eternal life Himself. I am convinced that if the Living Water were to get the attention, rather than the models we use, the world would find itself drawn more to the Kingdom of God.
>
> In organic church thinking, it is imperative that you create structure only when necessary. Life should dictate structure, not the other way around. We often say to church planters, "Do not organize 'it' until you have an 'it' to organize." In other words, do not begin with a structure and an organization. Begin with life and let the structure emerge naturally, driven by the needs and demands of the life.[2]

Models are God-given guides to assist us in our church-planting endeavors. They are very important and needed in global church planting. Though they are great blessings, they can become a bane to kingdom expansion, unless properly understood, examined, and gleaned for appropriate elements to be contextualized to a people group or population segment. Models have much to teach us but must be held lightly, especially before we enter the mission field.

## Defining Models

Before the construction of a bridge, architects and engineers develop a scaled-down version of the desired product. This small model guides them in the process of developing the actual bridge. In medicine, residents are exposed to various approaches toward the diagnoses and treatments of various diseases. These models are achieved by the implementation of various methods.

For church planters, a **model** is a form or expression of the local church that is culturally defined by both the church planters and the people they are serving, in light of the biblical parameters of what constitutes a church. As church planters consider the numerous contemporary and historic models, it is important that they recognize the strengths and limitations of those models in their original contexts as well as in the church planters' present contexts.

## Strengths

Understanding various church models offers several advantages. First, models provide a historical perspective of how the Spirit has worked in the past to birth churches in different contexts. Second, models assist in conceptualizing church-planting theories and enable the creation of strategies for evangelizing and assembling groups of new believers. Third, models provide church planters with points of reference from which they can begin their work. Having a good understanding of different models gives teams options for working in their various contexts.

## Limitations

Though the following example is fictional, it is based on actual church-planting stories. A church-planting team arrived in Europe from the United States, with several years of experience in planting churches in North America. Because the team had seen the Lord work in powerful ways through a particular model to birth three churches in the southwestern region of the States, the team members assumed that this model would meet with the same success in Brussels, Belgium. After all, they reasoned, other church planters in their area of the States had seen similar results with that same model as well. However, after laboring with much difficulty and not experiencing the expected results, they realized that it had not been effective to simply transfer a particular model from one mission field to another without proper contextualization. They had to reconsider their outreach strategy for the new context in Brussels.

> **"There was a time in history when it was enough just to follow a specific model, but that's no longer the case. We are going to have to learn to think and design on the spot."**
>
> —Bob Roberts Jr., *The Multiplying Church: The New Math for Starting New Churches* (Grand Rapids, MI: Zondervan, 2008), 77.

I am writing this section while on a flight from Montreal to Chicago. Just before takeoff I noticed that snow was beginning to fall. Scientists tell us that no two snowflakes are exactly alike. And the same can be said of churches. No two churches—even those based on the same model and in neighboring areas—are exactly alike because they are shaped by different church planters from specific cultural backgrounds and by the particular contexts in which the church-planting teams are working.

Based on these considerations, the first limitation of all church-planting models is that they are culturally specific. Any church birthed among new believers in Dallas, Texas, will differ from one birthed in the context of Brussels. The church planters will contribute their own passions, gifts, talents, and abilities, and the same can be said for the new believers. Also, there are many geographical, demographical, cultural, spiritual, historical, political, and linguistic differences between Dallas and Brussels. Models are uniquely shaped by the people and the contexts.

A second limitation to all models is the notion that no one model is *the answer* to all the problems facing church planters. There is no model that is the missing link to global evangelization. Beware of any church planter who advocates that he or she has the model that will work ef-

## On Model Selection

In his excellent article "Selecting a Church Planting Model That Works," Tom Steffen made the argument that there are differing philosophies behind model selection. The following is a brief excerpt from his work.

> There are three basic philosophies behind selecting a church planting model. Some prefer to single out a model that reflects their gifts, skills, and cultural backgrounds, and then find a people group that matches it. . . . Others prefer to select a popular model advocated by a church planter specialist and implement it among the target audience. Still others prefer to choose to conduct an environmental scan of a particular people group and craft a model to fit them.

Taken from Tom Steffen, "Selecting a Church Planting Model That Works," *Missiology* 22, no. 3 (July 1994): 368.

***Questions to Consider:***

1. Are there any other philosophies that you believe are behind selecting a church-planting model that Steffen did not mention?
2. Describe the strengths and limitations for each of the three philosophies listed.
3. Which of the philosophies are you more likely to embrace in your church-planting ministry? Why?
4. Of the church planters you know, which of the philosophies did they follow in planting churches?

fectively anywhere in the world. Though principles are universal, models must change from time to time, place to place, and people to people.

In the latter part of the twentieth century, the world was introduced to genetic cloning in a new way—what had historically been the stuff of science-fiction writers had become a reality. As I began to look around studying the work of church planters from across the globe, I noticed a striking similarity between the work of missionaries and biotechnologists.

Rather than allowing models to simply guide their work, many church planters were attempting to clone certain models. These models were ones that had proved very effective in certain contexts. Stuart Murray made an excellent and straightforward point when he simply stated, "Cloning more churches of the kind we already have will not do."[3]

## Ideal Types

You may recall in chapter two I discussed the role of ideal types when examining contemporary ecclesiologies. In this current chapter, I want to apply this tool to addressing models of church planting. Some time ago Bradley Weldy, a former doctoral student of mine, was writing a paper on church-planting models for my class. I had been lecturing along the lines of applying Max Weber's work to the understanding of models for church planting, and I encouraged Bradley to consider approaching his paper from this angle. He did, and he is the first person, to my knowledge, to write about ideal types and church planting. His paper influenced some of my thinking in this chapter. The full version of his excellent work can be found on my website at www.northamericanmissions.org.[4]

If we consider ideal types in order to better explain and understand models for church planting, we are essentially asking for a pure description of a certain model that only exists in theory. How such an ideal type manifests itself in the real world will vary from church planter to church planter and from context to context.

Although there are a myriad of models to choose from, in the interest of simplicity I decided to focus on four particular ideal types of church-planting models: traditional, cell, house, and Purpose-Driven. An examination of church-planting methods and models across the globe reveals the influence of these paradigms among contemporary church planters. Also, it is not unusual for church planters to draw from two or more of these ideal types to create an amalgam that the Lord uses to birth churches.

## Traditional

It is often difficult to place labels on church models. For the sake of simplicity, I am defining a traditional (conventional) church model as one that is generally the predominant expression in the United States and Canada. This church tends to be program driven and single pastor (or senior pastor) led. Its organizational structure typically includes several committees, and the primary small group is the Sunday school class. The Sunday morning worship service is generally understood as the most significant time in the church's life throughout the week, even though the church may have other weekly worship services.

A few of the books addressing church planting in the United States in the 1970s were written to guide church planters in planting a traditional model. Elmer Towns and Roy Thomas wrote two of these books.[5] While these works were very helpful, it was Jack Redford who attempted to codify a process by developing a nine-step strategic approach in *Planting New Churches.*[6] His "nine well-tested steps" are listed in the table below.

Figure 20.1 **Jack Redford's Nine Steps**

| | |
|---|---|
| Step 1: | Select the Church Missions Committee |
| Step 2: | Select the Area for the New Church |
| Step 3: | Prepare the Sponsoring Church |
| Step 4: | Cultivate the Mission Field |
| Step 5: | Start Home Fellowship Groups |
| Step 6: | Establish the Mission Chapel |
| Step 7: | Plan the Finances |
| Step 8: | Determine Facilities |
| Step 9: | Constitute the New Church |

## Cell

Numerous books have been written addressing the cell church model; one of the most comprehensive and influential works has been Ralph Neighbor's book *Where Do We Go from Here?*[7] Though Neighbor's work is not a church-planting manual (only one chapter is devoted to planting cell churches), it represents a model that has influenced many church planters.

A cell church consists of several small groups that meet frequently as individual cells in addition to regular gatherings with other cells on a frequent basis (e.g., weekly) for a celebration worship service. Each cell is interdependent with the other cells. The life of the church is in the cells and not in the large, corporate worship gathering. If the cell church fails to have the corporate gatherings, the church would continue because each cell individually participates in worship, evangelism, ministry, fellowship, and discipleship training. Even though shepherding and other matters of pastoral care take place in the cells, a cell church usually has a pastor(s) who oversees all the cells. A diagram of a typical cell model can be observed in figure 20.2. Bob Logan and Jeannette Buller have produced the *Cell Church Planter's Guide* for those desiring to plant cell churches.[8]

Figure 20. 2 **General Cell Church Structure**

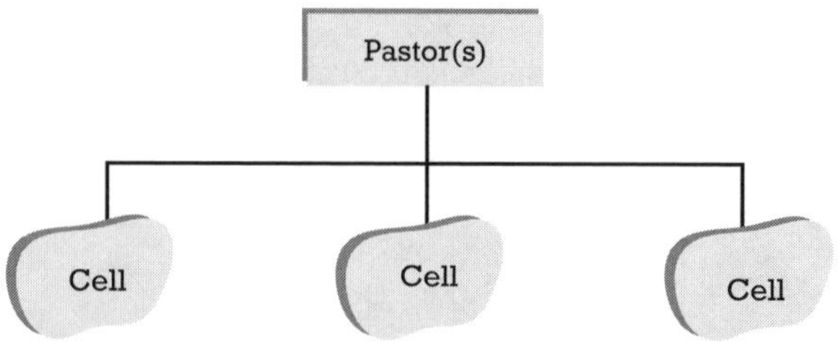

## House

House churches are as old as the first-century Church. It is not difficult to locate books related to house churches. Such works include Dick Scoggins, *Planting House Churches in Networks*; Felicity Dale, *Getting Started: A Practical Guide to House Church Planting*; Larry Kreider and Floyd McClung, *Starting a House Church*; and J. D. Payne, *Missional House Churches: Reaching Our Communities with the Gospel.*[9]

The house church model differs from the cell model primarily in two areas: pastoral leadership and autonomy. Though a house church may have as few members as one cell of a cell church, the house church would have its own pastor(s) and would be fully autonomous, even if part of a network of other house churches. A diagram of a typical network of house churches can be seen in figure 20.3.

Figure 20.3 **Network of House Churches**

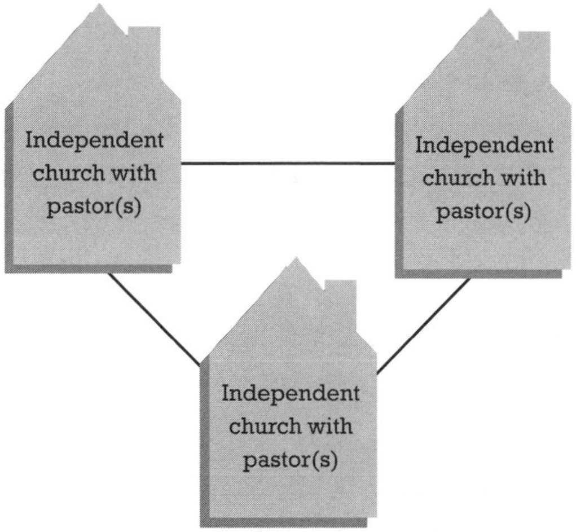

## Purpose-Driven

The name Rick Warren is familiar to the majority of the readers of this book. Warren, pastor of Saddleback Church in Southern California, planted the church in 1980. By 1995 he published the best-selling book *The Purpose-Driven Church: Growth without Compromising Your Message and Mission.*[10] Though the book was not a church-planting manual, it did tell Warren's story and philosophy of ministry that resulted in the birth of Saddleback Church. From his experience and church-planting paradigm, Warren began conducting Purpose-Driven church-planting conferences. Between the publication of the book and such conferences, large numbers of church planters, especially in the United States in the 1990s and early twenty-first century, began developing strategies to plant "Purpose-Driven" churches. Because of this unique paradigm, it is worthy of being categorized as an ideal type of model, with the contents of *The Purpose-Driven Church* describing it in detail.[11]

For Warren, churches should be focused on and organized around five biblical purposes: worship, evangelism, ministry, fellowship, and discipleship. After developing a core group to form the church, the church planters lead the church to have a public worship service that is described as a "launching" or a "going-public" event. Afterward, those present are assimilated into small groups. With the Purpose-Driven paradigm, the church planters develop strategies of moving unbelievers from the community to eventually becoming followers of Christ and leaders in the church.

> **"The answers are not found in our models, methods, and manmade systems but in the truth of God's Word and in being filled and led by the Sprit of God."**
>
> —Neil Cole, *Organic Church: Growing Faith Where Life Happens* (San Francisco, CA: Jossey-Bass, 2005), xxix.

## Panning for Golden Nuggets

During the California Gold Rush of the 1850s, many people traveled westward with the hope of finding their fortunes in gold. One method of looking for gold was known as *panning*. In a tedious process, a pan was used to scoop sediment from the bottom of a creek. Then with a swirling motion of the pan, the creek water would wash away the sediment and expose any small amounts of gold. The fortune hunter would spend time washing away great amounts of sediment in order to find a single golden nugget.

When it comes to models, church planters must operate as those panning for gold. As models are examined, church planters must sift through a great amount of sediment-like material that is not going to be relevant to their contexts nor complement their personalities and gifts. However, it is in this tedious process that church planters will find the golden nuggets that will be beneficial to their work. By holding on to models lightly and evaluating the elements for efficacy in communicating the gospel in different contexts, church planters will be in a healthy position for considering the world's multitude of models.

## A Framework for Understanding a Model

In his excellent article "Selecting a Church Planting Model That Works," Tom Steffen developed an analytical framework so that church planters could numerically evaluate various models.[12] Though Steffen's model has been influential in my development of a framework (see figure 20.4), I allow for more subjectivity and do not attempt to numerically evaluate the models to the degree that he recommended. Following Steffen's example, I have kept many of his categories while allowing for a focus on reproducibility and the consideration of needed resources to use the model.

Figure 20.4 **A Framework for Critiquing a Church-Planting Model**

| Stages of the Strategy | Biblical/ Theological Foundations | Reproducibility among the People in Your Context | Level of Resources Needed | Overall Strengths of Model | Overall Limitations of Model | Assumptions behind the Model |
|---|---|---|---|---|---|---|
| Pre-entry | | | | | | |
| Pre-evangelism | | | | | | |
| Evangelism | | | | | | |
| Post-evangelism | | | | | | |
| Phase-out | | | | | | |

***Key to Model Evaluation***

Biblical/Theological Foundations: (Poor, Fair, Good, Excellent)
Reproducibility: (Poor, Fair, Good, Excellent)
Level of Resources Needed: (Low, Medium, High)

An examination of the first column establishes the framework to understand any particular church-planting model. Here the models are scrutinized according to five stages: (1) pre-entry: methods of preparation for arrival on the field, (2) pre-evangelism: actions after arrival, but before the evangelistic work, (3) evangelism: methods of sharing the gospel, (4) post-evangelism: methods of following up with new believers/ churches, and (5) phase-out: procedures for raising up leaders while the team transitions to another location or people group to begin another church-planting strategy. Though a strategy rarely plays out in such a linear manner, for the sake of discussion, the chart is established in this fashion.

The next two columns evaluate the church-planting model at each of the five stages, in view of their biblical and theological support and in light of how reproducible the model is by the people. Column four evaluates the model at each of the five strategic stages in light of the amount of resources needed—money, people involved, and time commitment.

The last three columns are general observations of the overall model. It is here that church planters should ask themselves what are the strengths and limitations of the model for their contexts. The last column challenges the church planters to inquire about the assumptions behind the model. In other words, church planters need to know the history, context out of which the model was pioneered, and the personalities/ talents/gifts of the church planters who developed the model and saw it used effectively.

The following is an example of an evaluation of a fictitious church-planting model to provide an idea of how to use this tool. After the church planters studied a particular model that was used by a team in Lagos, Nigeria, they came to the following conclusions:

Figure 20.5 **An Example of the Use of the Evaluation Framework**

<table>
<tr><th>Stages of the Strategy</th><th>Biblical/ Theological Foundations</th><th>Reproducibility among the People in Your Context</th><th>Level of Resources Needed</th><th>Overall Strengths of Model</th><th>Overall Limitations of Model</th><th>Assumptions behind the Model</th></tr>
<tr><td>Pre-entry</td><td>Poor</td><td>Good</td><td>High</td><td rowspan="5">Very strategic model with a heavy focus on leadership development</td><td rowspan="5">Biblical/ theological foundations<br>High level of money involved</td><td rowspan="5">Pioneered for a highly educated, urban context<br>Church planters must be gifted with administrative gifts</td></tr>
<tr><td>Pre-evangelism</td><td>Fair</td><td>Good</td><td>High</td></tr>
<tr><td>Evangelism</td><td>Fair</td><td>Good</td><td>High</td></tr>
<tr><td>Post-evangelism</td><td>Poor</td><td>Fair</td><td>Medium</td></tr>
<tr><td>Phase-out</td><td>Poor</td><td>Good</td><td>High</td></tr>
</table>

With these results, the church-planting team has several critical matters to consider. First, this particular model has a shallow biblical and theological foundation. This limitation is a major problem. It may mean that a team can still benefit from some elements of the model if a proper foundation can be provided. Second, unless a team has access to a high level of resources (i.e., people, money, and time), it may be difficult to use this model. Third, if the team has someone gifted in the area of administration, some elements of this strategy may be useful. A careful evaluation using this framework gives church planters an effective structure for evaluating the strengths and limitations of various models.

### *Summary:*

1. Models are a blessing and very important to church-planting work.
2. Church planters should not go to a people with the intention of planting a specific model of church, but rather allow the model to develop within biblical parameters and in light of the context.
3. Models are shaped by their contexts and the church planters who use them.
4. It is important that church planters recognize that there are strengths and limitations to models.
5. There are at least four ideal types of models that church planters need to know in detail.
6. Models are not to be taken from one context and cloned in another context.
7. After embracing a biblical ecclesiology, church planters must learn how to "pan for the golden nuggets" when examining models.
8. It is helpful to use a framework to evaluate a model before using elements from it in another context.

### *Reflection Questions:*

1. In the opening of this chapter, I cited Neil Cole as stating that church planters should not begin with organization and structure. Do you agree or disagree with Cole's perspective? Explain.

2. Of the four ideal types listed in this chapter, which model are you the most familiar with, and which are you interested in the most? How will your familiarity with and interest in this model affect your church-planting work before your arrival on the field?
3. Using the framework that I have provided in this chapter, evaluate the present model you have in mind as you begin your church-planting work. What did you and your team learn from this exercise?

## *Important Terms in This Chapter:*

- Model
- Ideal types
- Traditional model
- Cell model
- House model
- Purpose-Driven model

Chapter 21

# COMMON OBJECTIONS TO CHURCH PLANTING

**Sadly, unexpected opposition sometimes comes from local evangelical ministers.**

—Ray Register[1]

The objections to church planting, especially in the United States, are many. Though most objections come from established churches that were planted decades ago, even some newly planted churches voice opposition to such missionary efforts. Many church planters find themselves having to give lengthy defenses for their activities.

Part of my training with church planters involves helping them understand the hearts of other brothers and sisters who voice opposition to church planting. They must be prepared to graciously respond to the concerns of others. So, in a sense, this chapter is written as an apologetic for church planting.[2]

In the first portion of this chapter, I address the issues of ignorance, turfism, and lack of kingdom vision as they relate to church planting. The latter portion of this chapter addresses many of the most commonly held objections to this Great Commission work.

Missionaries are passionate people. Therefore, before we begin, it is necessary to keep in mind that "a soft answer turns away wrath, but a harsh word stirs up anger. The tongue of the wise commends knowledge, but the mouths of fools pour out folly" (Proverbs 15:1–2). Though church planters mainly have the responsibility of building up the body of Christ through establishing new churches, they also have the responsibility of building up the body of Christ through their ministries to churches already established. We must guard our hearts when speaking to those in opposition to church planting. A gentle answer from the tongue of the wise is necessary for such a task and important in teaching other kingdom citizens about missions.

Just as the Lord has been gracious to us in our church-planting journey—sometimes, over many years—we must be gracious to others who are weighing the options of church planting for the first time. In some cases, you have been eating, drinking, and sleeping in the field of church planting for several years. The Lord has patiently allowed you to mull over the various theological and missiological matters for a long time. Make certain that you are sympathetic toward other kingdom citizens whenever you share your vision for making disciples, especially when others do not initially respond with the enthusiasm you desire. Remember, it is very likely your enthusiasm for church planting did not bubble up overnight.

> "Even though some people oppose the idea of church planting, we must do it anyway—because it's biblical."
>
> —Ed Stetzer, *Planting Missional Churches* (Nashville, TN: Broadman and Holman Publishers, 2006), 14.

## Ignorance

Many church planters are struggling with the fact that the majority of the churches across the United States and Canada are ignorant regarding church planting. To these churches, church planting is a novelty, some kind of fad or program that deserves little attention. Ironically, these churches exist today because of the faithful church planters of yesteryear who carried the gospel into pioneer territories.

Many churches need to be educated about church planting in general. I was reminded of this during a recent experience. In a class discussion in my Introduction to Evangelism and Church Growth course, I was addressing the topic of church planting. After some time of lecture and dialogue, a student raised his hand and politely made the following statement, "I don't mean to be rude, but what is church planting?" I had been speaking for about fifteen minutes on the topic and assumed that everyone knew what I was talking about. Remember, this student was not just any church member, but a leader, a seminary student. Also, this student was part of the Southern Baptist Convention, a denomination known for its emphasis on church planting!

A Vineyard church planter commented on this issue, "There is a huge job that needs to be done in communicating the need for church planting to the whole church, leaders and lay alike. It seems that there are only small streams from different denominations/church movements that are really committed to church planting. If vital churches are going to be started, the whole church needs to be educated."[3]

One church planter in Ohio observed the problem in his area: "I have found out that there seems to be a lack of helping pastors and churches understand what is expected and the levels of sponsorship they can do for planters. This takes time and training and relationship building but may not be done until they are looking for a church to sponsor a planter."[4]

Unfortunately, few churches will make the time to become involved in church planting. This planter from Ohio went on to say that denominational leaders should consider making regular visits to churches to educate them regarding church planting. One Southern Baptist church planter in Louisiana candidly stated, "One of the problems is a lack of education among SBC ministers and laity about church planting. The only thing they know about is church splits."[5]

## Turfism

**Turfism** is the idea that a certain geographical area is "our turf" and is off limits to any other group desiring to reach the same population. It is a gang mentality, diabolical in nature, stemming from pride, arrogance, and insecurity. It is amazing how many churches engage in this kind of possessiveness, believing they will reach all of the people living around their parish, yet reaching few to none!

I recall a time when I came face-to-face with this mentality. As a pastor for a rural church, I attended an associational meeting of several pastors. A meal was served, and I sat across the table from a well-respected, retired pastor in our association. We conversed for several moments. Since I was new in the area, this was our first encounter with one another.

After some time he began to inquire about an Independent Baptist church that had been meeting across the street from our property. Soon his frustration toward this congregation became apparent, and he exclaimed, "That's just like those Independent Baptists! They always plant their churches just across the street from our Southern Baptist churches!" I did not respond but continued to eat my dessert.

Some time later I attended another of these meetings, and during the dinner I again sat across the table from this man. The conversation was very pleasant as we conversed on a variety of issues. For some reason, the dialogue again became focused on "those Independent Baptists across the street." Again, in his frustration, he echoed the refrain that I had heard months before: "That's just like those Independent Baptists! They always plant their churches across the street from our Southern Baptist churches!" This time, however, I felt a response was necessary. The church that met across the street was reaching more people than we were reaching. Overall, I was impressed with its work.

In a very polite and respectful manner, I made the following comment, much to his surprise: "As long as they are faithfully teaching the truth of the Word and reaching people with the gospel, they are welcome to meet anywhere, even on our property." He did not respond to my statement. I then continued to eat my dessert. For dessert, that night, I think he was having humble pie.

> **"If the relationship between the mother and daughter churches remains strong, initiatives taken by the new church may challenge the planting church and lead to ecclesiological and missiological renewal."**
>
> —Stuart Murray, *Church Planting: Laying Foundations* (London: Paternoster Press, 1998), 262.

Turfism is extremely problematic in the United States. One church planter from Alabama remarked, "Many North American churches find themselves competitive, seeing the new church on the block as a threat and not a friend."[6] A church planter from Florida told me that even among those desiring church planting, there is irony: "Many say, 'Yes, we may need new churches, but not in my back yard.'"[7] Even in a pioneer area, a church planter encountered this issue. He wrote, "Many of the churches (even in Utah) are territorial."[8] We should hope that a new work reaching a different demographic segment would be welcomed into a particular area, but a church planter in North Carolina observed that this assumption is not always the case: "We have also found local churches to be either indifferent or openly hostile to the idea of starting radically different churches in their own backyard."[9]

## Lack of Kingdom Vision

By far the most problematic reason that most churches are not involved in church planting is a lack of kingdom vision. It could be argued that the prevalent turfism that exists throughout North America is related to this issue.[10] Many churches have a myopic view of church growth. Growth has become limited to the expansion of one body—their local congregation. Note the numerous times this lack of vision is mentioned in the following e-mails that I received from the field.

- The number one issue that we face is pastors and churches that are unwilling to partner with a new church start. We need churches to provide not only some financial resources but also churches that are willing to provide a core group of leaders either temporarily or permanently. We need more pastors with a Kingdom Vision than we currently have. (Church planter from Georgia)
- We have a shortage of churches with the vision to plant churches. In my eight years as a planter, it's taken this long to get the small number of churches in my association even to consider the possibility. This is both a pastor and church related problem. I'm not alone in this assessment. Our churches 40 years ago had a vision to plant and reproduce. Churches now are in either survival mode or 'ya'll come here' mode. (Church planter from Indiana)
- First and foremost is the apathy and lack of understanding about church planting from existing churches. Most existing churches have a very poor understanding of the Kingdom of God and His desire to see the Kingdom grow through

the multiplication of churches. Most existing churches (and pastors) are in a survival mindset and therefore have little interest for church planting. (Church planter from Kansas)

- Most of the parish ministry professionals I know have no vision for leading their congregations to see the worth of church planting. Either they have prostituted themselves to the big-is-best philosophy of church growth (i.e., to the exclusion of planting) or are too timid and fearful of personal loss and pain to fight the tide of corporate-minded laypersons. We need some model visionaries to take the heat, to make the way plain, and give permission to these guys to take risks and put money into missions/church planting. (Church planter from Kentucky)

## Responding to the Concerns

Responding to the objections to church planting requires, first of all, knowledge of the objections. Numerous excuses abound as to why we currently observe few churches involved. The purpose of this section is to address many of those objections and to offer brief rebuttals.

In their excellent resource *The Dynamic Daughter Church Planting Handbook,* Paul Becker and Mark Williams developed, by far, the most extensive discussion regarding how to respond to objections related to an established church planting another church.[11] These men compiled the many objections discussed below.

### We'll Lose Our Church Fellowship

Many churches are concerned about the loss of intimacy within their own congregations that might occur if they plant other churches. For years brothers and sisters have sat beside one another during worship services and Bible studies. They have laughed, played, and cried together, and their children are friends. Though the church should consist of strong relationships, true biblical fellowship does not include becoming inwardly focused. Healthy community is always missional and advocates the sending of missionaries to plant churches. What if the Church at Antioch would have been so passionate about the relationships that existed among the members and the apostle Paul and Barnabas that they would have resisted the leading of the Holy Spirit? But they obviously had a healthy understanding of church life and willingly sent out the church-planting team (Acts 13:1–3).

> **"You have to be prepared for the questions, objections, hesitations, reluctance and doubts that will be expressed when the topic of becoming a mother church is brought up."**
>
> —Paul Becker and Mark Williams, *The Dynamic Daughter Church Planting Handbook* (n.p.: Dynamic Church Planting International, 1999), sec. 1, p. 16.

## It Will Cost Too Much

This statement is one of the most common objections to church planting. Obviously, church planting can be expensive, but it does not have to be that way. This objection primarily relates to the church's definition of what constitutes a church. If church planting entails salaries, budgets, buildings, sound systems, mailings, and so on, then there may be a significant dollar investment required. Even if a church-planting strategy calls for a substantial amount of money, there are many avenues where funding can be found. For example,

- denominational resources
- mission agencies
- a bivocational church planter
- special offerings
- the core group

## We're Too Small

Many of the churches in the United States and Canada have fewer than one hundred members. In a day and age when the megachurch is still seen as the status for every church to achieve, many churches are constantly *waiting until they are larger* before they consider participating in church planting.

Recently, a church-planting pastor approached me for help with his work. Upon investigation, his work was no longer a church-planting ministry, but an established church of three years. Thinking his congregation was considering planting another church, I inquired about the plans they had made for the new work. His hesitancy to my inquiry quickly revealed that there were no immediate mission plans. After gathering his thoughts, he responded that the church was not ready to plant another church, but needed workers in a variety of areas. Knowing that this brother was trained in a denominational program that attempted to instill church multiplication within the hearts of church planters, I then inquired about future plans to plant the next church. His response was that he did not know, but that they were still too small to begin another work.

Few churches believe they are large enough to be involved in church planting. Again, this excuse raises the question, How large does a church need to be to begin another work? Clearly, there is no definite answer to this question. In practice, however, many congregations believe that the answer is *just a little larger* than they are presently. We must remember that God has proved himself to do immeasurably more than we can imagine, even with small things (Ephesians 3:20).

## We Can't Afford to Lose the Leadership and Workers

Though this objection is more prevalent in smaller churches, it is a common response. The irony involved in sending out the best leaders and workers is that the vacancies left behind in the mother church usually will be filled by those members who have been waiting to get involved. C. Peter Wagner commented on this when he wrote, "For the most part existing churches have unconsciously placed a ceiling on both clergy and lay leadership, and as a result upward mobility of new people into positions of ministry is difficult. But new churches open wide the doors of leadership and ministry challenges and the entire Body of Christ subsequently benefits."[12] Though mother churches give away some of their most faithful givers, leaders, attenders, and supporters, the Lord can raise up others to fill the empty positions.

On the other hand, those who are unable to use their gifts and talents to build up the mother church because there are few opportunities for them often become outstanding leaders in a new work. In one church where I served as a pastor, there was a couple who had a passion for leading believers in congregational singing and worship. There were few opportunities for them in the mother church; however, in the church plant the opportunities were limitless. They were sent out from the congregation and became very important leaders on the church-planting team.

## It Will Destroy Our Growth Momentum

Becker and Williams's words respond well to this objection:

> Too often pastors and churches are more concerned with the growth of their own corner of the kingdom, rather than the growth of the kingdom as a whole. It's true that daughtering a church may affect growth momentum of the mother church: it might decrease or it might increase. But the more important questions is: How will daughtering affect the growth of the Jesus Kingdom? The answer is clear: Christ's Kingdom will grow. The right thing then is to work for the building of His Kingdom,

and trust the Lord for what will happen in your own corner of the Kingdom. Not, "My kingdom come, my will be done" but, "Thy kingdom come, thy will be done."[13]

## What's in It for Us?

This objection reveals a selfish attitude that must be dismissed before any healthy church planting will occur. Unfortunately, many churches have adopted a capitalistic mentality toward the church. The church is seen as a business in which investments must be made, and at the end of the year the company cannot be in the red.

Again, a kingdom vision is required to overcome this objection. There are many joys and blessings that come from church planting. The church will be involved in seeing people come to Christ, new leaders develop, and fellowship deepen with the Lord and other brothers and sisters. The church will experience a fountain of blessings from the Lord as it is faithful to his mission.

## What If the Daughter Grows Larger Than the Mother?

There is a real possibility that the daughter church will grow larger than the mother. It is very likely that for the first few years the new church will exceed the mother church in the number of baptisms. Usually, newer churches grow faster than older, established churches.

Like many other objections, this one reveals a deeply rooted selfish attitude and insecurity. The simple answer to this objection is, "Let's hope the daughter church does indeed grow larger than the mother!" In humanistic terms, do not parents desire that their children exceed them in everything in life?

It is my fear that this objection can be found within the hearts of many pastors, though they may not voice it aloud. May the Lord heal us of this evil, and may we gain a kingdom perspective when it comes to church planting.

> **"Many pastors lack the vision for church multiplication because they simply have never given it serious consideration."**
>
> —Phil Stevenson, *The Ripple Church: Multiply Your Ministry by Parenting New Churches* (Indianapolis, IN: Wesleyan Publishing House, 2004), 66–67.

## Our Church Won't Go for It

Those holding to this objection may be right, but the church needs to change if this attitude exists. The leaders of the church, including lay leaders, will be the ones who will help lead the church past this objection. If the leaders are not supportive of church planting, then the likelihood of the church being involved is rare.

There are several things that pastors can do to help move their churches to be involved: Preach a series of messages related to church planting. Bring in church planters to share testimonies related to their work. Pastors can get involved in small tasks related to church planting and can then share those with the congregation. Get the church involved in a lower level of commitment. There are a variety of small tasks in which a church can participate.

## We'll Be in Competition with the Daughter

It has been said that it takes different kinds of churches to reach different kinds of people. Two churches can coexist within the same community and both reach different segments of that community. Competition is not found in the kingdom of God. Our struggle is with the Evil one, not with each other (Ephesians 6:12).

## But Pastors Get Kudos for Bigger Churches, Not Daughter Churches

Unfortunately, this statement is true. The North American Church is in an environment that fosters the belief that bigger is better. Becker and Williams believe that this objection may be one of the biggest barriers for mother churches.[14] Many church leaders will have to spend time in prayer overcoming this objection that may be hidden within their hearts. Denominational leaders need to begin rewarding those who are doing an excellent job planting other churches. They need to constantly tell the stories of the churches involved in church planting.

## Why Should I?

The simple answer is for the glory of God. The Bible establishes the example. Also, there are many lost people living in North America. Newer churches tend to reach more people with the gospel than established churches. Wagner went so far as to say, "*The single most effective evangelistic methodology under heaven is planting new churches.*"[15]

## But We Already Give Generously to Missions

This objection falsely assumes three things about church planting: (1) missions is something we can do by proxy, (2) missions is something that happens overseas and not here in North America, and (3) being involved in church planting means that a church has to give money.

Just because a church gives money to international missionary work does not mean that the church can neglect its responsibilities for missions here in North America. North America is also an enormous mission field. Though sometimes it is good for a church to give money to church planting, this is not always necessary and is not always the healthiest situation.

## I'd Like to, but I Just Don't Have the Time

There will never be enough time to plant churches if this is the objection. If church planting is a priority for us, then we will be intentional about making the time to be involved in missions.

## Shouldn't We Concentrate on Revitalizing Existing Churches?

This question represents another very common objection to church planting. Though revitalization is a very important and much needed ministry, it can be very difficult, time consuming, and expensive, when compared to church planting. One article comparing revitalization and church planting put it this way, "It is easier to have babies than raise the dead."[16] More churches reach more people with the gospel. In general, newer churches reach more people with the gospel than older churches do. Revitalization is needed, but not to the neglect of the missionary task of the Church. In fact, the irony is that as an inwardly focused church turns outward, the Lord blesses such faithfulness with spiritual growth.

## We Tried It Before and It Didn't Work

Ministry in general is difficult, and church planting in particular is extremely difficult. This objection cannot be one that hinders us from church planting. What if churches decided to stop doing evangelism just because they were unable to reach someone with the gospel? Think of inventors like Thomas Edison who spent years and a multitude of attempts to finally get an invention to work effectively. An unsuccessful attempt should not be an excuse to hinder future work.

## Joys versus Fears

Paul Becker and Mark Williams, in the following account, referred to the times of elation and concern when pastors lead their churches to plant other churches.

> Having and raising children is the most natural thing in the world—it's how God created us. A woman who has given birth will probably tell you that it is a normal, exciting and joyful experience. But it's not easy! God also created churches to give birth to other churches. Daughtering a church can and should be a normal, exciting, and joyful experience. But when a church gives its dollars, time, precious people and other resources to a new church, it's not easy.
>
> Fear of these sacrifices may cause a congregation to shy away from motherhood, and thus to miss the incredible joys of "parenting." Therefore, the first thing you will need to do as a leader is to cast the vision of daughtering a new church. Leaders need to lead the church to do what it ought to do for Christ.

Taken from Paul Becker and Mark Williams, *The Dynamic Daughter Church Planting Handbook* (n.p.: Dynamic Church Planting International, 1999), sec. 2, p. 1.

***Questions to Consider:***

1. Why do you think becoming a mother church is not easy?
2. Place yourself in the shoes of a pastor of a growing, established church. What do you believe are some of the concerns that come to his mind when he considers leading the church to plant other churches?
3. Now place yourself in the shoes of a pastor in a church that is declining. What do you believe are some of the concerns that come to his mind when he considers leading the church to plant other churches?

## The Leadership Just Isn't Available

The response to this objection is based on a definition of leadership. If someone believes that the only type of leadership that can be involved in church planting is someone of the "professional, well-educated clergy" type, then it may be difficult finding available leadership. If we look to the Scriptures—rather than to our culture—to determine our definitions of available leaders, then the number of leaders will increase. Regardless of our definition of available leaders, we must ask the Lord for the workers (Matthew 9:37–38), believing that he will make the provision.

## This Is a Bad Time for Us to Daughter a Church

This objection is similar to not having enough time. There obviously will be seasons in which it would not be wise for a church to enter into the ministry of church planting; however, for many churches a "bad time" is a bad excuse. There will never be a perfect moment. It is amazing that throughout the world in areas where the Church is persecuted and having "bad times," the Church is multiplying.

## We'll Daughter When Our Church Grows to "X" Size

This excuse is similar to being too small. What happens if the church never grows to "X" size? Churches of all sizes can be involved in church planting to some degree.

## Our Vision Is to Grow a Large Church

If, indeed, the vision is to grow one local congregation larger and larger, then extension and bridging growth must also be a part of this vision. Saddleback Church in Southern California has grown to megachurch status, but it has also been involved in planting numerous churches, long before it became a megachurch.

## I Don't Know How

The simple response to this objection is, "Learn!" There are numerous resources (e.g., books, conferences, websites) available to those interested in church planting. Many evangelical denominations are starting to embrace church planting as a healthy approach to church growth. Some have a resource person or department focused on the area of church planting. This objection is not as legitimate as it might have been fifteen to twenty years ago.

There are numerous objections to church planting, but none are sufficient to exclude a congregation from being involved in this wonderful way to advance the kingdom.

### *Summary:*

1. Three general reasons why people and churches are opposed to church planting include ignorance, turfism, and lack of kingdom vision.
2. There are numerous specific objections to church planting, and church planters need to know them and be able to respond to them in a Christlike manner.
3. Church planters need to recognize that when given the opportunity, they have the responsibility of equipping the saints in established churches by educating them about missionary work.

### *Reflection Questions:*

1. Have you been gracious to others who have not caught the church-planting vision? If not, why not?
2. Will you accept the responsibility that missions education within established churches is part of what you will do as a church planter from time to time?
3. Can you think of other objections to church planting not mentioned in this chapter? How would you respond to those objections?
4. Of all the objections listed in this chapter, which three do you believe are the ones you will most likely hear from others?

## *Important Term Used in This Chapter:*

- Turfism

Chapter 22

# CHURCH PLANTING IN URBAN CONTEXTS

If what God is doing in the world at large means anything to the church today, it should be clear that the phenomenon of urbanization is the work of God in preparing great multitudes of people for evangelization and the planting of tens of thousands of new churches.

—Roger S. Greenway[1]

Following the first three hundred years of the Church's existence, missionaries did a fairly good job at penetrating the rural communities, villages, small towns, and tribes scattered across the globe. However, the large urban environments, especially in the last two hundred years, have typically posed significant challenges. As of 2008 the majority of the world's population resides in the cities. As we move further into the twenty-first century, the great urban challenge will continue to impact global missions.

# An Urban World

The United Nations recently released some facts related to the present world population growth and the cities. Consider the following.

- The urban population passed the 1 billion mark in 1961. It took 25 years to add another billion urban dwellers and just 17 years more to add a third billion. Thus, the urban population reached 3 billion in 2003 and is projected to increase to 4 billion in 2018, 15 years later. By 2030, it is expected to be about 5 billion.
- The urban population in the less developed regions will increase from 2.3 billion to 3.9 billion over the next 25 years.
- Migration from rural to urban areas and the transformation of rural settlements into urban places are important determinants of the high urban population growth anticipated in the less developed regions.
- Urbanization is very far advanced in the more developed regions where in 2005 almost three-quarters (74 percent) of the population lived in urban settlements. The urban proportion in the more developed regions is projected to increase to 81 percent by 2030. In the less developed regions, the equivalent proportion was 43 percent in 2005 and is projected to rise to 56 percent by 2030.
- Africa and Asia were the least urbanized areas in the world in 2005 (38 percent and 40 percent, respectively). By 2030 Asia will rank first and Africa second in terms of the number of urban dwellers. Indeed, in 2030 almost 7 out of every 10 urban residents in the world will be living in Africa or Asia.
- The region of Latin America and the Caribbean is already highly urbanized, with 77 percent of its population living in cities in 2005. By 2030 that proportion is projected to reach 84 percent.

- In Europe the proportion of the population residing in urban areas is expected to rise from 72 percent in 2005 to 78 percent in 2030. In North America the increase in the proportion urban is projected to be from 81 percent in 2005 to 87 percent in 2030. In Oceania, the equivalent rise is from 71 percent in 2005 to 74 percent in 2030.
- The twentieth century witnessed the emergence of megacities, that is, cities with 10 million inhabitants or more. Since 1950 the number of megacities has risen from 2 to 20 in 2005. Two additional megacities are projected to emerge over the next decade, to reach 22 by 2015, among which 17 are located in developing countries.
- With 35 million residents in 2005, the metropolitan area of Tokyo was by far the most populous urban agglomeration in the world. After Tokyo, the next largest urban agglomerations are Ciudad de México (Mexico City) and the urban agglomeration of New York-Newark, with 19 million inhabitants each, followed by São Paulo and Mumbai (Bombay) with 18 million people each.
- In 2015 Tokyo will still be the largest urban agglomeration with 35 million inhabitants, followed by Mumbai (Bombay) and Ciudad de México (Mexico City) with 22 million people each, and São Paulo with 21 million inhabitants.
- Small cities, that is, those with a population of fewer than 500,000 people, were the place of residence of about 51 percent of all urban dwellers in the world in 2005.
- By 2030 three out of every five people on earth will likely reside in urban centers, and nearly half of the world's population will live in the cities of developing countries.[2]

## General Characteristics of Cities

Though the developed cities of the Western world differ in many regards from the developing cities of the Majority World, despite their locations across the globe, cities share some common sociological threads. By far, cities are places of influence, impacting areas of government, education, health care, information, entertainment, trade, industry, and warfare.[3] Cultural changes that happen in the cities eventually trickle down and impact small towns and villages. What begins in the cities affects the countryside. Larry Rose and C. Kirk Hadaway believed this urban effect is so strong that they wrote, "Often what happens in a single city so dominates a nation that what occurs elsewhere in the country is almost insignificant."[4]

Because of the influence that urban contexts hold over a people and the world, Tim Keller noted the emphasis church planters should place on reaching the cities. According to Keller, "In the village, you might win the one or two lawyers to Christ, but if you wanted to win the legal profession, you need to go to the city where you have the law schools, the law journals published, etc."[5] To put it more bluntly, Roger S. Greenway wrote, "The only conclusion we can reach is that at no time in history has it been more true than now that he who wins the city, wins the world."[6]

Paul G. Hiebert and Eloise Hiebert Meneses identified six general characteristics of all cities: scale, centers, diversity, specialization, hierarchy, and change.[7] First, cities are places of great scale. The size of cities is generally much larger than most towns and villages, with inhabitants organizing themselves in various ways. Megacites are massive population centers of at least ten million inhabitants, containing numerous social networks. Second, cities are centers of significance. The urban areas are centers of leadership, power, and authority. Third, cities are generally represented by a great amount of cultural, spiritual, political, and economic diversity. Even within ethnic enclaves (e.g., Little Havana in

Miami), there is great diversity. Fourth, cities are usually categorized by specialization. Cities are able to function, in large part, because of the various specializations which come together to create an overarching economic system. The general store of the small town seems to vanish in the cities and is replaced by numerous specialty stores. The local hospital in a small community may have a few general practitioners but generally does not provide the community with a multitude of specialists (e.g., endocrinologists, neurologists) who are more likely to be found in cities. Fifth, hierarchy also defines cities. The gap between the rich and poor, the powerful and powerless, and the educated and uneducated is much wider in the cities. Finally, in contrast to rural communities, change occurs in cities at a regular and rapid rate. Cities are constantly evolving, reorganizing and restructuring, growing and declining.

> **"Thus, while the world's populations have been migrating to the cities, the missionary has continued to gravitate to the countryside, partly because this is what the sending church still conceives of as 'real missionary work.'"**
>
> —Frank Allen, "Toward a Biblical Urban Mission," *Urban Mission* 3, no. 3 (January 1986): 6.

## Contrasting Urban Contexts

Though there are several urban commonalities, Francis M. DuBose noted that there are "fundamental differences" to be found among cities, with the greatest contrasts existing between First World cities and Majority World cities.[8] First, the social structures separate the powerful elite and the powerless masses, which typically are struggling for survival. In the Majority World, the Western concept of a majority middle class rarely exists. Second, the demographic realities of high birthrates exist.

Majority World cities are known for high birthrates, unlike their First World counterparts. Third, the economic realities greatly divide cities. Unlike the Western world, the Majority World did not experience an industrial revolution that helped produce a generally affluent, literate, majority middle class.

> **"Church leaders, missionaries, and prospective workers need to develop 'urban eyes' and the practical skills to do the research, plan the strategies, and carry out effectively God's work in cities."**
>
> —Roger S. Greenway, "Reaching the Unreached in the Cites," *Urban Mission 2*, no. 5 (May 1985): 5.

Fourth, Majority World political systems draw from multinational corporations that result in few financial resources remaining in county for development. Such partnerships send huge financial profits out of the country, leaving only enough behind for maintenance. Fifth, many cities have poor levels of education. Where financial resources are limited, education struggles and literacy rates are low. Sixth, many Majority World cities are still culturally defined by the colonial or precolonial periods of yesteryear, despite the fact that such cities have been influenced by capitalism and socialism. Finally, many Majority World cities are challenged administratively. Many city leaders are not experienced in city government, urban planning, or city maintenance.

## The Challenges of Urban Church Planting

For the urban church planter, the task of impacting the cities of this world for the kingdom of God is a great challenge. Though I am not able to include all of the dynamic factors that the urban missionary needs to be prepared for, I do believe the following paragraphs represent some of the major issues to be faced in any global city.

## Migration

**Migration** is the mass movement of a group of people from one particular geographical location to another location. Presently, the world is experiencing mass migrations of peoples within their own countries. For example, in the United States, many people are moving westward and southward, with cities in those regions rapidly growing, according to U.S. standards. In the Majority World, many villagers are traveling to the cities in the hope of finding a better way of life. Viv Grigg observed, "The greatest mission surge in history has entirely missed the greatest migration in history, the migration of Third World rural peasants to great mega-cities."[9]

## Immigration

**Immigration** is the moving from one country to another country by a person who then becomes a citizen of the foreign country. Though people are immigrating to a multitude of cities across the globe, the United States is the largest receiving country for immigrants today, and visible minorities compose over half of the population of Greater Toronto.[10] Though a bit hyperbolic, there is a great deal of truth to Ray Bakke's statement: "Today we know where 'all the nations' are—in the urban neighborhoods."[11] Though urban church planters will not necessarily have to travel land and sea to reach many of the unreached people groups of the world, they will have to cross substantial cultural gaps.

> "The greatest challenge to world evangelization is urban ministry."
>
> —James R. Engel, "Using Research Strategically in Urban Ministry," in *Planting and Growing Urban Churches: From Dream to Reality*, ed. Harvie M. Conn (Grand Rapids, MI: Baker Books, 1997), 46.

## The Realities of Urban Church Planting

Urban missiologist Roger S. Greenway wrote the following account describing the struggles of a missionary couple arriving in a city for the first time. This story is quick to point out that missionaries must not get so caught up in the romance of the city that they forget about the realities.

> It's sad to see young missionaries packing to go home, but it happens too often in the city. If the world's burgeoning cities are to be evangelized and urban churches multiplied, something better has to be done to train workers for the streets.
>
> Take Dick and Betty, for example. They lasted just two years in one of Latin America's largest cities. They had felt the call to overseas missions while Dick was in seminary. They heard about the rapid growth of urban populations and the modern frontiers that lie in the cities. So during their pre-field interviews, they indicated that they felt called to urban church planting and the board assigned them accordingly.
>
> But on the field they found that city life was more than they could take. First there was the noise, day and night, and the traffic, and the continual press of neighbors and the masses on the street. Dick felt they should mainly use public transportation, but that meant Betty was left for hours with the baby in a fifth floor apartment. They had never lived anywhere before without grass and a yard. Here there were only walls, corridors and an elevator. Their marriage began to show signs of strain. Prayer life suffered.
>
> Worst of all for Dick were the disappointments in starting the urban ministry he felt called to perform. He thought he had what was needed to begin. A Christian radio station had supplied him with a formidable list of names and addresses. These were of people who had responded to radio offers for free literature. Day after day Dick walked streets, climbed stairways and pounded on doors in pursuit of these people. But very little came of his efforts. Most were not home when he called, or had moved to other addresses, or refused to talk to him. A few were hostile. Some were already members of churches. The few he found who seemed genuinely interested in receiving instruction lived in widely scattered

parts of the city. There was not much chance of starting a church with them.

Dick and Betty began to have serious doubts about their place in the city. They visited various city churches and were impressed by the capable leaders. Many of the members were educated, successful people. Church programs were running smoothly and they could not see where their services were needed or wanted.

On the street, Dick sometimes found himself embarrassed or insecure. So little of what he had learned in seminary and in the small town church that Betty and he had attended seemed to help him now. Never had he seen so many kinds of people, languages, and cultures thrown together. He rubbed shoulders with the rich and poor, the educated and semi-literate. One moment he might be talking with an intensely devout person whose religion bordered on superstition, and a short while later he could be badgered by an aggressive communist defending ideological atheism. Challenged by their questions, Dick groped for the answers he had heard pastors use back home. But on the street the questions sounded different and the answers didn't fit. Dick's training had not prepared him for this.

Week after week, Dick and Betty prayed and anguished, trying everything they could think of to start a church. Then, after the most frustrating 20 months of their lives, they wrote to their board and asked to be reassigned outside of the city, or sent home. Urban ministry, they concluded, was not for them.

Taken from Roger S. Greenway, "Don't Be an Urban Missionary Unless . . ." *Evangelical Missions Quarterly* 19, no. 2 (April 1983): 86–87.

***Questions to Consider:***

1. Have you thought about some of these realities facing the urban church planter, or have you and your team been more caught up in the romance of the city?
2. Which of the challenges experienced by Dick and Betty are the ones that concern you the most? Are there others not mentioned in the story that are on your mind?
3. Do you agree with Dick and Betty that urban ministry was not for them? Explain.

### Poverty

Since the urban environment seems to amplify the problems of humanity, it should not be a surprise that poverty is a significant challenge for which the church planter must be prepared. It is estimated that by 2030 one in four people of the world will be squatters, or approximately two billion people.[12] Many of these people will continue to reside in the shantytowns and slums that typically form, sometimes overnight, on the perimeter of the cities of the world.

### HIV/AIDS

AIDS is a global problem, and the realities of the syndrome are nowhere more prevalent than in the developing Majority World. In 2007 the United Nations estimated that thirty-three million people in the world live with HIV.[13] Urban church planters have to be prepared to face the emotional turmoil that comes with working in such a plagued environment. Urban evangelism and church-planting strategies will be affected by contexts in which the life expectancy is brief and orphans and widows are commonplace.

> **"Moreover, roughly 90 percent of the world population growth is taking place in cities, mostly in the developing world."**
>
> —J. John Palen, *The Urban World*, 6th ed. (New York, McGraw-Hill 2002), 282.

## G.O.I.N.G. U.R.B.A.N.

I once wrote an article for the *Journal of Urban Ministry* in which I addressed some of the issues missionaries need to keep in mind as they "go urban." The remaining portion of this chapter has been taken from that article.[14] Using the acrostic **G.O.I.N.G. U.R.B.A.N.**, I suggest ten features that should characterize the urban missionary of the twenty-first century. These are individually discussed below.

## G: God Dependent

Has God called you to the great cities of this world to see disciples, leaders, and churches multiplied for the kingdom? Though all missionaries must respond to God with a reckless abandonment and a total dependence on him, the cities of this world amplify the need to make certain that a God dependency is at the heart of everything the church planter does. A daily dying to self and being filled with the Spirit are absolute musts (Ephesians 5:18).

In 2005 there were twenty **megacities** with populations of ten million or more, and the number of such cities is expected to rise with time.[15] Megacities are an incredible challenge to the church. An urban missionary recently told me that no amount of people or money could effectively reach her city. "Unless God moves," she noted, "there is no possibility of any urban transformation." Megacities are of such an overwhelming scale that it is obvious that nothing can be done in the flesh to effect positive societal transformation or to reach all the people with the gospel. The needs are so vast, the warfare so intense, and the cities of the world so diverse, that unless missionaries are dependant on the Lord in everything they do, they will have no kingdom impact in the urban contexts of the world.

> **"The planting and development of compassionate churches in every part of the city must be the long-term goal. This is the most effective solution to the multiple ills of the urban community."**
>
> —Roger S. Greenway and Timothy M. Monsma, *Cities: Missions' New Frontier* (Grand Rapids, MI: Baker Books, 1989), 55.

## O: Organizes according to Both Local and Global Strategies

For missionaries working in small towns and villages, a single strategy may be sufficient for the task of multiplying disciples, leaders, and churches. However, metropolitan areas require a different approach. There is no "one size strategy that fits all." Referencing Ray Bakke, Stan Guthrie wrote, "Cities are huge subsets, and we make mistakes when we approach them with a single strategy,"[16] Missionaries must work to develop a variety of strategies according to the people group, subculture, or population segment. Various strategies will also demand the use of different methods.

For the urban missionary, local strategies are not sufficient. These missionaries must capitalize on the significance of their locations for the Great Commission. The urban missionary must also work with missionaries in other world-class cities to develop global strategies. In some respects, people living in New York City have more in common with people in Paris, Beijing, and Tokyo than they do with those living in a small, Midwestern town in the United States.

Globalization, urbanization, and migration have all contributed to the unreached peoples of the world being scattered across the great cities of the world. Urban missionaries are working together to develop strategies to reach the Japanese in California, Brazil, as well as in Japan. Imagine the kingdom possibilities when a church planter in San Francisco connects a Japanese Christian businessperson with a missionary in Nagoya to assist in planting churches throughout that city. Consider the possibilities of what missionaries can learn from one another even though they are working in different countries. What if a church planter in Nepal was able to connect a Nepalese immigrant moving to Boston with a similar missionary in that New England city? North American churches and mission agencies that fail to cooperate miss a kingdom opportunity that has never before been available to the Church.

> **"Every year, close to 70 million people leave their rural homes and head for the cities. That's around 1.4 million people a week, 200,000 a day, 8,000 an hour, 130 every minute."**
>
> —Robert Neuwirth, *Shadow Cities: A Billion Squatters, A New Urban World* (London: Routledge, 2006), xiii.

## I: Incarnational in Witness

The positive influence and impact of the urban church planter will come through an incarnational preaching of the gospel that includes both verbal propositional truth (Romans 10:14–17) and significant social ministry (Luke 6:17–19). Wisdom for healthy contextualization of the gospel, for discipling new believers, and for leadership development will come partially from relationships established in the urban contexts. Failure to live among the people we are ministering to hinders the spread of the gospel. A neighbor, or insider, is usually given more credibility and is more likely to gain a hearing than an outsider. The urban missionary living among the people knows their concerns about the sanitation problems, crime, high cost of rent, and the poor educational system. Such a missionary understands the value of the summer and fall festivals because he or she rubs shoulders with the people throughout the rest of the year in the parks, marketplaces, apartments, or on the ball fields.

## N: Navigates Change Well

If there is anything that is constant in the cities of this world, it is change and change that happens rapidly. Urban missionaries cannot be creatures of habit. Though all missionary strategies must be flexible, urban strategies must be supremely flexible. Missionaries to the cities must be able to make adjustment and decisions "on the fly."

Those supervising the work of urban church planters would be wise in keeping this in mind, especially if they are attempting to supervise such work from a distance. The urban context is many times very fluid. Methods working today may not be effective later today.

## G: Grounded in a Biblical Missiology

Missionaries to the great cities must have a solid missiological foundation with deep roots into the Scriptures. A failure to ground missiology on anything other than the Word of God is a plan for urban failure. Urban missionary practice must be derived from the deep doctrinal truths of the Bible. Though there is a place for sociology, anthropology, and research (see below), the Scriptures must be the starting place and establish the parameters.

For example, the most critical issue in global church planting today is an ecclesiological issue. How an urban missionary answers the question, What is the local church? will affect everything he or she does to plant churches. The answer will affect the strategy developed, resources involved, methods used, and leaders developed. Any urban missionary planning on venturing to the field without a firm grasp on the truths of the Scriptures is, more than anyone else, subject to a missionary belief and practice devolving into pragmatism, syncretism, legalism, institutionalism, or full-blown heresy.

## U: Understands the City

Urban church planters must capitalize on all the resources that God has provided for them to become experts on their cities. As noted in chapter twelve, church planters need to understand their people geographically, demographically, culturally, spiritually, linguistically, historically, and politically. From the time the urban missionaries enter their cities to the time they enter the heavenly city, they must remain students of their cities by taking advantage of all the available sources of information.

Cities are like living organisms; each city has a pulse, or way of life, that differs from other cities and from small towns and villages. People interact, communicate, play, work, eat, travel, think, make decisions, worship, and raise their children differently in different cities and also in ways that differ from rural areas. The pulse of the urban context is not only influenced by the people who live there but also influences the people who live there.

> **"If the church wants to influence society, there is nothing more important for it to do than to reach large global cities."**
>
> —J. Allen Thompson, *Coaching Urban Church Planters: Growing Visionary Leaders, Vital Church and Multiplication Movements in the City* (New York: Redeemer Church Planting Center, 2005), 100.

## R: Relates Well to Diversity

Just as urban missionaries must be flexible and navigate changes with some ease, they also must be able to relate well to a diverse context. Paul G. Hiebert and Eloise Hiebert Meneses wrote, "We must see the city, therefore, not as a homogeneous place, but as hundreds of subcultural groups living and interacting with one another in the same geographic area."[17] On the same city block, the missionary may find the wealthy, street people, students, artists, prostitutes, single mothers, polygamous men, middle-class families, and drug dealers.

## B: Balances Urban Complexity with Missional Simplicity

Church planters should not allow the enormous size and complex nature of the cities to cause them to believe that complex strategies and practices are necessary. Urban missionaries need to keep it simple. Though the multiplication of disciples, leaders, and churches is difficult work, it can be very simple work. An examination of the Scriptures reveals the simple nature of the extension of the Church. A focus on the basics of missionary life and practice is what is needed for the urban environments. The more complex the methods and strategies used by the missionaries, the less likely the new believers and churches will be able to reproduce such methods and strategies. Keeping everything simple (in a biblical way) is what is needed to see the rapid dissemination of the gospel across the urban contexts.

## A: Apostolically Oriented

Effective urban church planters are applying a biblical model that is founded on the apostolic paradigm in the New Testament. An examination of the Scriptures reveals that the apostles, while serving on teams, were primarily involved in evangelism that resulted in new churches. Within those churches the apostles then developed biblically grounded leaders, with the expectation that those leaders would lead in the repetition of this process among their peoples and cities.

## N: Networks with Other Great Commission Christians

The urban environments of this world are too large, too diverse, too needy, too dark, and too significant for missionaries, churches, denominations, and mission agencies to work alone. There can be no lone rangers in the cities. The urban contexts allow missionaries to display to the world the love that exists in the body of Christ (John 13:34–35).

Networking with other Great Commission Christians is not a call for a contemporary urban ecumenical movement or a watering down of theological convictions for the sake of unity. Rather, it is a call to biblical harmony that has the potential to result in a healthy synergism to make a kingdom impact across an urban context. As I have looked across the globe to those working outside of North America, the practice of such kingdom networking is prevalent.

### *Summary:*

1. We live in a world with a majority urban population.
2. Urban growth will continue with the fastest growth occurring in Africa and Asia.
3. Cities have many commonalities.
4. Cities are strategic places for kingdom expansion.
5. Cities pose many unique challenges to church planters.
6. G.O.I.N.G. U.R.B.A.N. can assist the church planter in being better prepared for engaging the peoples of the world's cities.

### *Reflection Questions:*

1. Is reaching the city included in your church multiplication strategy? Why or why not?
2. What did you think about Tim Keller's comment, "In the village, you might win the one or two lawyers to Christ, but if you wanted to win the legal profession, you need to go to the city where you have the law schools, the law journals published, etc."? Do you think this is true? If so, does it apply to other areas of influence (e.g., education, entertainment)?
3. If your future plans involve urban missions, what concerns do you have at the present?
4. In addition to G.O.I.N.G. U.R.B.A.N., can you think of any other factors church planters need to consider before entering urban ministry?

## *Important Terms in This Chapter:*

- Migration
- Immigration
- Megacity
- G.O.I.N.G. U.R.B.A.N

Chapter 23

# TENTMAKING AND CHURCH PLANTING

Paul was a tentmaker, not because there was no other option, but because it was the best option to reach many segments of society. He wanted to be an example of how a Christian lives in this world. He wanted to earn the right to be heard based on his lifestyle, the careful building of relationships, being where the people were, working side-by-side with them.

—John MacArthur[1]

Because this chapter addresses money and missions, I must begin with some disclosure. I have been a bivocational minister; and I have been supported for the past thirteen years by churches. As a national missionary with the North American Mission Board of the Southern Baptist Convention, I am supported by the generous and sacrificial giving of numerous churches that compose my denomination. I share this information to let you know that I believe there is nothing inherently wrong with receiving financial support from other believers and churches for kingdom work. As I'll share later in this chapter, there is biblical evidence for such a model.

As the Church moves further into the twenty-first century, however, numerous challenges are before us that must cause us to rethink the way missionaries are being supported across the globe. The decline of Church membership and financial giving in the Western nations, the suspicions of unbelievers toward the Church, the diminishing authority of Church leaders, and the great need for more and more missionaries all point to the reality that the Church cannot rely only on fully funded church planters for fulfilling the Great Commission. We have always known this to be the case, both biblically and practically, but in many church-planting circles the ideology exists that without money, churches cannot be planted.

Also, I greatly fear that many reading this chapter will respond to my suggestions primarily out of pragmatic—rather than theological and missiological—convictions. For example, some reading this chapter will think, *Yes, you are correct. We need more church planters who are not relying on funding assistance from others.* It is out of the appeal for money that some will respond; but this is simply a pragmatic response. For example, a church-planting leader from the upper Midwest shared with me, "Many of the church planters are looking for a salary that cannot be met in our area. It is hard to tell a church planter that either he or his wife will have to work outside the church to make a living. For this reason we are looking very hard at bi-vo planters."[2]

> **"Tentmaking is not for everyone."**
>
> —Don Hamilton, *Tentmakers Speak* (Ventura, CA: Regal Books, 1989), 89.

Though there is nothing wrong with having a pragmatic response to this real and present need, my concern is that many will fail to see that there is a model in the Scriptures that should be the *primary reason* the Church considers the value of tentmaking, especially for Western nations.

## Defining Tentmaking

The word *tentmaking* stirs up a variety of images. For some the tentmaker is a missionary who travels land and sea to conduct mission work while supporting himself or herself by a skill or trade. Another person sees the tentmaker as a missionary doing covert activities in creative-access nations and thus compromising Christian integrity. For others a tentmaker is someone who ventures into a distant land to minister to others but is forced to earn his or her living through a secular occupation because of not being able to become a "real" missionary through a mission agency. Some may even understand the tentmaker to be someone who works for the Camping Superstore!

For additional information on tentmaking, I direct you to authors such as J. Christy Wilson Jr., Don Hamilton, Ruth E. Siemens, Tetsunao "Ted" Yamamori, Gary Ginter, and Patrick Lai—all who hold well-respected definitions of tentmaking. Also, the Lausanne Congress on World Evangelization in Manila in 1989 articulated its own understanding of tentmaking.[3]

Though there are various nuances that separate definition from definition, the common threads that run throughout the definitions articulated by the scholars mentioned above include the ideas that tentmakers are living and working in an overseas or cross-cultural environment, that a skill, trade, or some secular employment financially supports them, and that they are involved in religious (missionary) activity.

For my purposes here, I would like to broaden the definition to include Western nations and to restrict the definition to biblical church planting. My working definition of a **tentmaker** is *a missionary who is fo-*

*cused on evangelism that results in churches and who is financially supported by a marketable skill, trade, and/or other nonministerial source of income.*

A variation of tentmaking is bivocational missions. A **bivocational missionary** is someone who receives a portion of his or her salary from a church and/or denomination and another portion of salary from a non-clergy type of employment. Bivocational church planters can say that God supplies all of their needs. They understand that God is the source of all their finances—just as he is providing for fully funded church planters.

"However, to reach North American with gospel-preaching churches, we must use more bivocational church planters."

—Steve Nerger and Eric W. Ramsey, *Bivocational Church Planters: Uniquely Wired for Kingdom Growth* (Alpharetta, GA: North American Mission Board, 2007), 9.

## Great Commission Companies

The following excerpt is taken from Steve Rundle and Tom Steffen's work *Great Commission Companies: The Emerging Role of Business in Missions.* In the following passage, they referenced Church history as having various individuals who were businesspeople while they preached the gospel. They also referenced three reasons why few even consider the opportunity of creating businesses for both profit and kingdom expansion.

> Using business as a vehicle for missions and ministry is not new. The apostle Paul, for example, was a full-time leather worker during much of his missionary career. A study of his letters reveals that working was more than a way to support himself; it was a central part of his missionary strategy. Preaching the gospel for free added credibility to his message and served as a model for his converts to follow (see 1 Cor 9:12–18). . . . In the Middle Ages, Christian monks integrated work and ministry by tilling fields, clearing forests and building roads, while also tending to the sick, the orphaned and the imprisoned, protecting the poor, and teaching the children. . . . Even as recently as

the nineteenth century, many early Protestants such as the Moravians, the Basel Mission Society and William Carey integrated business and other secular occupations into their mission strategies.

So why then does this seem so new and unfamiliar? There are at least three reasons why today's missions community has been reluctant to work closely with business. First, there is the recent but deeply entrenched belief that "work" takes time away from "ministry." The closest a person can come to integrating the two is to pursue ministry on a part-time or bivocational basis, which is usually understood to mean wearing a work hat for part of the day and a ministry hat for the other part. . . .

Second is the closely related belief that a business can either serve society or make money, but not both. There is nothing new about this view, but it received a considerable boost in 1913 when the United States first allowed tax deductions for donations made to qualifying nonprofit corporations. This helped cement the perception that activities with high social or spiritual value—education, health care and humanitarian work—are not compatible with a profit motive. By implication evangelism and missions are the least compatible of all. . . .

The third reason business and missions are seldom combined is that it creates complications for a ministry's tax exemption. There are, to be sure, significant constraints in place to prevent people from abusing the tax codes. Nevertheless, secular nonprofits now routinely devote substantial portions of their resources to business activities. Those businesses serve many purposes, ranging from merely being a source of income to being an *integral part* of the ministry itself.

Taken from Steve Rundle and Tom Steffen, *Great Commission Companies: The Emerging Role of Business in Missions* (Downers Grove, IL: InterVarsity Press, 2003), 18–19, italics original.

***Questions to Consider:***

1. Do you agree or disagree with the three reasons why business as missions seems "new and unfamiliar" to many? Explain. Are there any other thoughts you would add to those of Rundle and Steffen?
2. Have you ever considered starting a business as a means to multiply churches? Is this option a future possibility for you?
3. What do you think are the strengths and limitations of planting churches from this paradigm?

## But in the West?

An examination of the most significant literature on tentmaking in the last several decades reveals that the focus is on non-Western nations.[4] One of the major arguments for tentmaking is that of the "creative-access nation." Because traditional missionary approaches are prohibited in certain countries, the Church needs a legitimate way to minister within these nations, and tentmaking provides a means of gaining entrée. In contrast, Western nations have been more open to missionary activities, and so tentmaking is rarely on anyone's mind unless there is a financial crisis facing a denomination or mission agency. When this happens, the Church considers tentmaking or bivocational options out of pragmatic, rather than theological and missiological, convictions.

> **"Being a successful tentmaker is one of the hardest jobs ever, but the rewards that come from being used by God to help others know him is worth all the effort, pain, and frustration."**
>
> —Don Hamilton, *Tentmakers Speak* (Ventura, CA: Regal Books, 1989), 89.

There are several reasons why tentmaking should be emphasized in Western contexts. Interestingly, much of the apologetic for tentmaking in creative-access nations is very applicable to nonrestrictive Western societies. Both J. Christy Wilson Jr. and Jim Reapsome have commented on the various strengths of the tentmaking paradigm.[5] Their writings have influenced my thinking in addressing North America, and I commend their work to you as well. There are at least eight specific reasons for the use of this paradigm in Western contexts.

First, there is biblical support for this model of mission work. A passage in which the concept is clearly portrayed is Acts 18:1–4.[6] After Paul arrived in Corinth from Athens and he was awaiting the arrival of Silas and

Timothy, he involved himself in ministry as well as tentmaking. During this time he met a Jewish man named Aquilla and his wife, Priscilla. Paul had two things in common with them: they had just arrived in the city, and they were of the same trade—making tents. Paul stayed with them and worked alongside them. Paul worked in his trade and preached the gospel. He remained in Corinth for eighteen months and witnessed the planting of the Corinthian Church. If the concept of tentmaker is going to be supported by biblical evidence, then the textual evidence requires the tentmaker also to be involved in church planting.

Second, the Western world, particularly the United States and Canada, has been experiencing many radical cultural shifts, especially throughout the twentieth century. Globalization, urbanization, postindustrialization, immigration, postmodernism, pluralism, and economic swings have created within our information-driven societies a stewpot of worldviews. Gone are the days when we could assume having the same cultural perspectives as our neighbors across the street. Even more astounding—gone are the days when we could assume sharing the same worldview and culture as our neighbors who are of the same ethnicity, speak the same language, and are of the same socioeconomic and educational level. Though some are quick to omit tentmaking from the missionaries to the West by pointing to the lack of cross-cultural dynamics involved in their work, it must be understood that all church planting is cross-cultural to some degree.[7]

> **"The future of North American church planting just might lie in the hands of farmers, salesmen, and teachers."**
>
> —Steve Nerger and Eric W. Ramsey, *Bivocational Church Planters: Uniquely Wired for Kingdom Growth* (Alpharetta, GA: North American Mission Board, 2007), 84.

Third, the potential for the missionary to develop credibility and to open a multitude of doors to preach the gospel increases whenever he or she enters into the world of the marketplace. For example, Steve Sjogren and Rob Lewin strongly admonished all church planters to get into the community via employment. They wrote, "You need to work no matter what your financial backing looks like. We encourage you to work outside the church until your plant reaches 200 in weekend attendance."[8] One church planter shared with me that though he did not have any problem receiving financial support for the ministry, he did not receive any money for working among his people group in the United States—so they wouldn't think that he was only loving and serving them because he was getting paid.

Many people in the West, particularly in the United States and Canada, have negative thoughts regarding the Church and money. In fact, one of the commonly heard excuses for why people are not interested in Christianity is because of their perception that "the Church is only interested in my money." Tentmakers are able to gain credibility in the eyes of those who labor alongside them by having "real jobs." The perspective of Jack Strong illustrates the point. Strong, who undertook a coal-mining job while serving as a vicar within the same parish, noted, "After priest and parishioners have scrubbed each others' backs a few times in the communal pithead bath-house, things could never be quite the same again."[9]

Along with credibility in the eyes of unbelievers come opportunities to share the gospel that would not be available if the missionary was outside of the marketplace. Postmodern cultural shifts have created a desire for authenticity and legitimacy in many areas of life. People are tired of being told empty promises by advertisers, educators, politicians, and religious leaders. There is a hunger for reality and genuineness. Gone are the days in the West where the clergyman was well respected and honored as an outstanding citizen with a calling that surpassed any secular form of employment.

I recall a counseling session in which I was ministering to a teenage girl and her mother. It was getting late in the evening, and the mother felt that they were intruding on my time. I told them that I was here for them and that I did not mind staying as long as they needed. To this the girl responded in semijest, "Yes, you are getting paid to be here."

Fourth, though the Church in the West is the wealthiest in the world, few financial resources are allocated to support full-time church planters for the long term. Tentmakers are able to avoid this dependency on a denomination, mission agency, or a church, thereby freeing up funds to be used in other areas of missions—particularly for missionary labors in the Majority World where the receptivity levels to the gospel are much higher, the needs are much greater, and the Church is growing the fastest.

Fifth, in a recent study I conducted of 190 U.S. and Canadian church planters and church-planting leaders, the most common critical issue they faced was a lack of finances. Many church planters found themselves receiving very little financial support to serve in such roles. Some felt called to a particular area but were unable to live among the people because of the cost of living and their small church or mission agency subsidy. Tentmaking allows for a source of income that could easily keep the missionaries out of poverty and allow them to relate socioeconomically to their people group while fulfilling the call to kingdom advancement.[10]

> **"However, since we have become normal, 'ordinary' people in our host culture, other people are open to us in ways they may not be to traditional missionaries."**
>
> —Chuck, tentmaker from Eastern Europe, in *Tentmakers Speak* by Don Hamilton (Ventura, CA: Regal Books, 1989), 68.

Sixth, the tentmaker is able to avoid the temptation of developing evangelism strategies that are subtly motivated by financial gain. During one conversation with a church-planting pastor from the Midwest, I was told that he was approaching the date in which his personal funding would begin to decrease, according to his denomination's policy. Though this individual's primary reason for being involved in church planting was to glorify God through making disciples, he did tell me that in the back of his mind was the prosaic reality that if his strategy did not result in quickly reaching others who would start giving tithes and offerings, soon he would be out of money to provide for his family.

Seventh, tentmakers are not restricted by many of the traditions, cultural expectations, bureaucratic policies, and red tape that, many times, accompany the reception of subsidy. There is much freedom found in the ministry of the tentmaker—freedoms that other church planters sacrifice when they serve with parachurch organizations. Tentmakers are not restricted by guidelines developed by policymakers who are miles away from the field and unfamiliar with the church-planting context.

Eighth, Wilson noted that tentmakers "have satisfactions of their own professional accomplishment which may balance the frustrations and discouragements which may arise in the course of Christian witness in different areas."[11] Many times in the West, church planting is a slow process, and certain personalities (including the personalities of those who fund church planters) have a difficult time when the work appears to be moving slowly. God has created within people a desire to take satisfaction in their accomplishments for the kingdom. Tentmakers are able to experience this satisfaction in knowing that they have put in a day's work and ministry, thus not separating the secular from the religious.

## Limitations for the Tentmaker

It would not be fair to discuss the advantages of tentmaking (and bivocational) missions and not address the limitations of such work. In his book *The Bivocational Pastor*, Luther M. Dorr observed some of the limitations of serving in this type of ministry.[12] Though he does not connect these limitations to church planters or tentmaking, they are as applicable to these two areas as well as that of bivocational pastors in established churches.

Such workers can find themselves with a lack of time to participate in the desired ministry activities. The amount of time devoted to a person's trade can detract from those activities related to church planting, unless the two are tightly wed. A second limitation is that there is a real possibility of a crisis of identity. Unless a holistic understanding of a calling in Christ and a healthy theology of work exist, the church planter may, at times, wonder if he or she is a missionary or a secular worker. Third, since time is limited, it is possible to neglect the family in the church-planting process. If not planned appropriately, there will be no time to spend with the spouse and children. Fourth, since such a person will generally have a full schedule, there may not be enough time for specific meetings related to the ministry.

## Biblical Responses to the Issue of Money

Responding to the financial issues related to mission work is no easy task. The relationship of money and missions has been discussed and debated for many years. In differing ministry contexts, church planters may have to rely on more than one source of finances. We see at least three ways the Lord met the financial needs of church planters throughout the Scriptures.[13] Examining the life of the apostle Paul, financial support came from three sources: churches (2 Corinthians 11:9; Philippians 4:15–20), individuals (Acts 16:15; Titus 3:13; Philemon v. 22), and his own labor (Acts 20:33–35). Because the present church-planting literature is not short on discussions revolving around developing financial partnerships with individuals and churches, I will direct the reader to the resources found in the bibliography and reserve the rest of this chapter for the latter issue.

F. F. Bruce noted that Paul served as a tentmaker "partly as a matter of principle, partly by way of example to his converts, and partly to avoid giving his critics any opportunity to say that his motives were mercenary."[14] A fourth reason Paul chose to abstain from receiving financial support was so that he could become all things to all people so he could win some (1 Corinthians 9:22).

> **"The objective of tentmaking is to put Jesus in front of those who have never had an opportunity to hear the truth about Him, or who have turned their backs on Him because of an encounter with some form of 'Christian religion.'"**
>
> —Patrick Lai, *Tentmaking: Business as Missions* (Colorado Springs, CO: Authentic Media, 2005), 4.

## Lukan Narratives

Two passages in the Book of Acts that offer substantial evidence for the apostle's tentmaking paradigm are 18:1–4 and 20:32–35. I have already addressed the former tentmaking passage in an earlier section, so I will briefly examine the latter passage.

The setting was in Miletus, and the audience was the elders of the Ephesian Church. Since Paul was in a hurry to arrive in Jerusalem before Pentecost, he sailed past Ephesus and called for the elders to meet him. In this farewell address, Paul's last words to the church leaders included his usual admonition to imitate his lifestyle: "And now I commend you to God and to the word of his grace, which is able to build you up and to give youthe inheritance among all those who are sanctified. I coveted no one's silver or gold or apparel. You yourselves know that these hands ministered to my necessities and to those who were with me. In all things I have shown you that by working hard in this way we must help the weak and remember the words of the Lord Jesus, how he himself said, 'It is more blessed to give than to receive.'"

By manifesting a healthy work ethic, Paul was able to avoid the accusation of avarice and truly show forth the example of a servant leader, as one who gives rather than takes.

## Corinthian Correspondence

There are several Corinthian passages that offer evidence for and explanation of Paul's tentmaking practice. In 1 Corinthians 4:12, Paul made the passing statement that he worked with his own hands.[15] In 1 Corinthians 9 the apostle made a very clear declaration that he indeed had the right to food and drink from the Corinthians (v. 4), but abdicated this right so as to not hinder the spread of the gospel (v. 12) and considered it a reward to preach the gospel without charge (v. 18). He made himself a slave to all so that he "might win more of them" (v. 19) and show his desire to "become all things to all people, that by all means I might save some" (v. 22).

## Thessalonian Correspondence

Paul maintained his tentmaking practice while in Thessalonica. In 1 Thessalonians 2:9 Paul reminded the Church that he and this team labored "night and day" so as not to burden them. Later, in his second letter to this Church, he repeated this fact and echoed his Corinthian abdication in conjunction with the problem that the Thessalonian Church had some members who were unwilling to work.

> Now we command you, brothers, in the name of our Lord Jesus Christ, that you keep away from any brother who is walking in idleness and not in accord with the tradition that you received from us. For you yourselves know how you ought to imitate us, because we were not idle when we were with you, nor did we eat anyone's bread without paying for it, but with toil and labor we worked night and day, that we might not be a burden to any of you. It was not because we do not have that right, but to give you in ourselves an example to imitate. For even when we were with you, we would give you this command: If anyone is not willing to work, let him not eat. For we hear that some among you walk in idleness, not busy at work, but busybodies. Now such persons we command and encourage in the Lord Jesus Christ to do their work quietly and to earn their own living. (2 Thessalonians 3:6–12)

## The Need for Marketable Skills, Trades, and Degrees

Unfortunately, the North American Church rarely assumes the possibility that church planters could be tentmakers. Even more unfortunate, many church planters do not consider the possibility of learning or developing a marketable profession, skill, or trade that would offer them both personal finances as well as a platform on which to penetrate a society with the gospel. By the time many individuals even consider the possibility of church planting, they are already on a track to professional ministry as a vocation, and the necessary change for some is too radical because they have come so far in their studies and plans.

Churches need to be educating their young people that the call to missions throughout the world demands that they prayerfully consider obtaining marketable skills and trades and earning college and graduate degrees that will best prepare them for the global marketplace. They need to be educating their people in solid theology and healthy missiology as related to work. Therefore, wherever they send their missionaries to plant churches in Western or non-Western nations, they will be better prepared to engage nonkingdom citizens with the gospel.

> **"We need to find jobs or design businesses that enhance our opportunities to work with nationals."**
>
> —Patrick Lai, *Tentmaking: Business as Missions* (Colorado Springs, CO: Authentic Media, 2005), 145.

Obviously, not all careers are effective for tentmakers; therefore, prayerful discernment should be used in the selection process. They need to consider careers that provide flexibility as well as many opportunities to interact with unbelievers.

## An Excursus: Personal Finances

I think it is important to conclude this chapter by sharing some of the findings of the informal research project that studied critical issues facing U.S. and Canadian church planters that I referenced earlier in this chapter. A few years ago, I sent an open-ended e-mail survey to 190 church planters in thirty-nine states and four provinces, asking, "What are the five most critical issues in North American church planting today?" Thirteen different parachurch, church, and denominational groups were represented. Of the findings, the most commonly mentioned critical issue facing church planters was that of finances.[16] Subsequent research by others and interactions with church planters and their supervisors have confirmed the findings from my informal survey work.

Fred G. King wrote, "Church planting is not the most financially lucrative ministry, but many will say it is the most spiritually rewarding.

The new pastor often finds himself in difficult financial straits yet expressing confidence, enthusiasm and trust in the all-sufficiency of God which frequently shines like a light in a dark place."[17] Despite their agreement with King and the fullness of the Spirit in their lives, North American church planters and their families face the issue of personal finances as a major concern. Arnell ArnTessoni offered a unique glimpse into this area of the life of the church-planting family in her excellent work *Gentle Plantings: A Personal Journal for Church Planters' Wives.* She wrote:

> There's probably not one of us who hasn't spent a worry-filled night tossing and turning thinking about money—or the lack of it. Gary and I found out two days ago that the salary support funding from our denomination has suddenly stopped and we're on our own, even though church giving isn't yet covering our church budget. After hearing the news my first instinct (which I only barely controlled myself from actually doing) was to grab Gary by the neck and shake him screaming, "We've got to do something! We're in the middle of our house lease! We've got to get money! Money! Go get that tin mug and hit the streets! We need money!"[18]

> "Kingdom entrepreneurs have a genuine desire to see communities of faith spring up in the spiritually driest places, and are willing to live and work in these places to make that happen. Rather than perceiving the business as a distraction from their ministry, kingdom entrepreneurs recognize it as the necessary context for their incarnational outreach."
>
> —Steven L. Rundle, "Preparing the Next Generation of Kingdom Entrepreneurs," in *On Kingdom Business: Transforming Missions through Entrepreneurial Strategies*, eds. Tetsunao Yamamori and Kenneth A. Eldred, (Wheaton, IL: Crossway Books, 2003), 229–30.

Many of the church planters in my study received a personal income from a denomination or a church. In most of the cases where such funding was provided, the finances were limited to a commitment of a few years at the most. The church planters entered into the church-planting work with the knowledge that at the end of the designated time, their personal funding would cease. In many of the cases, the expectation was that the church planter would become the pastor of the newly planted church. By the end of the financial commitment from the denomination or church, therefore, the new church was to be financially supporting the church planter/pastor.

Of the numerous e-mails that I received from the participants in the study, those related to personal finances contained many emotionally charged comments. The following are some of the responses that surfaced during the study. These statements are poignant.

- "Many church planters have only a short amount of time to become self-supporting. That is a pressure-cooker atmosphere that promotes much stress." (Church planter from New York)
- "We are supported, at this point, far better than the majority of planters in this area. However, the duration of support being three to five years is simply not long enough for most plants. Historically, it is the unusual plant that can become self supporting in that length of time." (Church planter from New York)
- "Financial resources from conventions and sponsoring churches are usually not adequate, especially for a planter who has a family." (Church planter from South Carolina)
- "[Certain groups] say that church planting is one of the highest priorities, but we make funding basically a two year-and-out plan. That may work in some areas but I don't think that is a

very good plan for the majority of church plants." (Church planter from West Virginia)

- "I have received more financial support than most of the church planters that I know. The problem for me is not the amount of support so much as the length of support. I am supported for three years. At the rate we are going there is no way our congregation will be able to support my family at the end of the three years. This is disturbing to say the least. There are times I think I would have been better off working a full-time job to support my family and not being dependent on support." (Church planter from California)

Many church planters have come to realize that the theory of a new church financially being able to support the church-planting pastor with a full-time salary is not always a reality by the time the financial support for the ministry ceases. Certain fields experience a slower growth rate than other fields. Also, some church planters may find themselves in areas where the church will never be able to support a pastor with a full-time salary.

### *Summary:*

1. There is biblical support for church planters receiving financial support and assistance from (1) churches, (2) individuals, and (3) marketplace employment.
2. Tentmaking and bivocationalism are two forms of marketplace employment. A tentmaking missionary supports himself or herself solely by a marketable profession. A bivocational missionary supports himself or herself by both a marketable profession and a church/denominationally related source of income.
3. The great need, especially in the Western world, is for missionaries to serve as tentmakers.

4. Though not everyone is called to be a tentmaker or to be bivocational, the advantages of marketplace missions outweigh the limitations.
5. Young people planning to serve in church-planting work need to obtain marketable degrees and professions from which they can carry out the Great Commission.

## *Reflection Questions:*

1. Is tentmaking or bivocational missionary work an option for you? Why or why not?
2. Can you think of other advantages or limitations to tentmaking or bivocational ministry not addressed in the chapter?
3. Do you have any concerns about serving as a tentmaker or bivocational missionary? Discuss these with your family and church-planting team.
4. What can you be doing now to prepare yourself with a marketable career that would give you a great platform to multiply churches?

## *Important Terms Used in this Chapter:*

- Tentmaker
- Bivocational missionary

Chapter 24

# MISSIONARIES OR PASTORS: WHAT ARE CHURCH PLANTERS?

The missionary, on the other hand, is essentially a wandering evangelist or teacher, and therefore he cannot be the pastor of a settled church; because he cannot both move about and be always at hand to serve the church in which he lives.

—Roland Allen[1]

Following my definition that biblical church planting is evangelism that results in new churches, a **biblical church planter** is simply one who is sent to preach the gospel and establish churches through making disciples from the harvest fields. Though churches can be planted with individuals and families that are already kingdom citizens, the church planter following the biblical paradigm of making disciples focuses on abundant gospel sowing in the hearts of those outside of the kingdom and allows the Holy Spirit to work in those hearts to birth kingdom citizens and new churches.

# Faulty Assumption

The North American Church has a significant and faulty assumption regarding church planters. In the United States it is not only assumed but also expected that if someone is going to plant a church, they will also pastor that church. The overwhelming majority of the church-planting literature, conferences, and training events geared to a U.S. audience presume this situation. Since at least the 1970s, the North American Church has categorized the plant-and-pastor model as the normative way to plant churches.

> "The apostolic planter can be most effective when not pastoring a local church (although the planter might be on staff at a local church). Instead, the apostolic harvest planter's main focus is on reproducing congregations."
>
> —Ed Stetzer, *Planting Missional Churches* (Nashville, TN: Broadman and Holman Publishers, 2006), 60.

One example of the practical outworking of such a paradigm is observed in the way churches, denominations, and mission agencies typically fund church planters. If planters receive financial support, the duration of the support will be for two, three, or maybe four years. Usually, the funding is established on a phase-out basis, with the church planter receiving 100 percent of the annual funding in year one, 75–50 percent in year two, and 25 percent in year three. Such a declining scale is founded on the plant-and-pastor model, with the assumption that the newly planted church will be able to provide the missing percentage for the planter/pastor after the first year.

## Two General Types of Church Planters

Though others specify church planters according to several different categories,[2] I separate contemporary church planters into two general types. Though there is going to be some overlap between the two types regarding characteristics, skills, and methods used, one fundamental difference exists. **Apostolic missionaries** do not plant-and-pastor churches, whereas **missional pastors** plant and remain as the pastors of those newly planted churches.

Before continuing, I need to be clear. All church planters must work to establish healthy foundations for newly planted churches and, most likely, will function pastorally for a season. Both apostolic missionaries and missional pastors must work for healthy church growth. Both types of church planters must work to provide healthy leadership for the new churches. Whether leadership comes from them remaining with the churches as pastors, obtaining pastors from other churches, or raising up pastors from among the new churches, all church planters are accountable for the health of the new churches.

### Apostolic Missionaries

The word *missionary* is derived from the Latin word *mitto*. The corresponding Greek word is *apostolos*, translated *apostle*, and refers to a person who is sent as a messenger.[3] By definition, a missionary is to be apostolic in his or her work. Practically, such an individual is involved in communicating the gospel to unbelievers, gathering new believers together to be the local expression of the body of Christ, and raising up pastors/elders from those newly planted churches. The apostolic missionary works to instill into the life of the new church a healthy understanding of what it means to be kingdom citizens, living according to a kingdom ethic, in a kingdom community.

So, why create the label "apostolic missionaries"? Isn't that redundant? The immediate answer is yes. However, though missionaries do many excellent tasks in the world, the word *missionary* has come to include many aspects of ministry not connected to church planting (e.g., school teaching, water purification, medicine, agriculture). The biblical example of an apostle maintains a focus on planting churches with people from the harvest. Apostolic missionaries, then, are primarily focused on the multiplication of disciples, leaders, and churches. Though missionaries may be involved in business or education or other tasks, they work through those means to share the good news and plant churches. Also, I am using the word *apostolic* to distinguish it from the plant-and-pastor model in order to communicate a nonpastoring paradigm.

My main reason for using the word *apostolic*, however, is to avoid any confusion regarding the biblical concept of the church planter. *Apostolic* is an adjective, like *pastoral* or *evangelistic* and communicates a function. But many in the Church today are wary of using the word *apostle* to describe anyone other than the Twelve and Paul, and the Church is more comfortable with the word *missionary*. So, I have added the adjective *apostolic* to *missionary* to be more palatable, and most importantly, more biblical in conveying the role of the missionary in the Church.

## Missional Pastors

Comparing the church-planting pastor with the apostolic missionary, Ed Stetzer was correct when he wrote, "The founding pastor has a desire to stay at one church longer than an apostolic harvest planter stays. The founding pastor has a pastor's heart, so he doesn't become restless to move on like the apostolic harvest planter. Ideally, the pastor will lead the new church to start others but will remain as pastor of the original church because he's a pastor with a missionary's heart rather than a missionary with a pastor's heart."[4]

Every pastor should be a missional pastor. However, I am specifically referring to a church planter who plants a church and then remains as its pastor. A missional pastor begins his ministry primarily functioning in an apostolic capacity. He is working in the harvest fields. As the Holy Spirit brings people to salvation, the missional pastor then gathers those new believers into a local expression of the body of Christ, still functioning in an apostolic manner. However, at this point, a role change occurs, with the church planter transitioning to that of pastor/elder. Following the planting of the church, a missional pastor works to instill within the newly planted church a healthy understanding of kingdom citizenship that will lead to the planting of other churches.

My church-planting experience has been in this category. In fact, as I write this chapter I am serving a church that was recently planted. The lead church planter has transitioned to serving as the lead pastor/elder and is doing an outstanding job leading this church to plant other churches. At the time of this writing, we have been blessed to send out church-planting teams to Cleveland, Ohio, and New Orleans, Louisiana, while working to raise up other church planters to go to the Pacific Northwest next year and Montreal the following year. In addition to sending out church-planting teams, we are presently working with another church planter in a nearby community in Louisville, Kentucky.

> **"The missionary is a temporary factor in any local area, and he should build the church in such a way that it will be able to continue after he has gone."**
>
> —Melvin Hodges, *The Indigenous Church* (Springfield, MO: Gospel Publishing House, 1976), 126.

The rise in the number of missional pastors in the past twenty years in North America has been one of the best recent gifts to the Church.

May the number of missional pastors continue to increase among church planters.

## The Need of the Hour

Despite the rise in the number of missional pastors over the past several years, the global need of the hour is for more apostolic missionaries, especially in the West. For the most part, the Church in the West has abandoned the role of the missionary in church-planting circles for that of the pastor. We must have *both*!

It is not my purpose here to attempt to convince you that the West is more a mission field now than it was a hundred years ago. Others—such as missiologists David Bosch (from South Africa), Leslie Newbigin (from England), Ed Stetzer (from the United States), Alan Hirsch (from Australia), and those at the Gospel and Our Culture Network (from the United States)—have written extensively on this shift from Christendom to post-Christendom realities and the need for the church to respond. Along with a mission field comes the need for apostolic missionaries.

When it comes to domestic missions, ironically, the Church in the United States and Canada still functions from a pastoral mindset and not an apostolic mindset. However, apostolic missionaries make up much of the North American church-planting force serving in the Majority World. In fact, few Western mission agencies will send anyone to another country to plant and pastor national churches, but rather they send apostolic missionaries.

Naturally, where the Church has been established for some time, as in Western contexts, we are going to see a rise in the number of church planters pastoring churches. Again, such an approach can be healthy and should be encouraged. Unfortunately, however, the Church in the United States and Canada is primarily focused on the plant-and-pastor paradigm. The pendulum in the church-planting world has swung far from the church planter as apostolic missionary and toward the church planter as pastor.

> **"Apostles are translocal rather than local leaders, and their focus is on mission rather than maintenance."**
>
> —Stuart Murray, *Church Planting: Laying Foundations* (London: Paternoster Press, 1998), 242.

## Biblical Support

I once taught a class in which I asked the students to offer the biblical evidence for both the plant-and-pastor paradigm and the apostolic missionary paradigm. Immediately, students began offering support for the latter but were practically silenced when it came to finding support for the former. Though most church-planting books written to a Western audience offer biblical evidence for church planting and challenge church planters to follow the biblical evidence, they improperly interpret the passages through a pastoral missiology and apply those passages to the pastorate.

Just as wearing glasses with blue-colored lenses will make everything appear to be blue, the Church in the West generally examines the Scriptures through pastoral lenses. Such a hermeneutic causes us to fail to properly interpret the New Testament in its historical contexts. All of Paul's letters to churches were written to newly planted churches. Though we refer to the writings to Timothy and Titus as the Pastoral Epistles, these three letters were not written to permanent pastors. Timothy was to remain in Ephesus (where there was a plurality of elders, Acts 20), help put things in order in the churches, and teach men to pass along the truths of the Scriptures to other men (1 Timothy 1:3; 2 Timothy 2:2). Titus was to remain on Crete and appoint elders in the churches (Titus 1:5).

Before continuing any further, again, I must remind you that it is my desire that the plant-and-pastor model will continue, as long as such planters are missional pastors. However, the weight of the biblical support for the church planter is clearly on the apostolic missionary paradigm. We must not fool ourselves into thinking otherwise.

## Missionary Paradigms

In the early twentieth century, Anglican priest Roland Allen compared the missionary methods of his day to those of the apostle Paul found in the New Testament. In the following excerpt, Allen noted that Western missionaries were leading the new churches to be too dependent on them.

> There is a still greater difference between his method of dealing with his converts and that common among us today. Indeed, I think we may say that it is in his dealing with his converts that we come to the heart of the matter and may hope to find one secret of his amazing success. With us today this is the great difficulty. We can gather in converts, we often gather in large numbers; but we cannot train them to maintain their own spiritual life. We cannot establish the church on a self-supporting basis. Our converts often display great virtues, but they remain, too often for generations, dependent upon us. Having gathered a Christian congregation the missionary is too often tied to it and so hindered from further evangelistic work. This difficulty unquestionably arises from our early training of our converts, and therefore it is of supreme importance that we should endeavour to discover, as far as we can, the methods of St. Paul in training his. For he succeeded exactly where we fail.

Taken from Roland Allen, *Missionary Methods: St. Paul's or Ours?* American ed. (Grand Rapids, MI: William B. Eerdmans Publishing Company, 1962), 82.

***Questions to Consider:***

1. Do you believe that contemporary church planters should follow the paradigm of the apostle Paul, or were such approaches only for the first century?
2. What practical issues do you think Allen was referring to when he wrote that the converts were too dependent on the missionaries?
3. Do you agree or disagree with the statement "For he succeeded exactly where we fail"? Explain your answer.

## Apostolic Missionaries

The ultimate apostle was the Lord Jesus (Hebrews 3:1). He provided an incarnational model of being sent from the Father (John 1:14). He reached people from the harvest, raised up leaders from those new believers, and sent them to the nations (Matthew 28:19). After the ascension, the New Testament reveals the work of Philip (not one of the Twelve) and Peter in the planting of churches (in Jerusalem, Samaria, and in Cornelius's house). The latter half of the Book of Acts and much of the New Testament give credit to the apostolic work of Paul (again, not one of the Twelve).

## Missional Pastors

If the biblical evidence clearly advocates an apostolic missionary role, then is there any evidence for the missional pastor paradigm as related to church planting? I only know of a few *possible* references to the plant-and-pastor approach to church planting, with one being an argument more from history.

In his first epistle, Peter referred to himself as both an apostle and a fellow elder (1 Peter 1:1; 5:1). If he was referring to his ministry in Jerusalem, then maybe he later functioned more in a pastoral role. We do know from the Book of Acts that Peter was significantly involved in the planting and growth of the Jerusalem Church.

The second possible example, though purely speculative, is that of Priscilla and Aquila. They were with Paul in the planting of the Church in Corinth and Ephesus. Also, the church met in their home in Ephesus (1 Corinthians 16:19). There is a historical argument that the churches of the day met in the houses of the elders. However, aside from the Jerusalem Church, the argument is not from the biblical text.

> **"The founding pastor wants to plant, grow, and stay long term."**
>
> —Ed Stetzer, *Planting Missional Churches* (Nashville, TN: Broadman and Holman Publishers, 2006), 62.

Another related example is James the brother of Jesus (Matthew 13:55, Galatians 1:19). Though not one of the Apostles, following the Ascension, he was most likely present in the upper room and participated in the birth of the Jerusalem Church. Sometime later, we also know that he held a significant leadership role in that Church (Acts 15:13; Galatians 2:9). Also, the Apostle John was significantly involved in the birth and leadership in the Church as well.

Does this lack of biblical support mean that the plant-and-pastor paradigm should be discarded? Absolutely not. However, especially in the West, we must allow this lack of support to give us pause and ask why this model dominates in the United States and Canada. If the Scriptures strongly support the paradigm of the apostolic missionary while our contemporary paradigms do not find firm biblical endorsement, change is needed. I am not advocating that the apostolic missionary is *the key* to solving all the problems facing the growth of the Church in the West. I am, however, saying that we must allow the Scriptures to guide us in both belief and practice, which means our theology, missiology, and institutions must also adjust accordingly.

Significant room must be made for the apostolic missionary. *The apostolic missionary paradigm must become the expectation for church planters regardless of their geographical location, with the plant-and-pastor paradigm being welcomed, yet the exception to the norm.*

> **"A foreign missionary should not be the pastor of a native church. His business is to plant churches, in well-chosen parts of his field, committing them as soon as possible to the care of native pastors."**
>
> —Rufus Anderson in *To Advance the Gospel: Selections from the Writings of Rufus Anderson*, ed. R. Pierce Beaver (Grand Rapids, MI: William B. Eerdmans Publishing Company, 1967), 99.

## Commonly Shared Characteristics of Church Planters

Aside from the Barnabas Factors I addressed in chapter fifteen, others have attempted to determine characteristics of effective church planters. In 1984 Charles Ridley, a professor of psychology at Fuller Theological Seminary, partnered with thirteen denominational groups to research the profile of a church planter. Ridley later published his findings in *How to Select Church Planters* and along with Robert E. Logan and Helena Gerstenberg produced the resource *Training for Selection Interviewing.*[5] From his research Ridley developed a list of forty-eight different performance dimensions of church planters. Later this list was reduced to thirteen essential qualities, and these have been extremely influential in practically every North American church-planting circle for evaluating potential church planters. According to Ridley, effective church planters manifest the following characteristics:

- Visionizing capacity
- Intrinsically motivated
- Create ownership of ministry
- Relate to the unchurched
- Spousal cooperation
- Effectively build relationships
- Committed to church growth
- Responsive to the needs in the community
- Utilize the giftedness of others
- Flexible and adaptable
- Build group cohesiveness
- Resilient
- Exercise faith[6]

## Three Universal Skills for Church Planters

There are three primary skills that must be used on a consistent and intentional basis by all church planters, regardless of the paradigm used. First, all church planters must be significantly involved in multiplying disciples through evangelism. In the early days on the field, church planters must spend the majority of their time in evangelism. Church-planting teams must hold each other accountable in this area, because it is the *most* important activity and yet is *always* the first area to be neglected for other important church-planting activities (e.g., administrative work, developing Bible studies, cultural exegesis, language development). Because the church-planting team is modeling what it means to be on mission for the King, then it must deliberately model intentional evangelism.

Second, church planters must be significantly involved in starting and multiplying small groups. Generally, the simpler the organizational pattern for these groups, the more easily they can be reproduced by others. Small groups are needed to reach seekers, instruct new believers, and develop leadership.

Third, church planters must be focused on multiplying leaders who are coming from the harvest (see chapter eight). An apprentice system must be established with the plan to raise up leaders from the small groups. These new leaders will be taught how to reproduce and guide their own small groups in the future. Mentoring and coaching potential leaders is a must, and modeling the kingdom ethic before them is essential (see chapter seven).

### *Summary:*

1. A biblical church planter is someone who is sent to preach the gospel and establish churches through making disciples from the harvest fields.

2. Unfortunately, in most North American church-planting circles, church planters are expected to plant and pastor new churches.
3. There are two general types of church planters: (1) missional pastors, who plant and pastor new churches while leading them to plant other churches; and (2) apostolic missionaries, who plant churches and raise up and equip pastoral leadership for those churches.
4. The urgent need of the hour, particularly in the West, is for more apostolic missionaries.
5. The weight of the New Testament evidence supports an apostolic missionary model for church planters.
6. Effective church planters share many common characteristics.
7. The three universal skills of all church planters are related to (1) evangelism, (2) starting and leading small groups, and (3) working to develop leaders from the people reached.

### *Reflection Questions:*

1. Why do you believe that the plant-and-pastor model is the expected paradigm to use in the United States?
2. What was your response to the arguments for the New Testament evidence pointing to the apostolic missionary model and not to the plant-and-pastor model? How does this affect your understanding of the church planter?
3. Do you see yourself as a missional pastor or as an apostolic missionary? Why?
4. Reread Ridley's thirteen qualities for church planters. Are these qualities in your life? Are there qualities missing from his list that you believe should be present in church planters?

## *Important Terms in This Chapter:*

- Biblical church planter
- Apostolic missionary
- Missional pastor

Chapter 25

# CHURCH-PLANTING MOVEMENTS AND CHURCH PLANTING

It's not about a church planting movement—it's about a Jesus movement!

—Bob Roberts Jr.[1]

Few topics in the world of missions today are as popular as that of **church-planting movements**. Since the turn of the century, denominations, parachurch organizations, local churches, and missionaries have been discussing, debating, and developing strategies that work toward the facilitation of such incredible amounts of church growth. According to a training manual produced by the International Mission Board, church-planting movements, or CPMs as they are commonly referred to, are important because they seem to "hold forth the greatest potential for the largest number of lost individuals glorifying God by coming into new life in Christ and entering into communities of faith."[2]

## Defining CPMs

David Garrison popularized the notion of CPMs at the turn of the twenty-first century in a small booklet published by the International Mission Board and later in his book *Church Planting Movements: How God Is Redeeming a Lost World.*[3] For Garrison, a CPM is "*a rapid multiplication of indigenous churches planting churches that sweeps through a people group or population segment.*" However, early in the twentieth century, Roland Allen had written of such movements in his classic *The Spontaneous Expansion of the Church.* According to Allen, "This then is what I mean by spontaneous expansion. I mean the expansion which follows the unexhorted and unorganized activity of individual members of the Church explaining to others the Gospel which they have found for themselves; I mean the expansion which follows the irresistible attraction of the Christian Church for men who see its ordered life, and are drawn to it by desire to discover the secret of a life which they instinctively desire to share; I mean also the expansion of the Church by the addition of new churches."[4]

Figure 25.1 **Common Characteristics in Every Church-Planting Movement**

1. Extraordinary times of prayer take place.
2. Abundant evangelism occurs.
3. Intentional planting of reproducing churches.
4. High view of the authority of God's Word is maintained.
5. Local people provide the leadership.
6. Lay leadership leads the way.
7. House churches are planted.
8. Local churches begin planting churches.
9. Rapid reproduction of disciples and churches occurs.
10. Healthy churches planted.

Figure 25.2 **Characteristics in Most Church-Planting Movements**

1. A climate of uncertainty exists in the society.
2. The society is insulated from outsiders.
3. There is a high cost involved for following Christ.
4. A bold fearless faith is manifested by the new believers.
5. Entire families are converted.
6. There is a rapid incorporation of new believers into churches.
7. Worship occurs in the people's heart language.
8. Divine signs and wonders occur.
9. On-the-job leadership training is used for new church leaders.
10. Missionaries suffer for their work.

The phenomenon that both men described was a move of the Holy Spirit among a sizable group of nonkingdom citizens to bring them to faith in a relatively short period of time, resulting in a large increase of new churches. The preceding two tables are adapted from Garrison's observations of common characteristics found in all CPMs[5] and common characteristics found in most CPMs.[6]

In addition to the lists included in Garrison's book, missiologist Jim Slack has documented nineteen common findings among confirmed CPMs. At the time of this writing, Slack has been involved in the assessment of twelve CPMs from across the globe, and his findings include the following:

1. Much prayer was provided for people's physical and spiritual needs among the new churches.
2. Preconversion dreams were common in the Islamic contexts; such dreams were used by the Lord to create a receptivity to the gospel.
3. Care for one another's physical needs was common in the churches for other brothers and sisters, as well as for the lost.
4. Little or no dependence on outside sources was found in third, fourth, and successive generations of churches.

5. The majority of pastoral leaders came from the people of the newly planted churches.
6. Most pastoral leaders were bivocational; a few were paid a full-time income.
7. Believers regularly confirmed having meaningful worship experiences in their churches.
8. The local churches gave their pastors permission to handle the ordinances; the pastors recognized themselves as pastor-evangelists; the churches sensed their autonomy as local congregations.
9. Evangelism and church planting occurred in the heart language of the people in the movement.
10. Local, on-site training was more effective than nonlocal training.
11. Indigenous church-planting principles were a major factor in the process of church multiplication.
12. Aside from the Kekchi, who constructed their own church facilities, the newly planted churches housed themselves in homes, offices, warehouses, barns, factories, schools, hospitals, health clinics, grain sheds, etc.
13. In settings where believers are persecuted, most of the churches maintained private (underground) worship sessions for about four to six months before becoming public, generally because of a burden for the lost.[7]

> "Leaders are the future of a church multiplication movement."
>
> —Robert E. Logan, *Be Fruitful and Multiply: Embracing God's Heart for Church Multiplication* (St. Charles, IL: ChurchSmart Resources, 2006), 97.

## CPMs in the West

The majority of the world's documented and undocumented CPMs are in the non-Western world. The only place in North America where extensive research has confirmed a legitimate CPM is in Cuba. For some time the Church has been experiencing a significant conversion growth and the multiplication of churches on this Caribbean island. Though I have not seen any documented research reports, Neil Cole, cofounder of Church Multiplication Associates (CMA), estimated that within the last seven years CMA has been involved in planting well over one thousand churches in thirty-six U.S. states and in thirty-one countries.[8] Outside North America, yet within the West, Garrison noted that in the late twentieth and early twenty-first centuries, Europe experienced CPMs among certain refugee populations in the Netherlands and among the Gypsies in France and Spain.[9]

Yet the majority of the world's CPMs have occurred in non-Western contexts. Because of this fact, from time to time, I have heard some people argue that the West will not experience a CPM. On the other hand, I have heard several people in the United States talk about CPMs in their areas. Upon investigation, however, what actually was occurring was a heightened interest in church planting and a few newly planted churches—nothing even close to a movement. If the Church began to experience such a movement of the Holy Spirit, what would it look like in places such as Western Europe (aside from Garrison's references), South Africa, Australia, New Zealand, Japan, Canada, and the United States?

Even a cursory comparison of the Western world with the Majority World quickly reveals fundamentally different social contexts. Generally speaking, the West is much more urbanized and secularized. Though there are many areas in which the extended family structures remain tightly connected, the West is known for a breakdown in the nuclear family and the extended family relationships.

Family-based conversion patterns are common in most CPMs. Such social networks exist in the West, but they are structured differently than their counterparts in areas of the Majority World. With the breakdown of these social bridges, the gospel will generally travel slower, and churches will not be planted at the rate witnessed in communities in which the family (nuclear and extended) connections are tight.

There is a high value placed on the individualization and privatization of faith issues in the West. Matters of religion are relegated to the private world, separate from the sphere of public life. The West can also be described as a post-Christianized context. Both good models and bad models of the Christian faith exist, but it is the poor models that pose some barriers for the rapid dissemination of the gospel. Missionaries have years of false gospels and hypocrisy to overcome.

> "What is the shortest possible route to plant a church that will spark a spontaneous movement to Christ?"
>
> —George Patterson, "The Spontaneous Multiplication of Churches," in *Perspectives on the World Christian Movement: A Reader*, eds. Ralph D. Winter and Steven C. Hawthorne (Pasadena, CA: William Carey Library, 1981), 603.

When the Western world is examined in light of some of the common characteristics found in most CPMs, clearly there are other contextual differences. At the time of this writing much of the Western world is not experiencing a prevalent climate of uncertainty. Even in light of global terrorism, the West is known for scientific and technological advancements, the best health care, wealth, and large amounts of food—all of which create an atmosphere of security, contentment, and comfort. Generally, the West does not fear wide-scale poverty, famine, disease, war, or natural disaster.

Few people in the West are insulated from outsiders. Globalization, urbanization, and advancement in telecommunication and the Internet have made the world a small place, especially for the West. As I write this chapter, I am sitting in my favorite coffee shop, connected to the Internet via a wireless system. I am able to do e-mail and communicate with people on the other side of the world or across town.

If e-mail communication is not sufficient, my cell phone is beside me. Within seconds I can talk to someone across the street or across the globe. Just recently, I read of the discovery of a new Brazilian tribal people group in the Amazon. To the journalist's knowledge, this group had never had any contact with the outside world. Though examples of isolation and semi-isolation and communication challenges exist in the Majority World, we are hard pressed to find as many examples in the West.

In most CPMs there is a high cost for following Christ. It is common to experience great loss of possessions, family, positions, as well as physical life. However, the Western world has been marked by and continues to witness the freedom of religion. In fact, serious religious oppression or persecution is difficult to find in the West. Though there are isolated examples of national and local government encroachment on religious freedoms, the West has yet to see the degrees of persecution and suffering for faith that exist in some areas of the Majority World.

As we have already seen in chapters seventeen and eighteen, the Methodists and Baptists experienced such movements in their early years, but what about today? With such radical social and cultural differences between the Western and Majority Worlds, what would CPMs look like in the West?

> **"Multiplication is what local churches must continue to do throughout their life cycle to ensure that the gospel goes forward in their country."**
>
> —Bob Roberts Jr., *The Multiplying Church* (Grand Rapids, MI: Zondervan, 2008), 60.

In the following four paragraph are my thoughts based on a sweeping generalization of the contextual makeup of Western nations. These are not *casual* speculations separated from theology, Church history, sociological and anthropological realities, or missionary principles and

## Spontaneous Expansion and Control

In his classic work *The Spontaneous Expansion of the Church*, Roland Allen discussed the elements involved in the rapid growth of the church across a people. In this excerpt, he discussed the matter of the missionary who, on the one hand, wants to witness such growth, but, on the other hand, wants to control the rate of growth.

> We fear it because we feel that it is something that we cannot control. And that is true. We can neither induce nor control spontaneous expansion whether we look on it as the work of the individual or of the Church, simply because it is spontaneous. "The wind bloweth where it listeth," said Christ, and spontaneous activity is a movement of the Spirit in the individual and in the Church, and we cannot control the Spirit.
>
> Given spontaneous zeal we can direct it by instruction. Aquila could teach Apollos the way of God more perfectly. But teaching is not control. Teaching can be refused; control cannot be refused, if it is control; teaching leads to enlargement, control to restriction. To attempt to control spontaneous zeal is therefore to attempt to restrict it; and he who restricts a thing is glad of a little but does not welcome much. Thus, many of our missionaries welcome spontaneous zeal, provided there is not too much of it for their restrictions, just as an engineer laying out the course of a river is glad of some water to fill his channels, but does not want a flood which may sweep away his embankments. Such missionaries pray for the wind of the Spirit but not for a rushing mighty wind. I am writing because I believe in a rushing mighty wind, and desire its presence at all costs to our restrictions. But if that is what we are talking about, it is futile to imagine that we can control it. Let us begin by acknowledging that we cannot. If we do that, we may escape from the confusion created by those who say that they have spontaneous expansion in their missions and welcome it and rejoice in it; and yet say also that they are sent to control and must control.
>
> By spontaneous expansion I mean something which we cannot control. And if we cannot control it, we ought, as I think, to rejoice that we cannot control it. For if we cannot control it, it is because it is too great, not because it is too small for us. The great things of God are beyond our control. Therein lies a vast hope. Spontaneous expansion could fill the continents with the knowledge of Christ: our control cannot reach as far as that. We constantly bewail our limitations: open doors unentered; doors closed to us as foreign missionaries, fields white to the harvest

which we cannot reap. Spontaneous expansion could enter open doors, force closed ones, and reap those white fields. Our control cannot: it can only appeal pitifully for more men to maintain control.

There is always something terrifying in the feeling that we are letting loose a force which we cannot control; and when we think of spontaneous expansion in this way, instinctively we begin to be afraid. Whether we consider our doctrine, or our civilization, or our morals, or our organization, in relation to a spontaneous expansion of the Church, we are seized with terror, terror lest spontaneous expansion should lead to disorder. We are quite ready to talk of self-supporting, self-extending and self-governing churches in the abstract as ideals; but the moment that we think of ourselves as establishing self-supporting, self-governing churches in the Biblical sense we are met by this fear, a terrible, deadly fear. Suppose they really were self-supporting, and depended no longer on our support, where should we be? Suppose self-extension were really self-extension, and we could not control it, what would happen? Suppose they were really self-governing, how would they govern? We instinctively think of something which we cannot control as tending to disorder.

Taken from Roland Allen, *The Spontaneous Expansion of the Church*, American ed. (Grand Rapids, MI: William B. Eerdmans Publishing Company, 1962), 12–13.

***Questions to Consider:***

1. Do you agree or disagree with Allen's argument that missionaries fear the rapid growth of the church because they cannot control it?
2. What concerns, if any, do you and your church-planting team have if you were to experience such rapid church growth in a short period of time?

practices. Speculation? Yes, but those of an experienced missiologist and minister of the gospel who lives in the West.

First, if the Spirit so moved in Western civilization, the conversion growth rates and numbers of newly planted churches would be slower than many of the places in the Majority World. Affinity lines, rather than family lines (especially in urban contexts), will probably be the primary social bridges by which the gospel travels from person to person. Such growth will also be slow because of the individualized and private approach to matters of faith and the fact that few people have a large number of friends in their affinity networks to share with.

Second, it is likely to happen among those individuals who are experiencing significant amounts of problems, upheaval, and change in their lives. Such people tend to be more receptive to the gospel. College and high school students, marginalized people, and the poor and powerless are the best candidates to be involved in such movements.

Next, first- and, maybe, second-generation immigrants tend to be receptive to the gospel, because they are experiencing significant and discomforting times of transition in their lives. Whether they are the Hispanic peoples settling in the rural communities of the United States or the Chinese migrating to the cities, the non-Anglo demographic are the most likely to be involved in CPMs.

Fourth, in my book *Missional House Churches: Reaching Our Communities with the Gospel,* I spent an entire chapter addressing house churches and CPMs, particularly related to the West.[10] Please understand that *house churches are not the missing link in Western CPMs.* However, the church planters involved in planting highly reproducible, simple expressions of the body of Christ will likely be the ones most poised to experience CPMs.

## Barriers to CPMs

I am very familiar with the roads in my neighborhood—so much so that whenever I drive down those roads, I know where the potholes and bumps are located. This knowledge only came about as a result of being familiar with the roads. Clearly, such knowledge makes my ride much smoother, and my vehicle's shocks probably appreciate it as well.

Knowing the barriers to CPMs allows church planters to drive the roads of church planting with knowledge of those obstacles to the multiplication of churches. Such knowledge allows us to develop strategies and apply methods that are designed to avoid the barriers.

In 2000 the International Mission Board of the Southern Baptist Convention identified nine obstacles to CPMs, which are discussed below.[11] Though we cannot manufacture a CPM, it is possible to erect barriers that would hinder the rapid dissemination of the gospel and the multiplication of churches.

## Extrabiblical Requirements for Being a Church

When church planters, churches, and denominations require extrabiblical standards for a local church to exist, the growth of these movements is potentially hindered. Examples of extrabiblical requirements are matters such as mandating worship expressions based on the missionary's cultural preferences, using leadership philosophies that were developed in the West, and demanding a designated "church" building as a meeting place. Though these practices may not be wrong, they are culturally defined and not necessarily healthy or helpful to other believers.

## Loss of a Valued Cultural Identity

When people are required to give up their cultures and embrace a foreign culture in order to become a follower of Christ, then movements are hindered. The cross is to be the only stumbling block church planters should set before people.

## Overcoming Bad Examples of Christianity

When believers set a poor example of Christian living, new believers may not want to be identified with them and so will not share the gospel. Some of these poor examples of Christianity are recorded in history and still negatively impact the hearts of some people, hindering the spread of the true gospel.

> "An obedient church has an inherent, God-given power to multiply, just as all other living things that God created."
>
> —George Patterson and Richard Scoggins, *Church Multiplication Guide: The Miracle of Church Reproduction*, rev. ed. (Pasadena, CA: William Carey Library, 2002), 12.

## Nonreproducible Models

The use of some church-planting models may not be reproducible by the people reached. For example, models using sound systems, PowerPoint, and nicely constructed buildings would be difficult to reproduce in areas with little access to electricity and property. Though certain models may be of a higher caliber and more efficient in particular contexts than other models, this does not necessarily guarantee they are best in facilitating CPMs.

## Subsidies Creating Dependency

Money can be used effectively for the advancement of the kingdom. The use of missionaries generally involves the need for financial resources to support them. However, the new believers and churches need to be self-supporting from the beginning. Outside funding that works to bolster growth often hinders long-term health. Financial resources should not be used to cause newly planted churches to become dependent on outsiders for their resources.

## Extrabiblical Leadership Requirements

Church planters must remember that the biblical requirements for church leaders are sufficient. Though there is nothing inherently wrong with advanced degrees and highly sophisticated leadership-training programs (these can be beneficial in certain contexts), missionaries need to recognize and embrace the sufficiency of the Scriptures on this matter. Whenever leadership requirements exceed biblical prescriptions, the potential for CPMs is likely to decrease.

## Sequentialism

Missionaries involved in CPMs have noted that rarely do church planting strategies play out in a linear fashion. Rather than missionaries arriving on the field, learning the language and culture, evangelizing, baptizing, and gathering new believers in churches in this sequential order, most reports have noted that these aspects happened in differing orders or even simultaneously. For example, in CPMs, language learning often occurs simultaneously with evangelism. Or, even before some people become believers, they participate in the ministries of new churches.

## Planting "Frog" Rather Than "Lizard" Churches

In the animal kingdom, lizards can be seen scurrying around in pursuit of their food; whereas, frogs simply wait for their food to come to them. **"Lizard" churches**, then, are those that are intentional about evangelism in their communities and marketplaces, rather than expecting the nonkingdom citizens to come to their gatherings to hear the gospel.

## Prescriptive Strategies

Church planters should not enter a field with a predetermined strategy developed in a classroom. Such a straightjacket approach hinders CPMs. Strategies need to be flexible and shaped according to the contexts.

> "It is my hope and prayer that if the sovereign Lord so desires to move across the North American continent, blessing His Church with church planting movements, you and I are participants rather than observers (or worse, hindrances) of such activities."
>
> —J. D. Payne, *Missional House Churches: Reaching Our Communities with the Gospel* (Colorado Springs, CO: Paternoster, 2008), 162.

## Recommended Shifts

*Apart from the sovereignty of God, church-planting movements will not occur anywhere in the West or anywhere in the world.* Though the Church cannot control the sovereignty of God or the contextual factors of the Western world, is there anything we can do to help facilitate CPMs in the West? The answer to this question is yes!

For some time I have been hearing the Western Church plead to the Lord for another Great Awakening. But what if the Lord of the harvest is not willing to send such an awakening across the Western world because the Church's theological convictions and organizations would not allow for healthy assimilation of the new believers into established churches and the multiplication of disciples, leaders, and churches? The Lord brought his children to the border of the Promised Land, ready to fulfill the promises given to Abraham centuries before. The children, however, were not ready to receive the blessings of God, but rather had to wander in the wilderness for forty years before they received the land. The Lord was willing, but his people were not—not willing to make the sacrifices to enter.

Throughout the world, especially in the West, a cycle of birth, rapid growth, stagnation, maintenance, decline, and rebirth has been a part of

Church history. Generally, a minority group becomes discontent with the majority group. Such a group breaks away and gives birth to a new movement that is typically marked with a zeal for evangelism and church multiplication (e.g., Moravians, Methodists, Baptists). After a period of rapid growth, this group begins to develop an inward focus, and growth begins to stagnate. The group begins to focus more and more on maintaining the structures it created to facilitate mission and less and less on the original vision and mission. Over time, this group begins to experience a decline in growth; it is during this time that other discontented groups begin to develop, voicing concern that what was once a movement has developed into a bureaucratic machine that has lost its original missional vision. The final stage is that a rebirthing process occurs with a breakaway group with a similar missional vision and zeal that marked the original group.

Though this cycle has been a pattern throughout Church history, it does not have to be the pattern for the future. The established Church must maintain what has been allowed to develop, but also must be missional.

The Church does have control of its theologies, missiologies, structures, strategies, and methods. For almost a decade I have been advocating that the Western Church make three particular shifts in order to help facilitate the rapid dissemination of the gospel and the multiplication of churches. Please note that *these shifts are not a magic formula to CPMs, nor are they the panacea to the problems facing church multiplication in the West.*

These suggested shifts have been developed in light of the Scriptures, missionary principles, in view of what the Spirit is doing in CPMs across the globe, and with an understanding of Church history. Again, they are not shifts that guarantee that such movements will occur, but rather attempt to "hoist the sails" and allow us to move with the Spirit's working.

## A Theological Shift

The first recommended shift is a theological one. Is the gospel sufficient to transform individuals and societies? Is the Holy Spirit able to seal, protect, and guide new churches? Is the Holy Spirit able to use everyday believers to preach the gospel, pastor, and multiply churches? Can a local church be biblically faithful, culturally relevant, vibrant, and make a significant impact for the kingdom while not being defined according to its size, budget, worship service, or programs? Can apostolic missionaries exist and plant churches in the West?

Until the Church is able to answer these questions in the affirmative *and* allow these convictions to guide missionary practices, it is unlikely it will ever be prepared for church multiplication. Unless the Church is willing to return to the simplicity of the gospel, the power of the Holy Spirit, and define the local church according to the simple biblical guidelines—rather than Western cultural preferences—it is unlikely that there will be global expansion. The Church must come to understand the Great Commission more in relational terms and less in institutional terms; with a simpler organization and less in terms of structure and bureaucracy; with more emphasis on biblical accountability and less allowance for member passivity; with more priority placed on community and less on acquaintances; as more dependent on equipping and sending the people of God for mission and less of a reliance on professional clergy.

A shift that emphasizes the apostolic nature of the missionary is required. As long as church planters are primarily understood and defined as pastors, multiplication and movement are not likely to occur. When a missionary begins to pastor a church, growth usually stagnates, and the zeal that once fueled evangelism is expended on ministry obligations within that local church.

## A Strategic Shift

The second recommended shift regards strategy. The Church must embrace a philosophy of church multiplication and not church planting by addition. William C. Tinsley correctly remarked, "Here lies a salient problem of the church: it is employing the wrong arithmetic function. It is attempting to penetrate a world of multiplication with simple addition."[12] Church-planting teams must be taught to think about how to reach their entire city, community, people group, or population segment by asking themselves how many churches do they believe are necessary for such a situation to occur. Missionaries should never be encouraged to believe that if they can plant a church of two hundred people, then their goal has been sufficiently achieved. Teams should be encouraged to work to plant multiple churches, especially more than one at a time. Such missionaries need to embrace the reproduction philosophy of the multiplication of disciples, leaders, and churches. The world is to be their parish, and they must be guided by a missional philosophy that wisely works toward reaching that entire parish!

## A Methodological Shift

For the most part, church-planting methods in the United States and Canada are *too* complicated. We must advocate and apply simple methods that are highly reproducible by new kingdom citizens. In light of the billions of nonkingdom citizens on this planet, it is unwise for church planters *not* to think about the reproducibility potential. I have seen church planters use methods that few, if any, of the people in the new congregations could use in planting other churches. The gifts, training, educational levels, talents, and expertise of the church planters were far above the capabilities of the new believers. If all the people knew about church planting was that which was modeled by the church planters, few would even consider planting other churches.

Generally, there is an inverse relationship between the degree of reproducibility and the technicality of church-planting methods. The more technical the methods used, the less likely the people reached will be able to use such methods to plant other churches.

All church-planting methods are reproducible to some degree as portrayed in figure 25.3. Even methods that require a great amount of money, people, highly gifted leaders, excellent public speakers, very gifted musicians, and outstanding administrators can be reproduced if such resources are available every time a church is to be planted. There is nothing inherently wrong with these methods. However, we must recognize that because many resources are involved, the technicality of the methods increases, leaving such methods with a low reproducibility potential. Highly complex methods should be few in number and not the norm for kingdom citizens.

Figure 25.3 **Reproducibility-Potential Guide**

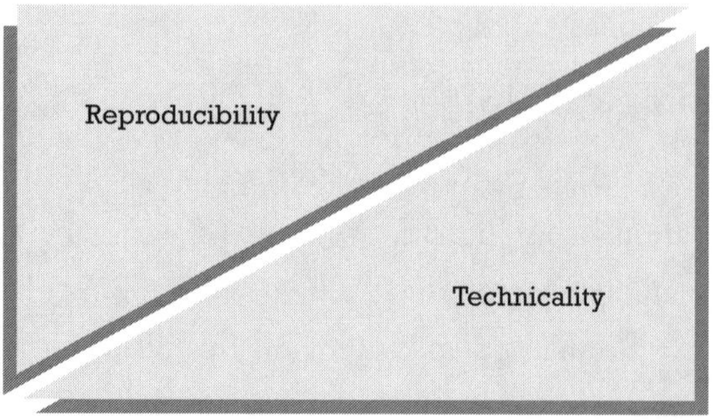


## Present Realities

CPMs usually do not occur overnight. Many times, missionaries spend entire lifetimes tilling the soil and sowing the gospel among a particular people before the Spirit births a CPM. In the latter part of the twentieth century, missiologist Donald McGavran noted that generally large movements of people came to faith only after a lengthy period of time of being exposed to the gospel message.[13] Clyde Meador also addressed this issue in his article "The Left Side of the Graph," in which he made the argument that many, if not most, of the CPMs in the world today were preceded by decades or even a century or more of faithful missionary labors.[14]

This situation was surely the case in Nagaland, one of the most Christianized regions on the planet. Paul Hattaway described the incredible movement of the Spirit among the Nagas in his book *From Head-Hunters to Church Planters: An Amazing Spiritual Awakening in Nagaland.* This unreached state of northeast India saw the first missionaries arrive in 1839, but it was in 1871 that the Ao people were the first of the Naga tribes to accept the gospel in significant numbers.[15] The first baptisms occurred and the first church was planted in Nagaland in 1872—*thirty-three years after the initial missionaries brought the gospel to the people!*

If research is correct, that the Lord usually works through a lengthy period of missionary service before the birth of a CPM, then church planters must understand that the task before them will usually not be accomplished in two to four years of missionary service—a common tenure among twenty-first-century missionaries.

### *Summary:*

1. According to David Garrison, a church-planting movement is a rapid multiplication of indigenous churches planting churches that sweeps through a people group or population segment.
2. Roland Allen was an Anglican priest of the early twentieth century who wrote about the spontaneous expansion of the church and the causes that hinder it.
3. Common characteristics of CPMs have been identified.

4. If CPMs occurred in the West, they would look different from what is presently reported in the Majority World.
5. CPMs cannot be created by church planters. Apart from the sovereignty of God, CPMs will not occur anywhere in the world.
6. Theological, strategic, and methodological shifts are recommended for the Church in the West to help facilitate CPMs.
7. There is an inverse relationship between the technicality of church-planting methods used and the reproducibility of those methods by new believers.
8. There are several barriers to CPMs that church planters must strive to avoid.

### *Reflection Questions:*

1. Do you agree or disagree that CPMs could occur in the West?
2. What would a CPM look like among the people you and your team are serving?
3. What changes (if any) in your church-planting methods are necessary to facilitate such movements?
4. Evaluate your church-planting methods by the Reproducibility-Potential Guide. Where do they fall along the line in figure 25.3? What would make your methods more reproducible by the people?
5. How long are you willing to labor among a people in order to see the multiplication of disciples, leaders, and churches?
6. Evaluate your church-planting team's strategy and methods in light of the barriers to CPMs.

### *Important Terms in This Chapter:*

- Church-planting movements
- Spontaneous expansion
- Frog churches
- Lizard churches
- Reproducibility-Potential Guide

# NOTES

### Chapter 1: Understanding Biblical Church Planting

1. Thom S. Rainer and Chuck Lawless, *The Challenge of the Great Commission* (n.p.: Pinnacle Publishing, 2005), 107–108.
2. C. Peter Wagner, *Church Planting for a Greater Harvest* (Ventura, CA: Regal Books, 1990), 11.
3. Stuart Murray, *Church Planting: Laying Foundations* (London: Paternoster Press, 1998), 30.
4. Ibid., 31, 34, 39.
5. Charles Brock, *Indigenous Church Planting: A Practical Journey* (Neosho, MO: Church Growth International, 1994), 30.

### Chapter 2: Ecclesiology and Church Planting—Part 1

1. Aubrey Malphurs, *Planting Growing Churches for the $21^{st}$ Century*, $3^{rd}$ ed. (Grand Rapids, MI: Baker Books, 2004), 25.
2. Charles Brock, *Indigenous Church Planting: A Practical Journey* (Neosho, MO: Church Growth International, 1994), 49.
3. For information on Rufus Anderson, see Jim Reapsome, "Anderson, Rufus," in *Evangelical Dictionary of World Missions*, ed. A. Scott Moreau (Grand Rapids, MI: Baker Books, 2000), 60. For information on Henry Venn, see Wilbert R. Shenk, "Venn, Henry" in *Evangelical Dictionary of World Missions*, ed. A. Scott Moreau (Grand Rapids, MI: Baker Books, 2000), 999.
4. Brock, *Church Planting*, 93.
5. Ibid., 89.
6. Stuart Murray, *Church Planting: Laying Foundations,* North American Edition (Scottdale, PA; Waterloo, Ontario: Herald Press, 2001), 30.
7. The work of Max Weber is discussed in *The Penguin Dictionary of Sociology*, $3^{rd}$ ed., Nicholas Abercrombie, Stephen Hill, and Bryan S. Turner (London: Penguin Books, 1984), 205.

8. Tom Julien, "The Essence of the Church," *Evangelical Missions Quarterly* 34 (April 1998): 148.
9. John E. Apheh, "Socio-anthropological Implications in Cross-Cultural Church Planting," *Asian Journal of Theology* 11 (1997): 285.
10. Robert E. Logan, *Be Fruitful and Multiply: Embracing God's Heart for Church Multiplication* (St. Charles, IL: ChurchSmart Resources, 2006), 33.

### Chapter 3: Ecclesiology and Church Planting—Part 2

1. Mark Dever, *What Is a Healthy Church?* (Wheaton, IL: Crossway Books, 2005), 35.
2. George W. Peters, *A Biblical Theology of Missions* (Chicago, IL: Moody Press, 1972), 209.

### Chapter 4: Holy Spirit and Church Planting

1. Millard J. Erickson, *Christian Theology Today*, unabridged, one-volume edition (Grand Rapids, MI: Baker Book House, 1985), 846.
2. John V. Taylor, *The Go Between God: The Holy Spirit and the Christian Mission* (New York: Oxford University Press, 1972), 4–5.
3. J. Terry Young, "The Holy Spirit and the Birth of Churches," in *The Birth of Churches: A Biblical Basis for Church Planting*, compiler/contributor Talmadge R. Amberson (Nashville, TN: Broadman Press, 1979), 171.
4. Tom Steffen, "Flawed Evangelism and Church Planting," *Evangelical Missions Quarterly* 34, no. 4 (October 1998): 434.
5. J. B. Lawrence, *The Holy Spirit in Missions* (Atlanta, GA: Home Mission Board, 1966), 9.
6. John Stott, *Christian Mission in the Modern World* (Downers Grove, IL: InterVarsity Press, 1975), 125.
7. Young, "The Holy Spirit," 170.
8. Roland Allen, *Missionary Methods: St. Paul's or Ours?* American edition (Grand Rapids, MI: William B. Eerdmans Publishing Company, 1962), 149.

### Chapter 5: Prayer, Spiritual Warfare, and Church Planting

1. E. M. Bounds, *The Complete Works of E. M. Bounds on Prayer* (Grand Rapids, MI: Baker Book House, 1990), 142.
2. Rick Love, *Muslims, Magic and the Kingdom of God: Church Planting among Folk Muslims* (Pasadena, CA: William Carey Library, 2000), 150, italics original.
3. Chuck Lawless, *Discipled Warriors* (Grand Rapids, MI: Kregel, 2002).
4. Bounds, *Prayer*, 143.
5. H. Gerald Colbert, "Spiritual Warfare in Church Planting: A Supplement to Basic Training" (Church Planting Network Resource): 6; article online at http://www.plantingteam.com/media/Sptl_Warfare_paper_w_ftnt3.doc; (accessed 9/1/08).

6. Robert E. Logan and Jeannette Buller, *Cell Church Planter's Guide* (St. Charles, IL: ChurchSmart Resources, 2001), sec. 1, p. 26.
7. Robert E. Logan and Steve L. Ogne, *The Church Planter's Toolkit*, revised (St. Charles, IL: ChurchSmart Resources, 1994), sec. 2, p. 6.
8. David Garrison, *Church Planting Movements: How God Is Redeeming a Lost World* (Midlothian, VA: WIGTAKE Resources, 2004), 177.

### Chapter 6: Evangelism and Church Planting

1. Robert E. Coleman, *The Master Plan of Evangelism*, 30th anniversary edition (Grand Rapids, MI: Fleming H. Revell, 1993), 97.
2. Transfer growth is moving people who are already followers of Jesus from one church to a new church. Though the latter church grows and is many times planted in this manner, the total unbelieving population among a people has not been diminished. The number of people within the kingdom of darkness still remains the same. Biblical church planting is about reaching people out of the harvest field.
3. Tom Nebel and Gary Rohrmayer, *Church Planting Landmines: Mistakes to Avoid in Years 2 through 10* (St. Charles, IL: ChurchSmart Resources, 2005), 56.
4. Harvey T. Hoekstra, *The World Council of Churches and the Demise of Evangelism* (Wheaton, IL: Tyndale House Publishers, 1979). For another historical account, see Arthur P. Johnston, *The Battle for World Evangelism* (Wheaton, IL: Tyndale House Publishers, 1978).
5. http://www.lausanne.org/lausanne-1974/lausanne-covenant.html (accessed 2/22/08). See also *Let the Earth Hear His Voice: International Congress on World Evangelization Lausanne, Switzerland*, ed. J. D. Douglas (Minneapolis, MN: World Wide Publications, 1975).
6. John R. W. Stott, *Christian Mission in the Modern World* (Downers Grove, IL: InterVarsity Press, 1975), 56.
7. Alvin Reid, *Introduction to Evangelism* (Nashville, TN: Broadman and Holman Publishers, 1998), 4, 5, 7.
8. J. I. Packer, *Evangelism and the Sovereignty of God* (Downers Grove, IL: InterVarsity Press, 1961), 97.
9. Wayne Grudem, *Systematic Theology: An Introduction to Biblical Doctrine* (Grand Rapids, MI: Zondervan Publishing House, 1994), 694–95.
10. This section was originally published in the May 2007 issue of the online periodical *Lausanne World Pulse*. See J. D. Payne, "Eight Principles of New Testament Evangelism," located at http://www.lausanneworldpulse.com/ themedarticles.php/700/05-2007.
11. Donald A. McGavran, *The Bridges of God: A Study in the Strategy of Missions* (New York: Friendship Press, 1955).
12. http://www.studylight.org/lex/grk/view.cgi?number=3624.

### Chapter 7: Discipleship and Church Planting

1. Robert E. Coleman, *The Master Plan of Evangelism,* 30th anniversary edition (Grand Rapids, MI: Fleming H. Revell, 1993), 173.
2. For more information regarding Life Transformation Groups, see Neil Cole, *Cultivating a Life for God* (St. Charles, IL: ChurchSmart Resources, 1999) and *Life Transformation Group Cards* available from www.cmaresources.org.
3. Cole, *Cultivating a Life*, 33–34.
4. Charles Brock, *I've Been Born Again, What Next?* (Neosho, MO: Church Growth International, n.d.). This resource can be ordered from the website www.churchgrowthinternational.com.

### Chapter 8: Leadership Development and Church Planting

1. David J. Hesselgrave, *Planting Churches Cross-Culturally: North America and Beyond,* 2nd ed. (Grand Rapids, MI: Baker Academic, 2000), 276.
2. Robert E. Logan and Neil Cole, *Raising Leaders for the Harvest* (St. Charles,IL: ChurchSmart Resources, 1992–1995), sec. 1, p. 9.
3. Ibid., sec. 1, p. 3.
4. Robert E. Logan and Tara Miller, *From Followers to Leaders* (St. Charles, IL: ChurchSmart Resources, 2007), 38.
5. Daniel Sinclair, *A Vision of the Possible: Pioneer Church Planting in Teams* (Colorado Springs, CO: Authentic Media, 2005), 236–37.
6. Henry Venn (1796–1873) was an early missiologist known for using this scaffold/building analogy.
7. Tom Steffen, *Passing the Baton: Church Planting That Empowers* (La Habra, CA: Center for Organizational and Ministry Development, 1993), 20.
8. Ibid., 25.

### Chapter 9: Strategy and Church Planting—Part 1

1. C. Peter Wagner, *Frontiers in Missionary Strategy* (Chicago, IL: Moody Press, 1971), 35.
2. http://www.m-w.com/dictionary/strategy (accessed 11/30/07).
3. C. Peter Wagner, *Strategies for Church Growth: Tools for Effective Mission and Evangelism* (Ventura, CA: Regal, 1989), 26.
4. Aubrey Malphurs, *Strategy 2000: Churches Making Disciples for the Next Millennium* (Grand Rapids, MI: Kregel Publications, 1996), 44.
5. Robert E. Logan and Steven L. Ogne, *The Church Planter's Toolkit* (St. Charles, IL: ChurchSmart Resources, 1994), iv–1.
6. Wilbert R. Shenk, *Changing Frontiers of Missions* (Maryknoll, NY: Orbis Books, 1999), 107.
7. Logan and Ogne, *Toolkit,* iv–1.

8. Edward R. Dayton and David A. Fraser, *Planning Strategies for World Evangelization* (Grand Rapids, MI: William B. Eerdmans Publishing Company, 1980), 16–17, italics original.
9. William Carey, *An Enquiry into the Obligations of Christians to Use Means for the Conversion of the Heathens* (London: Carey Kingsgate, 1961).
10. Basil Clutterbuck, "World Missionary Strategy," *London Quarterly and Holborn Review* 182 (January 1957): 30.
11. Edward R. Dayton, "To Reach the Unreached," in *Perspectives on the World Christian Movement: A Reader*, eds. Ralph D. Winter and Steven C. Hawthorne (Pasadena, CA: William Carey Library, 1981), 595.
12. Donald A. McGavran, *Understanding Church Growth* (Grand Rapids, MI: William B. Eerdmans Publishing Company, 1970), 356.
13. Michael Green, "Methods and Strategy in the Evangelism of the Early Church" in *Let the Earth Hear His Voice, International Congress on World Evangelization*, ed. J. D. Douglas (Minneapolis, MN: World Wide Publications, 1975), 165–66.
14. Roland Allen, *Missionary Methods: St. Paul's or Ours?* American Edition (Grand Rapids, MI: William B. Eerdmans Publishing Company, 1962); and J. Herbert Kane, *Christian Missions in Biblical Perspective* (Grand Rapids, MI: Baker Book House, 1976), 73–85.
15. For a description of such methods, see J. D. Payne, "Methods of Evangelism: The First 300 Years," *Journal of the American Society for Church Growth* 18 (Winter 2007): 55–77. This article is also available at www.northamericanmissions.org. Also, for a summary of the methods, see John Mark Terry, *Evangelism: A Concise History* (Nashville, TN: Broadman and Holman Publishers, 1994), 24–26.

## Chapter 10: Strategy and Church Planting—Part 2

1. Donald A. McGavran, *Understanding Church Growth* (Grand Rapids, MI, William B. Eerdmans Publishing Company, 1970), 360.
2. Hugo Culpepper, "Reflections on Missionary Strategy," *Southwestern Journal of Theology* 12 (Spring 1970), 29.
3. George Patterson, "The Spontaneous Multiplication of Churches," in *Perspectives on the World Christian Movement: A Reader*, eds. Ralph D. Winter and Steven C. Hawthorne (Pasadena, CA: William Carey Library, 1981), 603.
4. Edward R. Dayton and David A. Fraser, *Planning Strategies for World Evangelization* (Grand Rapids, MI: William B. Eerdmans Publishing Company, 1980), 32–33.
5. Ibid., 180.
6. C. Peter Wagner, *Frontiers in Missionary Strategy* (Chicago, IL: Moody Press, 1971), 31.
7. This is not to say that there are no genuine believers among nonevangelical groups, nor is it to say that all evangelicals are genuine believers.

8. Dayton and Fraser, *Planning Strategies*, 38. This percentage is drawn from a social theory known as the diffusion of innovation. For more information on this theory, see Everett M. Rogers, *Diffusion of Innovation* (New York: The Free Press, 1962).
9. Jim Montgomery, *DAWN 2000: 7 Million Churches to Go* (Pasadena, CA: William Carey Library, 1989), 77.
10. David Garrison, *Church Planting Movements: How God Is Redeeming a Lost World* (Midlothian, VA: WIGTAKE Resources, 2004), 251.
11. Ibid., 280.
12. Dayton and Fraser, *Planning Strategies*, 109.
13. C. Peter Wagner, *Strategies for Church Growth: Tools for Effective Mission and Evangelism* (Ventura, CA: Regal, 1989), 27.

### Chapter 11: Receptivity and Church Planting

1. Donald A. McGavran, *Understanding Church Growth* (Grand Rapids, MI: William B. Eerdmans Publishing Company, 1970), 216.
2. Ibid., 229.
3. Robert E. Logan and Neil Cole, *Beyond Church Planting: Pathways for Emerging Churches* (St. Charles, IL: ChurchSmart Resources, 2005), 47.
4. Ibid., 44.
5. Ibid.

### Chapter 12: Contextualization and Church Planting

1. Paul G. Hiebert, *Anthropological Insights for Missionaries* (Grand Rapids, MI: Baker Book House, 1985), 215.
2. David J. Hesselgrave and Edward Rommen, *Contextualization: Meanings, Methods, and Models* (Pasadena, CA: William Carey Library, 1989), 200.
3. Rick Warren, *The Purpose-Driven Church: Growth without Compromising Your Message* (Grand Rapids, MI: Zondervan, 1995), 160.

### Chapter 13: The Mother Church and Church Planting—Part 1

1. Thom S. Rainer, *The Book of Church Growth: History, Theology, and Principles* (Nashville, TN: Broadman and Holman Publishers, 1993), 212.
2. North American Mission Board, *New Churches Needed: A Step-by-Step Handbook for Planting New Churches* (Alpharetta, GA: North American Mission Board, 2001), iii.
3. For example, a simple examination of North American church growth literature from the past thirty years quickly reveals that the common notion of church growth is that which is related to expanding and maintaining the membership, leadership, and property of the local congregation.

4. Donald A. McGavran, *Understanding Church Growth* (Grand Rapids, MI: William B. Eerdmans Publishing Company, 1970), 63.
5. E-mail sent to author.
6. E-mail sent to author.
7. Aubrey Malphurs, *Planting Growing Churches for the 21st Century*, 3rd ed. (Grand Rapids, MI: Baker Books, 2004), 246.
8. A variation of this discussion of the evidence for church planting first appeared in my article "More Than 43,000 Southern Baptist Churches: Do We Really Need Another One?" *SBC Life* (June/July 2005): 4–5.
9. Malphurs, *Planting Growing Churches*, 380.
10. North American Mission Board, *New Churches Needed*, iv.
11. David T. Olson, *The American Church in Crisis* (Grand Rapids, MI: Zondervan, 2008), 146.
12. Ibid.
13. Phillip and Kandace Connor, *Who Is My Neighbor? Reaching Internationals in North America* (Princeton, NJ: Phillip and Kandace Connor, 2008), x.
14. http://www.odci.gov/cia/publications/factbook/geos/ca.html.
15. http://www.odci.gov/cia/publications/factbook/geos/us.html.
16. Olson, *American Church*, 146.
17. http://northamericanmissions.org/files/2008%20America's%20report-religious-landscape-study-full.pdf (accessed 9/1/08).
18. Taken from http://www.evangelicalfellowship.ca/NetCommunity/Page.aspx?pid=776 (accessed 9/1/08).
19. "Christianity on the Decline in Canada," *On Mission* (Fall 2008): 6.
20. C. Peter Wagner, *Church Planting for a Greater Harvest* (Ventura, CA: Regal Books, 1990), 11.
21. "Churches Die with Dignity," *Christianity Today* (January 14, 1991): 69.
22. Charles Chaney, "New Churches and the Unsaved," *Mission USA* (January–February 1995): 12.
23. North American Mission Board, *New Churches Needed*, 55.
24. Malphurs, *Planting Growing Churches*, 38.
25. http://www.adherents.com/rel_USA.html (accessed 2/18/05).

### Chapter 14: The Mother Church and Church Planting—Part 2

1. Rodney Harrison, Tom Cheyney, and Don Overstreet, *Spin-off Churches: How One Church Successfully Plants Another* (Nashville, TN: B&H Academic, 2008), 4.
2. J. D. Payne, "The Mother Church and Church Planting," *Journal of the American Society for Church Growth* 16 (Winter 2005): 31–59.
3. J. D. Payne, "Forget Number 1, Lead Your Church to Be Number 2151!" *SBC Life* (February/March 2006): 6–7.
4. Ed Stetzer, *Planting Missional Churches* (Nashville, TN: Broadman and Holman Publishers, 2006), 317, italics added.

5. Rick Warren, *The Purpose-Driven Church* (Grand Rapids, MI: Zondervan Publishing House, 1995), 111.
6. Jack Redford, *Planting New Churches* (Nashville, TN: Broadman Press, 1978), 79–80.
7. This resource can be ordered from www.dcpi.org or 800-255-0431.
8. Ralph Moore, *Starting a New Church* (Ventura, CA: Regal, 2002), 255–56.

### Chapter 15: Teams and Church Planting

1. Elmer Towns and Douglas Porter, *Churches That Multiply: A Bible Study on Church Planting* (Kansas City, MO: Beacon Hill Press of Kansas City, 2003), 146.
2. David W. Shenk and Ervin R. Stutzman, *Creating Communities of the Kingdom: New Testament Models of Church Planting* (Scottdale, PA: Herald Press, 1988), 43–44.
3. Greg Livingstone, *Planting Churches in Muslim Cities: A Team Approach* (Grand Rapids, MI: Baker Books, 1993), 112.
4. Ibid., 113.
5. Roger S. Greenway, "The 'Team' Approach to Urban Church Planting," *Urban Mission* 4, no. 4 (March 1987): 3.
6. Ibid., 4.
7. Ibid., 3.
8. J. D. Payne, *The Barnabas Factors: Eight Essential Practices of Church Planting Team Members* (Smyrna, DE: Missional Press, 2008).
9. At the time of this writing, this work is available online at www.dickscoggins.com.
10. Dick Scoggins, *Building Effective Church Planting Teams* (unpublished manuscript at www.dickscoggins.com), 81.
11. Adapted from Scoggins, *Church Planting Teams*, 82–83.

### Chapter 16: Early Moravians and Church Planting

1. J. Taylor Hamilton, *A History of the Missions of the Moravian Church during the Eighteenth and Nineteenth Centuries* (Bethlehem, PA: Times Publishing Company, 1901), xv.
2. Ruth A. Tucker, *From Jerusalem to Irian Jaya,* 2nd ed. (Grand Rapids, MI: Zondervan, 1983, 2004), 99.
3. Kenneth B. Mulholland, "Moravians, Puritans, and the Modern Missionary Movement," *Bibliotheca Sacra* 156 (April–June 1999): 226.
4. Ibid., 222.
5. J. C. S. Mason, *The Moravian Church and the Missionary Awakening in England 1760–1800* (New York: Boydell Press, 2001), 23.
6. Tucker, *From Jerusalem*, 99.

7. Colin A. Grant, "Europe's Moravians—A Pioneer Missionary Church," *Evangelical Missions Quarterly*, 12 (October 1976): 219.
8. J. E. Hutton, *A History of Moravian Missions* (London: Moravian Publication Office, 1922), 20–21.
9. Ibid., 182.
10. Gustav Warneck, *Outline of a History of Protestant Missions from the Reformation to the Present Time* (New York: Fleming H. Revell Company, 1901), 66.
11. David A. Schattschneider, "William Carey, Modern Missions, and the Moravian Influence," *International Bulletin of Missionary Research* 22 (January 1998): 12.
12. Ibid.: 9.
13. Stephen Neill, *A History of Christian Missions* (London: Penguin Books, 1964), 237.
14. David A. Schattschneider, "Pioneers in Mission: Zinzendorf and the Moravians," *International Bulletin of Missionary Research* 8 (April 1984): 65.
15. "Count Zinzendorf's Theory for Missions," *Christian History* (1982): 3.
16. Karl-Wilhelm Westmeier, "Becoming All Things to All People: Early Moravian Missions to Native North Americans," *International Bulletin of Missionary Research* 21 (October 1997): 174.
17. Mason, *The Moravian Church*, 24.
18. Hamilton, *Missions of the Moravian Church*, 209.
19. Schattschneider, "Pioneers in Mission": 66.
20. Walser H. Allen, *Who Are the Moravians? The Story of the Moravian Church,* 8th ed., revised (Bethlehem, PA: Department of Publications, 1981), 32.
21. William J. Danker, *Profit for the Lord: Economic Activities in Moravian Missions and the Basel Mission Trading Company* (Grand Rapids, MI: William B. Eerdmans Publishing Company, 1971), 73–74.
22. Colin A. Grant, "Europe's Moravians": 220.
23. Tucker, *From Jerusalem*, 112–113.
24. Kenneth Scott Latourette, *A History of Christianity: Reformation to the Present*, vol. 2 (Peabody, MA: Prince Press, 1953, 1975), 1024–1025.
25. Mulholland, "Moravians": 226.

## Chapter 17: Methodist Church Planting on the North American Frontier

1. Martin E. Marty, *Pilgrims in Their Own Land: 500 Years of Religion in America* (New York, Penguin Books, 1984), 171.
2. William Warren Sweet, *Methodism in American History* (New York and Nashville: Abingdon-Cokesbury Press, 1933), 42.
3. Ibid., 48.
4. Ibid.
5. Timothy K. Beougher, "Did You Know?" *Christian History* 2, no. 1 (1983): 4.

6. Charles Ludwig (*Francis Asbury: God's Circuit Rider*, xii) noted that in 1771 there were 600 American Methodists, while Mark Noll (*A History of Christianity in the United States and Canada*, 173) lists 300 in 1771. Regardless of the discrepancy between the figures, both closely agree on the number at the time of Asbury's death ("over 200,000" and "214,235," respectively). The point is well made that incredible growth occurred in this denomination.
7. Charles Ludwig, *Francis Asbury: God's Circuit Rider* (Milford, MI: Mott Media, 1984), xii.
8. Sweet, *Methodism in American History*, 187.
9. William Warren Sweet, *Religion on the American Frontier 1783–1840: The Methodists*, vol. 4 (Chicago, IL: The University of Chicago Press, 1946), 42.
10. Sweet, *Methodism in American History*, 145.
11. Paulus Scharpff, *History of Evangelism*, trans. Helga Bender Henry (Grand Rapids, MI: William B. Eerdmans Publishing Company, 1966), 102.
12. Charles Edward White, "Spare the Rod and Spoil the Church," *Christian History* 20, no. 1 (Issue 69): 28.
13. Ibid.: 30.
14. Ben Witherington, "Circuit Riders and Camp Meetings," *Ashland Theological Journal* 18, no. 2 (Spring 1987): 38.
15. Sweet, *Methodism in American History*, 149.
16. Horace M. De Bose, *Francis Asbury: A Biographical Study* (Nashville, TN: Publishing House of the M. E. Church South, 1916), 53.
17. Sweet, *Methodism in American History*, 101.
18. Peter Cartwright, *Autobiography of Peter Cartwright.* Introduction by Charles L. Wallis (Nashville, TN: Abingdon Press, 1984), 236.
19. Timothy K. Beougher, "Did You Know?" *Christian History* 14, no. 1: 3.
20. Ludwig noted that the allowance from 1784 to 1800 was only $64 per year. Charles Ludwig, *Francis Asbury: God's Circuit Rider* (Milford, MI: Mott Media, 1984), 158.
21. Ibid., 3.
22. Colin Brummitt Goodykuntz, *Home Missions on the American Frontier* (Caldwell, ID: The Caxton Printers, 1939), 259.

### Chapter 18: Baptist Church Planting on the North American Frontier

1. Robert G. Torbet, *A History of the Baptists,* 3rd ed. (Valley Forge, PA: Judson Press, 1963), 253.
2. Spencer Bidwell King Jr., "The Baptist Role in Winning the West," *Baptist History and Heritage* 6, no. 3 (July 1971): 155.
3. James E. Carter traces the evolution of the status of Baptist ministers from persecution to public acceptance in his article "The Socioeconomic Status of

Baptist Ministers in Historical Perspective," *Baptist History and Heritage* 15, no. 1 (Jan 1980): 37–44.

4. John Mason Peck, *Forty Years of Pioneer Life; Memoir of John Mason Peck: Edited from His Journals and Correspondence*, ed. Rufus Babcock (Carbondale, IL: Southern Illinois University Press, 1965), 93.

5. H. Leon McBeth, *The Baptist Heritage: Four Centuries of Baptist Witness* (Nashville, TN: Broadman Press, 1987), 224–25.

6. Ibid., 201.

7. William Warren Sweet, *Revivalism in America: Its Origin, Growth and Decline* (Gloucester, MA: Peter Smith, 1965), 128.

8. William Warren Sweet, *Religion on the American Frontier 1783–1840: The Methodists*, vol. 4 (Chicago, IL: The University of Chicago Press, 1946), 36.

9. John Taylor, *Baptists on the American Frontier: A History of Ten Baptist Churches of Which the Author Has Been Alternately a Member*, annotated 3rd edition, ed. Chester Raymond Young (Macon, GA: Mercer University Press, 1995), xi.

10. R. Stanton Norman, *The Baptist Way: Distinctives of a Baptist Church* (Nashville, TN: Broadman and Holman Publishers, 2005).

11. Robert G. Gardner, *Baptists of Early America: A Statistical History, 1639–1790* (Atlanta, GA: Georgia Baptist Historical Society, 1983), 62–63. It should be noted that H. Leon McBeth observed that Gardner made some corrections to these numbers in what I assume to be McBeth's personal copy of Gardner's work. Such changes reflect the following numbers: 60 churches in 1740 with 3,142 members and 979 churches in 1790 with 67,490 members. McBeth also noted that Gardner included the Keithians and Rogerenes, "whom many would not count as authentic Baptists." Despite these inclusions, McBeth was quick to add, "By any standards, this represents an unprecedented explosion of Baptists in the new land." See H. Leon McBeth, *The Baptist Heritage: Four Centuries of Baptist Witness* (Nashville, TN: Broadman Press, 1987), 206.

12. J. H. Spencer, *A History of Kentucky Baptists: From 1769 to 1885, Including More Than 800 Biographical Sketches,* revised and corrected by Burrilla B. Spencer, vol. 1 (Cincinnati: OH: J. R. Baumes, 1885), 210.

13. Roger Finke and Rodney Stark, *The Churching of America, 1776–1990: Winners and Losers in Our Religious Economy* (New Brunswick, NJ: Rutgers University Press, 1992), 59.

14. Torbet, *A History of the Baptists*, 253.

15. Spencer, *Kentucky Baptists*, 210.

16. George Washington Paschal, *History of North Carolina Baptists,* vol. 1 (Raleigh, NC: The General Board North Carolina Baptist State Convention, 1930), 305.

17. George W. Purefoy, *A History of the Sandy Creek Baptist Association from Its Organization in A.D. 1758 to A.D. 1858* (New York: Sheldon and Company Publishers, 1859), 42.

18. Spencer, *Kentucky Baptists*, 23.

19. Morgan Edwards, *Materials towards a History of the Baptists in the Province of North-Carolina*, vol. 4 (n.p., 1772), 18. This work is found in the Archives and Special Collections, James P. Boyce Centennial Library, The Southern Baptist Theological Seminary, Louisville, Kentucky. All spelling original.
20. C. Peter Wagner, *Church Planting for a Great Harvest* (Ventura, CA: Regal Books, 1990), 60–61.
21. Spencer, *Kentucky Baptists*, 309.
22. Paschal, *North Carolina Baptists*, 314.
23. Ibid., 319.
24. Taylor, *Baptists on the American Frontier*, 160.
25. Wagner, *Church Planting*, 62.
26. William Warren Sweet, *Religion on the American Frontier: The Baptists, 1783–1830* (New York: Henry Holt and Company, 1931), 9.
27. Ibid., 29.
28. McBeth, *Baptist Heritage*, 365.
29. Spencer, *Kentucky Baptists*, 53
30. Ibid., 41.
31. Ibid., 22.
32. Ibid., 39–40.
33. Ibid., 52.
34. McBeth, *Baptist Heritage*, 246.
35. For an excellent sociological treatment of the explosive growth of the Baptists across the frontier, see Roger Finke and Rodney Stark, *The Churching of America, 1776–1990: Winners and Losers in Our Religious Economy* (New Burnswick, NJ: Rutgers University Press, 1992), 71–86.

### Chapter 19: Family Matters and Church Planting

1. Aubrey Malphurs, *Planting Growing Churches for the 21st Century*, 3rd ed. (Grand Rapids, MI: Baker Books, 2004), 91.
2. For a discussion of these five most critical issues, see my article "Five Things Church Planters Wished Their Supervisors Knew," at http://northamericanmissions.org/files/Five-Things-Church-Planters-Wished-Article.pdf (accessed 7/23/08).
3. John M. Bailey and Sherri Jachelski, comps. and eds., *My Husband Wants to Be a Church Planter: So What Will That Make Me?* (Alpharetta, GA: North American Mission Board, 2007). Also available online at http://video.namb.net/cpv/cpwbooksmall.pdf (accessed 7/23/08).
4. Ibid., 18.
5. Ibid., 84.
6. Dave Smith, "Faith and Family," in *Church Planting from the Ground Up*, ed. Tom Jones (Joplin, MO: College Press Publishing Company, 2004), 154.

7. Joyce Jackson, "The Role of a Church Planter's Wife," in *My Husband Wants to Be a Church Planter: So What Will That Make Me?* comps. and eds. John M. Bailey and Sherri Jachelski (Alpharetta, GA: North American Mission Board, 2007), 48.
8. Arnell ArnTessoni, *Gentle Plantings: A Personal Journal for Church Planters' Wives* (Concordville, PA: The Church Planter's Network, 2001), 71.
9. Joel Rainey, *Planting Churches in the Real World* (Smyrna, DE: Missional Press, 2008), 96.

**Chapter 20: Models and Church Planting**

1. Tom Steffen, "Selecting a Church Planting Model That Works," *Missiology* 22, no. 3 (July 1994): 370.
2. Neil Cole, *Organic Church: Growing Faith Where Life Happens* (San Francisco, CA: Jossey-Bass, 2005), 126.
3. Stuart Murray, *Church Planting: Laying Foundations* (London: Paternoster Press, 1998), 161.
4. To read Bradley Weldy's work or download the pdf, see http://www.northamericanmissions.org/?q=node/374.
5. Elmer Towns, *Getting a Church Started* (n.p.: Impact Books: 1975). It is also available online at www.elmertowns.com; Roy Thomas, *Planting and Growing a Fundamental Church* (Nashville, TN: Randall House Publications, 1979).
6. Jack Redford, *Planting New Churches* (Nashville, TN: Broadman Press, 1978).
7. Ralph Neighbor, *Where Do We Go from Here?: A Guidebook for the Cell Group Church*, 10th ed. (Houston, TX: Touch Publications, 2000).
8. Bob Logan and Jeannette Buller, *Cell Church Planter's Guide* (St. Charles, IL: ChurchSmart Resources, 2001).
9. Dick Scoggins, *Planting House Churches in Networks* (Newport, RI: Fellowship of Church Planters, 2001); Felicity Dale, compiler, *Getting Started: A Practical Guide to House Church Planting* (n.p.: House2House Ministries, 2002); Larry Kreider and Floyd McClung, *Starting a House Church* (Ventura, CA: Regal 2007); J. D. Payne, *Missional House Churches: Reaching Our Communities with the Gospel* (Colorado Springs, CO: Paternoster, 2008).
10. Rick Warren, *The Purpose-Driven Church: Growth without Compromising Your Message and Mission* (Grand Rapids, MI: Zondervan, 1995).
11. Another reason for the contents of Warren's book being understood as an ideal type is that Warren clearly states in the book that the work does not tell of all the mistakes and problems he experienced along the journey in planting the church. Rather, the book was birthed out of much trial and error with the final product in the text being the desired type. (See page 28 of Warren's book.)
12. Tom Steffen, "Selecting a Church Planting Model That Works," *Missiology* 22, no. 3 (July 1994): 361–76.

### Chapter 21: Common Objections to Church Planting

1. Ray Register, *Back to Jerusalem: Church Planting Movements in the Holy Land* (Enumclaw, WA: WinePress Publishing, 2000), 118.
2. I first published the majority of this chapter as J. D. Payne, "The Mother Church and Church Planting," *Journal of the American Society for Church Growth* 16 (Winter 2005): 31–59.
3. E-mail sent to author.
4. E-mail sent to author.
5. E-mail sent to author.
6. E-mail sent to author.
7. E-mail sent to author.
8. E-mail sent to author.
9. E-mail sent to author. One exception to this situation is when established churches are involved in planting churches among different ethnic populations. For example, church planting tends to become more palatable to many Anglo congregations if the mission work is among a different people group.
10. I have included turfism as a separate category because it is a perceived reason for why most churches are not involved in church planting. Though a lack of a kingdom vision may be the true reason that many churches are turfish, nevertheless, many church planters attribute this problem to turfism.
11. Paul Becker and Mark Williams, *The Dynamic Daughter Church Planting Handbook* (n.p.: Dynamic Church Planting International, 1999), sec. 1, pp. 16–28.
12. C. Peter Wagner, *Church Planting for a Greater Harvest* (Ventura, CA: Regal Books, 1990), 20.
13. Becker and Williams, *Daughter Church Planting*, sec. 1, p. 20.
14. Ibid., 23.
15. Wagner, *Church Planting*, 11.
16. C. Wayne Zunkel, "It's Easier to Have Babies," *Brethren Life and Thought* 28 (Spring 1983): 78.

### Chapter 22: Church Planting in Urban Contexts

1. Roger S. Greenway, "Urbanization and Missions" in *Crucial Dimensions in World Evangelization*, eds. Arthur F. Glasser, Paul G. Hiebert, C. Peter Wagner, and Ralph D. Winter (Pasadena, CA: William Carey Library, 1976), 222.
2. United Nations, "World Urbanization Prospects: The 2005 Revision" (New York: United Nations, 2006), 3–5; http://www.un.org/esa/population/publications/ WUP2005/2005WUPHighlights_Final_Report.pdf (accessed 5/7/08).
3. Roger S. Greenway and Timothy M. Monsma, *Cities: Missions' New Frontier* (Grand Rapids, MI: Baker Book House, 1989), 108–110.

4. Larry L. Rose and C. Kirk Hadaway, eds., *An Urban World: Churches Face the Future* (Nashville, TN: Broadman Press, 1984), 32–33.
5. Tim Keller, "A Biblical Theology of the City," *Evangelicals Now* (July 2002) http://www.e-n.org.uk/p-1869-A-biblical-theology-of-the-city.htm (accessed 12/3/07).
6. Roger S. Greenway, *Apostles to the City: Biblical Strategies for Urban Missions* (Grand Rapids, MI: Baker Book House, 1978), 11.
7. Paul G. Hiebert and Eloise Hiebert Meneses, *Incarnational Ministry: Planting Churches in Band, Tribal, Peasant, and Urban Societies* (Grand Rapids, MI: Baker Books, 1995), 263–73.
8. Francis M. DuBose, "Cities Aren't All Alike," *Urban Mission* 3 (January 1984): 18–20.
9. Viv Grigg, "Sorry! The Frontier Moved," *Urban Mission* 4, no. 4 (March 1987): 13.
10. The sources of this data are www.un.org/esa/population/publications/2006Migration_Chart/2006IttMig_wallchart.xls and http://www.toronto.ca/demographics/ pdf/2006_ethnic_origin_visible_minorities_backgrounder.pdf.
11. Ray Bakke, *A Theology as Big as the City* (Downers Grove, IL: InterVarsity Press, 1997), 73.
12. Robert Neuwirth, *Shadow Cities: A Billion Squatters, A New Urban World* (New York: Routledge, 2006), 9.
13. Taken from "2008 Report on the Global AIDS Epidemic," p. 32; available at http://data.unaids.org/pub/GlobalReport/2008/jc1510_2008_global_report_pp29_62_en.pdf (accessed 9/3/2008).
14. J. D. Payne, "G.O.I.N.G. U.R.B.A.N. for the 21st Century Missionary," *Journal of Urban Ministry* 1 no. 1 (September 2008): 6–11; online at http://www.urbanministrytraining. org/journal/1.1.
15. United Nations, "World Urbanization Prospects: The 2005 Revision," p. 4; online at http://www.un.org/esa/population/publications/WUP2005/2005WUPHighlights_ Final_Report.pdf (accessed 4/28/08).
16. Ray Bakke in Stan Guthrie, *Missions in the Third Millennium: 21 Key Trends for the 21st Century*, revised and expanded (Colorado Springs, CO: Paternoster Press, 2000), 90.
17. Hiebert and Meneses, *Incarnational Ministry*, 271.

## Chapter 23: Tentmaking and Church Planting

1. Taken from the foreword of Don Hamilton, *Tentmakers Speak: Practical Advice from over 400 Missionary Tentmakers* (Ventura, CA: Regal Books, 1989), ix.
2. E-mail sent to author.
3. J. Christy Wilson Jr., *Today's Tentmakers: Self-Support: An Alternative Model for Worldwide Witness* (Wheaton, IL: Tyndale House Publishers, Inc., 1979);

Don Hamilton, *Tentmakers Speak: Practical Advice from over 400 Missionary Tentmakers* (Ventura, CA: Regal Books, 1989); Ruth E. Siemens, "The Vital Role of Tentmaking in Paul's Mission Strategy," *International Journal of Frontier Missions* 14 (July–Sept 1997): 121–29; Tetsunao Yamamori, "Tent-Making Mission," in *Evangelical Dictionary of World Missions*, ed. A. Scott Moreau (Grand Rapids, MI: Baker Books, 2000), 939–40; Gary Ginter, "Overcoming Resistance through Tentmaking," in *Reaching the Resistant: Barriers and Bridges for Mission*, ed. J. Dudley Woodberry (Pasadena, CA: William Carey Library, 1998); and Patrick Lai, *Tentmaking: Business as Missions* (Colorado Springs, CO: Authentic Media, 2005). For the Lausanne Congress on World Evangelization in Manila in 1989, see http://www.globalopps.org/downloads/Lausanne.PDF.

4. For some of the best books on the topic of tentmaking, see Roland Allen, *The Case for Voluntary Clergy* (London: Eyre and Spottiswoode, 1930); Hamilton, *Tentmakers Speak*; Lai, *Tentmaking*; Jonathan Lewis, ed., *Working Your Way to the Nations: A Guide to Effective Tentmaking* (Pasadena, CA: William Carey Library, 1993); Steve Rundle and Tom Steffen, *Great Commission Companies: The Emerging Role of Business in Missions* (Downers Grove, IL: InterVarsity Press, 2003); J. Christy Wilson Jr., *Today's Tentmakers: Self-Support: An Alternative Model for Worldwide Witness* (Wheaton, IL: Tyndale House Publishers, Inc., 1979); Tetsunao Yamamori and Kenneth A. Eldred, eds., *On Kingdom Business: Transforming Missions through Entrepreneurial Strategies* (Wheaton, IL: Crossway Books, 2003).

5. Wilson, *Today's Tentmakers*, 70–71; Jim Reapsome, ed., "Tentmakers," in *Evangelical Missions Quarterly* 32 (October 1996): 420.

6. There are several other passages that reveal that Paul was involved in a nonclergy type of business at times throughout his missionary work (e.g., Acts 19:11–12; 20:34; 1 Cor. 4:12; 9:6; 2 Cor. 11:27; 12:14; 1 Thess. 2:9).

7. I do not make light of the fact that for most North Americans, missionary work outside the continent is much more cross-cultural than missionary work done here. The point that I want to make is that cross-cultural mission work happens not only overseas but here at home as well.

8. Steve Sjogren and Rob Lewin, *Community of Kindness: A Refreshing New Approach to Planting and Growing a Church* (Ventura, CA: Regal, 2003), 172–73.

9. Jack Strong, "Into a Thick Wood," in *Tentmaking: Perspectives on Self-Supporting Ministry*, eds., James M. M. Francis and Leslie J. Francis (Leominster, U.K.: Gracewing Fowler Wright Books, 1997), 303.

10. Of course, for some the call to follow Christ is a call to poverty. But this calling is not the same for all. You only need to look at the New Testament to find both the poor and the wealthy in the same congregation (e.g., Philemon and Onesimus, James 2:1–7).

11. Wilson, *Today's Tentmakers*, 70–71.

12. Luther M. Dorr, *The Bivocational Pastor* (Nashville, TN: Broadman Press, 1988), 134–35.

13. I am thankful for the Fellowship of Church Planters, which delineated these three ways in one of its publications. See Dick Scoggins, *Building Effective Church Planting Teams* (Middletown, RI: FCPT, n.d.), 37–39. This resource can be downloaded or read online from the Fellowship of Church Planters' website at www.fcpt.org.
14. F. F. Bruce, *Paul: Apostle of the Heart Set Free* (Grand Rapids, MI: William B. Eerdmans Publishing Company, 1977), 220.
15. "We are fools for Christ's sake, but you are wise in Christ. We are weak, but you are strong. You are held in honor, but we in disrepute. To the present hour we hunger and thirst, we are poorly dressed and buffeted and homeless, and we labor, *working with our own hands.* When reviled, we bless; when persecuted, we endure; when slandered, we entreat. We have become, and are still, like the scum of the world, the refuse of all things" (1 Cor. 4:10–13, italics mine).
16. The top five most critical issues mentioned in order of importance were (1) finances, (2) leadership development, (3) unsupportive churches, (4) contextualization issues, and (5) family pressures.
17. Fred G. King, *The Church Planter's Training Manual* (Camp Hill, PA: Christian Publications, 1992), 14.
18. Arnell ArnTessoni, *Gentle Plantings: A Personal Journal for Church Planters' Wives* (Concordville, PA: The Church Planter's Network, 2001), 41.

## Chapter 24: Missionaries or Pastors: What Are Church Planters?

1. Roland Allen, "The Case for Voluntary Clergy" in *The Ministry of the Spirit: Selected Writings of Roland Allen*, ed. David M. Paton (Grand Rapids, MI: William B. Eerdmans Publishing Company, 1960), 163.
2. Ed Stetzer, *Planting Missional Churches* (Nashville, TN: Broadman and Holman Publishers, 2006), 53–75.
3. William David Taylor, "Missionary," *Evangelical Dictionary of World Missions*, ed. A. Scott Moreau (Grand Rapids, MI: Baker Books, 2000), 644.
4. Stetzer, *Planting Missional Churches*, 62.
5. Charles R. Ridley, *How to Select Church Planters: A Self-Study Manual for Recruiting, Screening, Interviewing and Evaluating Qualified Church Planters* (Pasadena, CA: Fuller Evangelistic Association, 1988); Charles R. Ridley and Robert E. Logan with Helena Gerstenberg, *Training for Selection Interviewing* (St. Charles, IL.: ChurchSmart Resources, 1998).
6. Ridley, *How to Select Church Planters*, 7.

## Chapter 25: Church-Planting Movements and Church Planting

1. Bob Roberts Jr., *The Multiplying Church: The New Math for Starting New Churches* (Grand Rapids, MI: Zondervan, 2008), 29.

2. *Stimulating and Nurturing Church Planting Movements* (Richmond, VA: International Mission Board, 2001), 9.
3. David Garrison, *Church Planting Movements: How God Is Redeeming a Lost World* (Midlothian, VA: WIGTAKE Resources, 2004), 21, italics original.
4. Roland Allen, *The Spontaneous Expansion of the Church* (Grand Rapids, MI: William B. Eerdmans Publishing Company, 1962), 7. This book was first published in 1927.
5. Garrison, *Church Planting Movements*, 172.
6. Ibid., 221–22.
7. Jim Slack, "Church Planting Movements: Rationale, Research and Realities of Their Existence," *Journal of Evangelism and Missions* 6 (Spring 2007): 41–43.
8. Neil Cole, "Case Study (USA): The Story of Church Multiplication Associates—From California to Chiang Mai in Seven Years," in *Nexus: The World House Church Movement Reader*, ed. Rad Zdero (Pasadena, CA: William Carey Library, 2007), 346.
9. Garrison, *Church Planting Movements*, 139.
10. See J. D. Payne, *Missional House Churches: Reaching Our Communities with the Gospel* (Colorado Springs, CO: Paternoster, 2008), 133–63.
11. This list is provided in David Garrison, *Church Planting Movements* (Richmond, VA: International Mission Board, 2000). This reference is from his booklet and not from his book by the same name, and I've summarized it in this section of the chapter.
12. William C. Tinsley, *Upon This Rock: Dimensions of Church Planting* (Atlanta, GA: Home Mission Board, 1985), 16.
13. Donald A. McGavran, *Understanding Church Growth* (Grand Rapids, MI: William B. Eerdmans Publishing Company, 1970), 297–98.
14. Clyde Meador, "The Left Side of the Graph," *Journal of Evangelism and Missions* 6 (Spring 2007): 59–63.
15. Paul Hattaway, *From Head-Hunters to Church Planters: An Amazing Spiritual Awakening in Nagaland* (Colorado Springs, CO: Authentic Publishing, 2006), 13–14.

# BIBLIOGRAPHY

## Books

Akins, Thomas Wade. *Pioneer Evangelism*. English Ed. Rio de Janerio, Brazil: Missoes Nacionais, 2002.

Amberson, Talmadge R., compiler. *The Birth of Churches: A Biblical Basis for Church Planting*. Nashville, TN: Broadman Press, 1979.

ArnTessoni, Arnell. *Gentle Plantings: A Personal Journal for Church Planters' Wives*. Concordville, PA: The Church Planter's Network, 2001.

Bailey, John M., compiler. *Pursuing the Mission of God in Church Planting: The Missional Church in North America*. Alpharetta, GA: North American Mission Board, 2006.

Bailey, John M., and Sherri Jachelski, comps. and eds. *My Husband Wants to Be a Church Planter: So What Will That Make Me?* Alpharetta, GA: North American Mission Board, 2007.

Becker, Paul, and Mark Williams. *The Dynamic Daughter Church Planting Handbook*. N.p: Dynamic Church Planting International, 1999.

Bright, Edna. *God Uses Ordinary People: A Memoir of Church Planting*. Franklin, TN: Providence House Publishers, 1998.

Brock, Charles. *Indigenous Church Planting: A Practical Journey*. Neosho, MO: Church Growth International, 1994.

———. *Let This Mind Be in You*. Neosho, MO: Church Growth International, 1990.

———. *Questions People and Churches Ask*. Neosho, MO: Church Growth International, 1988.

———. *The Principles and Practice of Indigenous Church Planting*. Nashville, TN: Broadman Press, 1981.

Bunch, David T., Harvey J. Kneisel, and Barbara L. Oden. *Multihousing Congregations: How to Start and Grow Christian Congregations in Multihousing Communities.* Atlanta, GA: Smith Publishing, 1991.

Bunn, Tim W. *God's Plan for Church Planting: Church Planting Manual Using God's Timeless, Supra-Cultural Principles.* Westminster, CO: IMD Press, 2008.

Burton, Jim, Norman Jameson, and David Wilkinson. *No Small Sacrifice: Church Starting in Urban North America, 1992 Home Mission Study.* Atlanta, GA: Home Mission Board, SBC.

Carlton, R. Bruce. *Amazing Grace: Lessons on Church Planting Movements from Cambodia.* Chennai, India: Mission Educational Books, 2000.

Chaney, Charles. *Church Planting at the End of the Twentieth Century.* Revised and Expanded. Wheaton, IL: Tyndale House Publishers, Inc., 1991.

———. *Church Planting at the End of the Twentieth Century.* Wheaton, IL: Tyndale House Publishers, Inc., 1982.

Cheyney, Tom, J. David Putman, and Van Sanders, general eds. *Seven Steps for Planting Churches: Planter Edition.* Alpharetta, GA: North American Mission Board, 2003.

Choy, Kathy, Elaine Furlow, Jim Newton, Phyllis Thompson, and Joe Westbury. *The Church Starts Here: Adult Home Mission Study 1988.* Atlanta, GA: Home Mission Board, 1987.

Cole, Neil. *Organic Church: Growing Faith Where Life Happens.* San Francisco, CA: Jossey-Bass, 2005.

———. *Cultivating a Life for God: Multiplying Disciples through Life Transformation Groups.* St. Charles, IL: ChurchSmart Resources, 1999.

Cole, H. Shelton. *Baptist Church Planting: A Primer for Answering Questions about Starting an Independent, Fundamental, Baptist Church.* Volumes 1 and 2. Great Barrington, MA: n.p, 1997.

Comiskey, Joel. *Planting Churches That Reproduce: Starting a Network of Simple Churches.* Moreno Valley, CA: CCS Publishing, 2009.

Conn, Harvie M., ed. *Planting and Growing Urban Churches: From Dream to Reality.* Grand Rapids, MI: Baker Books, 1997.

Cupit, Tony, ed. *Five Till Midnight: Church Planting for A.D. 2000 and Beyond.* Atlanta, GA: Home Mission Board, 1994.

Dale, Felicity, ed. *Getting Started: A Practical Guide to House Church Planting.* N.p.: House2House Ministries, 2002.

Estep, Michael R., ed. *Great Commission Church Planting Strategy.* Kansas City, MO: Nazarene Publishing House, 1988.

Faircloth, Samuel D. *Church Planting for Reproduction.* Grand Rapids, MI: Baker Publishing, 1991.

Fox, J. Mark. *Planting a Family-Integrated Church.* U.S.A: Xulon Press, 2008.

Francis, Hozell C. *Church Planting in the African-American Context.* Grand Rapids, MI: Zondervan Publishing House, 1999.

Garrison, David. *Church Planting Movements: How God Is Redeeming a Lost World.* Midlothian, VA: WIGTAKE Resources, 2004.

———. *Church Planting Movements.* Richmond, VA: International Mission Board, 2000.

Goslin II, Thomas S. *The Church without Walls*. Pasadena, CA: Hope Publishing House, 1984.

Gray, Stephen, with Trent Short. *Planting Fast-Growing Churches*. St. Charles, IL: ChurchSmart Resources, 2007.

Greenway, Roger S., ed. *Guidelines for Urban Church Planting.* Grand Rapids, MI: Baker Book House, 1976.

Griffith, Jim, and Bill Easum, *Ten Most Common Mistakes Made by New Church Starts.* St. Louis, MO: Chalice Press, 2008

Gupta, Paul R., and Sherwood G. Lingenfelter. *Breaking Tradition to Accomplish Vision: Training Leaders for a Church-Planting Movement.* Winona Lake, IN: BMH Books, 2006.

Harris, Richard H., compiler. *Reaching a Nation through Church Planting.* Revised Ed. Alpharetta, GA: North American Mission Board, 2005.

———, compiler. *Reaching a Nation through Church Planting.* Alpharetta, GA: North American Mission Board, 2003.

Harrison, Rodney. *Seven Steps for Planting Churches: Partnering Church Edition.* Alpharetta, GA: North American Mission Board, 2004.

Harrison, Rodney, Tom Cheyney, and Don Overstreet. *Spin-off Churches: How One Church Successfully Plants Another*. Nashville, TN: B&H Publishing Group, 2008.

Hattaway, Paul. *From Head-Hunters to Church Planters: An Amazing Spiritual Awakening in Nagaland.* Colorado Springs, CO: Authentic Publishing, 2006.

Herron, Fred. *Expanding God's Kingdom through Church Planting.* New York: Writer's Showcase, 2003.

Hesselgrave, David J. *Planting Churches Cross-Culturally: A Guide for Home and Foreign Missions.* Grand Rapids, MI: Baker Books, 1980.

Hesselgrave, David J. *Planting Churches Cross-Culturally: North America and Beyond,* 2nd ed. Grand Rapids, MI: Baker Academic, 2000.

Hiebert, Paul G., and Eloise Hiebert Meneses. *Incarnational Ministry: Planting Churches in Band, Tribal, Peasant, and Urban Societies.* Grand Rapids, MI: Baker Books, 1995.

Hodges, Melvin L. *The Indigenous Church: A Complete Handbook on How to Grow Young Churches.* Springfield, MO: Gospel Publishing House, 1976.

———. *A Guide to Church Planting: Practical "How To "Information on Establishing Mission Churches.* Chicago, IL: Moody Press, 1973.

Hogan, Brian P. *There's a Sheep in My Bathtub: Birth of a Mongolian Church Planting Movement*. Bayside, CA: Asteroidea Books, 2007.

*How to Plant a Church: A Study Guide*. Nashville, TN: Seminary Extension, 2001.

Hurn, Raymond W. *The Rising Tide: New Churches for the New Millennium*. Kansas City, MO: Beacon Hill Press, 1997.

Jackson, J. David, ed. *PlantLife: Principles and Practices in Church Planting.* Smyrna, DE: Missional Press, 2008.

Jackson, John. *High Impact Church Planting.* N.p.: Vision Quest Ministries, 2000.

Jones, Ezra Earl. *Strategies for New Churches*. New York: Harper & Row, Publishers, 1976.

Jones, Tom, ed. *Church Planting from the Ground Up*. Joplin, MO: College Press Publishing Company, 2004.

Keller, Timothy J., and J. Allen Thompson. *Church Planter Manual.* New York: Redeemer Church Planting Center, 2002.

King, Fred G. *The Church Planter's Training Manual.* Camp Hill, PA: Christian Publications, 1992.

Knight, Walker. *Seven Beginnings: The Human Touch in Starting Churches.* Atlanta, GA: Home Mission Board, 1976.

Kreider, Larry, and Floyd McClung. *Starting a House Church: A New Model for Living Out Your Faith.* Ventura, CA: Regal, 2007.

Lewis, Larry. *The Church Planter's Handbook.* Nashville, TN: Broadman and Holman Publishers, 1992.

Logan, Robert E. *Be Fruitful and Multiply: Embracing God's Heart for Church Multiplication*. St. Charles, IL: ChurchSmart Resources, 2006.

Logan, Robert E., and Neil Cole. *Beyond Church Planting: Pathways for Emerging Churches.* St. Charles, IL: ChurchSmart Resources, 2005.

Logan, Robert E., and Jeannette Buller. *Cell Church Planter's Guide.* St. Charles, IL: ChurchSmart Resources, 2001.

Logan, Robert E., and Neil Cole. *Raising Leaders for the Harvest.* St. Charles, IL: ChurchSmart Resources, 1992–1995.

Logan, Robert E., and Steven L. Ogne. *The Church Planter's Toolkit: A Self-Study Resource Kit for Church Planters and Those Who Supervise Them.* Revised Ed. St. Charles, IL: ChurchSmart Resources, 1994.

Love, Rick. *Muslims, Magi and the Kingdom of God: Church Planting among Folk Muslims.* Pasadena, CA: William Carey Library, 2000.

Ma, Jason. *The Blueprint: A Revolutionary Plan to Plant Missional Communities on Campus.* Ventura, CA: Regal, 2007.

Malphurs, Aubrey. *Planting Growing Churches for the 21st Century,* 3rd ed. Grand Rapids, MI: Baker Books, 2004.

Mannoia, Kevin W. *Church Planting the Next Generation: Introducing the Century 21 Church Planting System.* Indianapolis, IN: Light and Life Communications, 1994.

Maroney, Jimmy K., and James B. Slack. *Handbook for Effective Church Planting and Growth.* Richmond, VA: Foreign Mission Board, n.d.

McNamara, Roger N., and Ken Davis. *The YBH (Yes, But How?) Handbook of Church Planting: A Practical Guide to Church Planting.* U.S.A.: Xulon Press, 2005.

*Mission-Shaped Church: Church Planting and Fresh Expressions of Church in a Changing Context.* London: Church House Publishing, 2004.

Moerman, Murray, ed. *Discipling Our Nation: Equipping the Canadian Church for Its Mission.* Delta, BC: Outreach Canada Ministries, 2005.

Montgomery, Jim. *I'm Gonna Let It Shine!: 10 Million Lighthouses to Go.* Pasadena, CA: William Carey Library, 2001.

———. *DAWN 2000: 7 Million Churches to Go.* Pasadena, CA: William Carey Library, 1989.

Moore, Ralph. *Starting a New Church: The Church Planter's Guide to Success.* Ventura, CA: Regal Books, 2002.

Moorhous, Carl W., *Growing New Churches: Step-by-Step Procedures in New Church Planting.* Gary, IN: n.p., 1975.

Murray, Stuart. *Planting Churches: A Framework for Practitioners.* London: Paternoster Press, 2008.

———. *Church Planting: Laying Foundations.* North American Ed. Scottdale, PA: Herald Press, 2001.

———. *Church Planting: Laying Foundations.* London: Paternoster Press, 1998.

Myers, Lewis, and Jim Slack. *To the Edge: A Planning Process for People Group Specific Strategy Development.* Richmond, VA: International Mission Board, 1999.

Nebel, Tom. *Big Dreams in Small Places: Church Planting in Smaller Communities.* St. Charles, IL: ChurchSmart Resources, 2002.

Nebel, Tom, and Gary Rohrmayer. *Church Planting Landmines: Mistakes to Avoid in Years 2 through 10.* St. Charles, IL: ChurchSmart Resources, 2005.

Nerger, Steve, and Eric W. Ramsey. *Bivocational Church Planters: Uniquely Wired for Kingdom Growth.* Alpharetta, GA: North American Mission Board, 2007.

Nevius, John L. *Planting and Development of Missionary Churches.* N.p: The Presbyterian and Reformed Publishing Company, n.d.

Noel, Michael D., compiler. *Church-Planting Voices.* Camp Hill, PA: Christian Publications Inc., 1998.

O'Conner, Patrick. *Reproducible Pastoral Training: Church Planting Guidelines from the Teachings of George Patterson.* Pasadena, CA: William Carey Library, 2006.

*The Pastor's Helper for Growing a New Church.* Atlanta, GA: Home Mission Board.

Patterson, George, and Richard Scoggins. *Church Multiplication Guide: The Miracle of Church Reproduction.* Revised. Pasadena, CA: William Carey Library, 2002.

———. *Church Multiplication Guide: Helping Churches to Reproduce Locally and Abroad.* Pasadena, CA: William Carey Library, 1993.

Payne, J. D. *The Barnabas Factors: Eight Essential Practices of Church Planting Team Members.* Smyrna, DE: Missional Press, 2008.

———. *Missional House Churches: Reaching Our Communities with the Gospel.* Colorado Springs, CO: Paternoster, 2008.

Porter, Douglas, and Elmer Towns. *Churches That Multiply.* Kansas City, MO: Beacon Hill Press, 2003.

Rainey, Joel. *Planting Churches in the Real World.* Smyrna, DE: Missional Press, 2008.

Ratliff, Joe S., and Michael J. Cox. *Church Planting in the African-American Community.* Nashville, TN: Broadman Press, 1993.

Redford, Jack. *Planting New Churches.* Nashville, TN: Broadman Press, 1978.

Register, Ray. *Back to Jerusalem: Church Planting Movements in the Holy Land.* Enumclaw, WA: WinePress Publishing, 2000.

Ridley, Charles R. *How to Select Church Planters: A Self-Study Manual for Recruiting, Screening, Interviewing and Evaluating Qualified Church Planters.* Pasadena, CA: Fuller Evangelistic Association, 1988.

Ridley, Charles R., and Robert E. Logan with Helena Gerstenberg. *Training for Selection Interviewing.* St. Charles, IL: ChurchSmart Resources, 1998.

Roberts Jr., Bob. *The Multiplying Church: The New Math for Starting New Churches.* Grand Rapids, MI: Zondervan, 2008.

Robinson, Martin. *Planting Mission-Shaped Churches Today.* Grand Rapids, MI: Monarch Books, 2006.

Rogers, Glenn. *North American Cross-Cultural Church Planting.* N.p.: Mission and Ministry Resources, 2008.

Rohrmayer, Gary. *First Steps for Planting a Missional Church.* St. Charles, IL: ChurchSmart Resources, 2006.

Sanchez, Daniel R., ed. *Church Planting Movements in North America.* Fort Worth, TX: Church Starting Network, 2007.

Sanchez, Daniel R., Ebbie C. Smith, and Curtis E. Watke. *Starting Reproducing Congregations: A Guidebook for Contextual New Church Development.* Fort Worth, TX: Church Starting Network, 2001.

Schaller, Lyle E., *44 Questions for Church Planters.* Nashville, TN: Abingdon Press, 1991.

Scoggins, Dick. *Planting House Churches in Networks.* Newport, RI: Fellowship of Church Planters, 2001.

———. *Building Effective Church Planting Teams: A Handbook for Team Leaders and Mentors.* Middletown, RI: Fellowship of Church Planters, n.d.

Searcy, Nelson, and Kerrick Thomas. *Launch: Starting a New Church from Scratch.* Ventura, CA: Regal Books, 2006.

Sell, Alan P. F. *Church Planting.* Eugene, OR: Wipf and Stock Publishers, 1998.

Shenk, David W., and Ervin R. Stutzman. *Creating Communities of the Kingdom: New Testament Models of Church Planting.* Scottdale, PA: Herald Press, 1988.

Sinclair, Daniel. *A Vision of the Possible: Pioneer Church Planting in Teams.* Colorado Springs, CO: Authentic Media, 2005.

Sjogren, Steve, and Rob Lewin. *Community of Kindness: A Refreshing New Approach to Planting and Growing a Church*. Ventura, CA: Regal Books, 2003.

Steffen, Tom. *Passing the Baton: Church Planting That Empowers*. La Habra, CA: Center for Organizational and Ministry Development, 1993

Stetzer, Ed. *Planting Missional Churches: Planting a Church That's Biblically Sound and Reaching People in Culture*. Nashville, TN: Broadman & Holman Publishers, 2006.

———. *Planting New Churches in a Postmodern Age*. Nashville, TN: Broadman & Holman Publishers, 2003.

Stevenson, Phil. *5 Things Anyone Can Do to Help Start a Church*. Indianapolis, IN: Wesleyan Publishing House, 2008.

———. *The Ripple Church: Multiply Your Ministry by Parenting New Churches*. Indianapolis, IN: Wesleyan Publishing House, 2004.

*Stimulating and Nurturing Church Planting Movements*. Richmond, VA: International Mission Board, 2001.

Suarez, Gustavo V. *Connections: Linking People and Principles for Dynamic Church Multiplication*. Friendswood, TX: Baxter Press, 2004.

Sutter, K. *Keys to Church Planting Movements*. Bayside, CA: Asteroidea Books, 2008.

Sylvia, Ron. *Starting New Churches on Purpose: Strategies for the 21st Century*. Lake Forest, CA: Purpose Driven Publishing, 2006.

Sylvia, Ron. *HD Churches: Starting High Definition Churches*. Ocala, FL: High Definition Resources, 2004.

Thomas, Roy. *Planting and Growing a Fundamental Church*. Nashville, TN: Randall House Publications, 1979.

Thompson, J. Allen. *Coaching Urban Church Planters: Growing Visionary Leaders, Vital Churches and Multiplication Movements in the City*. New York: Redeemer Church Planting Center, 2005.

Tidsworth Jr., Floyd. *Life Cycle of a New Congregation*. Nashville, TN: Broadman Press, 1992.

Timmis, Stephen, ed. *Multipling Churches: Reaching Today's Communities through Church Planting*. U.K.: Christian Focus Publications, 2000.

Towns, Elmer. *Getting a Church Started*, 3rd ed. Lynchburg, VA: Liberty University of LifeLong Learning, 1993.

Towns, Elmer, and Douglas Porter. *Churches That Multiply: A Bible Study on Church Planting*. Kansas City, MO: Beacon Hill Press of Kansas City, 2003.

Viola, Frank. *So You Want to Start a House Church?: First Century Styled Church Planting for Today*. N.p.: Present Testimony Ministry, 2003.

Wagner, C. Peter. *Church Planting for a Greater Harvest: A Comprehensive Guide*. Ventura, CA: Regal Books, 1990.

Warren, Rick. *The Purpose-Driven Church: Growth without Compromising Your Message and Mission*. Grand Rapids, MI: Zondervan, 1995.

Williams, Melissa, compiler. *New Churches Needed Our Church Can Help!: A Step-by Step Handbook for Planting New Churches.* Alpharetta, GA: The North American Mission Board, 2001.

## Articles and Chapters

Allen, Frank W. "Kanuming, Philippines: An Urban Church Planting Model." *Urban Mission* 6, no. 2 (November 1988): 56–60.

Allen, Frank W. "Your Church-Planting Team Can Be Booby-Trapped." *Evangelical Missions Quarterly* 27 (July 1991): 294–97.

Apeh, John E. "Socio-Anthropological Implications in Cross-Cultural Church Planting." *Asia Journal of Theology* 11 (February 1997): 282–92.

Baker, Ken. "Power Encounter and Church Planting." *Evangelical Missions Quarterly* 26 (July 1990): 306–12.

Bateman, J. Keith. "A Ten-Point Plan for Producing Better 'Indigenous' Churches." *Evangelical Missions Quarterly* 42, no. 2 (April 2006): 152–54.

Beal, William C. "The Planting of the Evangelical Association in Western Pennsylvania." *Methodist History* 16, no. 4 (July 1978): 218–29.

Bessenecker, Scott. "Paul's Short-Term Church Planting: Can It Happen Again?" *Evangelical Missions Quarterly* 33, no. 3 (July 1997): 326–32.

Birkey, Del. "The House Church: A Missiological Model." *Missiology* 19 (January 1991): 69–80.

Blackaby, Henry. "The Birth of a New Church." *On Mission* 8, no. 3 (Summer 2005): 5.

Branner, John. "Five Approaches to Church Planting." *Urban Mission* 8, no. 2 (November 1990): 52–59.

Brown, Dan. "Church-Planting Movements in the Muslim World." *Mission Frontiers* 26, no. 1 (January–February 2004): 12–13.

———. "Is Planting Churches in the Muslim World 'Mission Impossible'?" *Evangelical Missions Quarterly* 33, no. 2 (April 1997): 156–65.

Caldwell, Stuart. "Jesus in Samaria: A Paradigm for Church Planting among Muslims." *International Journal of Frontier Missions* 17, no. 1 (Spring 2000): 25–31.

"Churches Die with Dignity." *Christianity Today* (January 14, 1991): 68–70.

Corwin, Gary. "Church Planting 101." *Evangelical Missions Quarterly* (April 2005): 142–43.

Downey, Steven. "What Are 'Best Practices' of Church Planting among Muslims?" *Evangelical Missions Quarterly* 44, no. 3 (July 2008): 368–73.

Dunaetz, David. "Transforming Chaos into Beauty: Intentionally Developing Unity in Church Plants." *Evangelical Missions Quarterly* 44, no. 3 (July 2008): 358–65.

Fehderau, Harold W. "Planting the Church in Congo, and the Emerging Situation Today." *Practical Anthropology* 8 (1961): 25–30.
Fisher, Ron. "Why Don't We Have More Church-Planting Missionaries?" *Evangelical Missions Quarterly* 14, no. 4 (October 1978): 205–11.
Fretheim, Arthur, Victor Fry, Kaye Pattison, and Robert Ross. "Leadership Forum: The 'Johnny Appleseeds' of Church Planting." *Leadership* 5, no. 2 (Spring 1984): 125–34.
Garrison, David. "Church Planting Movements: The Next Wave?" *International Journal of Frontier Missions* 21, no. 3 (July–September 2004): 118–21.
Giles, Greg. "New Church Nurture: A Task for Missions?" *Evangelical Missions Quarterly* 21, no. 2 (April 1985): 148–50.
Grady, Dick, and Glenn Kendall. "Seven Keys to Effective Church Planting." *Evangelical Missions Quarterly* 28, no. 4 (October 1992): 366–73.
Graham, Thomas. "How to Select the Best Church Planters." *Evangelical Missions Quarterly* 23, no. 1 (January 1987): 70–79.
Guy, Cal. "Southern Baptists and Church Planting/Growth." *Journal of Evangelism and Missions* 2 (Spring 2003): 79–86.
Hall, David. "10 Reasons Why Every Church-Planting Team Needs a Worship Leader." *Evangelical Missions Quarterly* 36, no. 1 (January 2000): 50–53.
Harsh, Norman. "Financial Resources for Church Planting." *Brethren Life and Thought* 36, no. 3 (Summer 1991): 221–26.
Hesselgrave, David J. "Essential Elements of Church Planting and Growing in the 21st Century." *Evangelical Missions Quarterly* 36, no. 1 (January 2000): 24–32.
Hiebert, Paul G. "Planting Churches in North America Today." *Direction* 20, no. 2 (Fall 1991): 6–20.
Higginbotham, Joseph. "The Generationally Indigenous Church." *RE:Generation Quarterly* 3, no. 1: 32–33.
Houghton, Graham, and Ezra Sargunam. "The Role of Theological Education in Church Planting among the Urban Poor: A Case Study from Madras." *Evangelical Review of Theology* 6, no. 1 (April 1982): 141–45.
Janzen, Warren. "5-10 Team: A Proposal for Church Planting." *Didaskalia* (October 1993): 69–75.
Jones, Juha. "Four Ways to Mentor Church Planters." *Evangelical Missions Quarterly* 44, no. 4 (October 2008): 488–91.
Kendall, Glenn. "Missionaries Should Not Plant Churches." *Evangelical Missions Quarterly* 24, no. 3 (July 1988): 218–21.
Kendall, Glenn. "Tiny Rwanda Shines as Example of Cluster Church Planting." *Evangelical Missions Quarterly* 26, no. 1 (January 1990): 136–43.
Kingdon, David P. "Church Planting in the New Testament." *Searching Together* 13, no. 4 (Summer 1984): 16–21, 39.
Kirby, Kenneth. "Church-Planting: Sow, Cultivate, & Harvest." *Fundamentalist Journal* 3, no. 4 (April 1984): 12–14.

Kuiper, Daniel. "Urban Church Planting and the Seminary." *Urban Mission* 10, no. 2 (December 1992): 39–48.

Lewis, Rebecca. "Strategizing for Church Planting Movements in the Muslim World." *International Journal of Frontier Missions* 21, no. 2 (Summer 2004): 73–77.

Logan, Robert E. "Innovative Ways to Plant Churches in the 21st Century." *Journal of the American Society for Church Growth* 12 (Winter 2001): 41–51.

MacDonald, John A. "New Structures for Cross-Cultural Church Planting." *Sewanee Theological Review* 37, no. 4 (1994): 381–98.

Machel, Edgar. "Will Church Planting Help a Denomination to Stay in Prime?: A Reflection about the Lifestyle of a Denomination and Church Planting." *Journal of the American Society for Church Growth* 13 (Winter 2002): 9–18.

"The Mass Media and Church Planting in Restricted Access Countries." *Evangelical Missions Quarterly* 29, no. 3 (July 1993): 278–83.

Murphy, Edward. "Guidelines for Urban Church Planting," in Arthur F. Glasser, Paul G. Hiebert, C. Peter Wagner, and Ralph D. Winter. *Crucial Dimensions in World Evangelization* (Pasadena, CA: William Carey Library, 1976): 233–53.

Nicholson, Steve. "Church Planting Is Difficult." *Cutting Edge* (Summer 1997).

Norden, Stephen M. "Sizing Up the New Church." *Reformed Review* 47 (Winter 1993 94): 114–19.

Norrish, Howard. "Lone Ranger: Yes or No?" *Evangelical Missions Quarterly* 26, no. 1.(January 1990): 6–14.

Ott, Craig. "Matching the Church Planter's Role with the Church Planting Model." *Evangelical Missions Quarterly* 37, no. 3 (July 2001): 338–44.

Payne, J. D. "Eight Principles of New Testament Evangelism." *Lausanne World Pulse* (May 2007); available at http://www.lausanneworldpulse.com/themedarticles.php/700/05-2007.

———. "From Scouts to Cultivators to Networkers: Connecting 'Lydias' and 'Pauls' in Western Pioneer Church Planting Strategy." *Evangelism Missions Quarterly* 43, no. 1 (January 2007): 82–89.

———. "Means of Evangelistic Growth: The First 300 Years." *The Journal of the American Society for Church Growth* 18 (Winter 2007): 55–77.

———. "P.L.A.N.T.S.: Equipping Seminary and College Students for Church Planting." *Lausanne World Pulse* (July 2007; available at http://www.lausanneworldpulse.com/themedarticles.php/783/07-2007?pg=all.

———. "4 Simple Ways to Be a Church Planting Deacon." *Deacon* 37, no. 2 (Winter 2006-07): 36–39.

———. "Ecclesiology: The Most Critical Issue in Church Planting Today." *Theology for Ministry* 1 (November 2006): 105–17.

———. "Forget Number 1, Lead Your Church to Be Number 2151!" *SBC Life* (February/March 2006): 6–7.

———. "The Mother Church and Church Planting." *Journal of the American Society for Church Growth* 16 (Winter 2005): 31–59.

———. "More Than 43,000 Southern Baptist Churches: Do We Really Need Another One?" *SBC Life* (June/July 2005): 4–5.

———. "The Art of Vision Casting for Church Multiplication." *Journal of the American Society for Church Growth* 16 (Fall 2005): 35–42.

———. "Missiology of Roland Allen." *The Journal of the American Society for Church Growth* 15 (Winter 2004): 45–118.

———. "The Legacy of Roland Allen." *Churchman* 117, no. 4 (Winter 2003): 315–28.

———. "Problems Hindering North American Church Planting Movements." *Evangelical Missions Quarterly* 39, no. 2 (April 2003): 220–28.

———. "Suggested Shifts in Preparation for the Spontaneous Expansion of the North American Church." *The Journal of the American Society for Church Growth* 14 (Winter 2003): 41–86.

———. "A Brief Biography and Missiology of Robert E. Logan." *The Journal of the American Society for Church Growth* 13 (Fall 2002): 29–65.

Phillips, Jere. "Funding New Churches." *Journal of Evangelism and Missions* 4 (Spring 2005): 23–38.

Reapsome, James W. "Church Planting and 'The New Man's' Life Style." *Evangelical Missions Quarterly* 19, no. 1 (January 1983): 68–71.

Reese, Robert. "Theological Considerations for Church Planting." *Journal of Evangelism and Missions*: 39–50.

Repkin, Nik. "Shaking the Dust off Your Feet." *Evangelical Missions Quarterly* 34, no. 3.

Rhennen, Gailyn Van. "Learning . . . Growing . . . Collaborating . . . Phasing Out." *Evangelical Missions Quarterly* 36, no. 1 (January 2000): 36–47.

Rommen, Edward. "Church Planting: Theory and Practice." *Evangelical Missions Quarterly* 20, no. 4 (October 1984): 387–89.

Rommen, Edward. "Planting in Tandem for Church Growth." *Evangelical Missions Quarterly* (January 85): 54–62.

Rowland, Trent, and Shane Bennett. "Qualifying for the Pioneer Church-Planting Decathlon." *Evangelical Missions Quarterly* 37, no. 3 (July 2001): 348–54.

Sawatsky, Ben. "What It Takes to Be a Church Planter." *Evangelical Missions Quarterly* 27, no. 4 (October 1991): 342–47

Schaller, Lyle E. "Why Start New Churches?" *The Circuit Rider* 3, no. 5 (May 1979): 3, 5.

Schindler, Deitrich. "Good-to-Great Church Planting: The Road Less Travelled." *Evangelical Missions Quarterly* 44, no. 3 (July 2008): 330–37.

Scoggins, Dick. "Reproducing House Churches: An Autobiographical Pilgrimage." *Urban Mission* (March 1994): 46–55.

Scoggins, Dick, and Dan Brown. "Seven Phases of Church Planting Phase and Activity List." *Evangelical Missions Quarterly* 33, no. 2 (April 1997): 161–65.

Seal, J. Paul. "Primary Health Care and Church Planting." *Evangelical Missions Quarterly* 25 (1989): 350–61.

"7 Steps to Planting a Vineyard Church." *Cutting Edge* (Spring 1997).

Snapper, David. "Unfulfilled Expectations of Church Planting." *CTJ* 31 (1996): 464–86.

Stanley, Brian. "Planting Self-Governing Churches: British Baptist Ecclesiology in the Missionary Context." *The Baptist Quarterly* 34, no. 8 (October 1992): 378–89.

Steffen, Tom. "Flawed Evangelism and Church Planting." *Evangelical Missions Quarterly* 34, no. 4 (October 1998): 428–35.

———. "Selecting a Church Planting Model That Works," *Missiology* 22, no. 3 (July 1994): 361–76

———. "Phasing Out Your Work: Make It a Plan, Not a Crisis." *Evangelical Missions Quarterly* 27, no. 3 (July 1991): 280–85.

Stetzer, Ed. "Do Church Planting Systems Help Church Planters?: A Summary and Study of the System That Southern Baptists Use to Support Their Church Planters." *Journal of The American Society for Church Growth* 15 (Winter 2004): 26–43.

———. "Multicultural Teams in Church Planting." *Evangelical Missions Quarterly* 39, no. 1 (October 2003): 498–505.

Stoffer, Dale R. "Church Planting: An Anabaptist Model." *Brethren Life and Thought* 39, no. 3 (Summer 1994): 210–22.

Thrall, Stephen, and Terry Smith. "Planting a Church in the Heart of Paris." *Urban Mission* 12, no. 4 (June 1995): 51–54.

Troutman, Charles H. "A Fallacy in Church Planting: A Fable." *Evangelical Missions Quarterly* 17, no. 3 (July 1981): 133–37.

Towns, Elmer. "Church Planting in the Urban Setting: The Key to Reaching America." *Journal of the American Society for Church Growth* 9 (Spring 1998): 41–51.

Towns, Elmer. "Contemporary Church Planting." *Journal of the American Society for Church Growth* 17 (Spring 2006): 48–56.

Towns, Elmer. "Planting New Churches." *Fundamentalist Journal* 2, no. 3 (March 1983): 50–51.

Westbury, Joe. "Missionary Scout: Exploring Western Canada to Plant New Churches." *SBC Life* 13, no. 5 (February/March 2005): 1–2.

Westbury, Joe. "Fertile Ground: Planting Churches in a Vast Mission Field—North America." *On Mission* 8, no. 2 (Special Issue 2005): 42–45.

Williams, Mark. "Daughter Church Planting Makes Sense." *Journal of the American Society for Church Growth* 14 (Spring 2003): 29–35.

Wilson, Linda. “Issues for Women in Church Planting.” *Evangelical Missions Quarterly* 39, no. 3 (July 2003): 362–66.

Wimber, John. “The Seven Constants of Church Planting.” *Cutting Edge* (Winter 1998).

Yamamura, J. K. “Planting the Church in Omitsu.” *The Japan Christian Quarterly* (January 1954): 151–53.

Zunkel, C. Wayne. “It’s Easier to Have Babies.” *Brethren Life and Thought* 28 (Spring 1983): 77–90.

# GENERAL INDEX

# BIBLICAL INDEX